Identity and Lifelong Learning in Higher Education

A Volume in I Am What I Become:
Constructing Identities as Lifelong Learners

Series Editors

Jo Ann Gammel, Sue Motulsky, and Amy Rutstein-Riley
Lesley University

I Am What I Become:
Constructing Identities as Lifelong Learners

Jo Ann Gammel, Sue Motulsky, and Amy Rutstein-Riley, Editors

Identity and Lifelong Learning in Higher Education (2020)
edited by Jo Ann Gammel, Sue Motulsky, and Amy Rutstein-Riley

Identity and Lifelong Learning in Higher Education

edited by

Jo Ann Gammel

Sue Motulsky

Amy Rutstein-Riley
Lesley University

INFORMATION AGE PUBLISHING, INC.
Charlotte, NC • www.infoagepub.com

Library of Congress Cataloging-in-Publication Data

CIP record for this book is available from the Library of Congress
http://www.loc.gov

ISBNs: 978-1-64113-885-7 (Paperback)

978-1-64113-886-4 (Hardcover)

978-1-64113-887-1 (ebook)

Printed in the United States of America

CONTENTS

PREFACE

I AM WHAT I BECOME

Constructing Identities as Lifelong Learners

Jo Ann Gammel, Sue L. Motulsky, and Amy Rutstein-Riley

There was a time, not that long ago, when adulthood marked the end of learning and the beginning of work and family, and retirement marked the beginning of decline. Identity was stable and often dictated by work, race, gender, and class. That time is no longer.

Today human growth and development does not peak at age 40 and decline at age 65. Emerging adulthood theory, with its new developmental stage following adolescence, suggests that adulthood does not even truly begin until the late 20s. Adult learning is no longer unidirectional from teacher to student, limited to brick and mortar settings or structured education programs, nor is it age restricted. Learning is ongoing throughout the lifespan and occurs in a variety of formal and informal settings. Along with the evolution of views on human development and learning comes a social constructivist perspective on identity. No longer is identity singular and fixed, but rather, identity is composed of multiple, intersecting layers that are dynamic and fluid. Identities are constructed and re-constructed through life experiences, in interaction with cultural

Identity and Lifelong Learning in Higher Education, pp. ix–xvi
Copyright © 2020 by Information Age Publishing

and relational contexts. To quote Ruthellen Josselson (1996), "Identity is what we make of ourselves within a society that is making something of us" (p. 28).

Learning and identity development are lifetime processes of becoming. The construction of self, of interest to scholars and practitioners in adult development and adult learning, is an ongoing process, with the self both forming and being formed by lived experience in privileged and oppressive contexts. Intersecting identities and the power dynamics within them shape how learners define themselves and others and how they make meaning of their experiences in the world. Understanding the importance of identity in learning is "critical to advancing our understanding of the learning process and our creation of effective, inclusive educational environments" (Zaytoun, 2005, p. 8).

INTRODUCTION TO THE SERIES

I Am Who I Become: *Constructing Identities as Lifelong Learners* is an insightful and diverse collection of empirical research and narrative essays in identity development, adult development, and adult learning. The purpose of this series is to publish contributions that highlight the intimate connections between learning and identity. Our aim is to promote reflection and research at the intersection of identity and adult learning at any point across the adult lifespan and in any space where learning occurs: in school, at work, or in the community.

Many of the contributions in this series examine identity and learning within marginalized and understudied groups. People from marginalized populations, whether based on gender, race, ethnicity, social class, sexual minority, disability status, or another identity, learn to perform their identities differently in diverse settings. Insights about how identity is constructed within diverse adult learning contexts can assist researchers and practitioners in understanding the socio-cultural factors that inform adult development, education and learning. Many of these works discuss how gender identity, race, class, ethnicity, sexual orientation, ability, religion, and the complex mix of these identities play a significant role in how learners define themselves and others and how their meaning-making shapes their experience in the world. In addition to chapters that span diverse identities, cultural contexts, and international settings, contributions also focus on identity development and adult learning at all points across adulthood, from emerging adults to the elderly.

The series aims to assist our readers in understanding and nurturing adults who are always in the process of becoming. We invite readers who are adult educators, adult development scholars, counselors, psychologists, social workers, and sociologists, along with education and training professionals in formal and informal learning settings, to revel in the rich array of qualitative research designs, methods, and findings, as well as autobiographies and narrative essays that transform and expand our understanding of the lived experience of people both like us and unlike us, from the United States and beyond.

OUR STORIES

As university educators, the three editors share interests within identity, adult development, and adult learning, although we have our own professional identities and particular scholarly interests. Jo Ann is an adult educator interested in mentoring adult doctoral students; Sue is a developmental and vocational psychologist interested in career transition, gender, cultural and relational identity, and sexual minority career development; and Amy is a sociologist focused on the wellbeing of adolescent and young adult girls. We proposed a volume on identity and lifelong learning that would highlight the many ways adults construct and change their identities as they encounter new contexts and new challenges. We envisioned chapters that would locate adult identity development and revision through formal or informal learning in professional, educational or community settings. These settings include higher education, adult or community education, professional development, or informal learning through transitions, cultural exploration, or life experiences.

Our call for proposals resulted in 150 responses, much more than the two dozen or so that we expected. We were astonished. We seemed to have struck a chord. With such a rich mix of stories to tell, we opted to create a series. The contributors are mostly, although not exclusively, higher education faculty members, administrators, and students interested in adult learning and development. The stories in this series are often deeply personal. Some are self-portraits exploring issues of transition, intersecting identities, and oppression. Others are qualitative research studies exploring teaching and learning experiences in specific cultural and international populations across the adult lifespan. Each chapter is a story of learners (who may be the author herself or her students) and each reflects on identity as it is considered and reconsidered in a particular learning environment.

OVERVIEW OF THE THREE VOLUMES OF THE SERIES

Volume One, *Identity and Lifelong Learning in Higher Education,* contains chapters by and about postsecondary educators and students. Chapters

selected for this volume include stories of traditional-age students in bachelor's degree programs, adult learners in community college and four-year
degree programs, graduate or doctoral students, and senior scholars reflecting on a lifetime of learning and becoming. Authors examine multiple and
intersecting identities using a variety of methods including autoethnography, phenomenology, and narrative research. Many employ a critical
lens such as feminism, critical race theory, or critical pedagogy to examine
issues of power in formal learning settings. Practitioners offer unique
pedagogical strategies based on new ideas that come from reflection and
rigorous research. Together these chapters enhance our understanding of
the inextricable link between learning and identity.

Chapters in Volume Two, *Identity and Lifelong Learning: Becoming Through
Lived Experience*, focus on identity and learning within informal settings and
life experiences rather than formal educational environments. The contributions showcase the many ways that identity development and learning
occur within cultural domains, through developmental and identity challenges or transitions in career or role, and in a variety of spaces from assisted
living facilities to makerspaces. These chapters highlight identity and
learning across the adult lifespan from millennials and emerging adults to
midlife and older adults. The studies take place in South Africa, Singapore,
and South Korea as well as in both rural and urban settings in the United
States. The authors examine cultural, relational and social identity exploration and learning through experiences of immigrant women, domestic
workers in two international contexts, hearing children of deaf parents,
African American career and family legacies, women becoming mothers,
artist identity formation, and women in career transition. Included in this
volume are phenomenological qualitative studies, autoethnographies, case
studies, and narratives that engage the reader about the myriad ways that
adult development, learning, and identity connect and influence each
other.

Volume Three, *Narratives on Becoming: Identity and Lifelong Learning*,
contains extraordinary essays that share a personal narrative lens or auto-
biographical/ethnographic methodology. Authors are from Australia,
Canada, China, Dominican Republic, Germany, Mexico, South Korea,
Turkey, and the United States, and include community workers, doctoral
students, and educators. Nearly half of the chapters are coauthored, collaborative stories. These chapters provide insights into the intersectional
identities and learning of writers, who discuss topics such as national
identity, parenthood, pedagogy for transformation, social justice, and the
intertwining of personal and professional growth. These authors present
powerful stories that identify the ways relationships, environments, culture,
travel, and values shape their identities, use literacy, teaching, and learning
as vehicles for experimenting with new identities, negotiate multiple

identities, contexts, and transitions involved in becoming, and construct meaning from the multiple paths that comprise the journey of lifelong learning.

Stories are powerful learning tools. Editing the chapters in this series has contributed to enlarging our own understanding of identity and lifelong learning and we hope it will do the same for our readers. Reading the contributions we received has made us reflect more deeply on our own identities and ways of learning. As qualitative researchers, we are used to attending to the voices of others and reflecting on our own positionality. Yet we were not prepared for the rich diversity of studies and narratives from authors who were hungry for the opportunity to tell their stories or those of others. We were often deeply moved by the power of these chapters and their ability to bring to light the voices of so many people in multiple cultural and educational contexts. We are honored to bring these voices to a larger audience through this series. "We need to tune in to the stories of change we hear all around us, the stories each of us tells ourselves about who we were, who we are now, and who we may be in the future" (McAdams, Josselson & Lieblich, 2001, p. xx).

OVERVIEW OF VOLUME ONE

Volume One, *Identity and Lifelong Learning in Higher Education,* presents personal narratives and research studies from colleagues who are university educators and students or who use post-secondary education institutions as a setting for their identity explorations. Each of the 19 contributions in this volume is unique in perspective and tone. Each is an appeal for greater awareness, respect for differences, and transformative change when underlying assumptions are disrupted.

Chapter 1, "Me and You, You and Me: Examining Student Perception and the Evolution of Teacher Identity in the Community College," by Morgan Halstead and Crystal Rudds, sets the stage for the following chapters. The authors, one a Black woman and the other a White woman, incorporate personal narrative and excerpts from student interviews in a study of their own teacher identities in relationship to positive and negative student outcomes. They acknowledge the messiness of intersectionality of ethnicity, gender, age, geography, parenthood, and the myriad positionalities in which these identifications result in privilege and oppression. The practice they are researching models a pedagogical stance and strategy for higher education faculty members who want to incorporate a process of reflection and connection with students, and who celebrate their students' participation in their own growth as teachers.

The chapters that follow cover the lifespan from adolescence and young adulthood through midlife and late adulthood. Chapter 2, by Amy Rutstein-Riley and Ann Mechem Ziergiebel, showcases The Girlhood Project at Lesley University in which traditional-aged undergraduates coconstruct the meaning of girlhood with middle school adolescents participating in an experiential learning program designed to explore identity, feminist consciousness, vulnerability, and allyship. The findings serve as a foundation for theorists and researchers interested in expanding knowledge about the interaction of gender identity with ethnicity, social class, and cultural factors. Alyson King and Allyson Eamer's study in Chapter 3 examines urban, racial minority undergraduate students from immigrant or lower socioeconomic status families attending a university outside of one of Canada's largest urban centers. Students share their perceptions of themselves becoming university students. The authors argue that part of identity formation occurs when a student has a sense of belonging to an academic community.

Chapters 4 and 5 are qualitative studies that focus on adult learners. Debbie Thurman and Jeff Savage, in Chapter 4, examine the resilience of first generation, Appalachian adult college students and shed light on identity development of students in a unique sociocultural context of place and class. Chapter 5 is concerned with bachelor's degree completion students, many of whom, upon finishing, described finding their identity, or purpose in life, as the most significant outcome of their educational journey. Jennifer Serowick's findings challenge student development research that focuses on traditional educational trajectories, in that her adult students discovered their identities, not in spite of their stops and starts, but because of their non-traditional pathways in academia.

Korean graduate student mothers earning their degrees in the United States while their husbands are in Korea are the subjects of a study by Ji-Yeon Lee and Hyesun Cho in Chapter 6. Their study explores the cross-cultural, transnational learning and development of these Korean female students. The students share their perceptions of gender, culture, and class within their identities. Marian Spaid-Ross and Caren Sax, in Chapter 7, offer an empirical study of the perspectives of adult learners over the age of fifty who enrolled in community college. They note themes of identity, belonging, transition, and self-efficacy through these learners' experiences of postsecondary education. In Chapter 8, Professor Emerita and adult educator, Judith Beth Cohen, offers her reflections and six lessons from a lifetime of teaching.

Chapters 9, 10, and 11 explore professional identity. Anne Graham Cagney explores teacher identity development in Chapter 9. Set in the context of large-scale structural changes to the Further Education and Training (FET) system in the Republic of Ireland, her study emerges from program evaluations where students reported significant learning that in some cases led to a change in their sense of self and identity as FET teachers. The study examines the nature of these student learning experiences for how they may promote perspective transformation. Chapter 10, by Michal Shani, Ilana Margolin, and Pninat Tal, reflects on the authors' own learning experiences in the context of a community of practice committed to creating a profound change in the teacher education system within their institution in Israel. They describe a longitudinal process of construction and re-construction of their multifaceted identities. Their chapter highlights Shani's story that represents, on the one hand, the process of becoming a teacher educator, and, on the other hand, the development of the professional and social identities of an ethical, diligent and talented person. Chapter 11, entitled "The Professor and the Closet," details a qualitative study exploring the experiences of gay, lesbian, and/ or queer identified faculty working in teacher preparation. Using a unique poetic display of her data, Lesley Siegel presents her findings as a conversation created using the words of her three study participants.

Through studies on classroom practice, many chapters offer new perspectives and innovative pedagogy for building relationships between students and teachers. Chapter 12 is a study by Emilie Clucas Leaderman, who examines the practices of faculty identified by undergraduate students as learner-centered. She offers suggestions for faculty development to promote changes in traditional modes of teaching. Ellie Fitts Fulmer, in Chapter 13, uses discourse analysis to examine written and verbal responses of student resistance in a course on multicultural issues. She offers an alternative approach to hearing students' responses in a binary (resistant/compliant) way. Her "course identities framework" provides a method instructors can use to reconceptualize and reframe resistance. In Chapter 14, Enid Larsen uses a living inquiry research methodology and parallels her personal learning experiences with those of the adult learners she guides through a process of reflection to earn credits for prior learning. She both describes and also models this Learning Autobiography process.

The stories in this series about identity and lifelong learning often describe powerful lived experiences. For example, in Chapter 15, Anjali Forber-Pratt vividly narrates her lifelong journey to reconcile her multiple identities. Before taking a leap of faith and traveling to India, her birth country and the place from which she was adopted, she says she identified only as a person with a disability. Revisiting her Indian identity, she began to experience a new, simultaneous development and integration of identities as a woman, a person of color, and an adoptee.

Many authors in this volume use a critical theory lens to illuminate issues of power for the reader. For example, Chapter 16 by Xóchitl Mendez, who has a disability, details actual dialogue along with her unspoken internal dialogue during a winter afternoon meeting between herself as a doctoral student and a professor. As she unpacks her vignette, a painful story unfolds. In Chapter 17, Ann Mechem Ziergiebel uses a feminist lens and paints a portrait, a narrative pentimento of revising her identity using the metaphors of dark and light, perspective, space, and composition to explore her journey from early intellectual bruising and silencing in school to her subsequent growth and empowerment. In Chapter 18, Kimberly D. Johnson gives voice to the invisible lives and experiences of African American women staff members in a predominantly White institution using Black feminist thought and critical race theory.

Writing from a social constructivist viewpoint, Kristen Linzmeier advocates reframing stereotypes implied in the term "non-traditional learners" in the final chapter, Chapter 19. She uses critical race theory and the concept of community cultural wealth as frameworks to counter traditional deficit views. She traces the story of Thalia, a 46-year-old immigrant and adult learner, striving to achieve her lifelong dream of becoming a certified teacher. Linzmeier thereby offers a new perspective on the role and responsibility of academia to provide a nurturing environment. She writes, "it isn't as simple as Thalia being able to create or choose an identity for herself. Her identity is dependent upon how she is defined by certain individuals, the environment, and the broader context of society." This powerful statement echoes throughout many of these portraits of identity and learning.

We are grateful to our authors for their contributions to the series *I Am Who I Become: Constructing Identities as Lifelong Learners* and to this first volume on *Identity and Learning in Higher Education*. We hope that these authors' insights will promote further research and influence pedagogy and practice in postsecondary institutions, resulting in more open, inclusive, democratic, and even transformative teaching and learning.

REFERENCES

Josselson, R. (1996). *Revising herself: Women's identity from college to midlife*. New York, NY: Oxford University Press.

McAdams, D., Josselson, R., & Lieblich, A. (Eds.). (2001). *Turns in the road: Narrative studies of lives in transition*. Washington, DC: American Psychological Association.

Zaytoun, K. D. (2005). Identity and learning: The inextricable link. *About Campus, 9*(6), 8–15. Retrieved from https://doi.org/10.1002/abc.112

CHAPTER 1

ME AND YOU, YOU AND ME

Examining Student Perception and the Evolution of Teacher Identity in the Community College

Morgan Halstead and Crystal S. Rudds
Malcolm X College

It was the winter of 2012. Two English teachers, also PhD students, crossed paths between their final interviews for a tenured position at a community college. One (Crystal), a Black woman whose experience teaching up to that point had been served at two public research institutions, the other (Morgan), a White woman transitioning from secondary education, grant coordinating, and the City Colleges of Chicago adjunct pool. Both of us were new to full-time teaching, to the tenure track, and the community college system. Both of us were about to become immersed in the challenging but rewarding environment of adult learners on an urban commuter campus, all the while completing ethnographic dissertations. Had our interviewers probed our sense of professional or "teacher" identity at the time, it might have been uncovered that our high levels of confidence were largely derived from previous successes in the classroom and a certain pride in our educational backgrounds.

Identity and Lifelong Learning in Higher Education, pp. 1–22
Copyright © 2020 by Information Age Publishing
All rights of reproduction in any form reserved.

I (Crystal) remember seeing Morgan that day in the lobby of the president's office. Her loose khaki pants suit struck a sharp contrast to my own choice of a black dress, stockings, and high heels. For some reason, our different attire got me wondering about the gender friendliness of the school. I wanted to be in a progressive atmosphere, so this was important to me. I had also observed the long row of photographs of former presidents (all African American) and was trying to decide what Black legacy I was stepping into. I had been educated and had taught at well-ranked, predominantly White institutions before this, and that year, Malcolm X College had a graduation rate of 9% (National Center for Education Statistics, 2015). I knew I could teach; what I did not know was whether I, fresh from university and non-native to Chicago, would be able to connect to students in need of so much remediation and so steeped in the life of their neighborhoods. Looking around at the dark gray halls of the old building, I was nervous.

I (Morgan), on the other hand, was thrilled! I felt sure of myself and of my abilities as a teacher, and I believed I had paid my dues. I had a 1-year old, a mortgage, and a belief in teacher-self (Zembylas, 2003). Students liked me. I thought I was perfect for the job. I thought that I was perfect for a community college *like this*; (and, here is where I will divulge completely) by this, I mean a community college populated by low-income, students of color. I thought they needed me, a good teacher who wanted to be there. At the time, Crystal was evidence that I was accepted. She was beautiful, professional, and ridiculously smart. We had much in common in where we were in our lives as we both were engaged in dissertation research that asked us to work with vulnerable populations. She seemed to connect with me too, which fed my confidence.

We firmly believe we came into our current institution as strong teachers. Yet, neither of us had an accurate sense of our outsiderness, our privilege/savior-complex, nor the limitations of our empathy. A driving factor behind writing this together is to underscore the importance that instructors continuously reflect on their self-perception as teachers and the gap between that perception versus their students' perceptions. Years later from our first meeting, we continue to be interested in constructions of teacher identities, especially those of community college instructors. Specifically, how can student perceptions impact the evolution and conscious shaping of the community college teacher's identity on an ongoing basis?

Here we explore our work as teachers, the situational context of teaching developmental and college writing to nontraditional learners, and our self-exploration as professors, activists, and mothers. Through a reliance on narrative inquiry, we synthesize critical reflection with selected student interviews, parsing out the relationship between constructed views of the self and the educational environment. This, in turn, leads us to argue that attention to student perceptions and deep reflection (beyond normative end-of-semester evaluations) can contribute valuable information for the identity development of the community college teacher in-progress. Moreover, this type of phenomenology can lead to critical consciousness on the part of the teacher *and the student*, and even be configured as a meta-pedagogy that helps other instructors and learners.

Three theoretical frameworks support our lens for our research methodology, writing, and ultimate themes: (1) phenomenology (2) critical pedagogy and (3) feminism. In terms of our methods, an investment in phenomenology and narrative inquiry led our approach and data gathering process. Phenomenology, especially its emphasis on the social (or shared) construction of knowledge, spaces, and identity, sees classroom outcomes as the effect of personal and historical contexts (Clandinin, 2006; Van Manen, 1990). Qualitative research arising from a phenomenological commitment should follow suit. Per Van Manen (1990), "Phenomenological human science is the study of live or existential meanings; it attempts to describe and interpret these meanings to a certain degree of depth and richness" (p. 11). We desired to challenge our own assumptions about our identity construction by interviewing students who had taken our classes during critical points in our evolution as teachers. The timing of the inquiry and the transient nature of our campus impacted the size of our subject pool. Essentially, our final subjects were selected because they were either still around or still enrolled, and they responded to our invitation. Four students, two of Crystal's and two of Morgan's, were interviewed separately using a semistructured set of questions. Their responses gave us a glimpse into how students may perceive us as teachers and mentors and how we still need to grow.

We interwove our stories as colleagues and teachers (who were also graduate students together) into this chapter and allowed the ensuing dialogue (a form of narrative inquiry) to help us interpret our identity development, especially in relationship to outcomes (both positive and negative) with students. This methodology supports our exploration of our teacher-identities in two important ways. First, as Van Manen (1990)[1] clarifies in exploring his own pedagogical self, "[reflecting] phenomeno-logically on experiences of teaching and parenting as a teacher or as a parent … [is an] attempt to grasp the pedagogical essence of a certain experience" (p. 78). Structurally, moving between our stories through the composing, revising, and editing processes forced us to continually revisit each other's experiences and deepened what we learned from each other. Second, we find narrative inquiry one of the most appropriate tasks when focusing on women's lives and perspectives. Bateson (1989) reminds us that the flow of women's lives is parallel to the ebb and flow of storytelling and, thereby, must allow for disjointedness and a bit of disorder:

> Women have always lived discontinuous and contingent lives…. The physical rhythms of reproduction and maturation create sharper discontinuities in women's lives than in men's…. As a result, the ability to shift from preoccupation to another, to divide one's attention, to improvise in new circumstances, has always been important to women. (p. 13)

We intentionally work through discontinuity to reflect on the ebb and flow of our identity making, our discourse with students, and redefinitions of our teacher-selves.

Critical pedagogy and feminist theory influence our praxis, specifically these disciplines' core tenets about decentered, transformative learning and activism. Critical pedagogy attempts to address the need for societal transformation through an emphasis on critical thinking, confrontation with rigid classist/capitalist/sexist/racist values and social justice. Divergent in practice, adherents argue the need for deep understanding of social contexts and consequences. McLaren (2007) described critical pedagogy as "[asking] how and why knowledge gets constructed the way it does, and how and why some constructions of reality are legitimated and celebrated … while others clearly are not" (p. 63). In education, some styles of instruction are celebrated, and some are devalued or punished. "Progressive professors [work] to transform the curriculum so that it does not reflect biases or reinforce systems of domination … [making] their teaching practices sites of resistance" (hooks, 1994, p. 21). The teacher who practices critical pedagogy intervenes into the education system at her own risk, not only by asking students to question the status quo of traditional learning paths but by positioning herself as colearner in the dialogue/inquiry. Side by side, students and teachers interrogate or address problems in a move towards greater consciousness and freedom.

Feminist theory offers an intersectional critique of identity, social relationships (such as those with students), and, of course, pedagogy. Though I, Crystal, identify as Black or African American, and I, Morgan, identify as White, we are both heterosexual, cisgender, married women, and mothers. We are able-bodied, middle class, and did not grow up in endangered communities. Neither of us were first generation college students, nor the first in our families to seek advanced degrees. We teach on a campus where the life struggles of our students are starkly different than our own, and feminist theory advocates for our acknowledging this, for acknowledging that our students live on the margins of society. Our students are single parents or single providers for other dependents. They are low income or "under class," often working more than one job to balance financial aid. They are frequently in need of developmental education and academic support before advancing to or while taking our classes; and recently, a larger number of students on our once predominantly African Latinx, some of whom are negotiating the uncertainty of being undocumented. What this means for feminist teachers is that space must be made in the classroom for divergent perspectives but also emotional vulnerabilities that might hamper self-actualization. Two central lenses for our feminist practice are the seminal works of bell hooks (1984) and Patricia Hill Collins (1990). hooks's (1984) assertion that "Feminists are made, not born" guides our thinking about the constructed nature of identity and teaching, how we are always in progress/process, just as our courses, hopefully, move or support students towards their own progression of feminist consciousness.

Feminism is also mothering, in terms of care, community, and patience. Collins (1990) recognizes that not just individual mothering but collective mothering is essential to feminism and community building. "Othermothering" is described as transformative for vulnerable communities:

> Such power is transformative in that Black women's relationship with children and other vulnerable community members is not intended to dominate or control. Rather, its purpose is to bring people along ... to "uplift the race" so that vulnerable members of the community will be able to attain the self-reliance and independence essential to resistance. (p. 132)

Collins' term "uplift" is a loaded term but an important one as we negotiate our attempts to support, nurture, engage, and connect while avoiding seeing ourselves as students' saviors. Furthermore, as English professors, we use feminism and critical pedagogy to guide students in questioning texts that expose hierarchical relationships in society. In this chapter, texts are also a lens for our students' interpretations of their experience with us.

The site of this study, an urban two-year college has an enrollment that has ranged between 4,000 and 7,000 students since 2014, 70% of whom are female. Many hail from high crime communities across the city, juggling jobs with single parenthood. Most utilize academic support services but do not have time for extracurriculars. Because most community college students are either on the developmental to credit track, or a career program track, for several years, institutional pressure often drives faculty to promote persistence and retention over other activities on campus, such as guest lectures. We mention these characteristics of our research site to emphasize the potential influence of the nontraditional student environment on student perception of teacher identity. We see this study, then, as a key contribution to the discussion of teacher identity and learning, especially given the lack of attention to teacher identity specific to the community college teacher. As noted by van Lankveld et. al (2016), there is a direct correlation between environment and teacher identity, which can reinforce or offset the stressors of higher education as a whole.

NARRATIVE I: WHY ARE WE HERE?

Fall 2012–2015: Crystal

Even though I had specifically confessed my lack of experience in developmental instruction during that final interview, the first semester at my college, I was thrown into the department's lowest level of developmental writing. I was terrible. By midterm, my entire class was failing, and I had to ditch the intellectualized approach I had conceived (like connecting Cornel West to grammar) and just get them through the final exam. My teaching persona was ineffectual; I did not know how to *act*. The professional reserve that I so carefully cultivated to manage my struggle with imposter syndrome at my former institution had only served to distance me from my current students' needs. Fast forward two years: I had shifted to a more approachable teaching persona, mostly to support the range of traumas students were bringing to the classroom; my dissertation was almost finished; and I had survived one of the saddest things about teaching on an urban campus, the loss of a sweet student to everyday gun violence. I finally was assigned an African American literature course, a chance to bring together my expertise, my belief in writing as a site of consciousness—a place where students could confront oppressive systems through self and communal discovery (Collins, 1990; Harris, 2004; Lunsford, 1991)—*and* an emphasis on Black feminism. From my vantage, the semester gave me a chance to affirm my identity as a professor who usefully employed critical pedagogy and my cultural identity as a Black woman.

My perception of myself in this class, however, that is, the identity components I thought I was expressing, apparently, did not fully translate. I thought I was communicating a progressive, feminist identity who purposely decentered herself to allow students to hone their comprehension of the topics. If I did, that is not quite what a former student recalled of me. N'ichelle, whom I interviewed for this project, didn't remember any of the strategies that I had used to provoke collaborative learning, such as abandoning the syllabus and allowing the students to decide the final project. Actually, what stood out most to her at the time was that I was also still a student.

In class, N'ichelle, often presented herself as self-deprecating. An older student, she described herself in the interview as a "different kind of learner" and explained this as someone who needed to write things down twice to remember them. Chuckling with me, she stated, "Back then, I just wanted everything to be simple … that's why every day when you came in there, I was like, '*Ugh, here she come.*' " It took her a while to embrace me, she said, until she saw "how serious I was about teaching and wanting the students to learn and to understand what it is [the class] was all about." N'ichelle used the word "serious" to describe me several times, as well as "straightforward" and "smart." Most interesting was her discussion of me as a woman; it seemed hinged on an identity composition I didn't realize I projected:

> Yeah, as a woman, you were just on point with carrying yourself. I mean, you were excellent to me. You were good. I used to look at you and say, I wonder what she does. You know, she's married, she's smart. I wonder what her social life is like. I used to wonder about that, because you used to be so vibrant, and all the time smiling, and I said, she's got to be okay. Every-body has days, but I knew with your personal life, you had help. You could go home and relax, and your husband would say, you gone be okay. I said, when I get where I'm trying to get, I'll put myself in a position to have a peaceful life like that.

She equated "carrying yourself" as a woman with access to social support and with the idea of a man being at home to provide affirmation. While I did share personal details with the class, I must have downplayed how lonely, in fact, getting through grad school had been for me while jug-gling marriage, teaching, and my college's tenure process. (I guess I did not mention my many near nervous breakdowns.) I also thought I had emphasized my ideological commitments more pronouncedly, yet N'ichelle focused more on the aspects of my identity she most aspired to.

In fact, although N'ichelle did articulate a definition of feminism ("a woman who makes sure the glass ceiling is not there"), when asked if I fit that definition, she reiterated her perception of me as "very smart" and that she was impressed that I knew so much and read a lot. I defended my dissertation the semester N'ichelle was in my class, and N'ichelle remem-bered this. She said it made her so proud to know that I was a "doctor" and had moved forward with my life: "I was like, wow, she's a doctor now, and I thought that was so amazing." Until this study, I had never directly asked a student how she saw me, relying instead on those vague semester evals: Ms. Rudds is cool or Ms. Rudds is nice. Talking with N'ichelle caused me to see that in some ways I was coming across just the way I wanted to, that is, as a caring but "serious" instructor who valued what happened in the classroom.

In other ways, parts of my identity seem effaced by N'ichelle's self pro-jection, because her projection centered on her esteem of literacy and what it took to be a good student. Even when it came to cultural identity, that is, our shared Blackness, N'ichelle expressed an idealized view of how teachers' personas functioned in the educational environment to her benefit or disadvantage. Her perception was that the difference between African American teachers and others was that African American teachers were more willing to slow things down when students didn't understand, and this was ascribed to culture rather than instructional technique. This was fine, right? I mean, it was why I was there to teach. And, yet, for some reason at the end of the interview, it felt like somehow N'ichelle and I had missed each other.

Spring 2012: Morgan

When I started the position, I felt sure of myself and of my abilities as a teacher and believed I had paid my dues to get here. I had a 2-year old, a mortgage, and a belief in teacher-self. I had already been working with Malcolm X as an adjunct. I did all that was asked of me, and my students liked me. I believed I brought something of value to them, clearly relying on a deficit perspective of the college and the students. I did not have a sense of my privilege nor the limitations of my empathy. I sometimes allow that belief to bubble up today. I am a good teacher, but part of reestablishing and understanding my teacher-identity is understanding my role in the social constructs that haunt my students.

During the three years of the tenure process, I continued to have a strong sense of my pedagogical skills. This was reiterated with approving feedback and compliments on student and administrative evaluations. The process, at the time, however, was antiquated and tedious, so I did not *grow*. I continued to do what seemed to work because the students reported confirmation of their positive experiences. According to students, they were learning. So, I must have been doing it right. Instead of critical reflection, I just did more stuff and over graded more papers to continue to prove myself to everyone. I went to every meeting, volunteered to take notes, achieved certifications, joined more committees, even leading the Cultural Diversity Committee. And, to be fair, in terms of retention and pass rates, the data suggest that my students generally did well in my classes. I also worked hard, often times believing that I worked harder than most of my colleagues and therefore was doing a good job.

My life outside of work also supported my confidence—I had an easy 2-year old, enjoyed two salaries between me and her dad, I had family support, and I was on my way to finishing my PhD with some rockstar advisors. I worked hard to make administration and other faculty members like me—this is a personality trait of mine that I still work to shake, the need to prove myself. What was driving me was the need to be liked but also a sense of being better, of getting it right. I was perfect for this job. And, then, I got pregnant with my second child.

LITERATURE REVIEW

Although identity was once considered a fixed or stable concept (Mead, 1934), education and learning research today supports the reality that teacher identity is ever-changing and "a relational phenomenon" (Beijaard, Meijer, & Verloopm, 2004, p. 108). Who we understand ourselves to be as teachers is a product of our evolving sense of self and our situational positions vis-à-vis others and our environment. Teacher identity can be compartmentalized into one's professional identity and one's personal identity (Day, Kington, Stobart, & Sammons, 2006; Izadinia 2013). Defining identity is a complex task, therefore, but as Bullough (1997) affirmed, "Teacher identity—what *beginning* teachers believe about teaching and learning as self-as-teacher—is of vital concern to teacher education; it is the basis for meaning making and decision-making" (p. 21, emphasis added). We will return to this distinction between "beginning" and "veteran" or more experienced teachers, but for the purposes of this study, most scholars would agree that teacher identity is a malleable schema that provides a core value system for a teacher's sense of "how to be" and "how to act" within the classroom, her professional field, and society at large (Sachs, 2005, p. 15). Beauchamp and Thomas (2009) have synthesized that we must also consider the impact of the type of learners an educational environment engenders, emotions that accompany particular teaching contexts, and the culture within academic disciplines and institutions (p. 184). This latter aspect of teacher identity makes for an even messier concept because of the intersectionality that comes into play in terms of ethnicity, gender, age, geography, parenthood, and the myriad positionalities these identifications result in relative to privilege and oppression.

Deep reflection is needed for teachers to improve or expand any praxis and is an essential element in teacher identity development. This should also lead teachers to consider their privilege and authority relative to society and their student population. This type of reflection may consist of journaling, conversations with colleagues and mentors, participation in focus groups, even responding to video observations. We favor narrative inquiry as a method of reflection, believing that question-based narratives allow teachers to express themselves while critically interrogating assumptions. Keeping in mind that "the nature of critical reflection can be an arduous task because it forces the individual to ask challenging questions that pertain to one's construction of individuals from diverse racial, ethnic, and cultural backgrounds" (Howard, 2003, p. 98), we see the responsibility of democracy-minded teachers to continuously check themselves and each other in the spirit of kindness and progress. This is just as important as teachers' awareness of their initial conception of their professional identity.

Within the literature, the bulk of studies on teacher identity focus on its application to preservice, K–12 teachers. This makes sense since institutions are continuously researching ways to support teacher identity development as teachers are entering the classroom. Studies on the development of teacher identity—usually relabeled "professional" or "academic" identity—within higher education are few (Archer, 2008; & Barnett & Di Napoli, 2008). But the higher education literature rarely, if at all, parses out how identities of community college teachers might differ or follow different trajectories (Townsend & Twombly, 2007). From a review of this subcategory of literature, we conclude that community college professors create identities in response to the tensions of administrative management, existence (or lack) of support from the academic community, and schisms in identity politics from student interactions, leading to disjointed, often disinterested selves (Cohen & Brawer, 2003; Brownell & Tanner, 2012; Levin, 2001). London (1978, p. 64) goes as far as describing faculty self-perception as "gangling, awkward, adolescent ... complete with problems of self-consciousness and self-identity." Indeed, community college professors teach more classes and are judged based on their retention outcomes, not teaching persona or style or ideological/political commitments. Although many community college professors have more than one master's or a doctoral degree, most are not required to publish or develop an independent line of research, which may reduce the incentive for deep reflection. Then, too, balancing four or five classes with committee obligations and office hours (our institution mandates seven hours per week) also limits the time we have to just sit down and *think*. Adjunct faculty have even less time and support. These realities of community college teaching deserve more consideration.

Furthermore, we note that within the research, a lot of attention is given to the impact of student *interactions* on teacher identity and not on the impact of student *perceptions* of teacher identity. Student interactions include conversations, activities within and outside the classroom, and any situation that places the teacher in behavioral relation with the student. Conversely, student perceptions have to do with the beliefs, impressions, observations, and memories the student has of a particular aspect of the learning experience, for which may or may not get shared. Akkerman and Meijer (2011) noted that discursively, the teacher is usually seen as the primary agent for describing and understanding teacher identity. This perspective may again be attributed to the emphasis of the literature on preservice or new teachers and the importance of assessing the actual effectiveness of those teachers from students' perspective versus students' understanding or construction of the teacher's teaching self. We would argue that for the veteran professor, it may be even more useful to gauge or consider student perception. Veteran professors (professors with seven years or more of experience) may naturally feel their identity, like their teaching methods, is solidified. Although one's personal identity will certainly continue to change, the presumption may be that one's professional identity is now stable based on validation from one's teaching career. Student perception, however, plays an important role (or should) in a true dialogic process in which, per Akkerman and Meijer, multiple voices are valued in the process of identity development (p. 314).

For democracy-minded professors, the connection between identity development and critical consciousness is preeminent. Giroux (1988) made clear that to truly recreate the classroom as a space for meaningful inquiry, teachers would have to evolve their own assumptions and strive to function as intellectual leaders. "Transformative intellectuals," in Giroux's thinking, "educate a citizenry in the dynamics of critical literacy and civic courage, [which] constitute the basis for functioning as active citizens in a democratic society" (p. xxxii). As mentioned above in our summary of critical pedagogy, this theoretical basis should drive teachers to acknowledge, and guide students in uncovering, the cultural politics of the day that in any way serve to suppress alternative forms of knowledge counter to the dominant order. This is more than the democratic classroom being framed under the context of civic learning or civic engagement. Obenchain, Balkute, Vaughn, and White (2016) offer a comprehensive review of the literature on how teachers conceive of their civic (or democratic) identities, concluding that preservice and secondary education teachers do not necessarily view good citizenship and an orientation toward social change or social justice as one and the same. We would more so take the part of Mirra and Morrell (2011), who connect the role of teachers to a civic agency in direct resistance to the current neoliberal climate of our education system, in which democracy is increasingly and disturbingly paired with a push for the marketization of individuals alongside a nationalism that denies difference. This kind of critical or civic consciousness is not achieved in isolation or at one juncture of the teaching career, but rather in relationship over time. As such, it mirrors and helps shape identity development, requiring continuous deep reflection and vulnerability. Our conviction in this connection fundamentally underlies both of our conceptions of what the ideal classroom looks like and our need to develop as teachers, especially in our attempts to foster critical thinking and egalitarian safe spaces in our community college classrooms. Whether we have been able to achieve this vision holistically and consistently is the motivation behind this research.

NARRATIVE II: LOST IN TRANSLATION

Fall 2016: Crystal

There I was, with grad school officially behind me, *"a doctor,"* tenured, and more confident in my pedagogy. Fall of 2016, I was teaching in my first learning community, a writing course paired with sociology. I had also planned *"the coolest black science fiction class ever"* and was excited about pushing myself to take more risks in the classroom. But there were days when the students would just stare at me, or when one of them would perform her construction of the "eager student" to impress me, even though I had overheard her dragging the class in the halls. Students in the learning community were giving my colleague and me grief about the amount of work and structure of the learning community. For a while, instead of trying to figure out if I were the problem, I retreated into an easier *"this is college"* stance, which only led to a bigger divide. I think I was hurt that the lesson planning I had put so much enthusiasm into was not going over.

After this inquiry, there are two insights I can now use to go back and reflect on that semester. One insight came from one of the lit students confiding in me that she and the rest of the class stayed confused because (in her words) "you don't talk like we talk." I was not from where they were from. This seemed code for perceived economic, geographic, and general lifestyle differences. It made me think about the examples I shared in class and how relatable they were. Was I so enthusiastic about the readings and theory that I, inadvertently, talked over their heads? Was there a way that I could have addressed my own *intraracial* privilege and intersectionality more directly?

I gained the other insight when I interviewed the second student for this project, an international student who had come to our college for one of its health programs. Self-identified as European and queer, Elise managed to find a sense of community on our predominantly Black and Latinx campus and exhibited the activism that I appreciated. She said she related to me being a woman but more so to "the kindness [I] would diffuse in the class somehow." But while my literature students disconnected due to class and cultural differences, Elise shared her dissonance in perceiving me as the LGBTQ ally I thought I was becoming:

> I got excited when I saw that we were going to talk about Caitlin Jenner
> and other gay-related titles, because I was interested in seeing and hearing
> people's reactions, and to be able to educate them if they said something
> wrong. But we didn't talk about who those authors were in depth, we talked
> about what they said and how. It felt like a try to show a sign of acknowl-
> edgment of the LGBTQ community but not a desire to go that route.

Upon reflection, Elise was exactly right. I had intended to create a space for dialogue about sexuality, but I was terrified I would not be able to contain the homophobic attitudes that might arise without shutting the whole class down. Meanwhile, I would overhear Morgan describing her literature classes and homegrown knowledge of Chicago. She also had been the advisor for our campus LGBTQ club. I thought, she knows what she's doing. Listen to how relatable she sounds! I allowed Elise to educate me on what an LGBTQ ally is and is not, and to make suggestions on how to be more visible. She reminded me that even as a "progressive," social justice-minded instructor, the positionality I occupy at the front of the classroom might not translate.

Spring 2013–2016: Morgan

My hubris came to an apex in the Spring of 2013. Things did not go downhill necessarily, but my overconfidence sshifted into "overworked," and I was not developing into a critically reflective practitioner. In reflection, getting to know Crystal, especially as she returned from her fellowship, was one shockwave to my false construct about myself. In my construct of her, she was like me, except that because she was Black she *must* connect with students better. This is what my dissertation research had told me, at least as I understood it. There were limits to my ideas about culturally relevant teaching (Ladson-Billings, 1994) and reality pedagogy (Emdin, 2016). However, my idea of her teacher identity was too simplistic an understanding of how student relationships and privilege work. As I learned over the course of our time together, especially being officemates, her identity as a person of color came with its own challenges and celebrations. I remember observing a number of students speak to her differently than me; some interactions seemed more personal and respectful, and some more personal and quite disrespectful, such as the two times I saw male students blatantly hit on her. And, therein lies a necessary challenge to the development of my teacher identity, the challenge to reimagine the complexities of how race, life experience, gender, and socioeconomic status transform how students receive me, and I need to work harder to avoid oversimplifying these constructs. In 2013, however, I was not there yet. It was still about me.

I was pregnant with my second child and hiding it because I was nervous about how this would work while I was midway through tenure and dissertation. There were days that I felt strong and that I was doing what I was meant to be doing; there were days that I was drowning. Drowning in work, in physical exhaustion, and in doubt. Suddenly, it did not feel like I was doing it all. It did seem like I was handling it, though. By the end of 2013, I walked my overdue baby belly across the stage to receive my diploma, finished year two of my tenure, had a second baby, took four classes during my one-semester, unpaid semester maternity leave (or as one male colleague commented, my "nice, long break"), and returned one semester later ready to work even harder. But somewhere in the tornado of doing stuff, I had lost any sense of mindfulness and presence. For two years, it was staying afloat, doing more, but engaging less. The students I had during those years are a blur. I was not reflecting; I was working. I did, in the end, receive tenure and finish my PhD, but it is clear to me now, neither of those things helped me become a better teacher. They just gave me a lot to do and two titles.

By the Spring of 2016, I was pretty overwhelmed with all of the work outside of my teaching. I was still stuck in the belief that doing more was what my students and the institution needed. I was running the Honors society, overseeing adjuncts, teaching overload classes, and working diligently to support my colleagues through curricular innovations, changes, and adaptations. My home life, and marriage for that matter, felt constantly chaotic as well. The two students I interviewed for this chapter were a bit swept up in that chaos, but they stuck out because of the way the made me stop, listen, and rethink my teaching and my self-perception.

Victoria and Ana both challenged me in different ways. Neither of them were difficult students; however, they both admit that they have been perceived as difficult in other classes with other professors. They encouraged me to rethink my pedagogical strengths and my White and class privileges. I was introduced to them in different, unconventional ways. Victoria became a part of an honors program for which I was an advisor, so before she was even in my classes, I worked with her scholarship applications, mentored her study groups, and chaperoned field trips. Victoria pushed my understanding on how educational structures, and the people who represent them, can fail undocumented students in terms of support and sensitivity. Ana, on the other hand, was first introduced to me when she had a complaint about an adjunct faculty member who I supervised. Later, she enrolled in my honors literature course where she shined. Ana led me to question my teaching methodology while suggesting ways that teaching literature can create conversations about feminism and students' self-efficacy.

To talk, I met Victoria in her place of employment, a community-based organization that helped support the neighborhood in terms of housing, education, environmental justice, and immigration matters. She worked most often with the youth projects, many of which were designed to combat violence, a well-known, consistent issue facing Chicago. I had attended the Women's March in Washington, D.C., with my mother and oldest daughter, a jubilant, invigorating experience. I did it for me, but I also believed I was doing it for my students. When I came back and discussed it with my class that January, Victoria had asked if I had seen the photographs and narratives detailing the experiences of the march, pointing me to author Luvvie Ajayi who argues, "White women and white bodies can hold space on streets and shut down cities 'peacefully' because they are allowed to. Black and brown people who march are assaulted by cops" (Ramanathan 2017). I am pretty sure that I might have tried to argue with that perspective. I do not know what I argued, but I am sure I did not listen enough. During our interview, I asked Victoria about this. She said she still thinks about this, "why people say, well, why do we need a relationship with the police. Why do we, being brown and black, have to go and forge a relationship? Caucasians don't have to." I pushed her a bit further on this tension because I wanted her honesty about the complexities in this imbalance, especially in terms of experiencing White teachers and professors:

> I wish white teachers knew that we were all different, that we have different lives. Some of our parents never went to school, period. Others had some college. Others don't even know how to handle or write an email or use a cell phone ... I wish teachers took more initiative to learn about us individually instead of trying to understand us as a whole."

I winced at that, not because she insulted me but because I was already thinking of defenses against this argument about teachers, especially White teachers. "But, I have so many students! I don't have enough time," I thought, thinking back to what is published about the community college teacher-self, the workload. I was also thinking about all the times I hoped that no student visited me during my office hours because I had "so much to do." How could I get to know my students if I focused on lesson planning and grading? I needed to be present, listening.

Thankfully, Victoria had not finished checking my privilege. Just recently, soon after she sent a text with information regarding the legal consequences, as much as anyone knew at the time, of President Trump's potential decision to eliminate DACA (Deferred Action for Childhood Arrivals). For DACA students, like Victoria, this was a concern she thought of daily. I did not. Nor was I prepared to help in any tangible way. When she sent me the text, I responded supportively, the best way I could. She followed up with, "Can we communicate this to the Wellness Center to foresee possible mental health support?" And, I did. And then, felt terrible for not having the wherewithal to think of that myself because I did not have to.

My interview with Ana revealed other misconceptions about my teacher-self. Ana is an incredibly smart and vivacious student from one of my literature classes. She stood out right away as the student who would shine in a discussion-based, reading heavy class. The class focused on, as she explains, "a lot about the American Dream and the paradox of what it means to be free but not be free in America." In fact, the class took place during the 2016 presidential election, allowing for some serious discussions about how multiple oppressions are not just found in Langston Hughes poems but are real, very alive concepts and actions happening now. I was hungry for those discussions, and they were too.

Feminism, in particular, was at the front lines of political conversations, so it was easy to connect students to the literature to augment these conversations. For me, it was essential that feminist theory and pedagogy guide my teaching. I had read the critiques of White, middle class feminists, Gertrude Stein and Simone de Beauvoir, about how feminism marginalized and White-washed experiences of women of color, but it was only something I understood academically. As a mother, however, I did develop a new consciousness of the connections of mother-work, reproductive rights, and othermothering. Ana argued that her own feminist conscience came into being as she also became a young mother:

> I considered myself a feminist before the class, but I had not connected it to literature and art. Being a feminist was something I started identifying with after my daughter was born. When I was pregnant, I had a doula, and she was like, well, how are you going to feed your baby and I said, you mean like Enfamil or Celiac? When I started breastfeeding, because it was something I was so unexposed to and ignorant to, I thought there have got to be so many other girls, my age who feel the same way. I became a breastfeeding peer counselor and, definitely, I think I would be wrong not to attribute [my feminism] to that community.

Like Ana, something shifted in my sense of feminist ideology upon becoming a mother; the idea of care developed, of course, but also the relationship between my body and space shifted. What Ana was identifying is an experience that I thought had separated me from students because I could afford a doula and lactation consultant, but in fact, the idea of care and body politics was not new to many of my mother-students. Feminist mothering is an important lens for me to use in my pedagogy, but I needed to hear more about my students' experiences as mothers, not to assume they needed to come to an understanding of this through me.

Ana said she connected with the socio-political and feminist themes of the class but another deeply personal theme also articulated a concept she was living and did not have a name for: double-consciousness.

> Being white, but being raised in black and Hispanic foster families, I was never fully anything. When it was convenient to be the white girl, I did not know anything about this or that. I was just a white girl. But, in my white

families, I am never fully white. I'm the ghetto girl—their language—because I somehow reflect black or Hispanic culture. Those traits were always interpreted as negative. In some of my classes, if I had something to say, there was a lot of stuff that I felt I could relate to, certainly not everything, but the assumption was you do not know, you don't know. And, I do not pretend to, but there was so much I did experience.

Growing up in foster homes, sometimes being raised by her sister, being a teen mom, Ana never felt like she fit in any group. Literature gave her some reassurance and language for her experience. Ana's perspective about herself was clearly mature, but it also revealed some of the perspectives I held about my students' experiences were myopic. Although the literature and focus of the class may have allowed for Ana to develop herself as a "transformative intellectual" (Giroux, 1988), without talking with her outside of class, my assumptions about her, partly because of her intelligence and race, did not fit her actual experience. When I focused on her in class, I took the feminist angle, which was an important angle but limiting in comparison to her reality.

I asked her about experiences she had with other assumptions, especially by professors. She explained one situation she considered unjust.

> I remember when we had a professor that mandated these downtown showings that were $25 to get into, and I specifically remember telling her, I don't have the money to go to this, and she was like, figure it out, it's part of your grade.

I understood her point, but even writing this, it is hard to grasp that $25 is something that cannot be achieved, but that is true for many of our students. These assumptions will follow Ana for years because of her Whiteness, and her class. Not long before the interview, for instance, as she was preparing to transfer to a four-year school that she had received a small scholarship for, she learned that she would have to put off her entrance. The issue was the $200 down payment that students needed to make before registering. On the phone with the admissions counselor, after asking if there were any alternatives to immediate payment, she was told, "If you can't come up with $200, you may want to rethink going to school here."

Both students were often frustrated with the actions, perceived motivations, and efforts of their classmates. This reflects my personal struggle (for many I suspect) to balance our support and patience with the pressure to teach at the "college-level." Victoria brought this up a lot,

> Sometimes it felt like the other kids didn't give anything. If you do not bother to take notes, to look at your notes, or to ask anyone else, if kids don't give their 50%, then why would I give my 50%?

Ana observed these frustrations in our class together, as well. She admitted, in fact, that she would get worried about other students. "Like someone would be missing something that you have explained seven times, but you were so patient with them. Maybe you were faking it, but you seemed to always believe it would all come together." It was a bit jarring to hear that both students called me patient, which is not a word I would have ever used to describe myself. Of course, I was pleased, but I also wondered if the patience I *performed* for the class was sometimes translating to frustration for other students. Was my image of othering/care translating differently for them?

My conversations with VIctoria and Ana also converged in their positive view of Malcolm X College as a safe space. Ana reported that the vast majority of her professors were some of the best she's experienced, that they were, "in general, phenomenal." Victoria felt less alone and more supported. She began her college career at a small liberal arts school, a place that on paper, she would have no trouble excelling at academically, but the space itself failed to support and uplift her. She explains,

> I feel like some of the students and teachers did not take enough time to say, hey, you are undocumented, let me see what resources I can find you. They were just like, hey, you are undocumented, you're on your own. Especially with the TRIO program because all of the friends that I identified with in other ways I couldn't hang out with because I couldn't partake in TRIO. In the end, Chicago was a friendlier place.

I had not expected to hear that from either of the them. That, Chicago, let alone the City Colleges of Chicago were the "friendlier place;" here too, I believed I was the beacon in a dark place, but in fact, there were more of us.

DISCUSSION AND CONCLUSIONS

In reviewing our narratives and interviews, we believe there are three themes that emerge in the context of our research question, how can student perceptions impact the evolution and conscious shaping of the community college teacher's identity on an ongoing basis? The themes we observe are teacher performance, the construct of the community college student and professor, and the misalignment of our self-identity and student perception. We carried images of what it meant to look like a *good* or *conscious* teacher, and we often strived to fit the image. In our narratives, there are several places that speak to this performance and how it actually fed into an inauthentic mold of the overworked, disconnected, or savior teacher, which is counter-productive to our beliefs in democratic, feminist classrooms. We find it more productive to foster critical reflection and presence, as well as spaces for vulnerability and honesty, especially in terms of privilege, the ability/inability to meet needs, and our own identity (mis)perceptions. In speaking with our students, there were clearly some parts of our pedagogical selves that rang true with students, but there were many traits about ourselves that we misconceived. Not that student perceptions are always more accurate, but they can provide crucial information for identity development if the instructor is open to change. In addition, by our asking and following up with students on their conceptions of cultural and political identities, and hearing them work through positive formulations, we were able to participate in their negotiation of critical consciousness, as well.

As our literature review shows, there is not enough research about identities of community college teachers as individuals with agency who foster relationships with students. Students managing environmental, financial, and family stressors, who also have educational deficits, may be selective in their attunement to teacher identity, gravitating more to model qualities versus political or ideological traits. Moreover, the community college experience is transient, and the contact students make with their professors—albeit sometimes life changing—is ephemeral. The result of all of these dynamics means that the impressions community college students are left with in terms of their teachers' identities do not always align with the identity the instructor may be trying to establish. Or rather, the impression the instructor thinks she is imparting may not completely "stick." Through our exchanges while writing this article, we came to the concurrence that, for us, teacher identity is a combination of our core values as educators and our performance of these values in classroom settings. However, we realized that our definition must necessarily include student perceptions to broaden how we see ourselves. We recognize that we, along with other composition professors in urban, open-admission sites, are part of a historical narrative, about which Laurence (1993) concludes,

> Each conversation will be historically informed by different personalities; different regions of the country; different classes, ethnicities, or races of students; different educational missions and traditions. And when we have this kind of knowledge to be gathered by more inclusive methodologies than those represented here, we will begin to read the texts, the institutions, and the field with more sophistication. (p. 270)

When we gather and tell such stories, we offer more breadth to the understanding of teacher development. This is a nod towards a critical metapedagogy, "a growing system of interwoven knowledge and methodology that continually adapts to the perceived writing needs of a student audience" (Golson & Glover, 2009, p. 1). As university and two-year professors, full-time and part-time, we must make space to formally reflect and reconnect with our students. We need to offer support and fund training, not only on the newest digital platform, but on effective reflective processes. By doing this, we gain more than end-of-the semester data about retention rates. We gain the fruits of dialogue and celebrate our students' participation in our growth.

NOTE

1. For a study involving a similar method, but focused on reflective primary school teachers, see Young and Erickson's (2011) "Imagining, Becoming, and Being a Teacher: How Professional History Mediates Teacher Educator Identity."

REFERENCES

Akkerman, S. F., & Meijer, P. C. (2011). A dialogical approach to conceptualizing teacher identity. *Teaching and Teacher Education, 27*(2), 308–319.

Archer, L. (2008). The new neoliberal subjects? Young/er academics' constructions of professional identity. *Journal of Education Policy, 23*(3), 265–285.

Barnett, R., & Di Napoli, R. (2008). Introduction. In R. Barnett & R. Di Napoli (Eds.), *Changing identities in higher education* (pp. 1–8). London, UK: Routledge.

Bateson, M.C. (2001). *Composing a life*. New York, NY: Grove Press

Beauchamp, C., & Thomas, L. (2009) Understanding teacher identity: an overview of issues in the literature and implications for teacher education, *Cambridge Journal of Education, 39*(2), 175–189.

Beijaard, D., Meijer, P. C., & Verloop, N. (2004) Reconsidering research on teachers' professional identity, *Teaching and Teacher Education, 20*, 107–128.

Brownell, S. E., & Tanner, K. D. (2012). Barriers to faculty pedagogical change: Lack of training, time, incentives, and ... tensions with professional identity?. *CBE-Life Sciences Education, 11*(4), 339–346.

Bullough, R. V. (1997). Practicing theory and theorizing practice. In J. Loughran & T. Russell (Eds.), *Purpose, passion and pedagogy in teacher education* (pp. 13–31). London, UK: Falmer Press.

Clandinin, J. D. (2006). *Handbook of narrative inquiry: Mapping a methodology*. Los Angeles, CA: SAGE.

Cohen, A. M., & Brawer, F. B. (2003). *The American community college*. San Francisco, CA: John Wiley & Sons.

Collins, P. H. (1990). *Black feminist thought: knowledge, consciousness, and the politics of empowerment*. New York, NY: Routledge Press.

Day, C., Kington, A., Stobart, G., & Sammons, P. (2006). The personal and professional selves of teachers: Stable and unstable identities. *British Educational Research Journal, 32*(4), 601–616.

Emdin, C. (2016). *For White folks who teach in the Hood ... and the rest of y'all too: Reality pedagogy and urban education*. Boston, MA: Beacon Press.

Giroux, H. A. (1988). *Teachers as intellectuals: Toward a critical pedagogy of learning*. Granby, MA: Bergin & Garvey.

Glover, T., & Golson, E. (2009). *Negotiating a meta-pedagogy: Learning from other disciplines*. Newcastle upon Tyne, UK: Cambridge Scholars.

Harris, R. (2004). Encouraging emergent moments: The personal, critical, and rhetorical in the writing classroom. *Pedagogy, 4*(3), 401–418.

hooks, b. (1984). *Feminist theory from margin to center*. Boston, MA: South End Press.

hooks, b. (1994). *Teaching to transgress: Education as the practice of freedom*. New York, NY: Routledge.

Howard, T. C. (2003). Culturally relevant pedagogy: Ingredients for critical teacher reflection. *Theory into practice, 42*(3), 195–202.

Izadinia, M. (2013). A review of research on student teachers' professional identity. *British Educational Research Journal, 39*(4), 694–713.

Kardia, D. B., & Wright, M. C. (2004). Instructor identity: The impact of gender and race on faculty experiences with teaching. *CRLT Occasional Papers, 19*, 1–8.

Ladson-Billings, G. (1994). *The dreamkeepers: Successful teachers of African American children* (1st ed.). San Francisco, CA: Jossey-Bass.

Laurence, P. (1993). "The vanishing site of Mina Shaughnessy's "Errors and Expectations". *Journal of Basic Writing, 12*(2), 8–28.

Levin, J. (2001). *Globalizing the community college: Strategies for change in the twenty-first century*. New York, NY: Springer.

London, H. B. (1978). *The culture of a community college*. Westport, CT: Praeger.

Lunsford, A. A. (1991). The nature of composition studies. In E. Lindemann & G. Tate (Ed.), *An introduction to composition studies* (pp. 3–14). New York, NY: Oxford UP.

McLaren, P. (2007). *Life in schools: An introduction to critical pedagogy in the foundations of education*. Boston, MA: Pearson/A and B.

Mead, G. (1934). *Mind, self and society*. Chicago, IL: University of Chicago Press.

Mirra, N., & Morrell, E. (2011). Teachers as civic agents: Toward a critical democratic theory of urban teacher development. *Journal of Teacher Education, 62*(4), 408–420.

National Center for Education Statistics. (2015). U.S. Department of Education. City Colleges of Chicago-Malcolm X College. Retrieved from https://nces.ed.gov/collegenavigator/?q=city+colleges&s=all&id=144166

Obenchain, K. M., Balkute, A., Vaughn, E., & White, S. (2016). High school teachers' identities: Constructing civic selves. *The High School Journal, 99*(3), 252–278.

Ramanathan, L. (2017, January 24). Was the Women's March just another display of white privilege? Some think so. *Washington Post*. Retrieved from https://www.washingtonpost.com/lifestyle/style/was-the-womens-march-just-another-display-of-white-privilege-some-think-so/2017/01/24/00bbdcca-e1a0-11e6-a547-5fb9411d332c_story.html?utm_term=.da27f0310cf4

Sachs, J. (2003). *The activist teaching profession*. Buckingham, UK: Open University Press.

Townsend, B. K., & Twombly, S. B. (2007). Community college faculty: Overlooked and undervalued. *ASHE Higher Education Report*, *32*(6), 1–163.

van Lankveld, T., Schoonenboom, J., Volman, M., Croiset, G., & Beishuizen, J. (2016). Developing a teacher identity in the university context: A systematic review of the literature. *Higher Education Research & Development*, *36*(2), 325–342.

Van Manen, M. (1990). *Researching lived experience : Human science for an action sensitive pedagogy*. Albany, NY: State University of New York Press.

Young, J., & Erickson, L. (2011). Imagining, becoming, and being a teacher: How professional history mediates teacher educator identity. *Studying Teacher Education*, *7*(2), 121–129.

Zembylas, M. (2003). Interrogating "teacher identity": Emotion, resistance, and self-formation. *Educational Theory*, *53*(1), 107–127.

CHAPTER 2

THE WORK OF GIRLHOOD

An Invitation to
Examine Self and Identity

Amy Rutstein-Riley
Lesley University

Ann Mechem Ziergiebel
Salem State University

"There is no leaving a piece of us at home," shares Black girlhood scholar Dominique Hill (2016, p. 1). As we all occupy intersectional identities, Hill is deeply interested in how and why we are often asked to leave one identity at home—identity being an important domain of this study. The Girlhood Project (TGP) is attentive to and curious about this same exploration. Now entering its 11th year, TPG invited Hill to provide further context to their multidimensional exploration of how girls ranging from middle school to college negotiate their emerging and evolving identities. Thus, our inquiry and subsequent discussion focuses on the following question emerging from negotiating complex domains through the TGP relational space: how does the experience of sharing our radical relational space to explore and coconstruct girlhood shape an examination of self?"

Identity and Lifelong Learning in Higher Education, pp. 23–38
Copyright © 2020 by Information Age Publishing

Components of our relational space include a multilayered service-learning and research program focused on the exploration of intersectional girlhoods in the context of intergenerational feminist girls' groups. In addition, the structure of TGP includes: an undergraduate course, "Girlhood, Identity & Girl Culture"; a companion advanced seminar, "Teaching and Research in Girls and Girlhood Studies" for teaching and research assistants; and girls' groups focused on the themes of identity development, critical media literacy, and body image. Girls' groups are a community collaboration between the principal investigator (Lesley University), and Somerville and Cambridge MA public schools, and are informed by feminist pedagogy and group process, critical race theory, intersectional feminism, and positive youth development.

If these layers are not enough, our emerging scholar model provides opportunity for undergraduate and graduate students to participate first as students, then as teaching and research assistants (TA/RAs), and finally as collaborators in the development of new teaching and learning strategies around complex concepts. Our model situates all participants in a participatory action research environment where the following domains become through lines: identity development, feminist theory, girlhood, power differentials, vulnerability, and negotiating allies. Our discussion focuses on four of these meaning making domains: identity through an intersectional lens; feminist consciousness; embodied vulnerability (mediating and celebrating the power of the body) and allyship (a lifelong process of building relationships based on trust, consistency, and accountability with marginalized individuals and/or groups).

THEORETICAL FRAMEWORK

The roots of our inquiry are deep, cultivated through the following theoretical underpinnings: intersectionality; feminist pedagogy; relational cultural theory; and transformational theory. Exploring the interrelationship of race, gender, and other social identities emerges from a social construction developed by law professor Kimberle Crenshaw (Cho, Crenshaw, & McCall, 2013)—intersectionality. Cho, Crenshaw, and McCall offer intersectionality as a social theory that examines how various biological, social and cultural categories such as gender, race, class, ability, sexual orientation and other axes of identity interact on simultaneous levels. Social interactions can create multiple systems of oppression and discrimination (Crenshaw et al., 2013). Crenshaw's theory grows out of her attempts to conceptualize the way law responds to issues involving both race and gender. She adds:

What happened was like an accident, a collision. Intersectionality simply came from the idea that if you're standing in the path of multiple forms of exclusion, you are likely to get hit by both (or many). (p. 2)

Getting hit by both (or many) forms of exclusion is an important investigation during TGP. Our appraisal allows our TA/RAs to examine what happens between college students and middle school students, and how the intersection of identity, body image, relationships, sexuality, and race surface from the girls' group sessions. Further, TA/RA's explore their own intersectional identities and coach both Lesley undergraduates and middle school students in coconstructing counternarratives that better represent their own lived experiences. Counternarratives occur when building on the experiences of others while seeing our experiences in a different light. These storied counternarratives contribute to identity, a fluid sense of self, combining the processes of being and becoming (Yugal-Davis, as cited in Riessman, 2008, p. 8).

Our feminist pedagogical experience in TGP welcomes identity fluidity, first by examining burdening historical stereotypes while choreographing desirable constructions of self through our teaching and learning settings. Norms and expectations are coconstructed and interpreted in multiple ways by all, illustrating feminist teacher Magda Gere Lewis's (1993) thinking:

Universities are both the site where reactionary and repressive ideologies and practices are entrenched, and, at the same time, the site where progressive, transformative possibilities are born. (p. 145)

Transformative possibilities are born in safe spaces where college students and middle school girls can explore their hopes, values, and choices cultivating feminist values respecting experiences and differences. Feminist values and ways of knowing assess power differentials and oppression, promoting critical reflection. Reflecting critically about power differentials grounds relational-cultural theory (RCT), a theory recognizing the significance of cultural context to human development (Miller, 1976). As a feminist theory, RTC privileges every voice while working through challenges and suspending judgments. Further, RCT explores connection and disconnection, theorizing that connections form or fail to form within cultural relationships. Additionally, RCT contends that persons with cultural privilege may appear more autonomous and self-sufficient (traits often valorized in a White patriarchal culture) while socially disadvantaged persons (whether by virtue, race, ethnicity, sexual orientation, or economic status) seek connection and empathy (Miller, 1976).

In addition, as our discussion reveals the depth of connection and empathy through our domains—identity, feminist consciousness, embodied vulnerability and allyship—TGP actualizes transformative learning, or perspective transformation through critical examination of our prior interpretations and assumptions to form new meanings. Mezirow (1997) discusses this paradigm shift from instrumental learning (mastering tasks, problem solving, manipulating the environment) to transformative learning (understanding purpose, values, beliefs, and feelings). And, what a shift it is! Challenging dominant narratives about girls and girlhood while, again, exploring their own intersectional identities provides a framework for transformation. Sadly, girl and girlhood dominant narratives include: girls are sexualized objects devoid of power and autonomy; girls are subjects rather than producers of their own experience; girls—by comparison to their male counterparts—are subordinate, simultaneously powerful, and devoid of power; and girls conform to the prevailing profile of a universal girl.

Yet, in authentic, safe spaces, girls create a counter-narrative around academic prowess—a praxis—reflecting their new story through visual and prose journaling, group design and feminist pedagogy. All members of TGP enter into spaces that define Mezirow's transformative learning theory (TLT): disorienting dilemmas; critical reflection; and, rational dialogue (Kitchenham, 2008). Again, these safe spaces respect experiences and differences—the egalitarian garden where connections and empathy grow. Let us examine the context for this fertile development.

CONTEXT

First, let us introduce our researchers. Dedicated to opening space for experiencing and exploring, researchers Amy Rutstein-Riley and Ann Mechem Ziergiebel bring passion, commitment, and expertise to middle school development and undergraduate mentorship. Amy Rutstein-Riley is an Associate Professor of Sociology and the Dean of Faculty at Lesley University. She is the principal investigator of TGP, a program that has evolved over the 11 years, the result of close collaborations with community partners, students, girlhood scholars, and middle school girls. Amy aspires to create equitable learning spaces where middle school girls, college students, peer mentors, doctoral teaching fellows and faculty each contribute to the coconstruction (shared meaning making) of knowledge about girls' and women's lives. This relational pedagogical framing requires ongoing critical reflection and a reflexivity (researcher's awareness) that place girls' and women's knowledge and development at the center and privileges understanding of self and others as essential to the collaborative learning in TGP. Amy is actively (if imperfectly) focused on attending to power in the learning community created by TGP. As a White, middle class, Jewish, heterosexual woman, she intentionally normalizes discussion about identity through an intersectional lens so that all participants engaged in TGP are invited to bring their whole selves into the learning experience.

Ann Mechem Ziergiebel is Field Coordinator at the School of Education, Salem State University, Salem, MA, where she coaches preservice educators in protocol driven relational practice, pedagogy, and assessment. Previously, Ann devoted 23 years to teaching middle school social studies and humanities in the Gloucester Public Schools, Gloucester, MA, while raising her four children. She recently completed her doctorate in Educational Studies at Lesley University, Cambridge, MA, focusing on adolescent visual voices across academic disciplines. Highlights of her research planted seeds for this discussion. Her commitment to educational equity—every child receives what he/she needs to develop to his/her potential—is deepened by the acknowledgement of her White privileged place. This position of white privilege demands scrutiny for bias and open spaces to include all voices.

Further, Ann's passion for open spaces and aesthetics in education is kindled by her family's artistic roots running through three generations of talented artists working in watercolor, oil, mosaic, sculpture, stained glass, and block print. Ann encourages her students—middle schoolers, preservice teachers and TGP participants—to explore the timeless links between history, literature, and visual arts while cultivating identity exploration. Her students are often found sketching in the footsteps of Fitz Henry Lane along Gloucester Harbor, or researching the artifacts of native civilizations at the Peabody Essex Museum in Salem, MA.

Now let us enter the TGP community of learning. We are a diverse university (undergraduate upper level sociology course) and middle school group. Our TA/RAs also present with multiracial (Black, Latina, and White) and sexual orientation pluralism. As most girlhood scholarship is grounded in the experiences of White, middle-class girls, problematizing Black and Brown girls, TGP scholarship is rooted in unpacking our experiences and how they shape what we know in our safe, power-diffused community. Our urban middle school partners present differently than our university population—the following demographic information is offered about the 2017 girls cohort: majority are non-White; age-span of Grades 6–8; some are returnees from previous year; many are expected to assist with childcare and other house-hold related tasks imposing restrictions on their personal freedoms; and while these girls may reject the concept of *machismo*, they do not necessarily label themselves as *feministas* (given the political and social limitations associated with the term).

Thus, it is in this charged community that TGP seeks to create connections through caring and power neutral environments and course coconstructed girls' group activities. This environment plays a critical role in mediating adolescent girls' dual needs for both independence and guidance (Rhodes, Davis, Prescott, & Spencer, 1996). Additionally, feminist psychologist Gilligan (1990) purports that relationships between girls and young adult women may be critical during the transition into adolescence as girls at this stage seek out and listen to older women. Further, Rhodes et al. (1996) contends that mentoring affects youth through three inter-related processes: enhancing youth's social relationships and emotional well-being; improving youth's cognitive skills through meaningful conversation; and promoting youth's positive identity development through role modeling. Along-side middle schoolers, while in mentoring roles, both TA/RAs and university students experience disorientation during our seven-week girls' group as behaviors, biases and expectations shift and sway for all participants in TGP. Managing disorientation is complex and relational as the discussion that ensues demonstrates. Our data collection for the following discussion includes focus groups facilitated by TA/RAs, critical incident reports and fishbowl discussions on weekly readings.

DISCUSSION

As gender is the organizing concept of TGP, four complimentary domains providing ballast and open spaces for meaning making (through disorientation) include: identity, feminist consciousness, embodied vulnerability and allyship. TGP course design is intentional, through the course syllabus on girlhood pedagogy and practice to coconstructed girl's group facilitation, inviting collaboration, critical reflection, and engaged dialogue through feminist group process. This strategic practice aims to see all participants as strong, fluid and intersectional—a practice supporting the work of feminist scholars Clonan-Roy and Jacobs (2017). Feminist youth development (FYD) (Clonan-Roy & Jacobs, 2017) is a critical consciousness model of female development based on the needs of girls of color. Stemming from positive youth development (PYD), which builds on the strength of the individual, their FYD model addresses the intersectionality that girls carry.

Clonan-Roy and Jacobs (2017) joined TGP for a powerful workshop reflecting on the competencies that develop and raise critical consciousness towards cultural capital and the power it wields. They offer six competencies that critically examine and strategically upend the social inequities that girls experience: confidence; character; connection; caring; contribution; and resistance. The research domains discussed in the following sections directly spiral through the work of FYD and emerge as vital lenses from which the complex work of girlhood is observed and propagated.

Identity

The quest for understanding self envelops the world of girlhood. Understanding self through story, organizing events from the past, remembering, wondering, and engaging in perspective taking contributes to the rich work of adolescent identity development. Educators and researchers Nakkula and Toshalis (2010), influenced by education theorist Vygotsky (1978), contend that authoring life stories is the productive imagining of self in a context. Powerfully articulating that individual psychological development is inherently a relational process, Vygotsky asserts that individual minds develop within the context of other minds by which they can be influenced. Thus, stories are pathways for integrating the influence of others. Let us listen to our university students discussing identity during focus groups facilitated by TA/RAs, critical incident reports and fishbowl discussions on weekly readings:

> Unpacking my white identity was hard for me and that was something I've never really had to confront before coming to this class and I think being in this class has helped me with that but that I know it's not anywhere close to being unpacked … but I think that's where I grew the most.

Further, as university students reflect on the pedagogical course framework, other identity threads are revealed:

> I think I had a personal turning point when we read Tatum and it was after that week's response on positive racial identity and multiracial identity and I was reading all the statistics of choosing not to identify with certain aspects of their identity—thinking about my socialization and how I didn't have a chance to develop any sort of racial and ethnic identity. I started to reflect on that a lot as to why I was struggling so much and why I didn't have it—as a kid it really wasn't talked about.

Another examination of self creates an emotional response:

> I feel like I have a turning point that happened—I think it was when I started to look in the mirror and see someone beautiful (starts to cry) … that's never happened to me until this class and it's hard to say out loud because I haven't done that yet and I know I seem like a very confident person but I'm not so this class helped me realize that—that it's okay to not be confident sometimes and when I started being happy is when I started to see changes in the way I facilitated groups.

Finally, racial identity becomes a lens requiring observing, listening and describing:

> I'm kind of thinking as we were reading *Black Girlhood Celebration* it felt like
> we were trying to work more with this work and I'm wondering where my
> place is as a white woman in this work and if I should be involved in this
> work. Is it for me or is this for them (middle schoolers) ... so I don't know
> and at one point I was like this is what I want to do now ...

Consider the disorienting dilemmas present in the discussion of race, privilege and historical context through gender and women's study activist Ruth Nicole Brown's seminal work, *Black Girlhood Celebration* (2009). Brown discusses a community of Black girls as a place to be, to feel loved, to dance—"a privileged outlaw space ... it creates a vibe amid a community as well as a spirit of artistic production or intellectual/spiritual discursive moments" (Perry, as cited in Brown, 2009, p. 107). Thinking about our guiding question—how does the experience of sharing this radical relational space to explore and coconstruct girlhood shape an examination of self—all participants in TGP go through a process of racial identity. In a society that emphasizes race, exposing TGP to the challenging and nuanced work of scholarship along with unpacking racial identity can prove both daunting and revealing. As our discussion ensues, the centering of gender and power connects deeply with identity exploration.

Feminist Consciousness

As discussed earlier, TGP is framed by feminist pedagogical concepts modeling: power as energy and capacity; community as a place that values autonomy and individuality; and leadership as shared purpose (Shrewsbury, 1993). Further, feminist consciousness assesses power differentials and oppression. Let us listen to our university students discussing feminist consciousness during focus groups facilitated by TA/RAs, critical incident reports and fishbowl discussions on weekly readings:

> The biggest word that stuck with me is empower—we don't needs to give
> power. They (middle schoolers) already have power, they just need to find
> it. We don't need to divvy it out ... rather, they need to find it. They already
> have a voice.

Continuing with the idea that cultivating voice and creating space in our girls' groups, another undergraduate states:

> Ruth Nicole Brown talks about mentoring versus creating the space keep-
> ing to the agenda to make space to reduce power differentials. This means
> not being in a teacher role. It's a fine line between a mentoring relation-
> ship versus teacher role, like telling the girls not to talk right now, it's a fine
> line to figure out. It's hard to figure out how to be structured and create
> space.

Another comment about power differentials displays the challenge of diffusing power:

> Going back to the idea of power—the idea that you have to take away your own to give it to someone else, that only one person in the room can have power—it's something I struggled with … just holding my own—being able to step up sometimes—allowing silence to persist.

And, continued wrestling with power, space and language is illustrated here:

> I believe I was afraid of stepping on people's toes for facilitation roles— stepped back too much and believe I did myself a disservice by stepping back …

Continuing with language and shared purpose, the following undergraduate shares:

> I think when you said cisgendered I think that's a big thing—it is a girls' group but it really is a hot topic right now—gender and the gender spectrum—and they might be in a community where that isn't discussed or welcomed—where transgendered is a dirty word.

A power link between feminist group process and identity is revealed in this fishbowl discussion:

> Asking questions is the most you can do for you and me. It's about unpacking privilege. Like Tatum talks about— forming a positive youth identity. I wish we had talked about it as an entire class. My white identity is affecting the entire group and class.

Truth, inquiry, and meaning making is the essence of feminist consciousness, the best situations occurring when this happens authentically while coconstructing a space to explore identities and celebrate shared experiences. Celebrating shared experiences invoking identity exploration while interrogating assumptions creates vulnerability— pressure to unlearn and be exposed to the possibility of distress (physically and emotionally). Hill (2016) expands our vulnerable state to a place called "embodied vulnerability"—the focus of our next discussion.

Embodied vulnerability. Hill (2016) enacts "embodies vulnerability" as an activity of assumptions. Her contention is that the intersection of race, gender are visible but seeing does not spark recognition. Hill's scholarship and teaching reflect her collective experience as an educator while inviting students to *see* her—aiming to center the body to the teaching/learning process (Black and lesbian). Recall that as we commenced this chapter, Hill implores us to leave no parts of ourselves at home, knowing that our socio-cultural context often requires a compartmentalizing of oneself. Listen to the possibilities (as shared in focus groups facilitated by TA/RAs, critical incident reports and fishbowl discussions on weekly readings) and potential hazards for bringing our whole selves to each interaction:

> Everyone's girlhood is different. It's not about projecting assumptions. I'm struggling because it's about my socialization and it's about someone else's girlhood. There are no similar girlhoods. I feel like it's contradictory. It makes me think of Dominique Hill. Because that's everything she talked about. Somebody asked her a question—when do you split—hold back—she tries to put her experience into everything because that's what the job calls for, her job is her life. Embodied vulnerability is confronting your own socialization—it's where we're showing our own vulnerability.

Uncomfortable spaces can be meaning-making spaces as well. Further thinking on discomfort and vulnerability follow:

> I think we're worried about becoming vulnerable. There's a fear of saying something, of being labeled a bad feminist, a fear of not knowing something— an uncomfortable space.

Continuing the rich mix of theory and practice, undergraduates research, design, implement and evaluate middle school girls' groups focusing on the intersection of identity, body image and critical media literacy. However, honest feedback in a focus group reveals:

> With our group we haven't really been vulnerable, we haven't said our genealogy, where we come from is not where we identify as, we haven't made the distinction between the two—we haven't touched up it at all—the girls could be in all different ethnic stages—to allow the girls to be vulnerable … we haven't reached steps of Tatum's positive racial identity development.

Critical to connecting theory to practice is the complex (and complexing) roles undergraduates face with facilitating and leading—undergraduates are often reminded that they are not teachers delivering content. Opening spaces for meaning making with inclusive activities requires complex, nuanced strategies, resulted in the following dilemma:

> Whose ideas get chosen and brought to the front and just navigating through that and then also in this facilitation role of course I have to compare it to my teacher role but just how much self things it was and so like I fell like in a teacher role—nothing is about you—everything is about the children … and in this role, it's a lot of self work. The first day I was like

"well shit this is gonna be about me too?" I think that surprised me in a good way but not just me and the other person but how much it's about me as well as them.

Vulnerability, embodied and psychological, opens up space and intention towards honesty and authentic experiencing of self with others. This is compelling and difficult work, enhanced with the development of intersectional allyship (embracing intersectional differences and similarities between the undergraduates and middle schoolers) along with intergenerational allyship (embracing the power dynamic occurring between younger and older people). TGP emphasizes the intersectional histories in feminist activism to prevent mistakes made by previous movements. This important framing continues in the following discussion of allyship's multiple constructs.

Allyship

The lifelong process of building relationships based on trust, consistency, and accountability with marginalized individuals and/or groups defines allyship, In a focus group, an undergraduate sums up her experience of using her voice effectively with marginalized individuals as being "a big thing for me, I still could and should use my voice ... still working through the way society suppresses and privileges identities ... I have been working through that. I journal a lot and doing it more. Having thoughts for yourself is important."

So what is allyship in TGP, a multigenerational, multiracial learning community...

Feminism and intersectional feminism does not equate allyship—it is not action—we need to apply what we're doing and thinking.

Another undergraduate adds;

It's learning to be an ally and combining your hopes for equity and unlearning and how that balance takes a lot of work and stress and a lot of people and questions, and without this space, none of us would have been able to accomplish this.

The perspective-taking stance of allyship is complex and rewarding. Educator Gehlbach (2013) defines perspective taking as "understanding the thoughts, feelings, and motivations of other people" (p. 119). Our thinking on perspective taking draws from the theoretical framework for understanding the social development of self, articulated by psychologist

Mead (1934). The ability of an individual to take the attitude of another toward herself/himself allows the individual to become self-aware—in Mead's words, *reflexive*. TGP examines reflexiveness as it cultivates the development of self-awareness. Reflexiveness is fostered through the use of language to communicate and through the ability to switch social roles. By switching roles, an individual takes on the perspective of the other person in that role, a critical characteristic of allyship.

Our undergraduate states, above, that allyship is "not an action"—it is applying multiple perspectives to your thinking. Checking yourself for biases and assumptions while listening *with* someone explores the "unlearning" process also mentioned above—the forgetting of an usual way of thinking. Here is another focus group comment:

> we all struggle with finding words and space in activities to talk about issues we're still working through, privileges that are still being realized ... if we don't talk about it, maybe the girls don't realize it ... we don't have whites-plaining.

Whitesplaining refers to the paternalistic stance given by Whites toward a person of color, often contributing their views on racist thinking. While rejecting condescending viewpoints, what the middle school girls do not realize about the connectedness or lack of connection with the under-graduates? How is allyship experienced in our multigrnerational groups? Consider these questions as this discussion transitions to analysis of our TGP experience with our guiding question— how does the experience of sharing this radical relational space to explore and coconstruct girlhood shape an examination of self?

ANALYSIS

Young women's identity development shapes adolescence—a critical juncture in the formation of a mature understanding of the self, including one's gender identity (Abrams, 2003). Researcher and feminist scholar Abrams (2003) contends that the past three decades have witnessed the concept of gender as a dynamic, socially constructed category replace traditional notions of gender as a fixed or biologically determined position. TGP, entering its 11th year, situates itself in the apex of postmodern identity development, where identities can be "assembled and disas-sembled, accepted and contested, and indeed performed for audiences" (Riessman, 2008). As we analyze our focus groups facilitated by TA/RAs, critical incident reports and fishbowl discussions on weekly readings, we apply thematic analysis—our primary attention is on "what" is said, rather than "how," "to whom" or "for what purposes" (Riessman, 2008).

The preceding discussion, viewing TGP through the meaning making lenses of identity, feminist consciousness, embodied vulnerability, and allyship, asserts that these narratives are performances of identity (Riessman, 2008). Performed through individual writings and group dialogues collected ethnographically in the TGP community, we witness three shaping practices emerging from our guiding question— how does the experience of sharing this radical relational space to explore and coconstruct girlhood shape an examination of self? These shaping practices include raising critical consciousness, understanding resistance and locating personal power. Let us examine a chart that provides undergraduate evidence for these shaping practices:

Raising critical consciousness, developing an awareness of how power circulates, connects to Hansen's (2011) concept of *cosmopolitanism*—the stance of global citizenship. A cosmopolitan perspective expands our capacity to be open to seeing the world as others do and hearing their ways of thinking and knowing (Hansen, 2011). As our undergraduate shares above, "taking space and making space" describes Hansen's model of listening *with* others. Further, our undergraduate is connecting to Freire's (2001) critical consciousness, knowing something from a certain position yet recognizing that this knowledge is fluid. Continuing, our undergraduate states, "you can have this theoretical knowledge and unless you practice it … what does it mean to have knowledge." This undergraduate discourse is the foundation for critical consciousness—empowering the powerless and paying attention to the intersectionality of multiple systems of oppression and discrimination (Crenshaw, 2004).

Continuing our analysis, understanding resistance contributes to a more interactive and engaged model of development and opens up the conversation about young womens' experiences across contexts and cultures (Abrams, 2003). Some scholars suggest that in their distance and alienation from idealized versions of femininity, young women who are marginalized along racial lines are better suited to reject persuasive images of female beauty (Abrams, 2003). As stated by our undergraduate, "changing social media—being able to change what we're thinking about media … so we can deconstruct …" is an important first step in resistance. Further study regarding whether dominant cultures may be less prepared to resist begs attention. Yet, our undergraduates are starting the conversation—"the girls that we work with are all effected by racism and by not giving it the attention it deserves, we're not doing any justice."

Giving voice to the effect of racism is the sound of locating personal power. Beginning to identify with ethnic and cultural identities, along with gender, sexual orientation, ability, age and other social constructs

Table 2.1.
Shaping Practices

Shaping Practice	Definition	Undergraduate Evidence
Raising Critical Consciousness	Developing an awareness of how power circulates	It's a growing experience and I need to hold myself accountable for the things I say—I try to do little check-ins with myself
		You can have this theoretical knowledge and unless you practice it ... what does it mean to have knowledge—taking space and making space
		One of the largest takeaways I have from the girls' group is learning the importance of a feminist pedagogy and all the things that can go wrong and all the good things that can come out of it
Understanding Resistance	Conscious and unconscious rejecting of social and cultural mandates concerning gender, race, class, and other axes of social difference	Changing social media—being able to change what we're thinking about media ... so we can deconstruct it
		The girls that we work with are all effected by racism and by not giving it the attention it deserves, we're not doing any justice
		I have come to understand intersectional feminism and where it came into play in my life
Locating Personal Power	Developing positive self-concepts and identifying with ethnic and cultural identities	Everyone has empowerment within themselves, everyone just has to find it—
		our job is to not give power but give them space to find it
		The building of interpersonal relationships between girls—just how important that is to the development of girlhood and to the identity of girlhood and how it is trivialized and not taken particularly seriously
		The idea that only one person can have power in the room and I think holding on to your power—it encourages others to do the same

cultivates the development of positive self-concept. Researchers argue that often, negative feelings about gender identity may be somewhat offset by a strong identification with ethnic and cultural identities (Abrams, 2003). "Everyone has empowerment within themselves, everyone just has to find it …" begins the undergraduate conversation of location within ourselves. As our undergraduate suggests, above, "our job is not to give power but give them (middle school girls) space to find it." Framed in feminist, constructivist and critical theory, TGP seems to succeed in providing space, safety and discovery for these powerful practices of raising critical consciousness, understanding resistance and locating personal power.

INSIGHTS

The shaping practices, above, are the roots of self-reflexivity and refinement of ideas and protocols. The TGP undergraduates and their learning community continue to explore and coconstruct girlhood, modeling the domains showcased earlier in this discussion—identity, feminist consciousness, vulnerability and allyship. From these stances emerge the raising of consciousness, the understanding of resistance and the locating of personal power. These results help us make new meaning from this inquiry guided by our research question: how does the experience of sharing this radical relational space to explore and coconstruct girlhood shape an examination of self? Additionally, our evidence indicates that sharing the radical relational space of the work of girlhood creates in our undergraduates an ongoing struggle and discovery of the intersection of gender and other salient identity statuses.

This thematic analysis showcases new meaning-making, broadening the discussion around the examination of self for undergraduates based on lived experiences and daily negotiations with social power and social difference. These findings can serve as a foundation for theorists and researchers who are interested in expanding knowledge about the intersections of gender identity with ethnicity, social class and cultural factors.

REFERENCES

Abrams, L. (2003). Contextual variations in young women's gender identity negotiations. *Psychology of Women Quarterly, 27*, 64–74.

Brown, R. N. (2009). *Black girlhood celebration*. New York, NY: Peter Lang.

Cho, S., Crenshaw, K. W., & McCall, L. (2013). Toward a field of intersectionality studies: Theory, applications, and praxis. *Signs, 38*(4).

Clonan-Roy, K., & Jacobs, C. (2016). Towards a model of positive youth development t specific to girls of color: Perspectives on development, resilience, and empowerment. *Gender Issues, 33*(2), 96–121. Retrieved from http://link. springer.com/article/10.1007/s12147-016-9156- 7

Crenshaw, K. (2004). Intersectionality: The double bind of race and gender. Retrieved from http://www.americanbar.org/content/dam/aba/publishing/ perspectives_magazine/women_perspectives_Spring2004CrenshawPSP. authcheckdam.pdf

Freire, P. (2001). *Pedagogy of freedom*. New York, NY: Rowman & Littlefield.

Gehlbach, H. (2013). Social perspective taking: A multidimensional approach. Retrieved from www.uknow.gse.harvard.edu/teaching/TC104-607.html

Gilligan, C. (1990). *"Girls at 11: An interview with Carol Gilligan."* Cambridge, MA: Harvard Graduate School of Education, in association with Harvard University Press.

Hansen, D. (2011). *The teacher and the world*. New York, NY: Routledge.

Hill, D. C. (2016). What happened when I invited students to see me? A Black queer professor's reflections on practicing embodied vulnerability in the classroom. *Journal of Lesbian Studies, 21*(4).

Kitchenham, A. (2008). The evolution of John Mezirow's tranformative learning theory. *Journal of Transformative Education, 6*(2), 104–123.

Lewis, M. (1993). *Without a word: Teaching beyond women's silence*. London, England: Routledge.

Mead, G. H. (1934). *Mind, self, and society from the standpoint of a social behaviorist* (C. W. Morris, Ed.). Chicago, IL: University of Chicago Press.

Mezirow, J. (1997). Transformative learning: Theory to practice. *New Direction for Adult Learning and Continuing Education, 75*, 5–12.

Miller, J.B. (1976). *Toward a new psychology of women*. Boston, MA: Beacon Press.

Nakkula, M., & Toshalis, E. (2010). *Understanding youth*. Cambridge, MA: Harvard Education Press.

Rhodes, J.E., Davis, A.A., Prescott, L.R., & Spencer, R. (1996). Caring connections: Mentoring relationships in the lives of urban girls. In B. Leadbeater & N. Way (Eds.), *Resisting stereotypes, creating identities* (pp. 142–156). New York, NY: New York University Press.

Riessman, C. K. (2008). *Narrative methods for the human sciences*. Thousand Oaks, CA: SAGE.

Rutstein-Riley, A., Walker, J., Diamond, A., Bryant, B., & LaFlamme., M. (2013). We're all straight here: Using girls' groups and critical media literacy to explore identity with middle school girls. In K. Harper, Y. Katsalis, V. Lopez, & G. S. Gillis (Eds.), *Girls' sexualities and the media: The power of the media* (pp. 263–283). New York, NY: Peter Lang.

Shrewsbury, C. (1993). What is feminist pedagogy. *Women's Studies Quarterly, 3&4*, 8–16.

Vygotsky, L. (1978). *Mind in society: The development of higher psychological processes*. Cambridge, MA: Harvard University Press.

CHAPTER 3

"ONE LAZY DAY WOULD CAUSE EVERYTHING TO COME CRASHING DOWN"

Stories From Underrepresented Students on Becoming a University Student

Alyson King and Allyson Eamer
University of Ontario Institute of Technology

INTRODUCTION

For most Canadian children and young people, seeing oneself as a "student" is commonplace. Once they reach their late teen years, however, many start to reconsider their learning trajectories and their future place in the world, and make important life decisions: whether to transition directly from high school to the work force; to pursue a higher education at a community college or university; or to pursue a trade. Our qualitative pilot study (funded by a Social Science & Humanities Research Council Small Research Grant) focussed on students who enrolled in a university located in a medium-sized working class city located one hour outside of

Identity and Lifelong Learning in Higher Education, pp. 39–57

one of Canada's largest urban centers. Demographically, these students tend to have lower entrance grades, be required to work and/or seek loans to attend university, come from immigrant or lower socioeconomic status families, be visible minorities, and commute to campus. This chapter will focus on what students say about choosing to pursue postsecondary studies, their experiences at university, and their perceptions of themselves as successful learners. We argue that part of this identity formation occurs when a student has a sense of belonging to an academic community.

METHODOLOGY AND DEMOGRAPHICS

Data were collected using concurrent surveys and interviews. Volunteers were solicited through purposeful selection to achieve equity regarding gender identification, first- versus fourth-year students, and ethnic or racial self-identification. The research used critical race theory (Crenshaw, 2011), resilience theory (Liebenberg & Ungar, 2009), and postcolonial/Indigenous paradigms (Smith, 2012) as theoretical frames of analysis to challenge the notion that "the social system is open and individual mobility can be attained through hard work" (Sleeter, 1993, p. 160). A total of 24 students (7 male and 17 female) took the survey, 13 of whom were first year students, while the other 11 were in their fourth year of studies. Additionally, eight female students (four in first year and four in fourth year) were interviewed; several male students were scheduled to be interviewed, but none kept their appointments. Three students participated in both the interview and the survey for a total of 29 individual participants. Although respondents were mainly aged 18 ($n = 10$) and 21 ($n = 8$), the full age range was from 17 ($n = 1$) to 25 ($n = 1$). Five students were permanent residents, four were Canadian citizens by naturalization, and 15 were Canadian citizens by birth. Of the 15 Canadian citizens by birth, all were born in Ontario. Students identified with a wide range of ethnicities, including Canadian, and several identified with multiple ethnicities, such as "Italian, German and Scottish" or "South Asian and West Indian." In the survey, students were asked a variety of questions including: the importance of their ethnic identity, their sense of belongingness, whether or not they had planned to attend university, and their experiences of feeling discriminated against in different locations. The interview questions were open-ended in order to allow individuals to elaborate on their particular experiences. In both the survey and the interviews, we tried to determine levels of parental support and educational background. Recent research suggests that family emotional support for students' educational aspirations and parental levels of education are more important than family finances in determining who enrolls and persists in higher education (Finnie, Sweetman, & Usher,

2008). In other words, when young people grow up with the expectation that they can go to university, they are more likely to do so. This suggests that, for those students who grow up expecting to attend university, a student identity may have begun developing before a conscious decision to attend is made.

LITERATURE REVIEW

Identity is a concept that encapsulates the individual's work of connecting oneself to a social community and locating oneself relative to a web of interrelationships. In the decades since Erikson (1959) first theorized the development of identity, researchers have linked it with, among other things, the process of organizing, meaning-making, achieving a sense of agency and acquiring higher cognitive capacity. Hoppes (2014) presented the questions that young people face as they transition into adulthood: "What is this life about? Who exactly am I in this moment? What are my personal and professional paths and where are they taking me? Am I prepared for the challenges ahead?" (p. 63). Blumenkrantz and Goldstein (2014) see college campuses as sites of initiation which can, through establishing mentoring relationships, facilitate the transition to adulthood without the digressions into self-destructive behaviors that have traditionally accompanied the transition from familial monitoring to self-monitoring. Other research focusses on the maintenance and/or modification of values and worldviews as the primary tasks of student identity development (Dean & Jolly, 2012; Flum & Kaplan, 2012; Kaufman, 2014; Sanders & Munford, 2016; Weidman, 2014). Our research is intended to capture the "variability of student experiences" (Strange, 2016, p. 17; see also, King, 2015) by exploring the stories of how underrepresented students at one Canadian university develop a university student identity and a sense of belonging to a university community.

THE DECISION: FAMILY SUPPORT AND ROLE MODELS

As noted above, parental education and the expectation that one will attend university are more important than simply socioeconomic background in determining who is most likely to enrol in and attend university (Finnie et al., 2008; King, Eamer, & Ammar, 2018). First generation students (those students whose parents have not had postsecondary education) illustrate the importance of family support for higher education despite parents' lack of experience with the system. In general, our research supports this finding. In the survey, we asked students about when and how they decided to go to university. Most of the students ($n = 18$) said that they had always planned to attend university, while a few ($n = 4$) indicated that they did not make the decision until they were in Grade 12. Beatrice (all names are pseudonyms), a first generation student, realized in Grade 11 that she had to start working harder in order to get into university. She was so looking forward to attending university that she visited the campus over the summer to become familiar with the facilities.

Family support for and commitment to students' educational aspirations are important to students' ability to deal with the stresses of moving away from home and university-level academic expectations. All students surveyed indicated that their parents emotionally supported them in pursuing their education, but some families were more supportive than others. For instance, Chaaya, a 23-year-old fourth-year student, immigrated by herself to Canada in order to attend university. She was born in India, but grew up in Abu Dhabi. At the time of the interview, she had been in Canada for three years. It was challenging to come by herself to a new country, but she found Canada to be warm and welcoming. Nonetheless, Chaaya faced some health and emotional challenges living alone in the university residence during her first winter in Canada. She says she always felt cold and wanted only to sleep, suggesting that she may have been experiencing depression. She was also diagnosed with diabetes. Unwell and alone, she failed one course and her GPA suffered. The following year, her parents came to Canada. The family has permanent resident status, but her well-educated parents have had trouble finding employment. Most of the family savings went to purchasing a house. At the time of the interview, she was living with her family and enjoying university much more because of being better able to focus on her studies. Having her parents nearby makes it easier to deal with problems. For example, her father picks her up on cold nights so she does not have to rely on the bus. Her parents encourage her to get good grades: "when they get furious, I'll be like oh I know I have to get much better scores next time." Her mother trained as a science teacher and gives her tips on studying and managing her time. Her sister, who is studying medicine in the United States, helped her to come up with a schedule for managing her time, but she continues to battle a low cumulative GPA. She now takes better care of herself by eating well and going to the gym before going home. She also tries to get most of her work done while at school and says that her family and her study group friends help her to persist in school. In spite of being diagnosed with a serious chronic illness, she blames herself for the academic difficulties in her first year, saying that she "should have just tried harder."

Not all families, however, were as dedicated to supporting their child. Twenty-one-year-old Dalia, an African immigrant studying health sciences, claimed that education was really important for her family, particularly for her father who was diagnosed with a life-threatening chronic illness while she was in high school. In spite of this, and the fact that both parents have university degrees, it was clear from the details of her story that it was her own initiative and determination that ensured her success at university. While Dalia was in first year, her family moved to another Canadian province. She had chosen originally to come to the university being examined in this study because it was far enough away from the family home (before their move to a new province) that she could live apart from her family to attend school, but still be close enough to visit; she chose to stay there even after her parents and brothers moved to another part of the country.

She did not receive any financial support from her parents in spite of being deemed ineligible for the Ontario Student Assistance Program (OSAP) on the grounds that her family's income was too high. Dalia often feels lonely on weekends and holidays because her immediate family now lives in a distant province, and she is not close with her extended family members who are more "culture focused" and believe she is too "Americanized." Her parents support her university studies, but her father employs "more of an intimidation type of thing." She and her mother work harder on their relationship now that they do not see each other every day.

Some students have family responsibilities that take time away from their studies. For instance, Anita, whose parents are divorced, lives with her father (who pays for her tuition), grandmother and sister, and is responsible for cooking dinner and cleaning the house. Her mother provides encouragement and is very supportive emotionally. However, Anita is ambivalent when speaking about her father: "with my dad, it is kind of just like he wants to see me do well but he does not necessarily show that he is proud."

While Beatrice's parents finished high school, neither completed a postsecondary education. Her mother attended college for a year and a half, but did not complete her program. Her dad started his own business, which failed, then took an online course, and is now starting a new business. Her parents are supportive and allow her to prioritize her school obligations; however, she has three much younger siblings, including one with Down syndrome and autism, so she is required to help look after them.

Parental support and family background are not the only determining factors. High school preparation and encouragement from teachers also play an important role. Dalia felt that high school did not adequately prepare her for university. She explained that she hated high school because she was so different from the other students as an immigrant. Dalia's family emigrated from East Africa to the United States and then to Canada where they have lived in multiple provinces. Her parents, from different parts of Africa, met in India while studying at university. In her American high school, Dalia felt her teachers tried to dampen her goal of becoming a doctor due to her race. She believes she was not supposed to aim to be an engineer or a doctor. Instead, she was expected to become a social worker or to enter a helping profession: "they just assume that … you're going to be [one of] those girls that is going to you know drop out of high school at some point and have kids." She gives the example of the high school chemistry teacher who, when asked to sign a letter in support of her volunteering in a hospital, discouraged her ambitions to seek a medical profession. However, having even one supportive teacher can make a difference. One of Dalia's high school teachers in the U.S. still checks up on her to see how things are going. This teacher's efforts mean a lot to her: "It's like she didn't have to do any of it and she always went above and beyond just because I think she knew that … coming into high school when you're an immigrant child it's very scary … so she kind of just took me under her wing." Additionally, her friends provide support and she knows she can count on them to help if she has a problem.

First generation students often struggle to navigate the university system and adapt to university studies. Nineteen-year-old Anita is attending university after taking a year off to work and upgrade her high school English and mathematics grades. At the time of the interview, she was three months into her first semester and she was finding the university workload to be heavy. She has two older siblings who went to college in Canada and both her parents finished high school. Her father attended university in Canada for a time, but did not complete his degree. Her family has lived in Canada for the last 15 years after moving back and forth between Canada and the West Indies for a few years. Similarly, Beatrice, an 18-year-old first generation student in her first semester of university, was born in Canada to parents with Filipino backgrounds. When she first arrived at university, she felt confident that she would do well, but was apprehensive of what might happen when she was under pressure, since she knew that some people dropped out during their first year. On the outside, she felt she looked "confident and bubbly," while on the inside she was anxious about making friends.

STARTING UNIVERSITY: MAKING FRIENDS AND FITTING IN

Several of the students interviewed indicated that when they arrived at university, they were simultaneously excited and nervous. In addition to adapting to a new school, new expectations, and finding new friends, many students also had to get used to living away from home. Even those who continued to live with their families now had to commute daily while also juggling school and work obligations. Both the survey and interview findings demonstrate that attending events such as orientation and becoming involved in student life helped in developing a sense of self as a university student and a sense of belonging to the university community.

While all the students felt at least a little bit nervous, a few felt lost when they first arrived. One first year student, Erin, stated that because she had not toured the school beforehand, she did not know how to find her way around. She did attend orientation, but since it took place at the downtown campus, she had trouble finding one of her classes at the other campus. After three months, she has only made two or three friends and feels lonely so she goes home every weekend to see her family and to work. She describes herself as shy and very busy with her horse and riding competitions. However, she also says that university studies are not as demanding as she thought they would be. She says that her high school teachers really tried to scare the students, but she finds that her schedule is not as busy or as difficult as she expected, even though her grades have gone down by about 10%. Although she now feels more comfortable at university because she understands what is expected, she is still too nervous to ask questions in class.

Students who participated in extracurricular or cocurricular activities were more likely to say that they were able to cope well with difficult courses, assignments or other challenges (see Table 3.1). Chaaya felt that everything was explained very well during orientation so she did not feel lost when classes started and she made several new friends. She was one of only a few enrolled in electrical engineering, but she did not socialize much with any of them because "people in my program, especially electrical, are not exactly sociable." In first year, she socialized primarily with international students who were also new to Canada. She felt that her first year was "pretty easy because most of it I already learned in my high school." This meant she was able to help out her friends in first year who were having trouble. However, the courses have gotten more difficult in the upper years. Chaaya used the peer tutoring service for one assignment, which she found helpful. She was a member of Engineers Without Borders and has volunteered for the African Student Society because a friend is the president. While she indicated that religion was important to her, she felt that it had little impact on her success at university. Similarly, she has not joined any Indian cultural groups due to not feeling welcome on the one occasion she attended a meeting. Instead, she prefers discipline-oriented groups that cut across culture and religion. Even though she is one of two women in electrical engineering, she does not feel disadvantaged; she feels she is treated the same way as all the other students.

Dalia's experience highlights the impact that race and ethnicity can have on fitting in on campus. She was on campus during orientation, but did not really understand what it was all about. She met few people in her

Table 3.1.
Nonacademic Activities and Ability to Cope

When you are faced with a difficult course, assignment, or other challenge, are you able to cope well?	Are you a member of, or have you participated in the activities of, any group or organizations in the past 12 months (e.g., a sports team, a hobby club, a community organization, an ethnic association, etc.)?	
	Yes, participated in group or organizations in the past 12 months	No, did not participate in any group or organizations in the past 12 months
Usually able to cope well	12	3
Sometimes able to cope	4	2
Not able to cope	1	0
TOTAL	17	5
No Response = 2		

first month of school because she was one of "the very, very few black girls" living in residence. For example:

> a guy approached me that was also black too and was "heyyy" … how are you? And he was like yeah I'm black too and I'm kind of lost and I was like me too! So we became friends and then slowly we started to make friends with more people. Like from our race. That way we didn't feel so … alone and weirded out cause … it's intimidating trying to go out and try to meet people, but … when you're with people that understand your culture then … it helps make it easier—you're both going through the same things you can be able to identify with [sic].

When asked if being of the same race or skin color is the same as having the same culture, she replied:

> it's like some intuition that you can always tell somebody that's African as compared to let's say somebody who's African American. It's just … mannerisms, the way they talk, the way … they approach you and it's weird cause [when] he approached me, I immediately knew he was African, even before he said a word. And I was African too so we were able to just immediately identify and he had an accent too so it was … as soon as he started talking to me I was … okay, phew, I know this person, … I was able to relate in some way at least.

She went on to explain that most of the Black African students at her university come from either Nigeria or Ghana. The region of Africa was important, she explained, saying that attitudes changed depending on what region of Africa students came from:

> I was born in Kenya ... [people would say] where's Kenya or something like that. But then, ... as soon as you say Nigerian, it's like OHHH KAYYY, like, hey, how are you, ... and it's even how they treat [you]. It's friendlier than if you're not.

She spoke with a Canadian accent during the interview, but she explained that when she spoke with others from Africa, she would use a different accent. This code switching was perplexing for some people who, based on her physical appearance, expected her to speak with a certain accent. She said that it was annoying that there was this categorization happening and said that it made it difficult to make friends: "if you ... are not from the same place you know immediately there's this barrier." She is a member of the African Student Association, but she says she is there not for support for herself, but to provide support to new students who may not immediately fit into its "cliques." Because she grew up in Kenya, she identifies more with her mother's Kenyan heritage than her father's Nigerian culture. Because there are fewer Kenyans at the university, she sometimes does not feel that she fits in due to her Kenyan accent. In spite of these challenges in first year and being shy, she has made a lot of

> really, really good friends. I did not speak with anybody [at first] but definitely with time ... when you make one friend then you make another friend and then you can slowly start to mix up with groups and now it's not just Africans I'm friends with. I'm friends with all types of races so that's definitely better than just being by myself from the beginning.

In spite of the divisions between the different groups of Black students, she says it is still much better than being in high school where you saw the same people every day and were expected to associate only with other Black kids. Because her parents had met in India and they were open to other cultures, she grew up feeling multicultural which gave her a different perspective. Dalia's experience illustrates the complexity of identity creation and belongingness when one does not fit neatly into a predefined category. This underscores the importance of flexible social boundaries, since, as intersectionality theory describes, each of us is the culmination of all our social locations: race, gender and social class, among other identity markers (Hankivsky, 2014).

Beatrice has not used any of the university's support services, but she expressed interest in seeking help through peer tutoring and volunteering at the outreach center. Her friends are supportive, but she does not often get to see those who did not go to university. Like herself, most of her friends who went to college or university live at home because school is "so expensive." She has four friends living in residence whom she visits after her night class before driving home. She only drives to school on the days she has her night class; otherwise, she takes the bus because she can use her bus pass (which is part of the ancillary fees). She considers herself agnostic, although her family does not know this because "I just don't want to give my grandparents a heart attack." Thus religion does not impact how she deals with challenges at university or in life. Similarly, her ethnic background does not impact her schooling or how she deals with challenges. She had minimal involvement in a Filipino-Canadian association while in elementary and high school, but she is no longer involved in any of its activities. She has not become involved in any on-campus groups or activities because she has been focussed on passing her courses. Her advice to incoming first year students: "It's not as bad as you think, but just don't expect everything to be really easy."

OVERCOMING CHALLENGES: ACADEMIC PREPAREDNESS, FINANCES, AND TIME MANAGEMENT

Half of the students surveyed felt that they were unprepared for university when they first started (see Table 3.2). Indeed, only those students whose self-reported secondary school grades were high felt that they were adequately prepared for university. This finding was also noted in the interviews. Dalia, who was discouraged by her teachers from pursuing medicine, does not feel that her Catholic high school prepared her for university. She acknowledges that she was at her "rebel stage" and that she "hated high school."

Table 3.2.
High School Preparation

Did high school prepare you for university?		
Average grade in Gr. 12	Adequately prepared me	Did not prepare me
90% + (A+ average)	3	0
80–89%	7	6
70–79%	2	6
TOTAL	12	12

Once they began meeting other students, teaching assistants (TAs) and professors, most respondents began to feel more comfortable in their classes. The next challenge was dealing with questions related to course materials. Many of the students were nervous about approaching their professors. Others worried they would be considered less bright than their peers if they approached the TA, or sought peer tutoring. Another significant component to adjusting to university studies was receiving the first set of grades. The rule of thumb for grades is that they drop by about 10% in first year. For many students, this proved to be a shock—especially if they failed their first set of tests or midterm examinations.

Anita, for example, feels she was not well-prepared for university because at high school there was much more "hand-holding." Teachers warned that this would not happen at university, but not much else was done to prepare the students for the independence needed for university. Frieda indicated that the same methods of studying and preparing assignments that worked for her in high school no longer served her well in university. In her lab courses, however, she did feel more prepared than other students. Six months into her program, she now enjoys her courses, is getting better grades, and likes the fact that the university is not as large as some others. She feels that the professors really care about their students and notes that attending orientation was useful in meeting others in her program.

In her fourth year of forensic psychology, Gail stated that high school did not prepare her well for university, especially in biology. She says that her Grade 12 biology class consisted largely of watching movies, so when she took first year biology in university, she lacked familiarity with the lab equipment and experiments. Similarly, she described her high school psychology and sociology assignments as consisting of only worksheets rather than essays. The only essays she wrote in high school were for English, a subject that she did not study at university. Although her mother was supportive and her grandmother provided financial assistance, Gail did not have any close family members who were able to provide advice or act as a role model during university. Gail and Hannah both chose their university because it was close to home, and they could save money by living with their family. Both found university scary at first, but are now comfortable and excited to be close to finishing their degree. Hannah, a first generation student, has parents who are supportive, but who do not really understand what it is like to study at university. Hannah paid for university herself and received scholarships and bursaries, but her parents helped when needed. Like Gail, she feels that her high school did not prepare her very well for university-level assignments. One example she gives is that in English class, she was taught to write very long essays with lots of detail, but in her university psychology essays, she is expected to be very concise and succinct.

Beatrice noted that most of her high school teachers prepared the students by simply warning: "you're on your own next year." Nevertheless, she felt well-prepared for university, having taken a number of high school courses related to her current field of study. Her high school social science courses allowed her to develop her essay writing skills and to become familiar with the terminology and concepts presented in her university courses. Chaaya also felt that her high school in Abu Dhabi prepared her well for her studies in electrical engineering; indeed, she had already learned in high school most of the first year curriculum. However, the courses gradually became harder, and she was dealing with health problems, so her grades have dropped since then.

Although finances seem to have little correlation with level of motivation to succeed at university, concern over finances (such as expenses for books, living, and tuition) was significant for eight students. Another eight said that finances were not a problem and five stated that working while in school was manageable. Perhaps not surprisingly, the one student who delayed her education to earn money was very motivated to succeed. Several students, who were faced with the challenge of trying to balance paid employment with school work, found it difficult to socialize and become involved in student life. Anita explained that she has not been able to socialize with any of the friends she made during orientation and only comes to campus to attend classes because she commutes almost 30 minutes from her family's home four days per week and typically works three days per week. During the Christmas holiday season, she worked more than 20 hours per week. She is careful to plan so that she does not have a shift scheduled the evening before an 8 a.m. class. She says that she has good time management skills and knows that "one lazy day would cause everything to come crashing down."

Beatrice works about 15 hours a week. She manages her time by scheduling work so that it does not conflict with school and so that she has one day a week with no class or work commitments. She also makes sure to do her readings prior to going to class, although she does not always understand everything she reads. At the time of the interview, she continues to enjoy university and feels confident that she is doing well, but is struggling with one course. Because she had friends in university before she started, she had been given sound advice, and felt that there were no surprises. She tries to follow her friends' advice to do the readings and homework, and to hand in all assignments on time, no matter how little they are worth, to avoid unnecessarily losing marks. She believes this advice has helped her to be successful. In terms of workload, she says the amount of homework was less than she expected compared to her friends at other universities.

Finances are also a challenge for Dalia; she does not get monetary support from her family, and has had to figure out for herself how to live affordably. She has held a job every year, starting in first year as a lab assistant through a work-study program. She now works in retail at a large shopping mall. She feels that her younger brothers count on her; indeed, she notes that she has had to grow up quickly as she was the one who had to keep the family together when her parents became ill.

REFLECTIONS ON SURVIVING UNIVERSITY STUDIES

After only one semester, the first-year students had already learned new strategies and were developing a sense of identity as a university student. Beatrice is one example. She believes that her diligence in taking notes during class has been important. In addition, she starts studying for midterms and tests early and works with her study group to quiz each other. When she did poorly on one midterm, she began to make even more detailed notes and began reviewing the material more often. The extra work paid off since her grade increased from 50% to 65% on the next test. While she did not put the same amount of effort into note-taking when reading the course text, she did try to link the ideas in the textbook with those mentioned in class. Her other course grades ranged from the low 80s to the low 70s, which she felt was in the normal range since she had been warned to expect a drop in grades in university. She describes benefiting from her friends as a source of academic help.

Another first-year student, Anita, said she loved the university experience, even though she does not have much time to socialize with friends or take part in campus activities. She has become part of a study group with three other young women. She says she would like to volunteer with orientation week activities because it would allow her to help other new students. After three months, she no longer finds her classes "scary." She says: "I [would] always want to sit at the back and not be the one that walks up and sits right in front of the teacher; however, it has definitely changed and I love it. I am excited for my next four years here.... I sit right at [sic] the front row." She feels that her courses are going well, with grades to this point ranging from the low 90s to the low 70s, with the better grades being in the courses she finds most interesting and engaging. She considered using the learning center for tutoring but had difficulties understanding how it worked and if there were costs involved. When faced with a poor grade after one midterm, she worked hard to stay positive and motivated, and continued to stay on top of course readings and assignments. Anita, who had taken a year off to earn money before starting university, maintained "the school mentality" by enrolling in night classes. In spite of this, she found the university workload much heavier than she expected.

By fourth year, most interviewees were comfortable with their academic identity and were happy to provide advice for new students. However, some students still did not feel a strong sense of belonging to the university community. Chaaya, for instance, made a number of friends in first year, but in her final year still does not feel completely comfortable at university. She says:

> there's a lot missing in [my] university life because back in India, my
> friends ... have a fixed schedule for instance [while] we have such a scat-

tered schedule. That is one reason I don't even get to see a lot of my
friends because when I have class, they don't have class and when they have
class, I don't have class.

In Canada, she explains, the social aspects of university studies are optional
and easy to miss, while in India there are no classes scheduled during
cultural festivals to encourage everyone to participate. For engineering
students especially, she says the workload is so heavy "that we cannot do anything other than study, study, study…. Like I used to go out a lot in my first
year, but in 2nd year, 3rd year, I'm barely getting any time to do anything."

By fourth year, Dalia is finding university easier because she is able to
manage her time better and she understands the system. She currently
works 25 hours per week, which she juggles by scheduling all of her courses
over a couple of days. Her advice for new students is to stay focused because
it is easy to get sidetracked, especially in the absence of familial monitoring.
Her family's struggles keep her focussed and motivate her "to go the extra
mile," because she remembers all they have been through. The support
of her best friend from high school also helps her to keep going through
difficult times. Her main academic support is a study group with friends.
The thought of approaching a professor intimidates her, but she is comfortable speaking with TAs. She has tried the peer tutoring service, but worried
that "if you don't know what's going on, I feel like someone else is going
to judge you." Having failed one course, she feels it is important to give
equal attention to all her courses, and not let any of them slide. Similarly,
she feels it is important to have a balance between studies and leisure
time. In her first semester, she spent all her time studying in the library;
then, in second semester, she focussed almost exclusively on her social life.
She felt that failing one course was partly due to a lack of connection with
the professor who she felt was unapproachable. She realized that when
she has to take another course with that same professor, she will need to
"get myself together, you know, don't take it personally." She has made a
plan to meet with the TA or get help from a friend if she continues to feel
uncomfortable speaking with that professor. When asked if she made the
right choice choosing this university over another, she said she was 100%
sure that she would make the same choice again. She feels that people at
her university have been "very, very helpful." Her final words of advice
are to stay focussed and be self-reliant: "you have to be the one to wake
yourself up at 6 in the morning to make it to an 8 A.M. class…. It teaches
you responsibility. Prioritizing is very important …"

Fourth-year forensic psychology student, Gail, comments that the
workload never gets lighter, so it is important to learn how to balance
extracurricular activities, work and "everything with school." Her primary
extracurricular activity is her sorority where she is in charge of all the

philanthropic events, such as working in the soup kitchen once a month. She joined the sorority in her second year because, as a commuter student, she felt like she was not "getting enough out of my university experience." Reflecting back on her four years, she wishes that she had done more volunteering, especially in her field of study. Although she feels she should have put more effort into studying and doing the readings, she makes a point of going to class regularly and completing all of her assignments. She also says that the main reason she has been successful is that she is "determined to succeed" in spite of the additional challenges of living with cystic fibrosis and having to find time for doctor's appointments, lung physiotherapy and other treatments.

Frieda comments that it is important to get involved in the life and culture of the university, which she describes broadly as participating in activities, clubs, school, and community volunteering, as well as student politics. Her advice to new students: "don't leave your studying to the last minute."

CONCLUSION

For the most part, all of the students in our study had similar feelings about starting university, particularly with respect to anxiety about being away from home, attending large classes, writing assignments and exams, and making new friends. The students who self-identified as visible minority were more likely to have lived outside Canada at some point in their lives, and thereby to have acquired international perspectives on education. The non-visible minority students tended to be from the region surrounding the university, with only one non-visible minority student coming from a city about four hours away. Most of the students who lived on campus tended to go home for the weekends. Only one student had full financial support from her parents; the rest worked to pay or help pay for tuition and living expenses. Among all the students, attending orientation was identified as important in making friends in first year, many of whom remained friends until fourth year. Joining clubs, teams or sororities was also deemed important. The one student on the survey who did not participate in orientation or join other student groups indicated that they do not have any friends at the university.

Although the survey results indicated almost equal numbers of students preferring to study with friends and those who did not, most of the students who were interviewed indicated that studying with others helped in achieving success in their courses. Navigating university services was challenging for many students. When asked which university supports had been helpful, most students indicated that one or more professors had been helpful in addressing their questions. Other sources of support included the online writing and math tools developed and made available by the university, the academic advisors in each Faculty, and self-organized peer study groups. The responses here suggest that being able to speak with professors and advisors in their home faculty is an important part of student success. Extending this, it suggests that professors and advisors have an important role to play in creating a sense of an academic community. Indeed, only six students said that they had used student learning center programs, such as peer tutoring and writing specialists, and even fewer had used other university centers or associations. Some students indicated that they were not sure if the services were free or how to access them. When asked what would help them to be successful, students indicated that the opportunity to speak with peers in classes would be very beneficial. Also included, but ranked less highly, were: a quiet place to think or study, fewer personal problems, encouragement from family and friends, and fewer financial problems.

As Smith (2012) notes, "[t]he idea of community is defined or imagined in multiple ways: as physical, political, social, psychological, historical, linguistic, economic, cultural and spiritual spaces" (p. 128). In the 21st century, academic communities are not the stereotypical "ivory towers." Academic communities are made up of people from diverse backgrounds who are shaking the foundations of the established institutions. This is not new, of course. Canadian universities have been evolving and opening their doors wider and wider (however slowly) since they were built, whether to admit women in the 1880s and 1890s or to provide increasing support for Indigenous students in the 2000s (Axelrod & Reid, 1989; Fallis, 2007; McKillop, 1994; Simpson, 2014; Strange, 2016). Becoming part of an academic community, whether it comes in the form of feeling like a scholar, developing new worldviews and mindsets, or exploring new opportunities for leadership and activism, allows young people to experiment with their identities and grow into adulthood in a space where safety nets and support systems are available. Dean and Jolly (2012) describe universities as the site of confrontations between new ideas and preexisting beliefs and worldviews, thus the existence of supports is key. This is not to say that all university communities are perfectly safe spaces and that there is not much work to be done still in opening the doors wider and supporting underrepresented students; rather, we argue that universities can provide unique liminal spaces between childhood and adulthood or between secondary school and careers where students can be independent while exploring (or "trying on") their identity(ies), and also developing skills needed for participation in the workforce and broader society. Furthermore, a student identity provides the foundation for future life-long learning, since postsecondary education is one of the four pillars of lifelong learning (LLL) in Canada (Grace, 2013).

The transformation that takes place within this liminal space is shaped by all stakeholders: the students themselves, their peers, their instructors and the administration and support staff who develop policies that support learning. Our findings support existing research which underscores the role of the professor. Dean and Jolly (2012) suggest that sensitivity on the part of instructors can assist in engaging students so that the identity development process can proceed. Flum and Kaplan (2012) underscore the role of the teacher in connecting school culture, curriculum and learning to the lived experiences of their students, arguing that identity develop-ment and academic learning occur reflexively and simultaneously when the student is viewed by the teacher as a whole person. Further, they report that postsecondary students whose identities were constructed through "active adaptation" rather than "passive unreflective compliance" were better adjusted socially and academically and had greater commitment to their chosen majors.

Universities are regularly challenged to become safer spaces and to be open to the growing diversity of people wishing to attend, just as students are challenged by professors, courses and new ideas encountered in their studies. While it is clear from the stories here and from the other research described herein that universities can do much more to support students and to increase diversity, it is also clear that the resilience and persistence of students are strengthened as they navigate their studies and adapt to new levels of independence and expectations of adulthood. Those who are classed as "mature" students often demonstrate higher levels of persever-ance from the time they are admitted. Often feeling out of place among younger direct entry students, mature students must adapt to being back in school and relearning how to study, write essays and exams, and so on, while continuing to juggle family commitments and employment. In the end, however, all students need to develop an identity as a student or a learner in order to succeed in and truly benefit from university studies.

REFERENCES

Axelrod, P., & Reid, J. G. (1989). *Youth, university and Canadian society: Essays in the social history of higher education.* Montreal & Kingston, Ontario, Canada: McGill-Queen's University Press.

Blumenkrantz, D., & Goldstein, M. (2014). Seeing college as a rite of passage: What might be possible. *New Directions for Higher Education, 166, Summer,* 85–94.

Crenshaw, K. (2011). Twenty years of critical race theory: Looking back to move forward. *Connecticut Law Review, 43*(5), 1253–1352.

Dean, K. L., & Jolly, J. P. (2012). Student identity, disengagement, and learning. *Academy of Management Learning & Education, 11*(2), 228–243. http://dx.doi.org/10.5465/amle.2009.0081

Erikson, E. H. (1959). Identity and the life cycle. *Psychological Issues, 1*, 1–191.

Fallis, G. (2007). *Multiversities, ideas, and democracy.* Toronto, Ontario, Canada: University of Toronto Press.

Finnie, R., Sweetman, A., & Usher, A. (2008). Introduction: A framework for thinking about participation in post-secondary education. In R. Finnie, R. Mueller, A. Sweetman, & A. Usher (Eds.), *Who goes? Who stays? What matters? Accessing and persisting in post-secondary education in Canada.* Montreal & Kingston, Canada: McGill-Queen's University Press.

Flum, H., & Kaplan, A. (2012). Identity formation in educational settings: A contextualized view of theory and research in practice. *Contemporary Educational Psychology, 37*, 240–245.

Grace, A. P. (2013). *Lifelong learning as critical action: International perspectives on people, politics, policy, and practice.* Toronto, Ontario, Canada: Canadian Scholars' Press.

Hankivsky, O. (2014). *Intersectionality 101.* Burnaby, British Columbia: The Institute for Intersectionality Research & Policy, Simon Fraser University.

Hoppes, S. (2014, Summer). Autoethnography: Inquiry into identity. *New Directions For Higher Education, 166*, 63–71.

Kaufman, P. (2014, Summer). The sociology of college students' identity formation. *New Directions For Higher Education, 166*, 35–42.

King, A. (2015). Exploring identity and multiliteracies through graphic narratives. *Diaspora, Indigenous, and Minority Education, 9*(1), 3–20. doi:10.1080/15595692.2014.952406

King, A. E., Eamer, A., & Ammar, N. (2018). Participation and persistence: An analysis of immigrant visible-minority students at UOIT. In B. Merrill, A.Galimberti, A. Nizinska, & J.González-Monteagudo (Eds.), *Continuity and discontinuity in learning careers: Potentials for a learning space in a changing world.* Rotterdam, The Netherlands: Sense Publishers/ESREA.

Liebenberg L., & Ungar, M. (Eds.). (2009). *Researching resilience.* Toronto, Ontario: University of Toronto Press.

McKillop, A. B. (1994). *Matters of mind: The University in Ontario 1791–1951.* Toronto, Ontario: University of Toronto Press.

Sanders, J., & Munford, R. (2016). Fostering a sense of belonging at school— five orientations to practice that assist vulnerable youth to create a positive student identity. *School Psychology International, 37*(2), 155–171.

Simpson, J. (2014). *Longing for justice: Higher education and democracy's agenda.* Toronto, Ontario: University of Toronto Press.

Sleeter, C. (1993). How white teachers construct race. In C. McCarthy & W. Crichlow (Eds.), *Race, identity and representation in education* (pp. 157–171). New York, NY. Routledge.

Smith, L. T. (2012). *Decolonizing methodologies: Research and indigenous peoples* (2nd ed.). London, UK: Zed Books.

Strange, C. C. (2016). Theories of diverse student success. In C. C. Strange & D. H. Cox (Eds.), *Serving diverse students in Canadian higher education* (pp. 13–22). Montreal & Kingston, Ontario: McGill-Queen's University Press.

Weidman, J., DeAngelo, L., & Bethea, K. (2014, Summer). Understanding student identity from a socialization perspective. *New Directions for Higher Education*, *166*, 43–51.

CHAPTER 4

HOW PLACE AND CLASS AFFECT IDENTITY DEVELOPMENT AS LIFE LONG LEARNERS

An Examination of Resilience in First-Generation, Adult College Students From Appalachia

Deborah (Debbie) Thurman
Tennessee Technological University

Jeffrey S. (Jeff) Savage
Cornerstone University

This chapter will focus on the role place and class play in shaping identify development for an oft-forgotten population. Moreover, the chapter will emphasize resilience as an antecedent factor in explaining identity development, especially the identity as a lifelong learner—a term that can be conceived of as all intentional learning that occurs across one's life

Identity and Lifelong Learning in Higher Education, pp. 59–77
Copyright © 2020 by Information Age Publishing

and includes "all types of learning—formal, nonformal, and informal" (Merriam & Bierema, 2014, p. 20). Specifically, this chapter will tell the story of adult college students from the Central and South Central Appalachian region of the United States as they navigate the challenging and unfamiliar world of higher education as first-time college students. The tension to be presented in this chapter is the lived experience of a group of people as they struggle to accept parts of their cultural identity (without judgment) while at the same time strive to improve not only themselves but also their chances of competing in a globalized society. At play in the development of these first-time college students, is the role of psychological resilience (a malleable characteristic) in helping them to become more than they have been and better than where they started. The role of resilience will emerge as a prominent theme in identity development from the people who participated in the transcendental phenomenological study that informs this chapter's message. We will overlay important values from higher education in this exposé as we do privilege the outcome of college completion as a result of an influential factor in the identity of Appalachian adults who have chosen higher education and lifelong learning as ways to become more than they are.

LITERATURE REVIEW

Background—Place & Class

In 1965 the United States Congress passed the Appalachian Regional Development Act establishing the Appalachian Regional Commission (ARC, 2017). Its mission was primarily to promote economic development for the 420-county region that follows the Appalachian mountain chain. That mountain chain extends 1,000 miles from northeastern Mississippi to southern New York State; it covers portions of 13 states, and just over 25 million people (ARC, 2017). The region is not homogenous in language or culture. Parts of the region have managed to succeed economically while some locations continue to lack basic infrastructure, such as roads, water, and sewer.

Much of the population of the Appalachian region lives in rural areas (42%) in contrast to about 20% in the rest of the United States (ARC, 2012). Of all 421 Appalachian counties identified by the ARC, 167 are in Central and South Central Appalachia, with 100 counties located in central and eastern Kentucky and Tennessee and a few counties in North Carolina (29) and West Virginia (7) (ARC, 2012). In envisioning the Central and South Central regions, think about eastern Kentucky and Tennessee (with a few counties in central Kentucky and south-central Tennessee), a little bit of western North Carolina, and small parts of Virginia and West Virginia (ARC, 2012). To be from the Central and South Central region of Appalachia is to have strong cultural capital (Yosso, 2005) in music, storytelling, family, kinship, and independence. However, over decades and centuries, these products of cultural capital—along with the natural barriers of the mountains in this region—have, at times, prevented outside influences to intersect with local culture; thus, generational strongholds have formed and sometimes, stagnation and resistance to change (Isenberg, 2016).

One of the remarkable descriptions of the Appalachian region is the fortitude of the people. Their consistent poverty and entrapment have contributed to an attitude of fatalism described as an inability to change their situation (Isenberg, 2016). However, the residents over generations have maintained a colorful culture that adds meaning to their lives. That culture involves music, story-telling, and dance (DeYoung, 1995; Tang & Russ, 2007).

One contributor to the region's poverty is low educational attainments, with only 17% of the population holding a college degree compared to over 24% nationwide (ARC, 2017). Researchers Bryan and Simmons (2009) found that influences of family history, low socioeconomic status, a lack of physical or technological access due to remote highway limitations, and the overall rural setting all contribute to the lack of college attendance. In fact, fewer students than the national average finish high school. Twenty-seven percent of Kentucky's students did not finish high school in 2012 (ARC, 2012).

Another contributor to poverty in the region can be found in the depletion of its natural resources of lumber, coal, and other natural materials for use in areas outside the region, most notably, the mining of coal to supply the United States' demands (Eller, 2008). The mining companies moved in and used strip mines that robbed the trees and topography of mountaintops, leaving the area vulnerable for flooding. Moreover, their deep mining under the earth held little consideration for the safety of the miners, garnering significant publicity from mining accidents or collapses. The miners who survived were left with black lung and other health issues. Mining companies pulled out, leaving devastation in their wake. Flooding from the strip mines continues to plague towns and communities in the region. For many students in Appalachia, education is often preempted or interrupted due to the financial needs of the family. At times, students must first meet the demands of "chores," such as caring for farm animals or food production before they can attend to homework. In areas where there are cash crops which support the family for an entire year, harvest time can mean no choice for the student and school attendance (Eller, 2008)

The poverty of the region is most profound on average in the Central and South-Central regions of Appalachia (ARC, 2017). In 2000, data indicated that 116 counties in Appalachia had a poverty rate that was 150% or more of the national average (ARC, 2012). The natural barriers to infrastructure specifically in this part of the broader Appalachian region have made it difficult to attract business, leaving the area dependent on fewer employment opportunities. The mountains create barriers for travel, education, economy, medical care, employment, and many other critical facets of life. The research subjects of this study are found in this Central and South-Central area of Appalachia.

Identity development in areas of deep poverty with strong generational and cultural controls can be a difficult evolution for individuals (Isenberg, 2016). The mountainous Appalachian area is just such a stronghold. Generations of deep-seated cultural reinforcement in land-locked areas have made pockets of population resistant to change. That resistance could merely be a result of poverty, or it could also stem from a threat to the parental culture. For parents, the status quo can be more comfortable than losing their child to an environment outside their culture (Isenberg, 2016).

Continuous generations of poverty can create a type of learned helplessness in identity development particularly if individuals feel that they may have passed the normal threshold of college entrance (Teodorescu & Erev, 2014). Adults desiring to complete a degree may have married early in life, had children before they intended, and become accustomed to limited financial resources that require spending all they earn to keep their families fed and housed. However, internal unrest for higher education may remain as a hopeful ticket out of restrictive cultural poverty. The participants in this research are strong individuals who desire something more than the norm in their culture. Some have acquired a desire for learning. One of the individuals studied described herself as "in the middle of nowhere" in Appalachia so she had to learn to be resourceful. The passion for learning among these individuals may have stemmed from learning exploration or from the encouragement of a teacher. Regardless of its inception, degree pursuit remains in the individual's unstated or stated goal set. That desire contrasts with a culture that does not value or does not encourage the pursuit of education (Bryan & Simmons, 2009).

Theoretical Framework

Resilience, as the basis for an explanatory, theoretical framework, found its basis in early longitudinal research by Garmezy (1971, 1991) and others (Garmezy & Crose, 1948; Garmezy & Rodnick, 1959; Garmezy, Masten, & Tellegen, 1984). Garmezy's (1971, 1991) research into the lives of schizophrenics revealed that mental illness of adults did not always translate into illness in their offspring. Some children of mentally ill adults were found to adapt fairly well to life despite their environment. Werner's (1989) longitudinal research into individuals living in adverse conditions also highlighted some cases in which people who had endured adverse circumstances able to develop in successful ways. More recently, the *Harvard Mental Health Letter* concluded that, after the traumatic events of September 11, 2001, some affected by the attacks with specific thinking habits were able to deal with the tragedy without counseling (Harvard Medical School, 2006).

Although there is a lack of a uniform definition of resilience, consistent research findings that some individuals or organisms can adapt well despite adverse environmental influences have led researchers to describe the construct of resilience as a focus on "good function or outcome in the context of risk or adversity" (Masten, 2014, p. 6) and "the capacity of a dynamic system to adapt successfully to disturbances that threaten system function, viability or development" (Masten, 2014, p. 10). Many methodological and operational definition issues remain to be worked out in the research and literature; however, the literature points to the critical role protective factors play in successful adaptation of resilient people. Regardless of the possible similarities among many positive psychological theories (resiliency, flourishing, hope, self-efficacy, optimism, self-determination), the importance of having access to and then applying adaptive, supportive, goal-oriented strategies cannot be overemphasized (Lopez, Pedrotti, & Snyder, 2014).

The construct of success is controversial within the literature on resilience, highlighting the issue of defining success: What is *success* and who gets to decide what it is? Typically, in psychological research, especially resilience research, success is defined either by a lack of maladaptive, dysfunctional behavior or by the presence of achievement—or, perhaps, by both (Masten, 2014). Students who earn a college degree are also more likely to earn higher salaries over their lifetimes, and are also more likely to achieve other positive life outcomes and be better adjusted psychologically (Weiten, Dunn, & Hammer, 2012). Moreover, for the participants in this study, earning a college degree, becoming educated, and "doing better" than their parents, were important goals, making the attainment of a college degree a valid definition of success. As Masten (2014) explains, as long as students have assets or protective factors that influence the relationship between risk factors and life outcomes, those life outcomes tend to, on balance, be more positive, adaptive, and achievement-oriented. Now, what kind of protective factors, in what combinations or amounts, and to what degree are all issues remaining to be worked out in the research on resilience, but according to Masten (2001), it is clear that the great surprise of resilience research is the ordinariness of the phenomenon.

Finally, resilience, an ability to endure serious difficulty without succumbing to hopelessness and helplessness, is a remarkable quality of the human spirit and can be interpreted as aspirational capital within Yosso's (2005) cultural wealth model. Some individuals are not able to rise above the circumstances of life. However, for others, a tenacity of spirit provides the impetus for dissatisfaction with the status quo (Masten, 2014). Those individuals want something more for themselves and their families. This characteristic is not based on vanity of spirit, but upon a burning desire to achieve. They do not want "something for nothing" but are willing to pay the necessary price for achievement. They have experienced life in the status quo, and it is not sufficient for them although they still love their families, their cultures, and their social capital that come as part of their Appalachian heritage. The research study included in this chapter reflects the theoretical perspective of resilience that shapes identity development as individuals use aspirational, linguistic, familial, social, and even navigational cultural capital to rise above constraints of poverty, negative influences, geographical barriers, and other challenges to bring about positive outcomes in their life via goal attainment. Identity for these Appalachian first-generation college (FGC) students can be seen through Orbe's (2008) characterization that students develop a sense of self through the "dialectical tensions" that make up the reticular forces of their lives.

PROBLEM, PURPOSE, AND QUESTIONS

The problem investigated in this study included the obstacles to completion of college degrees experienced by working, first-generation adult college students or recent graduates in the Central area of Appalachia and the resilience demonstrated as these students attempted to overcome the complexities of college life and complete their four-year college degrees. The main purpose of the current study was to understand what allows some people from austere backgrounds to thrive and succeed despite limitations of geography, culture, family, and identity. The main author's (Dr. Thurman) experience growing up and living within the Appalachian region about which she writes provided the main motivation for situating the study within this culture. The recent scholarship on class (particularly low class Whites) produced by Isenberg (2016) and the anecdotal treatment of hillbilly culture by Vance (2016) provided further support for studying an important but often-maligned and forgotten segment of the U.S. population as they struggle to thrive in spite of their cultural identity and the prejudices others read into this culture (Isenberg, 2016). Higher education scholarship on the continued struggles of first-generation college students (Abdul-Alim, 2013; Horwedel, 2008) along with the need for more research about adult students in higher education (Compton, Cox, & Laanan, 2006), especially in light of the changing demographics of college students (McGee, 2015), provided the lens used for this research study. The specific focus of the current study and was to understand and uncover the lived experience of working, adult, first-generation students and recent graduates in the Central and South-Central area of Appalachia in their pursuit of a four-year college degree. The study focused on the resilience displayed by these adult students in the face of obstacles experienced as they worked to obtain a four-year college degree in a nontraditional setting.

The questions guiding the research project were as follows:

1. What have participants experienced regarding the phenomenon (Creswell, 2013, p. 81)?

    a. How do the life complexities of first-generation, working, adult college students from Appalachia influence their ability to persist in college?

    b. What perceived internal and attributed external resources (psychological or otherwise) do students possess that have helped them to persist in the face of obstacles (resilience)?

2. What contexts or situations have typically influenced or affected participants' experiences of the phenomenon (Creswell, 2013, p. 81)?

    a. What are the students' perceived cultural supports or hindrances in pursuing their educational goals?

    b. In what way has parental nonattendance at college shaped Appalachian adult student college experiences?

METHOD

Design

We selected a qualitative, transcendental phenomenological design for the current research because we intended to present the essence of lived experience through the voices of participants in how they dealt with challenges (to include their ability to overcome these challenges) they faced in pursuit of a college degree. Moustakas (1994) described phenomenological research as "[t]he transformation of an individual or empirical experience into essential insights" (p. 27). His research philosophy indicated that the researcher should intentionally use his intuition and diligently strive to remove bias when researching with a transcendental phenomenological design (Moustakas, 1994). Researchers must be absorbed in hearing voices of participants without allowing bias from their own experience to enter into the research. This description reflects the difference in hermeneutical phenomenology (the researcher becomes part of the research) and transcendental phenomenology—the researcher, using epoche, removes her bias and chooses merely to listen to the participants (Creswell, 2007; Moustakas, 1994). Qualitative research, in the transcendental phenomenological tradition, allowed us to "construct a rich and meaningful picture of a complex, multifaceted situation (Leedy & Ormrod, 2016, p. 251) by hearing the voices of adult students (Moustakas, 1994) through intentional listening. To ensure authenticity and dependability (O'Leary, 2017), we used methodological triangulation, employing three methods of assimilating information: individual interviews, journaling, and focus groups. Pseudonyms were chosen at the onset by each participant and continued throughout the study.

Participants and Setting

We chose participants from four specific locations in a university degree program in counties located in Central and South-Central Appalachia where a state university offers an off-campus evening program. The state university providing the education program from which participants were drawn is in the middle and eastern area of Tennessee. It serves a 42 county area, and 36 of the counties that it serves are in the Appalachian region.

We purposely selected the study participants based on their experience of being a working, adult, first-generation college student in the third or fourth year (junior and senior years) of study in an area of Central and South-Central Appalachia. We considered recent graduates for the participant pool. Students were not deselected based on gender, age, race, or any other criteria. In addition, we selected students from one of the four programs in the counties indicated above. Furthermore, we used *first-generation college student* as a selection definition. In regards to this study, we defined a first-generation college student as a college student whose parents did not attend college at all (Byrd & MacDonald, 2005). We used a self-report procedure in which students provided information about their background to choose the participants. All of the students completed a demographic survey to supply descriptors of their parent's educational attainment, their work status, where they attend classes, and to indicate if they would like to be a part of a research study. We selected a sample of 11 participants from the responses to the survey. Eleven participants, all older than 25 years, met the criteria, began, and completed the study. Individual interviews were conducted at or near the locations where the students attended the university classes.

The definition used for "adults" in the current the study was anyone 25 years of age or older (Kasworm, 2003). The adult students chosen for this study were marginalized due to their culture (Isenberg, 2016; Vance, 2016), their status as "working," (Jacobsen, 2009), and standing as parents of young children (Berger, 2016). Each participant had completed or were currently enrolled in the final two years of university coursework. The university courses were held at satellite community college locations within the region. Many of the courses were compressed into five-week segments, creating an intense and rigorous program for disciplined adult students. The adults studied were (a) working at least 20 hours per week, (b) first-generation students (neither parent had attended college), (c) in the third of fourth years (junior or senior) of college or recent baccalaureate graduates, (d) In Central or South-Central Appalachia based on the designations of the Appalachian Regional Commission (2012). The participants were not deselected based on gender, age, race, or any other criteria as long as they had experience the phenomenon of the study and were participating (or had recently completed) the accelerated program offered by the university based in the region (Moustakas, 1994). Five were married, five were non-parents, three were single parents, three were "empty nesters," nine had earned their baccalaureate degree, two were male, nine were female, one was African American, and one was an elected official.

Procedures and Data Analysis

The data analysis process first required the development of a portrait of each participant using descriptions of their resilience and challenges. Because of the large volume of data, the importance of making meaning of the data was a critical component. Commonalities among the eleven portraits began to emerge allowing for groupings of those common descriptions. using guidance by Moustakas's "horizonalization" (1994, p. 95), which refers to the use of significant statements to help in describing the experience of the phenomenon. The themes were evident once we developed summary descriptions from student comments. Groupings could then be made, such as, "resilience," "how school and work blended," and "pivotal situations." As themes emerged from the groupings, we identified clusters of uniformity. The clusters, such as financial hardship, could also be grounded in the poverty and geography of the region or their current underemployment.

RESULTS

Question One: What have participants experienced regarding the phenomenon (Creswell, 2013, p. 81)?

The life complexities of working adult, first-generation university students in Appalachia were considerable. For those participants who were working full-time and primarily underemployed, the stressors were difficult, yielding only a poverty-level salary in most cases. Employment choices in the region were scarce, so it was necessary to keep the work that they had, despite the fact that it was unsatisfactory. The participants knew that there was more "out there" somewhere for people with degrees. However, they were unqualified for those jobs without a baccalaureate degree.

As adults, and in some cases with children to feed and care for, the participants did not have the luxury of leaving home to go to a university, sometimes hours away, and becoming full-time students. One participant, Clara, was still attending classes and had a job in a hospital pharmacy. She lived 1.5 hours from the main university campus, making it difficult for her to attend the main campus. The branch campus where the university offered the baccalaureate degree program was five minutes from her employment. Even so, she said, "I have to be real aggressive to get my work done so I can get out on time and get here to class." Isabella further revealed, "If my school had been further away from my work, I would have had to reconsider or take out more loans to pay for gas and things like that."

Students also did not have the luxury of parents or financial aid to pay for their education. To return to school, Lucy left work that she could "do in her sleep" because her employer was not willing to work around her class hours. She took a $26,000-a-year pay cut to begin a job that required "a learning curve" and long hours. She also cut living expenses; she "took out satellite TV" and "took things down to the bare basics." Also, in only two cases did they have employment that might help by paying for a few classes.

As first-generation students, students knew little of the processes and language of the university. The satellite community college campuses where some of the participants had earned associate's degrees had small classes and many one-on-one opportunities to get help with anything they had encountered. The university, on the other hand, was different in many ways. Students had to enroll on their own, needed to learn new and different processes from those at the community college, dealt with many campus-based personnel issues, and overall had to handle most situations without guidance. John described his multiple-semester effort to attend the main campus of the university several years prior as a first-generation student. First, he tried registering but each semester his schedule would appear to be online, but before the semester began, it was gone from view. Finally, one semester, he went to campus, registered, and actually started. However, that effort revealed more frustrating events for this first-generation student:

I didn't know I had to take e-mail. If I had known that I had to take an e-mail address. I just went and registered and they never said. The first math class that I had in the class the teacher would talk how we discussed this and discussed that and I would be sitting there and I ask, "Our class is just Tuesdays and Thursday isn't it?" She said, "Yeah." The whole semester we went through homework assignments and stuff that they had did and I felt like I was going to this classroom every day that I had never been through it before. It was all Greek to me. Well, it wasn't Greek to me. I understood it but in a semester I would go into class and never missed a day of class. Finally, I walked in the class one day and there was nobody there so I see some students out and I asked them about it and they said, "It is finals week." Oh really? So, I go to my advisor and it is like yeah it is on your e-mail. What e-mail? That is when I found out I had to take an e-mail. I didn't know this whole semester. We got all of that worked out so I went back home and I logged into it and all these math assignments and videos and all this stuff just started, that whole semester of class. Luckily, my final had not been yet. It was the next day, but I would have missed it. I kind of felt like that was something that maybe they should have said, "Remember your finals." Of course, I know in college that you are supposed to be the responsible one. Of course now after I learned the system, I was good, but nobody ever showed me how things worked. It was very frustrating, the whole deal with them over there

As students in Appalachia, participants in this study still encountered the deep cultural influences of family members who did not value education. During the interviews, several participants mentioned "losing friends" due to pursing higher education, simply because friends did not understand why participants wanted to pursue education or because friends were intimidated by the change in those attending school. Lilly mentioned enduring the jealousy of her supervisor. She said, "She is just very negative about everything. She doesn't seem to want me to go further in my education." Sue revealed losing most of her friends because of pursuing higher education, partly due to time constraints and priorities and partly due to jealousies and growing intellectual differences. Participants also mentioned family members as not understanding the need for further education. For example, Sue's already difficult relationship with an alcoholic father became even more troublesome. He criticized her for not taking time for him. She stated, "My dad is a selfish person and he really gets on my nerves." Feelings of guilt and shame (often perpetrated by parents or others in one's inner circle) for participants in the study were common and palpable. Becoming more educated than one's family resulted in conflicting emotions for both participants and their families, with a tension between being proud of achievements and growth but also jealous of and uncomfortable with what "being educated" would mean for family and culture.

The geography of the region also created time constraints and hazards as students traveled to classes. Although Lucy was taking classes at a branch campus, she still had a lengthy commute on narrow, curvy roads to attend classes. She noted that she dreaded slow traffic in her rush to get to class on time, adding a layer of stress over an already anxiety-filled experience.

The perceived internal and attributed external resources that the participants found in themselves (as reflected in the interviews and journaling) revealed their stamina and resilience. To endure the additional stress that now accompanied these full-time students meant they had to reach deep into themselves and rely on their faith or their support systems to persist. Several participants mentioned that learning communities comprised of other students made a big difference. Some described times they wanted to quit, but peer pressure from other students influenced persistence to the next class. A unique feature for most participants included overcoming maladaptive tendencies born from having very little idea about college success. Chief among these bad habits was procrastination. In responding to this reality, students were forced to develop time-management skills they did not know existed. As an example, consider Lucy, who started work at 6 a.m., had a two-hour break in the afternoons and had to be at the station to give the evening news before she left for class. She would try to study during the afternoon break and then study at her mother's home during evenings that she stayed with her ill mother. Lucy would share what she was learning to ensure that her mother knew that she had Lucy's attention, "She asked me constantly, I felt like I was back in elementary school, "What are you reading?" and "What is it about?" Dorothy described the internal qualities that aided her in her education, "I found myself at 27 without a job, divorced, no education, and kind of starting all over, so that is it, starting all over. So, I think starting there and rebuilding a little bit at a time gave me the confidence."

Question Two: What contexts or situations have typically influenced or affected participants" experiences of the phenomenon (Creswell, 2013, p. 81)?

The participants frequently spoke of family members who affected them in negative ways. Two specifically spoke of addicted fathers whom they chose not to be involved in the lives of the participants for this study. Many fathers of participants in this study demonstrated poor interpersonal skills, were often inebriated and were usually critical of their daughters. One of the students had to endure the embarrassing ordeal of an inebriated father who came to her commencement. Others spoke of brothers who did not understand why they needed to pursue education. Another negative and pervasive influence was the death of a mother. Several students' mothers had died, often removing the lone supportive influence. Two students dealt with seriously ill mothers, and one had to endure a terminally ill wife of 23 years whose health superseded (but did not replace) his academic work. Billy Bob described this emotional experience:

> Yeah, my wife dealing with cancer has been a real struggle. Cause, not near what she is going through, but trying to focus on a class while this was going on was mentally challenging. It is hard knowing your wife is sick in the next room while you are trying to look stuff up on the computer or spending time that you could be spending with her, but like I say, she was real supportive of what I was doing and she was encouraged it. So that worked out but it made it tough.

Poverty was a palpable theme that influenced almost every student in this study—it was a daily issue for most of them. Amy described her need for loans to keep a car running, in addition to paying for classes, "I took a lot of loans. I took out the max amount of loans to take care of my car and to take care of my bills so I am still facing financial concerns now and in the future now that I have to start paying back my student loans." Isabella could not afford internet at home because she had no full-time job and no benefits. She described one obstacle that she had to overcome. "I was staying at work so late working on stuff because I didn't have internet elsewhere. I could go over to the local truck stop. I could use their Wi-Fi, which I did do a few Saturday mornings." Every semester when payment for classes came due, students made difficult choices about priorities related to school and life. Interestingly enough, many students' family member made sacrifices to help their siblings complete school, sometimes the same family members whose self-conscious jealousy served as a roadblock or hindrance in other situations.

Adult students who participated in this study nearly always mentioned time lost with family and friends. Friends "unfriended" them on social media or would criticize them for various reasons, causing the students to ignore what had previously existed as a valuable social network to make room for studying and other schoolwork. Time to assist children with homework was difficult to find. "The stress of leaving my one child [with a learning disability] at home and not being able to be there and help her with her homework" was constantly troubling to Lilly who had personally experienced the same disability. Often, the parent was gone to class while the children had to study or help one another. Study time was lost when family situations or work situations had to be a priority. Time lost sleeping was nearly a daily issue. Sue described part of her week in this way, "Monday, Tuesday, and Wednesday were always the worse because I would work until eleven Monday and then work seven to four on Tuesday and then go to class from nine to five and then come in to work and work until seven to four the next day. I was like a zombie for those three days." Weekend time had to be sacrificed to write papers or study for exams while the family wanted to do a fun activity. On the positive side, participants frequently mentioned family or friends who came to their rescue, either to mow their yard, encourage them, hand them a little money, or stand by them throughout the program and cheer for them at commencement. One had an ill mother who was glad to have her daughter study at her home and share what she was learning. However, near the end of the program, she began to ask how much longer it would be. That mother, albeit very ill, managed with family help to attend commencement. Lucy described the overwhelming thrill of seeing her ill mother in the stands during commencement, cheering and waving.

Nearly every person mentioned the importance of the learning community as a support system. Some mentioned faculty members who were sensitive to their individual issues. The community even shared textbooks with one another if necessary when funds were low. They gave technological support to at least one of their members who had little experience with computers and developing presentations. The learning community rarely complained outside their small circle about the work involved or specific faculty members. It was as if they had their heads down and were pushing through the situations.

Parental nonattendance at college was reflected in their inability to understand completely what the working adult, first-generation, Appalachian student was experiencing. They had little regard for the tedious processes and issues surrounding university attendance. Only a few of the participants mentioned supportive parents. Some mentioned that had the parents lived long enough to see the participant attending a university, they most likely would have been proud of them; they simply lacked the frame of reference for how to help or even how to be supporting. In this area of Appalachia, life is hard, and many times, employment in coal-mining and other hard situations, shortened the life of parents. Not having parents who attended college hurt in two ways: (a) it added to their poverty, meaning that the students could not depend on parents to help with "exorbitant" college tuition but also (b) parents lacked the internal, psychological resources to help their children.

Perhaps one reaction after reading the results of this study might be that many challenges faced by these Appalachian FGC students are similar to just about every college student or those faced by other first-time college attendees. While that would be an accurate statement, it would miss the distinctive tensions and hindrances faced by these Appalachian adult students. First, there is the strong connection to family (Bryan & Simmons, 2009) that is both a support system and also a barrier based on the lack of academic capital families often have to understand higher education. Moreover, the distinctive linguistic accents and speech patterns of Appalachian student speech, is often viewed, maliciously and incorrectly as "hick," redneck, or "poor white trash" (Isenberg, 2016; Webb-Sunderhaus, 2016). Steele's stereotype threat research, usually thought to apply only to African American minorities (Steele, Spencer, & Aronson, 2002), nonetheless has explanatory power for all people who find themselves disenfranchised or disempowered by others (Spencer, Logel, & Davies, 2016). Simply put,

> When members of a stigmatized group find themselves in a situation where negative stereotypes provide a possible framework for interpreting their behavior, the risk of being judged in light of those stereotypes can elicit a disruptive state that undermines performance and aspirations in that domain. (p. 415)

The tension experienced by these Appalachian students to use cultural capital (aspiration, speech, family, and social structures) that is undermined by others' negative assessment of these very forms of support produces a kind of stereotype vulnerability that requires a unique resilience (found in these same ridiculed forms of capital) to overcome their genuine barriers to post-secondary attainment.

DISCUSSION

Revealed in the research were themes related to how first-generation college students who are also working adults construct and change their identities in ways related to their marginalized, understudied, and disenfranchised culture. One enduring theme was the lack of value placed on education in these students' families; a second distinct theme was poverty, both in their own families of origin, and in the region; and a third engaging theme was student unrest with their current identities, an unrest that compelled further achievement in the form of higher education. For these individuals, living life without a baccalaureate degree would leave them unsatisfied with their identities. Specifically, this research emphasized the role of positive deviance (Patterson, Grenny, Maxfield, McMillan, & Switzler, 2008) as an adaptive strategy of resilience that addressed how identity can be constructed within adult learning contexts. Specifically, positive deviancy describes positive anomalies—examples of those "like us" who succeed despite what empirical research and practical experience would say are significant constraints (LeMahieu, Nordstrum, & Gale, 2017). Much of our contemporary conversation is built around what is wrong, who is to blame for it, and why we should be afraid of both. Positive deviancy would suggest that instead of focusing on all the antecedent and consequent variables that predict or lead to underachievement for a particular group, researchers and practitioners (and policymakers) should focus on examples of people from these groups who succeed and why they do so. Individuals from Appalachian roots have unique challenges that are rooted in the poverty, low educational achievement, cultural limitations, and topographical restrictions that are part of the region (ARC, 2012); nonetheless, these same individuals possess strong cultural wealth, including family, language, aspirations for autonomy, mastery, and purpose, and galvanizing social support. In other words, many of the regions' citizenry may have more than the normal level of obstacles to overcome but also a unique set of support structures from which to draw.

SUMMARY

The overall purpose of this study was to understand the essence of life complexities for first generation, adult college students from Appalachia who were trying to work and pursue what was often a life-long dream—earning a college degree—and how this pursuit shaped their identities as lifelong learners. We desired to uncover, hear, record, and then share with others the perceptions, attitudes, motivations, and resilience (the lived experience) that these participants demonstrated as they endured difficult life circumstances in pursuit of something significant to them. Every participant in this study represented the message behind the powerful words attributed to Benjamin Disraeli: "I have brought myself, by long meditation, to the conviction that a human being with a settled purpose must accomplish it, and that nothing can resist a will which will stake even existence upon its fulfillment" (as cited in Nightingale, 2005). Every participant faced some difficulty, obstacle, challenge, setback or classic risk factor as defined in the research literature; yet, each one, due to personal, internal resources, or the help from some other person or the social system, was able to persist in the face of difficulties to achieve something important to that person. In pursuit of their goals, however, something else happened: Each person developed human capital none had expected. One person bought a house; one was building a new house; six had received promotions or new jobs; three were able to move from the remote areas where they lived to an urban dwelling; and most experienced family pride (even if complicated and nuanced) in their accomplishments. Beyond that, though, each participant learned new confidence in his own abilities and potential. Each person gained more respect in her workplace. In short, each student transformed into something he or she never thought would happen—each became a purveyor of hope for others on their difficult journeys through the complexities of life.

REFERENCES

Abdul-Alim, J. (2013). Dream big: Partnership programs make college a reality for first-generation students. *Diverse Issues in Higher Education, 6,* 18–20.

Appalachian Regional Commission. (2012). The Appalachian region: A data overview from the 2006–2010 American community survey. Retrieved from http://www.arc.gov

Appalachian Regional Commission. (2017). Appalachian Regional Commission: History and region; education and training/data reports. Retrieved from http://www.arc.gov

Berger, K. S. (2016). *Invitation to the lifespan* (3rd ed.). New York, NY: Worth.

Bryan, E., & Simmons, L. A. (2009). Family involvement: Impacts on post-secondary educational success for first-generation Appalachian college students. *Journal of College Student Development, 50*(4), 391–406.

Byrd, K. L., & MacDonald, G. (2005). Defining college readiness from the inside out: First-generation college student perspectives. *Community College Review, 33*(1), 22–37.

Compton, J. I., Cox, E., & Laanan, F. S. (2006). Adult learners in transition. *New Directions for Student Services, 114,* 73–80.

Creswell, J. W. (2007). *Qualitative inquiry & research design: Choosing among five approaches* (2nd ed). Thousand Oaks, CA: SAGE

Creswell, J. W. (2013). *Research design: Qualitative, quantitative, and mixed methods approaches* (4th ed.). Thousand Oaks, CA: SAGE.

DeYoung, A. J. (1995). Constructing and staffing the cultural bridge: The school as change agent in rural Appalachia. *Anthropology & Education Quarterly, 26*(2), 168–192.

Eller, R. D. (2008). *Uneven ground: Appalachia since 1945.* Lexington, KY: The University Press of Kentucky.

Garmezy, N. (1971). Vulnerability research and the issue of primary prevention. *American Journal of Orthopsychiatric Association, 41*(1), 101–116.

Garmezy, N. (1991). Resiliency and vulnerability to adverse development outcomes associated with poverty. *American Behavioral Scientist, 34,* 416–430.

Garmezy, N., & Crose, J. M. (1948). A comparison of the academic achievement of matched groups of veteran and non-veteran freshmen at the University of Iowa. *The Journal of Educational Research, 41*(7), 547–550.

Garmezy, N., Masten, A. S., & Tellegen, A. (1984). The study of stress and competence in children: A building block for developing Psychopathology. *Child Development, 55*(1), 97–111.

Garmezy, N. & Rodnick, E. H. (1959). Premorbid adjustment and performance in Schizophrenia. *Journal of Nervous & Mental Disease, 129*(5), 450–466.

Harvard Medical School. (2006). *Resilience*. Retrieved from http://www.health.harvard.edu/newsletter_article/Resilience

Horwedel, D. M. (2008). Putting first-generation students first. *Diverse Issues in Higher Education, 25*(5), 10–12.

Isenberg, N. (2016). *White trash: The 400-year untold history of class in America*. New York, NY: Penguin Books.

Jacobsen, M. H. (2009). *Encountering the everyday: An introduction to the sociologies of the unnoticed*. New York, NY: Palgrave Macmillan.

Kasworm, C. E. (2003). Setting the stage: Adults in higher education. *New Directions for Student Services 102*, 3–10.

Leedy, P. D., & Ormrod, J. E. (2016). *Practical research: Planning and design* (11th ed.). Hoboken, NJ: Pearson.

LeMahieu, P. G. Nordstrum, L. E., & Gale, E. (2017) Positive deviance: Learning from positive anomalies, *Quality Assurance in Education, 25*(1), 109–124.

Lopez, S. J., Pedrotti, J. T., & Synder, C. R. (2015). *Positive psychology: The scientific and practical explorations of human strengths* (3rd ed.). Thousand Oaks, CA: SAGE.

Masten, A. S. (2001). Ordinary magic: Resilience processes in development. *American Psychologist, 56*(3), 227–238.

Masten, A. S. (2014). *Ordinary magic: Resilience in development*. New York, NY: The Guilford Press.

Merriam, S. B., & Bierema, L. L. (2014). *Adult learning: Linking theory and practice*. San Francisco, CA: Jossey-Bass.

McGee, J. (2015). *Breakpoint: The changing marketplace for higher education*. Baltimore, MD: John Hopkins University Press.

Moustakas, C. (1994). *Phenomenological research methods*. Thousand Oak, CA: SAGE

Nightingale, E. (2005). The strangest secret: How to live the life you desire [CD Lecture]. Niles, IL: Nightingale-Conant (original recording 1956).

O'Leary, Z. (2017). The essential guide to doing your research project (3rd ed.). Thousand Oaks, CA: SAGE.

Orbe, M. P. (2008). Theorizing multidimensional identity negotiation: Reflections on the lived experiences of first-generation college students. In M. Azmitia, M. Syed, & K. Radmacher (Eds.), *The intersections of personal and social identities. New Directions for Child and Adolescent Development, 120*, 81–95.

Patterson, K., Grenny, J., Maxfield, D., McMillan, R., & Switzler, A. (2008). *Influencer: The power to change anything*. New York, NY: McGraw-Hill.

Spencer, S. J., Logel, C., & Davies, P. G. (2017). Stereotype threat. *Annual Review of Psychology, 67*, 415–437.

Steele, C. M., Spencer, S. J., & Aronson, J. (2002). Contending with group image: The psychology of stereotype and social identity threat. In M. P. Zanna (Ed.), *Advances in experimental social psychology* (Vol. 34) (pp. 379–440). San Diego, CA: Academic Press.

Tang, M., & Russ, K. (2007). Understanding and facilitating career development of People of Appalachian culture: An integrated approach. *The Career Development Quarterly, 56*, 34–46.

Teodorescu, K., & Erev, I. (2014). Learned helplessness and learned prevalence: Exploring the causal relations among perceived controllability, reward prevalence, and exploration. *Psychological Science, 25*(10) 1861–1869.

Vance, J. D. (2016). *Hillbilly elegy: A memoir of a family and culture in crisis*. New York, NY: HarperCollins.

Webb-Sunderhaus, S. (2016, September). "Keep the Appalachian, drop the redneck": Tellable student narratives of Appalachian identity. *College English, 79*(1), 11–33.

Weiten, W., Dunn, D. S., & Hammer, E. Y. (2012). *Psychology applied to modern life: Adjustment in the 21st century* (10th ed.). Belmont, CA: Wadsworth.

Werner, E. E. (1989). High-risk children in young adulthood: A longitudinal study from birth to 32 years. *American Journal of Orthopsychiatric Association, 59*(1), 72–81.

Yosso, T. J. (2005). Whose culture has capital? *Race, Ethnicity and Education, 8*(1), 69–91.

CHAPTER 5

"I KNOW THERE ISN'T ANYTHING I CAN'T DO"

Adult Learners Find Identity Through Bachelor's Degree Completion

Jennifer Serowick
Lesley University

INTRODUCTION

One of the primary reasons I attended college was because it was simply in my life trajectory. In my mind, and for most people I knew, life went something like this: high school graduation, four years of college, job(s), graduate school, marriage, kids, career, and retirement. My trajectory thus far has been, with some exceptions, exactly as it was programmed for me. So when I think back to college, I remember my bachelor's degree as an important time in my life that led to growth, maturity and a foundation for my employment prospects, but not one that particularly defined me, nor my identity. In fact, later in life, it was mostly the reputation of my college, rather than my personal experience there, that defined its importance in my future. The question we ask each other is, "where did you go

Identity and Lifelong Learning in Higher Education, pp. 79–100
Copyright © 2020 by Information Age Publishing
79

to college?" followed by "what was your major?" I do not ever recall being asked, nor thinking about, how college shaped my identity nor my perspectives on life-long learning.

The fact that I do not look back on my college experience as a particularly defining moment in my identity formation somewhat belies student development research in higher education. Scholarship surrounding identity development of college students is central to the field of higher education. It is widely accepted that college is a crucial time for young adults to answer the question "who am I?" through a series of developmental milestones described by psychologists and theorists across decades (Jones & Abes, 2013). While identity development is complex and ongoing, the process can be defined as essentially discovering one's purpose in life (Heshmat, 2014). In my experience, it was long after college that I discovered my purpose and in fact, as identity theorists agree, I am still in a life-long discovery process of that purpose (Heshmat, 2014; Jones & Abes, 2013; Josselson, 1998). The contrast of my experience with college and the pursuit of my identity, and that of what I would guess to be many people who pursue a traditional education trajectory, became striking to me through my research with adults who travelled a very different path to bachelor's degree completion.

For the participants in my recent research into adult degree completion, education was far from programmed (Serowick, 2018). Due to their complex lives and family circumstances, these individuals stopped and started college often across decades. The process of having to struggle to earn their degrees led to so much more than a diploma to hang on the wall. *Where* they attended became much less important than the fact *that* they attended and that, ultimately, they finished. In finishing, many of them also described finding their identity, or their purpose in life, as being able to learn anything as evidenced by their success with degree completion. While not the sole focus of this research, identity development as life-long learners through bachelor degree completion emerged as one of the most important results of earning a bachelor's degree for the participants in the study. Contrary to traditional student development research however, identity formation for the participants in this research was far from sequential (Jones & Abes, 2013).

This chapter will provide an overview of my research and findings with a group of women who completed bachelor's degrees after multiple stops and starts with a particular focus on the themes that emerged related to identity development and lifelong learning. The reader will "hear" from several participants whose stories most poignantly reflect how degree completion assisted in their identity construction as lifelong learners—the answer to the question "who am I?" While student development theories often focus on the early years of college as foundational for identity development, theorists agree that identity formation is ongoing, highly individualized, and is best revealed through personal stories (Jones & Abes, 2013; Josselson, 1998). In addition to their personal narratives providing insight into identity formation, I am also sharing participant stories here because I promised them I would. Because they knew the impact their journeys had on themselves, they wanted to share them with other adults still in the struggle, with the hopes that their stories could inspire and motivate others to finish.

DESCRIPTION OF THE PROBLEM AND SIGNIFICANCE OF THE RESEARCH

Adult students, typically defined as over the age of 25, make up 40% of current postsecondary enrollment and are predicted to experience growth at higher rates than traditional-aged students through 2020 (Gast, 2013). Because of their increasing presence in higher education, research on adult students, part of a larger student body often referred to as nontraditional, is plentiful. The problem is that despite its volume, something seems to be missing from the data because higher education has still not solved the problem of adults leaving higher education without degrees. In fact, adults continue to complete degrees at a lesser rate than their traditional, first-time college peers at about 33.7% compared to 54.1% (American Council on Education [ACE], InsideTrack, NASPA—Student Affairs Administrators in Higher Education [NASPA], National Student Clearinghouse, & University Professional and Continuing Education Association [UPCEA], 2015). This completion problem has led to approximately 35 million Americans who have started college but not completed a degree or certificate (Erisman & Steele, 2015). Besides the national concerns of a having a large population of people with credits but no degree, there are widespread implications for individuals that include both financial and personal. There is no shortage of data on this population, yet, moving adults successfully to graduation remains a problem.

While the aim of the research was to add to existing information about adult degree completion, the study did uncover at least one finding not often highlighted in the literature. The focus of this chapter is that finding—that for these participants, the journey to a bachelor's degree was more than the pursuit of a credential; it was the pursuit of their very identities as lifelong learners. Prior to expanding on the identify development of the participants involved in this research, this chapter will provide a brief background into the topic of degree completion to provide the context in which these participants' stories live.

THE IMPORTANCE OF A BACHELOR'S DEGREE: LITERATURE REVIEW

Increasing the number of Americans with bachelor's degrees has become a national priority for global competition, national economic health, workforce preparation, and individual economic mobility and well-being (Burns, Crow, & Becker, 2015). Economic predications signal that by 2018, 63% of all jobs in the United States will require some level of postsecondary education which equates to 22 million new college-educated workers (Burns et al., 2015). At current completion rates, by 2025, the country will experience a shortage of 16 million college graduates (Burns et al., 2015). When employers cannot fill positions, the economic impact is significant. In 2008, for example, the education gap resulted in a gross domestic product loss of approximately $2.3 trillion (Burns et al., 2015). The impact is magnified each year as the number of college graduates continues to decline. In addition to the economic implications, Americans over 25 years without a college degree are three times as likely to be in poverty as those with at least a bachelor's degree (Burns et al., 2015). The following sections will outline the importance of a degree at the state, federal and individual levels.

Benefits to State and Federal Economies

College graduates positively impact the financial health of states and nations by creating a competitive and healthy workforce. For example, because of their increased income, college graduates pay higher income tax, which contributes to increasing state and federal budgets (Council for Adult and Experiential Learning [CAEL], 2008; Schneider & Yin, 2011). Alternatively, low levels of college completion carries a high direct cost, adversely affect the U.S. economy and contributing to socioeconomic inequity (Paulson, 2012). Additionally, the job market is changing such that employers who used to demand technical expertise are now demanding employees who have more well-rounded skills including communication skills, problem solving, and critical thinking. By 2020, approximately 15 million jobs will require a baccalaureate degree but only about 3 million Americans will have a degree (Angel & Connelly, 2011; National Adult Learner Coalition, 2017). Increasing the numbers of college graduates will benefit employers, the workforce, states, and the nation, but also, impact individuals and their quality of life.

Benefits for the Individual

The benefits of a college degree are numerous, although the financial benefits tend to be a primary driver of bachelor's degree completion.

Workers with a bachelor's degree earn about $20,000 more per year than workers with a high school diploma or a General Educational Development (GED) certificate (Ryan & Siebens, 2012). Over a lifetime, this could mean a college graduate could earn approximately a half million more than a high school graduate (Schneider & Yin, 2011). Because of the financial benefits which include higher income and access to health insurance, college graduates live longer, are healthier, and have healthier children (from infancy to adulthood) than high school graduates or even adults with some college but no degree (Robert Wood Johnson Foundation, 2009). Finally, the more educated one is, the less likely one is to be unemployed. Adults with less than a high school degree experience 7.6% unemployment while adults with a bachelor's or higher see a 3.9% unemployment rate (Aud, Wilkinson-Flicker, Kristapovich, Rathbun, Wang, Zhang, & National Center for Education Statistics, 2013).

College graduates also see multiple intrinsic benefits. They tend to experience a greater sense of control over their lives, better social standing and higher levels of emotional and social support from friends and peers, increased social mobility, and an overall higher quality of life (CAEL, 2008; Robert Wood Johnson Foundation, 2009). Finally, adults are living and working longer than ever. In fact, 71% of people between 25 and 70 plan to work past retirement age thereby giving them more time to enjoy the benefits of a college degree (Kuh, Kinzie, Buckley, Bridges, & Hayek. 2007).

For adults, however, as was true for the participants in this research, returning to earn a degree, regardless of the benefits, becomes complicated as life layers on complexity.

METHODOLOGY

Overview of Phenomenology

In order to study adult student degree completion, which appears from the research to be the exception rather than the norm, this study used a phenomenological approach. Phenomenology facilitates discovery and description of the "essence" of a phenomenon through the multiple lenses of individuals who have shared that experience (Creswell, 2007; Mertler & Charles, 2011; Sokolowski, 2000; Vagel, 2014). Through interviews with adults who have experienced degree completion, both commonalities and differences were sought, keeping the founding principle of phenomenological research in the forefront: "there are multiple ways of interpreting the same experience, as well as multiple meanings that can be derived from that experience" (Mertler & Charles, 2011, p. 205). Exploring these multiple meanings allows insight into how a phenomenon is actually lived rather than how it is presented through data, models, frameworks, and conceptualizations (Vagel, 2014). This approach, therefore, had the potential to enhance existing literature related to this population.

Phenomenological research is often used to study a problem when it is important to understand several individuals' shared experiences of the same phenomenon and when the understanding of the experiences is important "in order to develop practices or policies, or to develop a deeper understanding about the features of the phenomenon" (Creswell, 2007, p. 60). Sokolowski, a phenomenologist, describes the value of this approach not only for organizations that serve a specific population, but for the participants and those who share in the experience: "The identity of the thing is there not only for me but also for others, and therefore it is a deeper and richer identity for me" (Sokolowski, 2000, p. 32).

Research Questions and Interview Protocol

Research questions for phenomenological studies are limited and open ended (Creswell, 2007). The following two questions and sub-questions guided this research:

1. What were returning adult students' experiences with degree completion?

    a. What events led adults to stop out the first, and any subsequent unsuccessful times?

    b. Who influences returning adult students in bachelor's degree attainment?

    c. What situational factors influence returning adult students in bachelor's degree attainment?

2. How did returning adult students experience degree completion?

    a. Why do adults stop out and return to higher education multiple times?

    b. How were they ultimately successful in bachelor's degree attainment?

Because one of the philosophical principles of this type of research is to start without presuppositions, the primary interview questions were broad and related closely to the two research questions. Interview questions sought to illicit information from participants that would allow for the description of the essence of the degree completion experience. Participants were asked to describe their early educational experiences, motivations for attending college, reasons for stopping and starting, and people who may have influenced them. They were also asked to reflect on their graduation and describe what they perceived to be the factors that ultimately led to their success. Finally, they were asked to reflect on the value of their degree and experience, and to offer advice for other adult students.

Participants were selected from three institutions, all with variations of programs geared toward adult learners. Participant selection criteria included: (1) completed a degree within the last five years, (2) were over the age of 24 when they graduated, and (3) at some point in their education, stopped then started again. Because data collection was through one-on-one in-depth interviews, a small sample size allowed a diverse perspective without being so large as to make it difficult to reduce the data into a detailed composite description of a successful adult learner (Creswell, 2012). While the sample was not representative of the general adult student population, the students selected provided information that lent to an in-depth understanding of the factors they attributed to their success and therefore could provide guidance for future students and colleges looking to improve completion.

Participant Overview

A total of nine participants were identified. Participants ranged in age from 25 to 55 and attended between two and four institutions. All but three of the participants attended their first institution immediately after high school and the total time to bachelor's degree completion ranged from seven to 36 years. Although neither gender nor ethnicity were variables in the research, all of the respondents were women, and all but one Hispanic/Latino participant, were white. Pseudonyms were used for participant confidentiality.

Data Collection and Analysis

Phenomenological data analysis consists of several steps that allowed for the "reduction" of factors to only those related to the phenomenon being studied (Creswell, 2007; Klenke, 2008, Vagel, 2014). Data were first categorized into nodes, or groupings that reflected the core ideas related to degree completion, and then the nodes reduced again into larger groups of meaning. The larger groups were organized into clusters of themes that contributed to understanding the essence of the phenomenon. Once themes were developed, transcribed interviews were reviewed again to verify that no themes had been overlooked until the data were "saturated" with no new themes emerging (Creswell, 2012; Mertler & Charles, 2011).

Finally, combining descriptions from each participant, a narrative of the "essence" of the phenomenon was developed. Both common and divergent themes were included to explain the phenomenon from a holistic perspective. The composite summary sought to describe the shared experience to allow readers to have a sense of empathy with the participants and an overall understanding of what it might be like to experience returning to college as an adult (Creswell, 2007).

RESULTS

Study results, presented via descriptive analysis that is central to phenomenology, included narrative descriptions for each participant, an overview of the themes, and a composite summary of the essence of the central phenomenon. The next three sections of this chapter will present a summary of the original study results as they relate to identity development through life-long learning. The first section will provide three of the nine participant stories that best illustrate the concept of identity development through degree completion. The second section will provide a summary of the themes that emerged through the data analysis and their relation to identity formation. Finally, the composite description that captures the essence of the phenomenon of degree completion as an adult learner is presented.

THEIR STORIES: BEFORE AND AFTER

One participant, Emma, described the potential benefits of sharing success stories. She said "in those stories people would relate ... to hear how people feel different about their before and after. That's a powerful story. A powerful message." Following are narrative descriptions of three of the participant's stories that best illuminate a common thread of identity construction through higher education. As Emma noted, their reflections on their experience illustrated significant changes between their perceptions of themselves before they earned their degree versus their reflections on who they became in the process of finishing the degree.

Anne: Writing Her Own Story

Anne, 55 years old, pursued her degree on and off for 15 years. Anne's pursuit of a bachelor's degree was tumultuous for decades as she struggled to find her identity, or her purpose in life, beyond serving the roles of mother, wife, and daughter. Along the way, Anne experienced repeated barriers as her priorities shifted between her daughter, her relationships, and her work. Influenced deeply by others who treated her poorly, she points to her mother as the foundation for her damaged self-esteem: a mother who once told her that she would never amount to anything and that she "was too dumb to even be a secretary." Her low self-esteem, combined with no strong guidance in high school, led Anne to the conclusion that college was very important for other people, but not for her. With no vision of herself as an educated person, her priority after high school was to redefine herself, fit-in, and escape the world in which she was raised:

> I don't think I had been away from my mother's dysfunctional home long enough for me to gain my own identity. I still thought I was who she always told me I was ... kids step into the shoes we set out for them ... I don't think I had two of the same shoes.

After high school, Anne joined the military but left before her service ended because she became pregnant. Anne's baby, and her new role of mother, brought an altered reason for earning the degree. She began to see it as a means to provide her child with a life different from the one she had. While her pattern of starts and stops continued, she never gave up hope that she would eventually have a better life.

Years passed, relationships came and went, marriages came and went and with each struggle, Anne's determination increased. Anne began to experience success in community college that provided the catalyst for an ultimate shift in her self-esteem. Eventually, Anne's life became settled. She was in a stable marriage, and her daughter had gotten through college and enrolled in law school. Sending her daughter to college had been a major milestone. Anne knew there was no way her daughter would travel the same road she did. She described one emotionally charged interaction with her daughter:

> In 6th grade she came home from school and she said to me, "Do you know you don't *have* to go to college?" And I said, "Oh, but *you* do".... I couldn't give her that quarter inch ... I knew ... that wasn't even an option.

Once she had seen her daughter through, however, Anne began to think that it could be her turn. A supportive employer with tuition reimbursement provided a stable foundation that would change her life.

The change began with completion of her associate's degree. As she experienced success, her motivations toward her degree changed again as her entire perspective on life shifted. She began to feel valued in and out of the classroom and the support of her peers and faculty provided the stability she lacked in her early years. She saw value in what she did even in a secretarial position. Anne had discovered a love of learning and the increase in self-esteem and confidence she earned from the associate's degree drove her to continue to her bachelor's.

Life was still hectic as she earned her bachelor's, but finally understanding the value of the degree for herself kept it as a priority. She believed the difference, besides the fact that she was experiencing success and loving school, was that she was finally doing something for herself. She had spent her life revolving her world around others. This shift in priorities allowed her to at last seek her identity. She described the shift after earning her associates:

> I started to realize I have a lot to offer … I'm not going to be relegated into the fringes of society … I don't bother with [my mother] but she raised me and I believed what she told me about myself. I realized … and my daughter was in her 30's … but I realized I am going to write my own story. And my story is a successful daughter, a happy marriage, a bachelor's degree. I want to have fulfilling work. And I'm doing it. I'm just doing it. And I fought for it.

After finishing her bachelor's degree, Anne still found herself wanting more as she envied the masters graduates at her commencement day. Her life's responsibilities clearly still weighed on her and she cited her need to care for her husband as a reason for not continuing in a master's program. At the time of her interview, while her degree had not had an immediate impact on her job and income, she was on a track towards a position that without her degree, she would not be travelling.

Anne's journey is one of stops and starts in college, but more importantly, was a journey of transformation. With distance and time, and the motivation of a child for whom she wanted better, she was able to build her self-esteem and create a new identity as a successful, valuable woman. The transformation is apparent in her recollections. When asked to describe her early feelings about herself and education, she said she felt like "just totally a loser." As her friends went off to college, she recalled she "was happy for everybody but that just was not going to happen for me." When asked to reflect on the value of her experience with education after her bachelor's, she described it as "fantastic. I learned so much. I know there isn't anything I can't do."

Joanne: Liberation Through Learning

After 15 years and three institutions, Joanne earned her degree at 32 years old. Joanne's experience with degree completion evolved as an ongoing struggle with her identity as an independent woman in her quest to finish the degree. When asked to reflect on her earliest perceptions of college, she had difficulty recalling specifics because her mentality then was so far from her current mindset. She described that distance: "Because my perspective is totally different now … it's hard to remember what molded it then." She described herself in her early years both as a "go with the flow" type of person but also driven to succeed. Although she recalled ambivalence towards college leading up to her high school graduation, once she decided to pursue her bachelors, she did not waver: "it's not like I was back and forth about it. I'm sure once I decided to go I was on that path." However, once on that path, she struggled to fit in.

Joanne was used to supporting herself in a family where she always received what she needed, including college tuition, but had to earn her own money for anything she wanted. Unwilling to lose the independence she felt from having an income, she continued to work when she went to college. She felt out of place, however, with other students who did not work and were solely focused on their studies and the social life of college. Since she was already supporting herself with a decent job, she began questioning the value of the degree and as result, felt disconnected from the learning. She never questioned, however, her ability to succeed. That self-confidence vanished, however, when she became involved in an abusive relationship with someone she met while still in college.

The combination of the relationship, her lack of connection at school, and her plummeting self-confidence led to her leave college. Rather than choosing to leave, she recalled feeling forced to abandon her hopes of college. Never a problem in her early life when she did what she wanted and supported herself, in the throes of abuse, she lost her ability to make her own choices as well as her financial independence. She described that time as feeling that the degree itself was not lost to her, but was something that was taken from her. No longer self-sufficient nor pursuing her own goals, Joanne's identity was shattered. For the first time in her life, she felt like a failure.

Fortunately, she was able to leave the relationship and as soon as she found stability, her aim was to take back that failure. In the journey to take it back, however, she experienced anxiety, stress, and fear that she would continue to disappoint people, another effect of her abusive relationship. Despite her diminished self-esteem, as soon as she could, she went back to college. Once there, she found that her perception of the value of a degree had changed. The shift coincided with many changes in her life, but notably, her financial status. In her first attempt with college, her parents had saved enough money that they could provide college as a necessity. After Joanne's divorce, with the loss of the college fund, the price of the degree "suddenly mattered."

College shifted for Joanne to one of those items in life that she now had to finance on her own. She reflected that only without the security of having her education financed, did she at realize the value of that education. Above all else, however, Joanne's return to college allowed her to regain her freedom and independence, an experience that she described as "liberating." Earning the degree led to freedom of thoughts and learning; freedom to seek a better job or additional education; freedom to raise her children on her own terms and push her children towards education; and importantly, earning the degree gave Joanne the freedom she had previously lost, to control her own destiny.

Emma: I Can Learn Anything

Emma, 54 years old, was in and out of college for 32 years. Higher education was elusive in her experience. Wrapped up in the larger question of her life's purpose, it came and went as she pursued her passions and interests believing her circuitous path would lead to her destiny. Growing up, the noise of her large family, their liberal ways, her brother's mental illness, and an overall philosophy of every-person-for-themselves was too loud to allow her to think for herself. After high school, she did what she thought she should by attending her local community college. But staying close to her disruptive home stunted her ability to start to discover her identity. She reflected:

> I think if you go off to school, then you can separate from family. You can start to self-identify. And that wasn't happening … I'm still living at home, I'm waiting tables, I'm taking a few classes, I don't know what I'm going to do. I think if I had that differentiated experience, that would have made a big difference for me.

When she finally did move away from her home, she found that without a stable foundation, and in the absence of anyone in her life guiding her, she stumbled around for years pursuing interest after interest, seeking her calling in life.

Emma experienced a turning point when she discovered what she thought was her professional calling was actually her clinging to a desire to repair her family. For years, she pursued psychology in school, always returning no matter how many times she stopped out. It was not until she was ending a serious relationship and was in couple's therapy that a counselor pointed out that perhaps it was not psychology she was pursing, rather, the idea that she could fix her past. Coming to the realization that psychology was not her true passion set her free from her own expectations of earning the college degree. It was at that point, that she stopped going altogether and experienced a shift in her feelings about earning her degree.

No longer able to connect the degree to what she perceived as her work calling, Emma's pursuit of a degree transformed from education as a means to fulfilling work, to a source of shame. At the end of her journey, she was able to identify the absence of the degree as a feeling that a physical part of her was missing. She compared it to "the tin man without a heart," and questioned the pressure she felt to complete the degree. She reflected on her feelings that people can be complete without a bachelor's degree:

> What you are and who you are and how you've lived your life is fantastic. Instead of, you're not complete ... so you can fix cars but you're not complete because you didn't finish those 4 years. It's a shaming thing. And I felt shamed. And I don't think that's useful.... You can live a really good life without a college degree if you're not shamed about it.

Her conflicted feelings were apparent however, as she described how it was to finish her degree:

> in some ways, there's a completion ... something that is tied up. It's complete ... I know from myself and other people who didn't finish it's as if ... we feel bad about ourselves.... Like we're less than ... we're not as smart.... And if you finish in a way that's valuable for you, studying something that intrigues you, that really lights you up that makes you hungry for more. That's fantastic. It completes something. That's what it did for me. It completed something....

This struggle between the shame of the absence of the degree and the completeness she felt when she earned the degree, was not evident however in her reflections about the value of her own degree in the end.

> I certainly wanted to finish, but it was very different in that I was learning ... I understood how to learn, and that I would continue to learn because now I loved to read and I want to explore and I want to continue to have that journey.... It's a part of my mind I taught to function. I can use that as a tool and take that anywhere.... I may have had the capacity, [been] as smart as other people ... but I hadn't connected that capacity. I hadn't engaged that capacity. I engaged the capacity and because of that ... I can learn anything. That's what I came out with. I could learn anything ...

She credited the shift in her experience to increased structure both in the classroom and in her life. She found a good balance between independence and structure with faculty who encouraged her to explore and learn things she was enthusiastic about, but at the same time, always checked in with her. She also found structure that maturity and stability lent her as an adult. Working for the same employer for years, and supporting herself, she created a foundation that she did not have as a child. She reflected that although she developed as a confident, independent, resilient woman who could travel alone, and support herself, what she lacked was consistent structure and guidance.

When asked to reflect on the entire experience, Emma described her experience as very personal; one that she would not have changed because she felt it was the entire journey, not the destination that defined her. Although unable to see it while she was struggling with finding herself, once she had finished, she was able to see that each experience along the way contributed to her growth:

> every learning experience adds up … [my hometown] community college wasn't any less valuable then the [out-of-state] community college [or] my desire to be an actress. It's all part of the desire to learn. [We need] to instill in adults that every little piece of their college or undergraduate that they gather is incredibly valuable because in it, was their desire to learn. So instead of diminishing it … or thinking of it as incomplete, that all of those things are pearls. Or the rocks that light the way. All of those metaphors. These are a part of your journey…. I own it.

Claiming the experience as her own was a turning point. Once she stopped trying to complete the degree for external reasons (to fix her family, to measure up to others, to get a job), she started to see the value in it for herself. That was evident in the way Emma described her graduation: "what it's done for me is that it became less this external thing … the degree to get the job … I wanted it for something very personal. I became personally fulfilled … I did it for me."

Emma's journey through degree completion was transformative in that she discovered herself along the way. Her upbringing provided her with the tenacity to never give up; her soul-searching values led her to try each new path as it presented itself; her intelligence gave her the curiosity and ability to learn; and finishing the degree, allowed her to fully "engage" every piece of herself in what she felt was a completion of heart, soul and mind. When asked to describe the journey and the value of the degree, Emma stated simply and with great emotion, "The word that comes to me is immeasurable."

FINDINGS: CENTRAL THEMES

While each participant's experience was unique, six central thematic areas emerged from the women's stories that offer a representation of common experiences in the phenomenon. While not all themes are common to all participants, they emerged as important structures in the phenomenon. The thematic areas include: (1) unstable early college experiences, (2) pattern of stops and starts end with a final tipping point, (3) success results from focus on internal versus external value of the degree, (4) sense of shame and low self-esteem, (5) influence of family and relationships, and (6) personal value outweighs professional value of the degree. Themes and sub-themes are described briefly below in relation to identity development.

Theme 1: Unstable Early College Experiences

For many of the women, unstable postsecondary preparation combined with a lack of direction and connection to the college experience contributed to the first and subsequent stop outs. Despite the unstable foundation, six of nine participants attended college directly after high school, experienced obstacles and dropped out, many of them in their first year. The remaining three participants worked or went to the military for several years prior to starting college but still described their first college experience as being fraught with obstacles. The subthemes related to early instability include the following: (a) lack of precollege direction in family and high school environment, (b) lack of connection between aspirations and academics, and (c) lack of engagement in college life during first attempts.

Theme 2: Pattern of Stops and Starts Ends With Final Tipping Point

Shifting situational circumstances in each of the women's lives created barriers that contributed to multiple stops and starts for years until a final tipping point that served as a catalyst for ultimate success. Common obstacles included financial and employment factors, changing roles in family and relationships, and a continued lack of direction. These obstacles were overlapping, intersecting, and circular. All participants, however, also identified a tipping point—a moment in life where they found clarity as to why the degree was important and why they wanted it. The subthemes that emerged related to obstacles and tipping points include the following: (a) transforming financial and employment status, (b) shifting family or relationship status, and (c) finding the right institutional fit at the right time.

Theme 3: Success Results From a Focus on the Internal Versus External Value of the Degree

One of the interview questions asked participants to reflect on what was different in their last attempt that they believed lent to their success.

Overwhelmingly, the women indicated that in addition to shifting situational circumstances, that they experienced success when the intrinsic value of the degree outweighed the external pressures. While participants described similar stressors of prior attempts in college, they described that positive forces present in their last experience outweighed the stressors that once kept them from completion. The barriers were similar: balancing work and responsibilities with being in school; financial stressors; a lack of self-confidence; and the strain of feeling that they still did not fit in a traditional college world.

Despite the barriers, all of the women also described the successes and positive forces that tipped the balance in favor of completion. Positive forces at work for each women included both external and internal factors. External factors that motivated students included employer support and financing, support from family, children and friends, and adult-oriented institutions that support learning and completion. Internal factors were more numerous and included the following: (a) learning sparks a passion for the coursework and connections to life, (b) success and momentum leads to increased self-confidence, and (c) motivation to complete becomes internal versus external.

Theme 4: Sense of Shame and Low Self-Esteem

Many participants in this study experienced a sense of shame and reduced self-esteem in the absence of the degree. While this concept overlaps in several other themes, the strength of the experience of shame itself emerged as an important aspect of the journey. Some believed that the shame came from societal pressure to have a degree but others internalized their stop outs as repeated failures and their inability to complete what they started which developed into low self-esteem and a lack of confidence. Shame emerged in several ways reflected in the following subthemes: (a) worry that repeated failures disappoint people, (b) shame leads to conflict about the value of the degree, and (c) the shame of past failures persists through graduation despite success.

Theme 5: Influence of Family and Relationships

The participants in this study were all influenced greatly (both positively and negatively) by parents, children, colleagues, and friends. While relationships and children were also part of the situational factors described above that led to stops and starts, many women specifically discussed the strong influence that others had on their decisions related to attending school. It emerged in the data enough so that it warranted a separate thematic section. The influence of others emerged in three subthemes that include the following: (a) parents engrain attitudes about higher education in their children at an early age, (b) adults with children want them to travel a different path, and (c) peers and colleagues exert explicit and implicit pressure and support.

Theme 6: Personal Value Outweighs the Professional Value of the Degree

When asked to reflect on the sum of their journey in degree completion and the value of the experience, participants overwhelmingly pointed to personal over professional value as the most important outcome of degree completion. Subthemes include the following: (a) limited financial and employment impact, (b) desire and confidence related to life-long learning, and (c) primary value of the degree is personal and intangible.

IDENTITY DEVELOPMENT AS LIFE-LONG LEARNERS

The six themes that emerged in the research align with the most distilled definition of identity formation as seeking the answer to the question: "Who am I?" (Jones & Abes, 2013). The basic goal of identity development is to find and hone strengths and interests that can ultimately be applied to pursuing one's purpose in life (Heshmat, 2014). That development can be stalled early in life if individuals are at odds with the values and experiences of those around them as was true for many of the participants in this research. Rather than choosing identity, individuals absorb the values and norms of those around them and "these values may not be aligned with one's authentic self and create unfulfilling life" (Heshmat, 2014, para. 1). This misalignment of values was evident in participant's early educational experiences and the influence of family and later, spouses, friends and coworkers.

Many of the participants described their patterns of stops and starts and a general feeling that they were not college material or could not find the value of their studies. Psychologist Shahram Heshmat (2014) points out that "A lack of a coherent sense of identity will lead to uncertainty about what one wants to do in life" (para. 1). When participants discovered their interests and their ability to learn, they were at last able to bring into alignment their true interests and talents with their purpose in life. Josselson (1998), a psychologist who applied Erik Erikson's early identity development theory to women describes the process of identity formation for women that aligns with experiences of study participants:

> Identity in women cannot be simply named, for it resides in the pattern that emerges as a woman stitches together an array of aspects of herself and her investments in others. A woman is, then, not a "this" or a "that" (mother, lawyer, wife, secretary, etc.), for these can only be pieces of herself. A woman is how she weaves it all into a whole, articulating herself in the world with others and simultaneously making private sense of it.
> (pp. 29–30)

Josselson's definition illuminates the process the women commonly experienced but lends a validity to the journey that many of participants were not able to realize. Because many viewed their stops and starts as repeated failures and discordant with societal expectations of educated individuals, they experienced great stress and feelings of shame. Discovering the intrinsic value of earning their degrees, rather than focusing on external pressures and norms, seems to have been what allowed these participants to finally put all of their pieces in a coherent whole.

COMPOSITE DESCRIPTION: ESSENCE OF THE PHENOMENON OF ADULT DEGREE COMPLETION

The following composite description sought to describe the "underlying structure" of the shared experience (Creswell, 2007, p. 62). While the individual descriptions provide the stories of each participant, and the themes aim to summarize the commonalities, the composite description includes both common and invariant meanings to describe the overall essence of the phenomenon. Therefore, the passage below is neither one participant's story, nor all of their stories, rather, an effort to reflect the possible lived experience of an adult who experiences the phenomenon of completing a bachelor's degree.

Even before they finished high school, the odds for success in college were against them. They were either not empowered to identify and pursue their interests, nor able to because of a lack of direction, support, guidance or finances. As a result, when they eventually started at college, they did so with no direction, no passion, and no belief in themselves. Once they got to college, they did not last long. They were too far away from home or too close to home. They were too unfocused and it was too expensive. With no connection to college, life easily interrupted pursuit of the degree and they dropped out. They had a series of unsatisfying jobs and felt inferior to others who were no smarter, but carried the badge of a college education. They tried college repeatedly but each time, life got in the way until a final tipping point. They got divorced; they got sober; they got a good job that would pay; they moved across the country; their kids grew up and out; they let go of their past failures; their boss screamed at them for the last time. For the last time, they tried again.

This time, they had a personal, single-minded focus to finish. In a supportive adult-friendly institution, they took one course, then the next, and they did well and they loved learning. Each success built their momentum and self-confidence and they eventually succeeded. In their reflections, they described a journey of sacrifice, shame, and perseverance that helped them ultimately find their identity. They broke from the molds of their past, driven to live a different life from their upbringing. Their beliefs shifted from "college is not for me" to a "why not for me?" approach. They found their direction, their calling, their passions—their very identities—and stability in the structure and success of school. They described themselves as having a new mindset at the time of completion because the pursuit of the degree became more about them. Above all the outcomes of earning the degree, each of the women described how the experience opened her mind to life-long learning, a transformation they all found life altering.

IMPLICATIONS

This research aligns with what higher education knows to be true about the barriers for students who complete bachelor's degrees as adults, but brings into primary focus the intrinsic importance of earning a degree. The implication of this study, therefore, is to shift the conversation from *what* adults experience to *how* they experience it. Primarily, it is important to understand that education is only a part of the whole of an individual's life and that an adult's ability to tend to that part is constantly shifting. Adult educator Ralf St. Clair (2008) researched underrepresented adults' decisions to participate in higher education. He summarized the struggle for institutions to develop strategies that account for students' complicated lives:

> The challenge for those interested in participation is to find a fluid way of looking at participation that takes into account the complexity of identity, and yet still produces concrete insights that can be used to shape policy and approaches. (p. 19)

St. Clair challenges adult education practitioners to think in flexible ways when trying to design programs that appeal to adult learners. This research, and the stories of the participants, suggest that the key is in the "complexity of identity." Higher education would benefit from embracing the lifelong process of identity development and help prospective adults see how completion of the degree holds significant internal value in the process of finding the answer to "Who am I?"

In addition to providing the supports and flexibility for adults to handle the barriers of complex and evolving lives, institutions can shift the conversation from "college is not for me" to "why not me?" Rather than articulating the value of the degree primarily in terms of better employment prospects or increased earning, or simply something that needs to be finished at a prescribed time in life, higher education could focus on the possibility of the degree leading adults to develop their identities into lifelong learners. This can be accomplished by continued sharing of success stories so adults can envision themselves being successful and let go of the shame they may feel from their past. Psychologists Susan Jones and Elisa Abes (2013) suggest that "the study of identity may be considered an investigation into the stories of one's life; as an individual constructs a sense of self, tempered by the external world, a story unfolds and gets written" (p. 6). If adults could realize the potential of higher education to provide a path to identity development as lifelong learners, then perhaps we could enable more adults to finish, thereby instilling them with the ability and the confidence that they can truly be or do anything.

REFERENCES

American Council on Education [ACE], InsideTrack, NASPA—Student Affairs Administrators in Higher Education [NASPA], National Student Clearinghouse, & University Professional and Continuing Education Association [UPCEA]. (2015). Postsecondary outcomes for non-first-time students. Retrieved from http://www.insidetrack.com/2015/04/07/great-data-now/

Angel D., & Connelly, T. (2011). *Riptide: The new normal for higher education.* Lexington, KY: The Publishing Place.

Aud, S., Wilkinson-Flicker, S., Kristapovich, P., Rathbun, A., Wang, X., Zhang, J., & National Center for Education Statistics. (2013). The condition of education 2013. Retrieved from http://nces.ed.gov/pubsearch/pubsinfo.asp?pubid=2013037

Burns, B., Crow, M., & Becker, M. (2015, March/April). Innovating together: Collaboration as a driving force to improve student success. *Educause Review*, 10–20.

Council for Adult and Experiential Learning, & National Center for Higher Education Management Systems. (2008). *Adult Learning in Focus: National and State by State Data*. Retrieved from http://www.cael.org/pdfs/state_indicators_monograph

Creswell, J. W. (2007). *Qualitative inquiry & research design: Choosing among five approaches* (2nd ed). Thousand Oaks, CA: SAGE.

Creswell, J. W. (2012). *Educational research: Planning, conducting, and evaluating quantitative and qualitative research* (4th ed). Upper Saddle River, NJ: Pearson Education.

Erisman, W., & Steele, P. (2015, June). *Adult college completion in the 21st century: What we know and what we don't.* Washington, DC: Higher Ed Insight.

Gast, A. (2013). Current trends in adult degree programs: How public universities respond to the needs of adult learners. *New Directions for Adult and Continuing Education, 140,* 17–25, doi:10.1002/ace.20070

Heshmat, S. (2014, December 8). Basics of identity: what do we mean by identity and why the identity matters? [Web log post]. Retrieved from https://www.psychologytoday.com/us/blog/science-choice/201412/basics-identity

Jones, S. R., & Abes, E. S. (2013). *Identity development of college students: advancing frameworks for multiple dimensions of identity.* Retrieved from https://ebookcentral-proquest-com.ezproxyles.flo.org

Josselson (1998). *Revising herself: The story of women's identity from college to midlife.* Retrieved from https://ebookcentral-proquest-com.ezproxyles.flo.org

Klenke, K. (2008). *Qualitative research in the study of leadership.* Bingley, UK: Emerald Group.

Kuh, G., Kinzie, J., Buckley, J., Bridges, B., & Hayek, J. (Eds.). (2007). Piecing together the student success puzzle: Research, propositions, and recommendations. *Association for Study of Higher Education (ASHE) Higher Education Report, 32*(5), 1–182.

Mertler, C. A., & Charles, C. M. (2011). *Introduction to educational research* (7th ed). Boston, MA: Pearson Education.

National Adult Learner Coalition. (2017). *Infographic: Fast facts on adult learners.* Retrieved from http://www.cael.org/alert-blog/fast-facts-on-adult-learners

Paulson, A. (2012). *Transition to college: Nonacademic factors that influence persistence for underprepared community college students* (Doctoral Dissertation). Available from ProQuest Dissertations and Theses database. (UMI No.3546033)

Robert Wood Johnson Foundation, Commission to Build a Healthier America. (2009). *Education and health* [Issue Brief 6]. Retrieved from http://www.commissiononhealth.org/PDF/

Ryan, C. L., Siebens, J., & U.S. Census, B. (2012). Educational Attainment in the United States: 2009. Population Characteristics. Current Population Reports (pp. 20–566). Retrieved from http://www.pathwaylibrary.org/ViewBiblio.aspx?aid=20616

Schneider, M., Yin, L., & American Institutes for Research. (2011). *The high cost of low graduation rates: How much does dropping out of college really cost?* Retrieved from http://www.air.org/resource/high-cost-low-graduation-rates

Serowick, J. A. (2017). *A phenomenological description of bachelor's degree completion for returning adult students* (Doctoral dissertation). Available from ProQuest Dissertations & Theses Global. (UMI 2007197376). Retrieved from http://ezproxyles.flo.org/login?url=https://search.proquest.com/docview/2007197376?accountid=12060

Sokolowski, R. (2000). *Introduction to phenomenology.* New York, NY: Cambridge University Press.

St. Clair, R. (2008) Beyond the barriers: Understanding decisions to participate in continuing higher education among under-represented groups. *The Journal of Continuing Higher Education*, 56(1), 15–24.

Vagel, M. D. (2014). *Crafting phenomenological research*. Walnut Creek, CA: Left Coast Press.

CHAPTER 6

"I'VE FOUND MY OWN IDENTITY HERE!"

Korean Graduate Student Mothers' Identity Transformations in the U.S. Higher Education Context

Ji-Yeon Lee and Hyesun Cho
University of Kansas

INTRODUCTION

According to Open Doors Report (2015), the number of international students in the United States has increased by 10% for the past decade to a record high of 974,926 students. The number of South Korean students in 2015 was the third largest (6.5%), followed by Chinese (31.2 %) and Indian (13.6%) students. Given that the population of South Korea is less than one twentieth of that of China or India, Korea being third in attendance in U.S. higher education highlights the popularity among Koreans of studying abroad. In particular, there has been an increase in the number of Korean married women with children enrolled in American graduate school

Identity and Lifelong Learning in Higher Education, pp. 101–118
Copyright © 2020 by Information Age Publishing

programs while their husbands reside in Korea. This unique phenomenon has few parallels represented by other international student populations in the United States. Nonetheless, there is a paucity of empirical research that has focused on the lives of these Korean mothers who play roles as both degree-seeking international graduate students and primary caregivers. To this end, this chapter aims to examine these women's lives in the U.S. higher education context by providing insight into the intersectionality of gender, culture, class, and identity in these women's experiences of lifelong learning.

CONCEPTUAL FRAMEWORK

This qualitative study is drawn from a social constructivist approach to conceptualizing mother's agency in lifelong learning. A social constructivist approach considers identity and learning as an inherently integrated process (Garrett & Baquedano-Lopez, 2002; Watson-Gegeo, 2004). From this perspective, lifelong learning is grounded in the learner's participation in a social practice that constitutes the communicative realms they inhabit. In a similar vein, social identity is multifaceted, dynamic, cross-cultural, and transnational (He, 2010; Jeon, 2010).

From the social constructivist approach to be adopted here, agency is understood as the "socioculturally mediated capacity to act" both in its production and in its interpretation (Ahearn, 2001, p. 112). Rather than conceptualizing agency as an individual capacity, we believe that agency relies on both sociocultural conditions of possibilities and constraints as well as the individual's ability to exert her beliefs, values, and dispositions in response to particular contexts (Cho, 2014). In other words, agency is not a free will of the individual. This perspective places agency within its social context, including past history, current situations, and future prospects. It also recognizes agency with regard to the affordances and constraints of a particular context (van Lier, 2002).

In short, agency refers to one's capacity to act contingent upon the sociocultural context in which an individual is situated (Cho, 2016, 2018). Thus, it is important to contextualize processes of the individual's meaning-making in the larger structural, historical, and socio-cultural context as it would be beneficial to examine the intersection of gender, culture, and class.

Korean Mothers' Role in the Family

During a typical day, mothers are barraged on a number of fronts with demands on their time and energy. In particular, challenges faced by most married Korean women in their own country are numerous, including taking on responsibilities of ancestor worship and living up to the expectations of deference to their mother-in-law concerning family matters (Chong, 2008). In addition, most married women with children have responsibilities in contemporary Korean society, that of "status-production" and "intensive mothering" (Chong, 2008, p. 78). This is manifested through a strong emphasis on their children's education. Based on the Confucian value of education, Korean mothers are known to have an unusual zeal for education, which is commonly called the "diploma disease" (p. 79). Obtaining a degree from a prestigious university is perceived as the key to success in Korean society. Even elementary students' mothers are expected to keep abreast of up-to-date information about the college entrance exam and private exam preparatory institutions called *hagwon* as well as the recruitment of English and math tutors for their children.

Park (2010) labeled Korean middle-class mothers as "manager mothers" who play the newly intensified maternal roles for children's education in the context of Korea's neoliberal transformation. The changing landscape of Korean neoliberalism is at the intersection of globalization that has intensified Korea's incorporation into neoliberal personhood, which spurs migration among the privileged (Park & Lo, 2012). In other words, Koreans are expected to be self-sufficient citizens who are independent and not in need of government social services. For example, an increasing number of middle-class Korean families have sent their school-age children to an English-speaking country as English has become a pivotal tool in developing human capital with which people can survive in the global world (Jeon, 2012; Shin, 2016). In the era of neoliberalism, language and learning are not seen as integral to identity; instead increasingly viewed as marketable resources, commodities, and/or skills (Cameron, 2005; Park & Lo, 2012).

In the context of Korea where private education has been prevalent, manager mothers are responsible for their children's education, including collecting information about study abroad and managing their children's extracurricular schedule. According to Statistics Korea (2015), $18 billion were spent by parents for their children's private education in South Korea. This indicates that about $240 per month per K–12 student were spent on average. Research has shown that Korean mothers believe that their support will determine not only their children's academic achievement but their future in general (Chong, 2008). Therefore, one of their weighty responsibilities as a mother is viewed as preparing their children for the globalized world (Chong, 2008; Song, 2012).

With contemporary Korean mothers' roles in mind, this study aims to investigate the role and agency of Korean mothers in the United States with regard to lifelong learning as graduate students at an American university. More specifically, the following research questions guided the study: (1) What do Korean mothers experience while raising children alone and pursuing a graduate degree at an American university? (2) What are the perceived challenges faced by these student mothers at home and in academy? (3) In what ways do mothers meet with obstacles as full-time graduate students and primary caretakers? And (4) How do mothers perceive themselves as a result of their experiences in the United States?

METHODS

The focal participants in the study are four Korean female graduate students at a Midwestern university in the U.S. who are married with children while their husbands reside in Korea. These four participants can be categorized into two groups: one group is in a Master's program—students who had full-time jobs as English teachers in Korea and took two years of study leave to move to the U.S. with their school-age children (Kyungmi: 42 years old with 9-year-old and 12 year-old children, Bitna: 43 years old with 7-year-old and 11-year-old children). The other group includes doctoral students with preschool age children (Jinhee: 36 years old with 1-year-old and 4-year-old children, Sujin: 39 years old with 3-year-old and 7-year-old children) whose husbands have finished their degrees and returned to Korea to work.

The two primary methods for this research are participant observations and in-depth interviews over the course of four semesters. This type of qualitative longitudinal study can allow participants to have their voices heard (Henderson, Holland, McGrellis, Sharpe, & Thomson, 2012). Drawing on the social constructivist framework, it is assumed that people make meaning in socially constructed realities. A constructivist approach to this qualitative longitudinal study also allowed the researchers to pinpoint experiences and perspectives that were meaningful to participants each semester on their program and ground the data in their perceptions of reality.

Furthermore, the close relationship the second author had with each participant allowed her to collect their rather intimate personal stories. The second author attended the same university with the participants (and studied in the same discipline with the three of them at the time of the study), resided in the same on-campus housing, sent the children to the same elementary or preschool, and (in case of all but one) attended the only Korean church in town. As a result, she was able to observe many of their life events from their arrival until their last day when they left for Korea or another state. All interviews were semistructured and conducted in Korean.

FINDINGS

The Dilemma of Motherhood

All women in this study are married with two children and are economically stable, if not affluent, with their and their husband's combined
incomes. They are also academically capable of pursuing a graduate degree
in the United States. Based on traditional gender norms influenced by
Confucian values in Korean society, Korean women are expected to marry,
have children, and raise a family (Chong, 2008; Kendall, 1996). In addition
to these social pressures, contemporary Korean women are expected to
work for additional, but indispensable, family income mainly due to their
children's private education. While assuming these responsibilities, many
women also have the desire for personal growth and development, which
often translates into obtaining an advanced degree in an English-speaking
country, such as the United States (Rhee, 2006). The achievements and
challenges experienced by these Korean women, particularly as mothers,
are highlighted in the following section.

Investing in Children's Education in the United States

In Korea, one of the most important roles of a mother is to "manage" her
children's education (Chong, 2008, p. 79; Park, 2007). Academic achievement is measured largely by which prestigious university one attends and,
in turn, what career one practices. In attending a top-tier university and
getting employed to start a desirable career, English plays a gatekeeping
role in order to accommodate the effects of globalization and neoliberalism
(Jang, 2015; Park & Lo, 2012). As a consequence, one of the achievements
perceived by Korean mothers in the study was their children's significant
improvement in learning English after a few years of residing in the United
States.

Kyungmi, the mother of a 9- and 12-year-old, was very proud of her children's success in English learning, particularly in speaking and listening.
She attributed this accomplishment to the amount of time that her children
spent daily using English in the United States. She described her children's
improvement in English with much enthusiasm:

> My younger one wanted to say something in English and started to imitate
> the sounds of English in six months [after we came here]. I know that my
> older one does not easily adapt to a new environment and does not try
> something unless he is one hundred percent sure, so he was reluctant to ex-
> press himself. But one day, when I happened to be listening to his conver-
> sation with friends, he said everything he wanted to say [in English] even

though he has some accent. At the moment, I realized the value of our two years staying here [in the United States].

Kyungmi passionately expressed her pride in her sons' improvement in English and even analyzed the reason for the children's success by indicating the importance of "falling into the sea of English" or studying English in the immersion environment. Similarly, Bitna detailed how her two children's English had improved in the U.S. with a tremendous sense of pride. Not only did she help her children focus on English language skills, but she indicated other reasons for their improvement, including an emphasis on creativity and self-expression in American elementary schools. Bitna also described the personality of her two sons in detail and the areas of English skill improvement for each child.

Some may argue that these mothers pay close attention to children's education and monitor their progress because they are experienced English teachers in Korea. However, they are very typical Korean mothers in that they are practicing intensified maternal roles in their children's education in order to accomplish their mission of upward class mobility in the highly competitive Korean society (Park, 2010). In fact, despite their children's significant improvement in English, both Kyungmi and Bitna were not certain that they were "doing enough" as an "educational manager." Their concern included the potential challenges faced by their children when they return to the highly competitive atmosphere in Korean schools. Kyungmi mentioned that she had their children study four major subjects (Korean, math, social studies, and science) according to the Korean national curriculum while staying in the United States. Bitna also prepared for her children's return to Korea so they would not fall behind their future classmates. In other words, one of the most important achievements for these mothers is their children's educational attainment not only in English but in preparation for returning to Korea.

Playing a Role as a Mother-At-Home

The mothers in the study appreciated the opportunity to play the role of "mother-at-home" in the United States. When these women were living in Korea, they did not have much time to stay home with their children, primarily because they worked full time and partly because children stayed outside of the home until late night due to lessons in private academic institutes. If the kids are not old enough to go to school, they are taken care of by their grandparents or a babysitter while their mother is at work. Generally speaking, Korean children have very limited time to spend with their working mothers, let alone their fathers. The four participants' children were no exception to this "parent-less" lifestyle before moving to the United States. As a result, these mothers were very grateful for the opportunity to spend more time with their children at home. They admitted that they cooked more often than they did in Korea in which many restaurants or ready-made foods were always available at reasonable prices. In addition to being a full-time graduate student and education manager of the children, the mothers expressed their satisfaction about being a mother waiting for her children at home and making homemade meals for them.

Despite their overall satisfaction about their role as mothers, the participants still found their situation to be challenging. The mothers of preschoolers, in particular, felt sorry that their children had to be in daycare all day, not getting full attention from mothers. Their guilt as mothers was evident when they compared their children with those of stay-at-home mothers or with those who had both parents in the United States. For example, Sujin said:

> I am feeling sorry for my children because I am not always available to them because of my study. My mother was a stay-at-home mother and paid full attention to me and my siblings while we were growing up. When I compare my kids with others who have stay-at-home mothers and even with myself who had my mother, I really feel sorry for my kids.

By comparing herself to her mother and other housewives around her who were committed to their student-husband and children's academic success, she felt inadequate for her own children's upbringing. It is well-documented that Korean mothers feel guilty when what they are doing (e.g. studying and/or working) does not conform to traditional gender norms: father outside as a breadwinner and mother as a housewife (e.g., Chung, 2015). Although contemporary Korean women are "literate, well-educated, and enjoying the rewards of postwar economic affluence and the technology of modern life" (Chong, 2008, p.66), they are heavily influenced by "modern maternal ideology" (*hyŏndaep'an mosŏng ideologi*) in Korean society. According to this ideology, the mothers always need to be an "ideal" mother. As a consequence, working mothers feel insufficient and limited to fully support their children's education and well-being. Jinhee shared her feelings when she described how her daughter had changed since her husband returned to Korea upon his graduation:

> I feel sorry for her because I'm doing my studies with her sacrifice.... For the six months after her father was gone, she became quiet and emotionally unstable. She was a vocal girl last year, but this year her preschool teacher told me that she is very shy. I think that's because her father is not here. I told the teacher that I'm studying here without her father and

she almost cried, saying that it was a very difficult situation, and she said,
"Don't feel too guilty." Well, I didn't feel guilty before, but I realized that's
how others think about me.

It should be noted that how others (e.g., the child's teacher) perceive
them as single parent-student in a foreign country influences the way the
mothers perceive themselves. In the context of neoliberalism, it is the
family that should be responsible for their social mobility (Song, 2010).
Neoliberalism demands individuals to be self-managed citizens who take
responsibility to improve themselves (Park, 2007). For Korean mothers,
this social ethos translated as the importance of her ability to promote her
children's educational attainment (Park, 2007). Park (2007) argued that
"this is the meeting point between the South Korean neoliberal project of
producing self-managed citizens and the emerging discourse of [education]
managing mothers" (p. 207).

In sum, the mothers with school-age children were satisfied with their
children's successful improvement in English, one of their major goals
during their stay in the U.S. as sojourners. As "education managers," they
also pushed their children to prepare for their return to Korea by studying
major subjects based on the Korean national curriculum. As depicted in
Chung (2015), single parenthood enhanced their independence as the
head of the household thereby having ample opportunities to engage
in the decision-making process as a parent. Nonetheless, they felt that
their time and energy were not still sufficient for their children and thus
felt guilty about pursuing their advanced degree in a foreign country at
the expense of children's social and emotional support from their family
members, including husbands.

The Challenges of Studenthood

The four women in the study identified themselves as not only mothers
but also as experienced teachers or graduate students at an American
university. The first sentences of these women's self-introductions for the
interviews were as follows: "I have worked for fifteen years as an elementary
school teacher" (Kyungmi); "It has been almost sixteen years that I have
worked as a secondary school English teacher" (Bitna); "I am a third year
Ph.D. student in the Educational Leadership program" (Jinhee); and "I
came here in 2006 because of my husband's school transfer to KU and two
and a half years have been passed since I started my study in 2009" (Sujin).
They then shared their educational background or work history, the reason
for moving to the United States, and the makeup of family members. In
other words, they mentioned their academic or professional careers before

their family members in their self-introductions. By others, they were called not only "somebody's mother," the most common title used when referencing a married woman with children in Korea, but a *sŏnsaengnim* ("teacher"), a commonly used title for graduate students in Korea as well as for school teachers. The following section delineates the participants' experiences as full-time international graduate students, inexorably intersected with the maternal role they play in the household.

As a Student—Compromise

Kyungmi and Bitna are master's students in Teaching English to Speakers of Other Languages (TESOL), and Jinhee and Sumin are doctoral students in Educational Leadership and TESOL, respectively. In addition to being a full-time student, all of them participated in other activities, like volunteering for their children's classroom (Kyungmi) and the Korean church (Bitna as a choir member, Sumin as head of the Sunday school, and Bitna, Jinhee and Sumin serve lunch on Sundays).

As international students with F-1 visa status, they shared similar challenges, including learning academic English, while adjusting to different cultural norms and expectations, and taking at least 9 credit hours to maintain the student visa, to name a few. Moreover, as Asian female students, they often struggled with the prejudice and stereotype that Asian women are less independent (Green & Kim, 2005) than their Western counterparts. Regarding the academic culture at an American university from doctoral students' perspectives, Jinhee's comment aptly described different educational expectations between the two countries:

> In America, doctoral students choose their own research topics and pursue their dissertation topic. I think this is a difference between American and Korean graduate programs. In Korea, the academic advisor clearly decides on everything, saying, "Mr. X, do this and Ms. Y, do that, and we will publish a book that combines the two." So I didn't have opportunities to develop my own research interests. Lack of academic training makes it more difficult for me [to study here]. Korean academic culture is to follow the advisor, but that's not the case here. That's why there is a clash between the two cultures.

This finding corresponds with Kim's (2007) study that discussed the discrepancies between expectations of Korean students and their American advisors, such as Korean students' passivity in initiating communications between advisor and advisee, and the perception of the academic advisor as an absolute authority figure. In Korea, the hierarchical relationship between professor and graduate student is highly rigid and stratified. It is not uncommon that Korean graduate students are viewed as "servants" of their academic advisors. Thus it was extremely difficult for Jinhee and other participants to overcome this passivity thereby taking the initiative for their own research and adjusting to less-formal or less-authoritative teacher-student relations at an American university.

Despite the cultural discrepancies inherent in academia, however, the participants in the study have accomplished their goals as students. The question remains as to how these women were able to accomplish their tasks as students under pressures as "single" mothers. The recurrent themes in their narratives and participant observations reveal that their changed perception of their modified roles as a mother and a student as well as efficient time management helped them achieve their academic goals. First of all, they readily accepted their obstacles due to their familial responsibilities rather than constantly comparing themselves to those who had no "burdens on their shoulders." Jinhee explained how she managed her time during the school semester in comparison with other students' circumstances:

> I took comprehensive exams this semester so were under tremendous time pressure, as you know. I could study only while my daughter was in daycare. So I focused on my study during the day, and what happened was that it enhanced my concentration on work. I seem to be more efficient than other male students or single female students. I should admit my limitations and understand what I can do or cannot do. If I start to compare my situation with others, that leads me nowhere but to frustration. This is not only true when you study as a mom, but also when you work for a company as a woman.

Although comparing herself with other students who generally had more hours of study without the responsibilities of child rearing and domestic housework, she had come to accept her situation as a mother and stop comparing herself with her peers in the graduate program. Sumin made a similar comment with a smile, "*I dare not to compare myself with other single students.*" These attitudes may be explained in terms of "satisficing"—a compound of "satisfy" and "suffice." In the study of tenure-track female faculty members with children, Ward and Wolf-Wendel (2012) applied this term to their research participants which refers to their making decisions that are good enough, or adequate, if not the best, in the field of economics. They argued that "in the case of women with children, satisficing is used as a way to manage work responsibilities to the best of their abilities and in ways they might not have had to if there were fewer roles to play and responsibilities to juggle" (p. 42). In that regard, these mothers are taking advantage of this (somewhat gendered and dismissive) form of "satisficing," in that they figured out what they needed to do and how much they could do under the given situation and managed their time and work as efficiently as they could.

"Buffering" is another concept used to explain similar women's achievements. It refers to the "negative effects of stress or failure in one role can be buffered by successes and satisfaction in another role" (Ward & Wolf-Wendel, 2012, p. 43). For example, the feeling of happiness or relief that these mothers get while spending time with their children can ease their tiredness from school work. Or their sense of accomplishment from school work can help them overcome their weariness from taking care of their children. However, these women can be easily trapped in what has been called "negative spillover" (Ward & Wolf-Wendel, 2012, p. 44). For instance, stress from study causes impatience with children's mistakes, or stress from housework can transfer to their study and yield an unsatisfactory product. This negative spillover was observed in the student mothers' interactions with their children in the study. By accepting their limitations and employing a strategy of maximizing their time efficiency, however, the mothers in the study seemed to survive and thrive in these two "greedy institutions" of motherhood and academia that demand "exclusive and undivided loyalty" (Ward & Wolf-Wendel, 2012, p. 41).

The tension between motherhood and selfhood depicted in this study confirms the existing literature on student mothers in other cultures (e.g., Bosch, 2013; Cooper, 2007; Estes, 2011; Guillory & Wolverton, 2008; Pare, 2009). The findings demonstrate a constant interplay between the "ideal student norm" and the "ideal mom norm" in which participants in higher education are expected to have the ideal student norm, regardless of their maternal role. Perhaps the most notable finding of the study is manifested in the role and agency of these Korean women as the heads of household, independent from their husbands in a foreign country.

As a Head of Household—Independence

One of the prominent changes reported by the participants when they became "single" mothers in the U.S. was their independent lifestyle. Although all of them mentioned some obstacles in raising children or taking care of household matters without their husbands' help, they all valued this experience of "standing alone." Kyungmi whose husband returned to Korea upon completion of his one-year sabbatical leave mentioned that she did not have an opportunity to "live a real life" when her husband was staying with her in the United States. She commented on the differences between the life with and without her husband:

> When my husband was here [in the United States], he took care of everything: all household matters, utility bills, and even ordering at a restaurant. I didn't like that. In fact, I thought that I was missing many opportunities to live a real life [in the United States]. After he left, I was a little bit scared at first when I filled my car with gas because, you know, all I did was studying, nothing else, even getting gas in the car. I mean, you can learn not only from books but also from your experience of everyday life, but he didn't give me a chance. Now he is not here and I have all these opportunities.

Without her husband's presence and help, Kyungmi had the opportunity to live independently. In a similar vein, when Jinhee compared her life before and after her husband returned to Korea upon his graduation, she felt a strong sense of accomplishment and freedom, and in turn, finding her own identity. The following quote from Jinhee encapsulates the experience of the Korean student mothers in the study:

> My achievement is my strong independence. I found my own identity here. When I lived with my husband here, I had no bank account under my name. The car is also under my husband's name. Because only he drove, he bought anything he wanted while grocery shopping. I lived just like a ghost [yuryŏng in'gan]. He didn't let me have a credit card, saying that I spend too much money. I didn't have a driver's license, and I didn't have a personal checking account, unlike everyone else. I was completely financially dependent on my husband until he returned to Korea. [After he left,] I got my own driver's license, and had my own checks made at the bank. I go grocery shopping by myself and buy what I want to eat.... Anyway, I have found my own identity in the U.S.

In the quote above, Jinhee perceived her sense of independence as her utmost achievement. Although she was pursuing a doctoral degree in the United States, and even earning salary as a graduate research assistant, she confessed that she lived without a strong sense of self while living with her husband. With possessing her own driver's license and checking account, she was enjoying financial and emotional independence from her husband.

This is interesting to note because, in the case of Korean middle-class families, it is usually the wives, not husbands, who manage household matters, including finances. Contemporary Korean wives are perceived as "the managers of domestic consumption" (Kendall, 1996, p. 115). As budgeters, women manage the family incomes and expenditures, and as consumers, they purchase everything from milk to a new house (see Nelson, 2000). As noted earlier, Korean women are actively involved in children's education as an "education manager mother" while they also attend to family rituals or other kin-related duties, especially for in-laws as a representative of the family. Korean wives actively carry out housework not only inside the home (e.g., cooking, cleaning) but outside the home (e.g., banking, purchasing goods, arranging children's extracurricular activities, organizing family events).

When Korean women live overseas as sojourners, however, their roles seem to revert to more traditional duties inside the home with which men usually take over the household matters requiring contact with the outside world. This is especially the case for full-time housewives who accompany their husbands for an advanced degree from an American higher education institution. Due to their perceived lack of English proficiency, it may be challenging for them to communicate with people such as tellers, clerks, waiters, or customer service representatives. Further, limited social networking means they have fewer places to visit and fewer people to learn from or receive support. Their visa status prohibits them from getting employed in the U.S. whereas F1 student visa holders can work on campus. Usually, a husband who speaks English has more access to social network, mainly through the university, and can bring in income and take care of household matters outside the home while his wife cannot help being dependent on her husband much more than she was in Korea. He has a credit card, writes checks, signs a rent contract, deals with bills over the telephone, orders in a restaurant, and even talks to the children's teachers at a parent-teacher conference. After a year or two in the United States, women seem to take on such tasks as they become adapted to the new environment. However, what they do in the U.S. is still much less than what they typically do in their home country.

One may find that these women are different from traditional Korean housewives in several regards: their English is proficient enough for admission into an American graduate program; they have ample opportunities to interact with people in school or in the community, and; they may work and earn a salary as a teaching or research assistant on campus. Therefore, it can be expected that the participants in the study who are capable of academic work in the U.S. would be able to function as capable individuals outside the home and enjoy their independence. Yet, Kyungmi and Jinhee continued to be dependent on their spouses until their husbands' return to Korea. They did not play a role as a decision-maker in their households until they lived on their own with their children. Thus Korean wives' dependence on their husbands in the U.S. does not stem solely from their lack of English skills, few opportunities to make money, or limited social networks. Despite their capabilities, the participants were still playing limited roles at home while living with their husbands in the United States. This reflects the patriarchal structure of Korean families that is not easily changed within one or two generations. Regardless of the wife's educational background, income, or other qualifications, the husband is the head of household and her primary role is to support him and raising the children. If a wife violates this gender order, she is often accused of being the source of family conflict (Chong, 2008). The findings reveal that once the husbands left for Korea, the wives in the study became fully independent and gained individual agency by playing dual roles as the primary caregiver and a graduate student in the United States.

IMPLICATIONS

The findings of the study report that the Korean student mothers attempted to resolve the tensions between their multiple identities as mothers and graduate students. It is revealed that these mothers tried to fit themselves into both mother and student ideal norms and ended up reinforcing the ideologies of intensive mothering that marginalize them (Estes, 2011). This gives mothers a feeling of imperfection in playing the dual roles (Chung, 2015). While the possible solutions would include the improvement of support for these student mothers on campus, such as maternity leave or childcare, Bosch (2013) argues that this type of solution is too simplistic as it implies student mothers are deficient and limited, in need for special treatment (p. 27).

Rather, more empirical research should pay attention to the cultural norms and expectations embedded in students' home culture that may result in tensions between the roles that student mothers play in and outside the higher education context. Such inquiry will help challenge the monolithic and deficit discourse about marginalized student mothers in U.S. higher education. In addition, since this study examines the international student mothers who were successful in their academic endeavors, it would be worthwhile investigating the experiences of mothers who have not completed their degree and the reasons behind their decisions. Further empirical studies on culturally and linguistically diverse student mothers' experiences with isolation and marginalization in the U.S. higher education can inform university administrators and instructors about how to create more inclusive and supportive environments for student mothers who continue to face formidable barriers to the successful completion of their degrees.

CONCLUSION

This qualitative study explores the experiences of four Korean student mothers who are pursuing their graduate degree in the United States. Using in-depth interviews and participant observations over the course of four semesters, the study elucidates the personal narratives of Korean female graduate students as student mothers. The data highlight the symbolic nature of both roles—mother and student—which is often in conflict with the sociocultural environment in which each role is performed.

As mothers, the participants closely monitored their children's English language development and encouraged their children to academically prepare for their return to Korea. Compared to their busy life in Korea where they had full-time jobs, these mothers could spend relatively more time at home with their children in the United States. However, they still felt that the absence of their husbands, which resulted in raising children as single mothers in a foreign country, was a daunting challenge to overcome. As students, they had to cope with the cultural differences in the expectations and norms of the Korean and American academic environments. Playing dual roles as a mother and student was a double burden for the participants requiring a balance between family and school responsibilities. The Korean mothers in the study were not free from the pressures of intensive mothering, the perception that mothers feel guilty when pursuing their own academic goals with less time, energy, and attention to their children (e.g., Pare, 2009). Their predicament was exacerbated by the complex, intersecting axes of hierarchy and patriarchy, both at home and in the U.S. higher education context.

Despite the myriad challenges faced by them, however, Koran graduate student mothers in the study valued the experience of independence, and gained a strong sense of accomplishment from "finding their own identity" in their words. They asserted that they underwent personal transformations, thereby becoming independent, resilient, and capable individuals during their graduate studies in U.S. higher education. All of them reported that they gained an enhanced sense of self-esteem and confidence through their stay without their husbands in a foreign country.

By investigating the lives of Korean mothers who have completed a graduate degree in the United States, this chapter also answers two questions as to why *Koreans* come to accept this transnational lifestyle and why Korean *women*, in particular, pursue it. Koreans are immersed in neoliberal ideology wherein they are expected to be self-sufficient citizens who are independent and not in need of government social services. As education managers, Korean mothers particularly choose to be transnational families in pursuit of educational attainment for their family while committing themselves to social status maintenance, or upward class mobility.

The trend continues as Korean married women are still willing to sacrifice themselves for their family's social advancement in the turmoil of the modern Korean history. These mothers who struggle to negotiate their agency and roles between motherhood and selfhood may appear to be selfish by some (e.g., Pare, 2009), but their efforts are ultimately made for their family's prosperity, especially their children's academic attainment. It is not our intention to undermine these women's achievements by describing them as the victims of the neoliberal, patriarchal Korean society. As noted previously, all participants have returned to Korea, armed with a graduate degree earned in a timely manner while their children's English proficiency has advanced to a satisfying degree. They have fulfilled personal enrichment and intellectual development that had been traditionally reserved for the privileged classes, mostly dominated by men. Their experience as mothers, heads of household and international graduate students for over two years in the U.S. has several positive impacts on their lives, not only for their increased earning capacity in the Korean job market but for their enhanced sense of self-esteem and personal growth.

One consensus among scholars about the landscape of Korean modernity is its "compressed" process (Abelmann, 2003, p. 281). South Korea is a dynamic, fast-changing society in which education is highly regarded and a zeal for academic achievements is extremely intense from an early age. As such, how this new phenomenon of transnational motherhood affects the status of women in Korea merits attention. Will this trend continue with Korean mothers shouldering the double burden of motherhood and the pursuit of selfhood? Will the stories of Korean women change in their daughters' generation? How do their stories have an impact on our understandings of lifelong learning and identity in the transnational world? Our hope is that this study lays a foundation for such an important line of inquiry as it sheds light on the intersectionality of gender, culture, class, and identity in lifelong learning by examining the experiences of Korean graduate student mothers in the U.S. higher education context.

REFERENCES

Abelmann, N. (2003). *The melodrama of mobility: Women, talk, and class in contemporary South Korea.* Honolulu, HI: University of Hawaii Press.

Ahearn, L. M. (2001). Language and agency. *Annual Review of Anthropology, 30,* 109–137.

Bosch, B. (2013). Women who study: Balancing the dual roles of postgraduate student and mother. Retrieved from http://ro.ecu.edu.au/theses/592.

Cameron, D. (2005). Communication and commodification: Global economic change in sociolinguistic perspective. In G. Erreygers (Ed.), *Language, communication and the economy* (pp. 9–23). Amsterdam, Netherlands: John Benjamins.

Cho, H. (2014). Enacting critical literacy: The case of language minority preservice teacher. *Curriculum Inquiry, 44*(5), 677–699.

Cho, H. (2016). Racism and linguicism: Engaging language minority pre-service teachers in counter-storytelling. *Race, Ethnicity and Education. 20*(5), 666–680. doi:10.1080/13613324.2016.1150827

Cho, H. (2018). *Critical literacy pedagogy for bilingual preservice teachers: Exploring social identity and academic literacies.* Singapore: Springer.

Chong, K. H. (2008). *Deliverance and submission: Evangelical women and the negotiation of patriarchy in South Korea.* Cambridge, MA: Harvard University Press.

Chung, Y. (2015). *Cross-cultural adaptation in the discourse of education and motherhood: An autoethnography of a Korean international graduate student mother in the United States* (Doctoral dissertation). The Pennsylvania State University, State College, PA.

Cooper, C. W. (2007). School choice as 'motherwork': valuing African-American women's educational advocacy and resistance. *International Journal of Qualitative Studies in Education, 20*(5), 491–512. doi:10.1080/09518390601176655

Estes, D. K. (2011). Managing the student-parent dilemma: Mothers and fathers in higher education. *Symbolic Interaction, 34*(2), 198–219. doi:10.1525/si.2011.34.2.198

Garrett, P. B., & Baquedano-Lopez, P. (2002). Language socialization: Reproduction and continuity, transformation and change. *Annual Review of Anthropology. 31,* 339–361. doi:10.1146/annurev.anthro.31.04042.085352

Guillory, R. M., & Wolverton, M. (2008). It's about family: Native American student persistence in higher education. *The Journal of Higher Education, 79*(1), 58–87.

Green, D., & Kim, E. (2005). Experiences of Korean female doctoral students in academe: Raising voice against gender and racial stereotypes. *Journal of College Student Development 46*(5), 487–500.

He, A. W. (2010). The heart of heritage: Sociocultural dimensions of heritage language learning. *Annual Review of Applied Linguistics, 30,* 66–82.

Henderson, S., Holland, J., McGrellis, S., Sharpe, S., & Thomson, R. (2012). Using case histories in qualitative longitudinal research. *Timescapes methods guides series 2012 Guide No. 6.* Retrieved from http://www.timescapes.leeds.ac.uk/assets/files/methods-guides/timescapes-holland-case-histories-in-ql.pdf

Jang, I. C. (2015). Language learning as a struggle for distinction in today's corporate recruitment culture: An ethnographic study of English study abroad practices among South Korean undergraduates. *L2 Journal, 7*(3). Retrieved from http://escholarship.org/uc/item/8nb0q2d4

Jeon, M. (2010). Korean language and ethnicity in the United States: Views from within and across. *The Modern Language Journal, 94*(1), 43–55. doi:10.1111/j.1540-4781.2009.00982.x

Jeon, M. (2012). Globalization of English teaching and overseas Koreans as temporary migrant workers in rural Korea. *Journal of Sociolinguistics, 16*(2), 238–254. doi: 10.1111/j.1467-9841.2011.00527.x

Kendall, L. (1996). *Getting married in Korea: Of gender, morality, and modernity.* Berkeley, CA: University of California Press.

Kim, Y. (2007). Difficulties in quality doctoral academic advising: Experiences of Korean students. *Journal of Research in International Education, 6*(2), 171–193. doi:10.1177/1475240907078613

Nelson, L. C. (2000). *Measured excess: Status, gender, and consumer nationalism in South Korea.* New York, NY: Columbia University Press.

Open Doors Report. (2015). Retrieved from https://www.iie.org/en/Why-IIE/Announcements/2016-11-14-Open-Doors-Data

Pare, E. R. (2009). *Mother and student: The experience of mothering in college* (Unpublished doctoral dissertation). Wayne State University, Detroit, MI.

Park, J. (2010). Chogi yuhak gwa kuigook hu ŏnŏ jŏgŭng (Pre-college Study Abroad and Language Adaptation After Returning to Korea). *Korea Joongwon Language Society Spring Conference Proceedings*, 179–186.

Park, J. S. (2010). Naturalization of competence and the neoliberal subject: Success stories of English language learning in the Korean conservative press. *Journal of Linguistic Anthropology 20*(1), 22–38. doi:10.1111/j.1548-1395.2010.01046.x

Park, S. (2007). Educational manager mothers: South Korea's neoliberal transformation. *Korea Journal 47*(3), 186–213.

Park, J. S. Y., & Lo, A. (2012). Transnational South Korea as a site for a sociolinguistics of globalization: Markets, timescales, neoliberalism. *Journal of Sociolinguistics, 16*(2), 147–164. doi:10.1111/j.1467-9841.2011.00524.x

Rhee, J. E. (2006). Re/membering (to) shifting alignments: Korean women's transnational narratives in US higher education. *International Journal of Qualitative Studies in Education, 19*(5), 595–615. doi:10.1080/09518390600886379

Shin, H. (2016). Language 'skills' and the neoliberal English education industry. *Journal of Multilingual and Multicultural Development, 37*(5), 509–522. doi:10.1080/01434632.2015.1071828

Song, J. (2012). The struggle over class, identity, and language: A case study of South Korean transnational families. *Journal of Sociolinguistics, 16*(2), 201–217. doi:10.1111/j.1467-9841.2011.00525.x

Song, J. (Ed.). (2010). *New millennium South Korea: Neoliberal capitalism and transnational movements*. New York, NY: Routledge.

Statistics Korea. (2015). Retrieved from http://kostat.go.kr/portal/eng/pressReleases/1/index.board?bmode=read&aSeq=352520

van Lier, L. (2002). An ecological-semiotic perspective on language and linguistics. In C. Kramsch (Ed.), *Language acquisition and language socialization: Ecological perspectives* (pp. 140–164). New York, NY: Bloomsbury.

Ward, K., & Wolf-Wendel, L. (2012). *Academic motherhood: How faculty manage work and family*. New Brunswick, NJ: Rutgers University Press.

Watson-Gegeo, K. A. (2004). Mind, language, and epistemology: Toward a language socialization paradigm for SLA. *The Modern Language Journal, 88*(3), 331–350. doi:10.1111/j.0026-7902.2004.00233.x

CHAPTER 7

LEARNING DOESN'T STOP AT 50

Lifelong Learning for Older Adults

Marian Spaid-Ross
Palomar College

Caren L. Sax
San Diego State University

INTRODUCTION

I always hoped that someday I would return to college. One day I took a giant leap of faith and decided to apply and enroll in a community college to complete an associate's degree in sociology with a dream of transferring to a four-year institution. I can remember the very moment when I received a welcoming letter from the institution inviting me to a new student orientation. By the time the first day of the semester arrived, I was excited about the educational journey I was about to embark on.

During the two years that I attended the community college, I developed a network of institutional support and services that assisted me in obtaining my educational goals. My participation in an adult student support group, including

Identity and Lifelong Learning in Higher Education, pp. 119–139
Copyright © 2020 by Information Age Publishing
All rights of reproduction in any form reserved.

weekly individual tutoring and monthly counseling workshops, addressed some of my challenges with managing the multiple roles and responsibilities in returning to college.

After completing my degree at the community college, I applied to a four-year institution and was accepted. As an older undergraduate adult student at the university, I recall having difficulty balancing family obligations, work, and my role as a college student. I scheduled a meeting with a professor, Dr. Sanders, who appeared welcoming and supportive and provided me with the knowledge, and resources to help me deal with these challenges. Dr. Sanders described various student services and programs that were offered at the institution, including an adult learner mentoring program. Through this program, faculty serve as mentors by hiring older adult students as teaching assistants. As a result of our conversation, Dr. Sanders offered to hire me as a teaching assistant and agreed to serve as my official mentor. I participated in this mentoring program, which provided support from additional faculty and an opportunity to network and gain access to other adult learner groups at the institution. At the end of two years, I attained my educational goal of earning a bachelor's degree in sociology.

During the following summer, I entered a faculty internship program that offered access to faculty mentors from various institutions. I selected a faculty mentor from my discipline and was given an opportunity to serve as a teaching assistant for one semester. After the semester ended, I was recommended by the faculty mentor for a teaching position at the community college. Today I continue to teach at a local community college where I mentor other older students and continue to advocate for institutional and community support to design and facilitate workshops for older adult learners who decide to enter or return to college.

The first author's personal experience was a prime motivator for undertaking this research. In addition, her ability to relate to and empathize with the participants during the interviews supported the insightful analysis of the data. This chapter offers an empirical study of lifelong learning derived from the perspectives of adult learners over the age of 50 who enrolled in community college, noting themes of identity, belonging, transition, and self-efficacy through postsecondary education. While the experiences of these adult learners are the primary focus of the research, the authors used the analysis to offer recommendations for postsecondary institutions for recruiting and welcoming older adult learners as valued members of their campus.

CONTEXT FOR THE STUDY

One of the most important shifts in the early 21st century is the aging of the American workforce (U.S. Census Bureau, 2014). The population is projected to age over the coming decades, with "the percentage of the population that is aged 65 and over expected to grow from 15 percent to 24 percent, an increase of 9 percentage points" (p. 4). This demographic phenomenon is assured as 78 million Baby Boomers, born between the years of 1946–1964, become eligible for retirement over the next 20 years (American Association of Community Colleges, 2015). Some of these individuals who have not retired are considering extending their work lives even longer, as they face concerns about finances and long-term care costs, while others may want to continue working to stay active and productive (MetLife Mature Market Institute, 2012).

Community colleges have considerable history serving adult learners, that is, those over age 25. Federal grants provided under the Higher Education Act of 1965 and the Older American Act of 1965 created college programs and services addressing workforce development for older Americans (Fishman, 2010). The Council for Adult and Experiential Learning found that "more than 30 percent of the adult population are untouched by postsecondary education and in 35 states, more than 60 percent of the population does not have an associate's degree or higher" (Ewell, Kelly, & Klein-Collins, 2008, p. 6). During 2010, 38.3% of Americans between the ages of 25 to 64 earned a 2-year or 4-year degree (Lumina Foundation, 2012). At that time, funding was allocated through the Health Care and Education Reconciliation Act to improve the capacity of community colleges to support the adult learner and their educational attainment, and in turn, "ensure the success of individuals in the workplace and safeguard our country's prosperity in the global economy" (U.S. Department of Education, Office of Vocational and Adult Education, 2012, p. vii). However, shortly after that report was issued, further research found that older workers, that is, over age 55, "are less likely to engage in training at community colleges than younger workers, and that they enroll at lower rates in credential or degree-granting programs at public two- and four-year colleges" (Council for Adult and Experiential Learning, 2013, p. 108). Cruce and Hillman (2012) noted that postsecondary institutions have yet to respond to this demographic change due to the lack of empirical information on the educational preferences of older adult learners. As a result, public postsecondary institutions may be losing intergenerational knowledge and additional revenue by not tapping into the older adult student market. And, older adult students may be missing out on valuable educational and social opportunities.

This study considered the specific needs and challenges of adult learners over the age of 50 enrolled in community college and explored the range of supports and resources they identified to foster a positive sense of belonging and realize successful learning outcomes. In turn, some recommendations are offered for older adult students in this particular age demographic as they navigate their paths toward completing their educational and vocational goals. Additional suggestions are offered for the institutions to improve their outreach to and support for this population. The primary research question that guided this phenomenological exploration was: What is the experience of the adult learner who is 50 years or older at a community college? Additionally, the following subquestions were explored: How do older adult learners perceive their community college experiences? What institutional factors facilitate success or present barriers to an older adult learner's positive college experience? The study was delimited in that it did not attempt to specifically compare the experiences of older versus younger or more traditional students.

GUIDING CONCEPTUAL FRAMEWORKS

Although a review of the literature did not produce any theories specific to the college experiences of older adult learners, several theoretical frameworks were utilized to guide this research that address individual growth, belonging, and the transition into and out of different experiences. Schlossberg, Lynch, and Chickering's (1989) theory of marginality and mattering explained marginality and mattering as a "sense of not fitting in" (p. 9), which can heighten students' feelings of uneasiness and depression and create unhealthy levels of self-consciousness. Their theory indicated that student success is influenced by a sense of mattering or belonging and offers a construct to explore this further. On a related dimension, Schlossberg's theory of transition defined transitions as "a process over time that includes phases of assimilation and continuous appraisal as people move in, through and out of it" (Schlossberg, Waters, & Goodman, 2006, p. 55). Supporting research by Goodman, Schlossberg, and Anderson (2006) suggests, "The process of these life transitions fosters learning and development and that a transition can be said to occur even if an event or non-event results in changed assumptions about oneself" (p. 111).

Another relevant theory, Strayhorn's (2008) theory of belonging, based on Maslow's (1943) hierarchy of needs, suggested that "belongingness" (Strayhorn, 2008, p. 30) is essential to one's individual growth as a person and existence within a community. Strayhorn's model posited that a student's feelings associated with belonging with regard to one's peers in and outside of the classroom at the institution is a crucial part to the college experience. Subsequent research by Strayhorn in 2012 provided further clarification: "The absence of belonging is marginalization, isolation, or alienation from others" (p. 17).

RELEVANT LITERATURE

In reviewing research addressing adult students, much of the literature includes those who are 25 years and older, versus traditional students who attend college immediately after graduating from high school at age 18. Adult students generally face three kinds of barriers before enrolling in postsecondary education: situational, dispositional, and institutional (Cross, 1981). Situational barriers include a lack of knowledge about the campus resources and services, and may include facing personal mobility, health problems, and managing responsibilities for family caregiving. Dispositional barriers are often perceived as beliefs regarding their own ability to be successful, as well as questioning their sense of belonging while attending college. Strayhorn's (2008) Theory on Belonging maintains that a student's sense of belonging is "based on an individual's psychological needs and that satisfaction of such needs affects behaviors and perceptions" (p. 4). Similarly, Deutsch and Schmertz (2010) found that female college students, who returned to college after the age of 24, found a sense of belonging or connectedness through a community of academic and social support. Students felt supported within their classrooms and developed a broader understanding of the social climate of the institution.

Institutional barriers often manifest themselves through inflexible class schedules, campus accessibility, and complex enrollment and financial aid procedures. Pusser and colleagues (2007) found that the "institutional response to the needs of older adult learners are neither generally systematic nor empirically based or fail to address the diversity in identities, characteristic and needs" (p. 7). As a result, adults are often institutionally invisible, marginalized, and taken for granted or systematically ignored by the field of higher education (Sissel, Hansman, & Kasworm, 2001). Postsecondary institutions continue to develop and implement practices and policies that target an extremely broad adult student population. By not being aware of the specific support and resource needs of the older adult learner within postsecondary institutions, colleges may be limiting or decreasing opportunities for student success.

Understanding the needs and interests of older adult learners is particularly important to community colleges because they enroll many more adults than do four-year institutions (Bragg, 2011). The most recent analysis on student enrollment in community colleges year-round was from 2013–2014. The analysis indicated that in 2013–2014, 9.8 million undergraduates were enrolled in public two-year colleges (National Center Education Statistics, 2015).

Community colleges are popular with adult learners for many reasons: the relative low cost; the mission to serve less-academically prepared and lower-income students; their flexibility in scheduling where and when courses are offered; and the occupational and technical skill focus with close ties to local employers. The introduction of the applied baccalaureate degree at the community college may result in educational and career opportunities for the adult learner beyond the community college to the bachelor's level (Townsend, Bragg, & Ruud, 2009). For older adults, the community college can be a powerful place for additional education, skills, and training/re-training that provides adults with a pathway toward a 21st century career.

METHODOLOGY

Qualitative research is a method for "exploring and understanding the meaning individuals or groups give to a social or human problem" (Creswell, 2009, p. 4). Given the exploratory nature of this study, a phenomenological framework was used to better understand the older adult's perspectives about their time enrolled in college through analyzing their varied experiences both within and outside the classroom. Phenomenology describes how people portray things and experience them and how they experience what they experience (Patton, 2002). A phenomenological approach, with the college experience being the phenomenon, created an opportunity for the voices and stories from older adult college students to be revealed and shared in hopes of "gaining a deeper understanding of the nature and meaning of [their] everyday experiences" (Van Manen, 1990, pp. 9–10). Creswell (1998) proposed a process that requires the researcher to: (a) understand the philosophical perspectives behind the approach, especially the concept of studying how people experience a phenomenon; (b) develop questions that explore the meaning of that experience for individuals and asks them to describe their everyday lived experience; (c) collect data from individuals who have experienced the phenomenon under investigation; and (d) conduct the phenomenological data analysis.

Participants

A specific subgroup of older adult students who were enrolled in a California community college were identified using the following selection criteria: (a) students who were 50 years and older, and (b) enrolled full-time or part-time in a community college. Flyers were distributed through deans at three community colleges. One hundred adult learners applied for the study and 20 participants were selected based on their availability to participate. As the first author received each respondent's inquiry, she contacted them via e-mail, and in some instances, by telephone, to confirm that the respondent met the study's criteria and was available to be interviewed. The researcher selected 20 participants from three community colleges in southern California, who were each interviewed individually.

Complete confidentiality and privacy was promised to the participants both verbally and in writing, as required and approved by the university institutional research board where the research was supervised by the second author. The interviews took place at an office on the community college campus where participants were enrolled. At the time of the interview, the participants were asked to sign the approved informed consent form, which detailed the purpose, procedures, benefits, duration, confidentially, incentives, right to ask questions, and participation in the study. During all interviews, participants were informed of the responsibility of the researcher to protect the rights, safety, and welfare of the participants in the study. If a participant decided to not participate, he/she was free to withdraw consent and stop participation at any time. All participants were informed that their information would be kept confidential by using assigned numeric codes and secured in a locked cabinet in the researcher's office until the end of the study.

Data Collection and Analysis

Situated in the phenomenological research tradition, in-depth semistructured interview questions were used for data collection. The interview protocol was designed to explore and understand how an older adult learner perceived his/her college experience. In framing the interview protocol for the one-on-one interviews, the researcher designed a set of specific questions derived from a review of literature, which added focus and meaning to the research questions. Questions were field tested with four older adult learners who met the participation criteria. Their responses were not included in the study. Collecting the information in this way allowed the researcher to draw meanings from specific responses and to use participants' own language to describe and explain their experiences. Each interview lasted about 60 minutes.

After the data collection process was completed, all recorded interviews were transcribed by a professional transcriptionist, resulting in about 250 pages of data. The first author read the transcriptions and made initial notations to gain a general understanding of the older adult learner's community college experience. The researcher bracketed out her thoughts and assumptions into the margins of the transcripts. She then revisited the comments that were written in the margins at the end of each transcript to ensure that the data were analyzed according to the experiences of the participants. The researcher used initial and axial coding as the primary coding strategies for data analysis, making notes on colored post-it notes while reading to compare and contrast interview data. The next phase of the analysis involved axial coding to sort, synthesize, and organize the data, resulting in categories and themes based on recurring patterns. This reassembling process helped to identify relationships surrounding the axis of the category (Charmaz, 2006). Coding and categories were then discussed with the second author who helped to refine the emerging themes. After the themes were agreed on, direct quotes and phrases were used to describe and capture the participants' perspectives and feelings.

FINDINGS

Based on the comments shared, all participants were very open to being interviewed, gave their time willingly, and were excited to share their story with someone eager to listen. Many expressed appreciation in having their voices heard, knowing that information would be shared with postsecondary institutions. Overwhelmingly, every participant was interested in the researcher's goals and the purpose of the study, hoping to contribute to increasing the institution's knowledge and awareness of the importance of supporting other older adult learners who wanted to attend college.

The study's participants included 15 women and 5 men, with 17 of the 20 identifying themselves as Caucasian, two as African Americans and one as Hispanic. They ranged in age from 50 to 74 years. Sixteen participants attended college part-time and four attended full-time. Students had different goals for attending college, including 10 who were pursuing a degree, four who enrolled in a certificate program, and six who enrolled for personal enrichment.

Four major themes were identified: (a) Do I Fit in Here? (b) Returning to College is not Easy; (c) Navigating the Institution; and (d) Interactions with Faculty and Peers Make a Difference. Subthemes to support the major themes and quotes from the participants are included to provide further insights into their experiences.

Theme 1: Do I Fit in Here?

Questioning whether or not they fit in at the college was a common concern. Participants felt a need to identify with another older adult learner and wished they would be recognized and accepted as a fellow student at the institution. Ms. W stated, "As I looked at all the young kids that were here, it made you feel like, what was I doing here with all these young kids?"

When asked about major challenges she was facing, Ms. G responded after taking a moment to think about it: "I would think it is fitting in in the classroom." A majority of participants expressed that there were visible differences, such as age and appearance, that influenced their feelings of fitting in. Several of the participants shared that they initially felt out of place because most of the students at the college are younger. One of the participants stated, "The first day that I walked on campus, I remember thinking to myself, all these kids! I saw them as younger than my own children. Most of them looked like they were right out of high school." Another participant shared that she had a friend who entered college and left after a week due to her fear of what younger students would say about her appearance. Ms. F explained, "I had a friend that was really uncomfortable because she was older and fat. She didn't want kids to laugh at her. I think she just thinks that because they are so much younger."

After entering/or returning to college, some of the participants talked about being anxious, stressed, scared, intimidated, uncomfortable, and overwhelmed. Mr. C shared, "It's really intimidating to come on the first day of class. For me, it was intimidating to walk up to a big campus that I didn't know anything about; it was kind of intimidating." Ms. O expressed similar feelings:

> Overwhelming to the say the least; I came to college because I had done 19 years of prison. My first week I got lost all over the campus, and I was afraid to ask for directions. To this day, I am still a little overwhelmed and intimidated with the abundance of young students.

Many of the participants felt that participating in classes with younger students who do not share similar life experiences created a sense of doubt as to whether they even belonged within the classroom. Ms. F's reaction regarding her first day attending classes with younger students makes this feeling clear:

> I feel like as soon as I walk into a classroom, they think, oh god, she's old. There is a part of me that wishes that they would talk to me and not view me like I have something contagious: my age.

Other participants described their feelings of not being accepted by fellow students within the classroom. Mrs. G said, "I sometimes feel isolated because a lot of the students don't talk to you because you are as old as their mom or grandmother. I think they tend to isolate themselves from me because I am older." Ms. L shared her observation: "A lot of them will be embarrassed if they use the F word when they see grandma is sitting next to them."

Some participants shared specific strategies to deal with these types of feelings of not fitting in. For them to be successful in obtaining their educational and/or vocational goals, they provided examples, such as modifying their attire on campus, utilizing websites that provide information on student evaluations of professors before they register for courses, and enrolling in multiple colleges. Mr. A said that when he wants to be recognized and accepted as a student peer within the classroom environment, "I wore shorts because teachers don't wear shorts to class. And, that makes me look like a student, right?" Ms. M used the internet to learn more information:

> I look at the website, Rate My Professor, when deciding which course and professor I will choose. I just do everything I can to find out about them before I sign up for a class because I feel like then I won't have a difficult time.

Instead of shopping for professors, Ms. R shopped for colleges:

> I started going to one college because the teachers were totally different; if you had a medical excuse, a valid one, they wanted to work with you, they really wanted you to succeed, they wanted you to pass the course, which was totally different than the other instructor I had at another college, so I decided to go to both colleges.

Theme 2: Returning to College Is Not Easy

This theme portrays some of the challenges experienced by the participants and the impact imposed on their ability to fully engage in the pursuit of their educational, vocational, and personal goals. Three subthemes support this larger theme: (a) cognitive and physical challenges; (b) balancing school, home, and work; and (c) facing financial hardship.

Cognitive and Physical Challenges

Many of the participants shared that they have cognitive and/or physical challenges that often interfere with their learning. One participant explained that her return to college was difficult due to a medical condition. She needs to self-administer various medications throughout the day and, as a result, sometimes experiences a lapse in memory. Ms. E shared that it frustrates her when she does not do well on an exam. She said, "I've done the work, I have done the homework, but I go into class to take the test, and I don't recognize anything." Ms. O described some of her cognitive challenges with learning:

> First, I guess because of my age, it is harder now to learn than when I was in my twenties going to nursing school. It used to be that listening to the lecture and briefly reading the chapter was enough. Now I have to read and reread and record the lecture and do a lot more hours of work.

Ms. R said that she requires accommodations that will address her specific learning needs within the classroom, explaining:

> I have a learning disability. I learn from having visual examples. You show me something how to do it and let me do it in front of you. Then I can go and teach someone else. If you say you learn it like this using a book it doesn't work for me. So, that is a real problem for me.

Ms. E admitted: "I am very nervous about next year because all of my classes will be in the evening. Because of the medication and my health, I don't retain anything. I'm even worse in the evening than during the day."

Some participants described physical challenges in returning to college, such as dealing with their access to the classrooms and mobility around campus. Some felt frustrated when expressing their concerns to staff and faculty. Ms. R stated, "I think for me as an older adult, it's a long distance to walk from class to class. They used to have a shuttle that would take people who have disabilities from point A to point B."

Balancing School, Home, and Work

Overwhelmingly, participants described their daily effort with trying to manage their various roles, such as being a wife, mother, grandmother, caregiver, father, employee, and student. In some instances, the responsibilities of family and work produced difficulties with their ability to manage time. Ms. L stated, "By the time you have grandkids and kids, and I still work part time, you have an awful lot on your plate; sometimes it becomes a little bit difficult to get the homework done." Ms. P described her family responsibilities as a major challenge:

> The major challenge for me particularly is making sure I have the study time I need because I am older and I've had an established life and I have 8 grandkids and 4 children and a husband that I've always been attentive to his needs.

The majority of the participants stated that they value education and are determined to have a better life for themselves; however, balancing the responsibilities of family, life, and work is sometimes difficult. Ms. O is a daughter, caregiver, employee, and student; she depicted her daily life:

> I live with my mom. I take the bus every day and it takes me an hour by bus to get to this college. Recently, I have become my mother's caretaker; she fell down and broke her hip, so I take care of her needs. I know exactly what time I need to leave here to get to class on time and what time I am going to get home after classes.

Facing Financial Hardship

Many respondents spoke openly about the lack of money presenting a major challenge to their completion of their educational goals. They stressed financial hardship as a barrier that prevented them from having access to resources. Ms. K stated, "I was too late for the financial aid deadline; it would have helped with the cost of books and the cost of living so that was really difficult."

Ms. O revealed, "After serving 19 years in prison, I came to college. I was considered an out-of-state student, so I was only allowed to go to school part-time. I didn't have the money to even buy a bus pass." Mrs. D explained her feelings regarding the financial support that is needed for her to pursue a degree:

> If I decide to get my bachelors or master's degree, the thing that would stop me from doing it would be money. I have to have at least 12 units to get full funding, so when I went to a full-time job as opposed to a part-time job, I had to drop my units that I was carrying and lost funding.

Theme 3: Navigating the Institution

A pervasive theme that described how students navigated the institution was through the utilization of student support services and programs. Every participant agreed that accessing these services at the college contributed to having a positive experience. Ms. P explained that taking advantage of student programs, such as the reentry program, created a positive college experience.

> Everyone has been extremely helpful. This particular college has an adult reentry program, and there's a young lady, I don't know if she was assigned to me, but she has guided me through what classes I need to get to achieve

my goal. She's been supportive, they've had orientations for adult reentry, which has been most informative. It's just been 100% positive experience being here. It's just been wonderful.

Mr. M shared that when he returned to college he had registered in the reentry program, praising the program and the staff: "I thought when I came back I would just have to figure things out on my own, but they got me in a good direction and helped me figure out a plan."

Ms. W described how she utilized and relied on the support from the tutoring center when she was having difficulty with her math courses:

I went to the tutorial center four days a week. I'd go before class and come back after class. As a matter of fact, some of the tutors were calling me by my first name because I was in there every day. I can't say enough about the tutorial center!

Ms. D explained how using the career and learning center on campus was helpful in serving her educational and health needs on campus. "I used the career center, the writing lab and the learning center. The learning center up north also has health services. I use all of these services."

Only a couple of the participants either did not have information on student support services offered at the college, or chose not to utilize them. Ms. O explained:

I think there are a lot of resources for us at this college but it is not always out in the open. Only a few older adults at this college had any idea that they existed. Some of them learned about student services and resources from faculty within their classroom.

Mr. H shared that even though he has a medical disability he chose not to utilize the disabled student programs and services at the college, stating, "I have two cracked disks, so I do have a disability placard. I haven't taken advantage of any other services because I don't really know how to go about it."

Theme 4: Interactions With Faculty and Peers Make a Difference

A prominent theme that emerged during the study was the impact that interactions with faculty and peers had on the older adult student's experience within the classroom, both positive and negative. Three subthemes included: (a) interactions with faculty; (b) context of classroom climate; and (c) interaction with peers within the classroom.

Interactions With Faculty

Describing positive experiences with one of her professors, Ms. S stated: "My keyboarding teacher was almost like I had her to myself. I always had so many questions. She would sit down next to me, read the assignment, and we would find the answer together." Mr. T was positive in his description, claiming he had no problems: "The professors treat me just like any other student, no favoritism. Being able to relate to the professors because they are my age is easier, so that makes me feel more comfortable." Ms. R described her good relationships, claiming that they "have written me recommendations and some have even gone on to be mentors to see how I am doing and to keep me on track."

Some of the individuals faced negative classroom experiences. Ms. H shared her interactions from an online class:

> [The teacher] was not very friendly with students or me. She was rude with comments that she wrote back. I don't think they really know the student's age, the way she talked to you like you're a kid, so maybe they need to look up the student's age. I did not appreciate the online teacher, so I will never take another online class.

Regarding a face-to-face class, Ms. M felt that one of her instructors was focusing only on the younger students: "Teachers appear that they are addressing the younger generation rather than the older generation, and sometimes I get the feeling that I am wasting the younger generation's money." Similarly, Ms. F felt that she was not recognized nor encouraged by the faculty as a student within the classroom, saying that "It felt like it wasn't really my turn, and that he wasn't really referring to me and that it was meant for everybody else but me."

Context of Classroom Climate

Classroom climate is "the intellectual, social, emotional, and physical environments in which our students learn" (Ambrose, Bridges, DiPietro, & Lovett, 2010, p. 170). Since the classroom is a social and emotional environment that can promote or hinder learning, a faculty's ability to create a positive and inclusive setting is key for fostering successful outcomes. Further, a faculty's response to student behaviors may determine or change the climate within the classroom. Participants expressed their feelings on how faculty addressed behaviors by students within the classroom. For example, Ms. F shared how inappropriate behaviors by students in the classroom interfered with her learning: "I was in a couple classes with some really disruptive younger students. It made it impossible for me to concentrate, and if you looked around, other people couldn't focus on what they were doing." Mr. A shared a conversation he had with a professor regarding students whom he considered disruptive to his learning:

> I was a student at another college and I had problems. My problems were that the kids didn't pay any attention to the teacher and were disruptive in class. They giggled and they laughed, and it was always in the back of the room. I talked to the teacher about it, and he said he knew of it, but nothing changed so I left.

Many of the participants shared that they are unique adult learners with varied life experiences that contribute to their college experience. "When you're 60 and they are only 18, I find the fact that I am older I am much more disciplined." Ms. D explained how older adult life experiences have better prepared her for a student role and meeting course expectations:

> I think life experience, organization, some basic things like planning ahead, things you learn from common sense. You have to plan your time, you have to plan for emergencies, don't wait until the last minute. One of the first lessons I learned coming back to college is to figure out what the professor wants and give it to them. You have to be here, you have to show up and be ready.

Likewise, Ms. P stated that she felt comfortable in the classroom: "I am taking this course because the professor likes to hear from the older students and see what they have experienced."

Interactions With Peers Within the Classroom

Ms. G described how peer-to-peer interactions within a classroom have influenced her experiences: "There have been a lot of classes where you don't interact with them. They go about their own thing and stay in their own groups." Ms. W described her first day classroom experience as cordial. "No one went out of their way to introduce themselves or anything, but I did meet with a girl and I asked her if I missed a class if I could call her, and she said, 'oh yeah.'" On the other hand, Ms. B described how some students responded to her in class. She said that when she asked questions, "the kids totally freaked out if you ask too many questions." Ms. J found that she had more meaningful interactions in the tutorial center than in the actual classroom, while Ms. O explained how she felt with working with younger students within the classroom:

> When an instructor wants us to work in groups, and I am dealing with students that are so young and don't want to do the work. Sometimes it's difficult or no one wants to pair up with me because of my age.

Ms. W described the types of students she has seen over the years within various college classrooms.

> When I was at another college, we were all there to learn, there was no monkeying around, and when the teacher said he'd be back in 20 minutes, everyone would have a quick smoke and coffee to stay awake because they had to work, but they were all there to learn. And what I miss seeing in the classes at this college is that the kids are here to learn, but not with the intent or with the same enthusiasm to learn.

Overall, the students who participated in this study had positive experiences at the community college. They seemed highly motivated to succeed in obtaining their educational and vocational goals. The majority who were the most successful were those who had the best supports from the institution and who had figured out how to balance their other responsibilities for family and work. Additionally, many experiences and perspectives were similar across the students and they believed that education will lead to a new career and a better life. A few of the participants were impacted financially as a result of their life experiences, and the majority of participants believed education is the key to having a sustainable economic future.

LESSONS LEARNED

The findings from this study provided a shared insight into the meaning of the college experience among the participants. The older adult students in this study were highly motivated to succeed in their educational goals, although enrolling in college led to them to ask many questions of themselves, including whether or not they even belonged there, if they could fit in with students who were much younger, if they were acknowledged and valued by the faculty and fellow students (or deserved to be), and if, by using available student support services, could they navigate the college more effectively to reach their goals.

For those participants who questioned their decision to return to or enter college for the first time, identifying with other older students was helpful. Joining programs like the re-entry program helped them to connect to others who were questioning their place at the college. Schlossberg's (1989) Theory of Marginality and Mattering provided additional insight regarding the older adult's feelings of fitting in at the institution. Clearly, the degree to which they felt like they mattered influenced their perception of their college experience and was important to their successful completion of their educational goals. These students' feelings of not fitting in at the institution were characterized as feelings of stress, intimidation, and discomfort. A feeling of fitting in within the classroom environment was important to these students' learning experiences, their perception on whether they were accepted or marginalized, and whether or not they would continue to pursue their goals at the college.

Strayhorn's (2008) model on belonging emphasized that when a student does not feel welcome, they often infer that they do not belong. In this study, the participants seemed to express that belonging was not as important as fitting in at the institution. In other words, they seemed to equate belonging with having the right to be there, but questioned if they fit in. It became apparent from analyzing the participants' responses that their perceptions of fitting in had changed soon after their first day of attending college. Fitting in for the older adult student meant that they were able to participate on a level playing field with their peers and in the eyes of their faculty. Strayhorn's (2012) research that described the absence of belonging as feeling marginalized, isolated, or alienated seemed to be factored into their views of how they interacted with their peers and if they felt valued and appreciated by both their peers and the faculty. They knew they had the right to be there; they just were not sure if others felt the same way.

The majority of students who felt they had the best supports from the institution and their family seemed to be the most successful. Schlossberg et al's (2006) theory of transition provided a lens by which to view their journey into, through, and out of college. For most of the participants, returning to college was often challenging. The coexistence of family responsibilities and commitment to work while being a college student created barriers. Juggling roles and responsibilities on a daily basis inter- fered with their ability to manage their time effectively and devote the amount of effort required to be a successful student. Facing the three types of barriers, that is situational, dispositional, and institutional (Cross, 1981) required the students to use their personal skills, life experience, and social capital to find ways to overcome these challenges, and they often felt better equipped to do so. Students described how the right classroom climate and the appropriate student support services made the difference for them in feeling successful. Programs that specifically targeted the needs of the older adult learner removed many of the barriers that these students faced, and could, in many cases, be easily implemented by community colleges.

RECOMMENDATIONS FOR PRACTICE

Important recommendations on how to support older adult students' community college experience have been generated from this study.

Suggestions are offered to institutions, faculty, and staff as they consider how to better embrace this population of students.

An Institutional Landscape of an Inclusive Student Culture

Older adult students need to feel that they fit in and are considered part of the student landscape at the institution. A simple recommendation for community colleges and their administrators is to include visual images of older adult students on all college websites, brochures, and other college materials. By including visual images of older students on their marketing materials, they are acknowledging the importance of having these students' knowledge and experience as an integral part of the undergraduate's learning experience. Demonstrating intergenerational interaction as a valued component of the community college experience would go a long way in attracting older students to campus.

Older Adult Student's Financial Aid Programs, Scholarships, and Resources

Some participants were barely able to afford their tuition and textbooks and shared that without financial aid and college resources they would find it harder, if not impossible, to continue their educational goals. Colleges might consider offering designated scholarships, fee waivers, and subsidized funding opportunities to meet the educational needs of the older adult student. Additionally, designing educational funding seminars specifically for older adult students may be helpful in their understanding of the funding options and the steps required to obtaining financial aid.

Older Adult Student Mentoring Program

Student support services should consider offering an older adult student mentoring program to provide a pathway of support, featuring mentoring, networking, and adult student fellowship. Adult student mentors would include experienced peers who had previously participated in the program and are using the mentoring experience as part of their service learning at the community college. The goals of this mentoring program would be to welcome and support the newly enrolled or returning older adult student and provide an opportunity for them to meet and build peer relationships with other students and faculty to feel welcomed.

Older Adult Learner Recruitment and Retention Campaign

The educational and environmental benefits for community colleges being considered an older adult friendly institution must include enhancing support services and resources targeted to these students. Institutions might consider offering a series of workshops to focus on the issues identified by the newly enrolled or returning student, including a series of mini-workshops on skill building, handling stress, time management, financial resources, and exploring sustainable careers.

As the United States population continues to age over the next several decades, the older population will become more racially and ethnically diverse. Understanding this demographic shift is important because an increasing proportion of older Americans continue to access postsecondary education. Community college leaders, faculty, and staff need to recognize that older adult student needs are becoming more critical as these students return to college. Extra support is necessary to maximize the opportunities for growth by adult students who are degree seeking, or interested in career, technical, and extended education programs. Community college leaders need to advocate for serving the older adult learner by implementing services, financial resources, and other supportive programs to attract and retain older students as they pursue their educational, vocational, and personal goals.

THE REST OF THE STORY

Taking another, and even larger, leap of faith, I applied for a doctoral program at age 60. Building on my positive experiences from my undergraduate and graduate degrees, I had the internal and external resources to enter the program with more confidence. Having peers in the program who were at least closer to my age, but more importantly, who each brought many years of experience working in postsecondary education, made me feel as if I belonged and had a right to be there. Finishing my doctoral degree by researching the experiences of fellow adult students stemmed from a desire to learn more about the specific needs, resources, and services that support adult students as they pursue their educational goals. By conducting this research, I discovered that institutions, faculty, staff, and peers play a significant role in shaping the adult student's perception of belonging at the institution. The experience further reinforced the value of pursuing lifelong learning, a benefit at any age.

REFERENCES

Ambrose, S. A., Bridges, M. W., DiPietro, M., Lovett, M. C., & Norman, M. K. (2010). *How learning works: Seven research-based principles for smart teaching.* San Francisco, CA: Jossey-Bass.

American Association of Community Colleges. (2015). Plus 50 programs in practice: How AACC's Plus 50 Initiative is helping community colleges transform programs and services for adults age 50 and over. Retrieved from http://plus50.aacc.nche.edu/Documents/Plus50_Programs_in_Practice_2015.pdf

Bragg, D. (2011). Chapter 9: Examining pathways to and through the community college or youth and adults in higher education. In J. C. Smart & M. B. Paulsen (Eds.), *Handbook of theory and research* (Vol. 26, pp. 355–393). New York, NY: Springer. doi:10.1007/978-94-007-0702-3-9

Burton, K., Golding, L., & Griffiths, C. (2011). Barriers to learning for mature students studying HE in an FE college. *Journal of Further and Higher Education, 35*(1), 25-36.

Charmaz, K. (2006). *Constructing grounded theory: A practical guide through qualitative analysis.* Thousand Oaks, CA: SAGE.

Council for Adult and Experiential Learning. (2013). *Tapping mature talent: Policies for a 21st century workforce.* Retrieved from http://www.cael.org/pdfs/TMT_21stCentury_Policies_Full_Report

Creswell, J. W. (1998). *Qualitative inquiry and research design: Choosing among five traditions.* Thousand Oaks, CA: SAGE.

Creswell, J. W. (2009). *Research design: Qualitative, quantitative, and mixed methods approaches.* Los Angeles, CA: SAGE.

Cross, K. P. (1981). *Adults as learners.* San Francisco, CA: Jossey-Bass.

Cruce, T., & Hillman, N. (2012). Preparing for the silver tsunami: The demand for higher education among older adults. *Research Higher Education, 53,* 593–613. doi:10.1007/s11162-011-9249-9

Deutsch, N., & Schmertz, B. (2010). Starting from ground zero: Constraints and experiences of adult women returning to college. *Review of Higher Education, 34*(3), 477–504.

Ewell, P., Kelly, P., & Klein-Collins, R. (2008). *Adult learning in focus: National and state-by-state data.* Chicago, IL: Council for Adult and Experiential Learning. Retrieved from http://www.cael.org/pdfs/state_indicators_monograph

Fishman, S. (2010). Older learner programs in Ohio: Policy and practice implications. *Educational Gerontology, 36,* 654–675.

Goodman, J., Schlossberg, N. K., & Anderson, M. L. (2006). *Counseling adults in transition: Linking practice with theory* (3rd ed.). New York, NY: Springer.

Lumina Foundation. (2012). *A stronger nation through higher education.* Indianapolis, IN. Retrieved from http://www.luminafoundation.org/ publications/A_stronger_nation_through_higher_education.pdf

Maslow, A. H. (1943). A theory of human motivation. *Psychological Review, 50*(4), 370–396.

MetLife Mature Market Institute. (2012). *Transitioning into retirement: The MetLife study of baby boomers at 65.* Retrieved from https://www.metlife.com/assets/cao/mmi/publications/studies/2012/studies/mmi-transitioning-retirement.pdf

National Center Education Statistics. (2015). *Total 12-month enrollment in degree-granting postsecondary institutions, by control and level of institution and state or jurisdiction.* Retrieved from: https://nces.ed.gov/programs/digest/d15/tables/dt15_308.10.asp

Patton, M. Q. (2002). *Qualitative research and evaluation methods* (3rd ed.). Thousand Oaks, CA: SAGE.

Pusser, B., Breneman, D. W., Gansneder, B. M., Kohl, K. J., Levin, J. S., Milam, J. H., & Turner, S. E. (2007). *Returning to learning: Adults' success in college is key to America's future.* New Agenda Series. Indianapolis, IN: Lumina Foundation for Education.

Schlossberg, N. K. (1989). Marginality and mattering: Key issues in building community. In D. C. Roberts (Ed.), *Designing campus activities to foster a sense of community* (pp. 5–15). New Directions for Student Services, No. 48. San Francisco, CA: Jossey-Bass.

Schlossberg, N. K., Lynch, A., & Chickering, A.W. (1989). *Improving higher education environments for adults.* San Francisco, CA. Jossey-Bass.

Schlossberg, N. K., Waters, E. B., & Goodman, J. (2006). *Counseling adults in transition: Linking practice with theory* (2nd ed.). New York, NY: Springer.

Sissel, P. A., Hansman, C. A., & Kasworm, C. E. (2001). The politics of neglect: Adult learners in higher education. *New Directions for Adult and Continuing Education, 91,* 17–27.

Strayhorn, T. L. (2008). Fittin' in: Do diverse interactions with peers affect sense of belonging for black men at predominantly white institutions? *NASPA Journal, 45*(4), 501–527.

Strayhorn, T. L. (2012). *College students' sense of belonging: A key to educational success.* New York, NY: Routledge.

Townsend, B. K., Bragg, D. D., & Ruud, C. M. (2009). Development of the applied baccalaureate. *Community College Journal of Research and Practice, 33*(9), 686–705. doi:10.1080/10668920902983601

U.S. Census Bureau. (2014). *An aging nation: The older population in the United States.* Washington, DC: Author. Retrieved from https://www.census.gov/prod/2014pubs/p25-1140.pdf

U.S. Department of Education, Office of Vocational and Adult Education. (2012). *Adult college completion tool kit.* Retrieved from http://www2.ed.gov/about/offices/list/ovae/resource/adult-college-completion-tool-kit.pdf

Van Manen, M. (1990). *Researching lived experience: Human science for an action sensitive pedagogy* (2nd ed.). Albany, NY: State University of New York Press.

CHAPTER 8

LESSONS FROM A LIFE AT SCHOOL

Judith Beth Cohen
Professor Emerita, Lesley University

As a young newly minted teacher I read *Summerville, A Radical Approach to Childhood* (1960) and fell in love with the English progressive school founded by A. S. Neill back in 1921. No grades, no boring classes, a community where kids and adults were equal. I longed to be part of such a utopian project. Now, some 50 years later when I reflect on my career teaching at both progressive and traditional institutions, it seems like a collage created of many shapes and colors. Yet my belief in an intimate face-to-face community where the topics emerge from the lived experiences of students and teachers has not wavered.

LESSON 1: IMPROVISE

As a young idealist, I began teaching in a special education classroom for "disturbed" children who had been removed from "normal" schools. Though my charges showed no physical signs of disability, no one questioned this labeling and segregation. Children were bused away to a

Identity and Lifelong Learning in Higher Education, pp. 141–149
Copyright © 2020 by Information Age Publishing
All rights of reproduction in any form reserved.

separate building to be taught by specially trained teachers. That was me. With my newly acquired master's in psychology and education, I was drawn to those kids. My mother suffered from mental illness, and though I could not cure her, maybe I could prevent them from suffering such adult misery. My training, my reading and my own bitter experience motivated me to work where kids spend most of their time, in school. Each child had a separate lesson intended to keep them up to grade level in our small, colorless classroom rented from a church school. All kids were White—there were no classes in art, music or gym and the curriculum was mine to create. Timmy, a skinny, jittery little guy who could not seem to concentrate, was cheerful and compliant; Bobby, a rather overweight, healthy looking boy was squeezed into this little desk, and Amy, a thin girl, wiggled in and out of chairs and resisted any direction. Our principal, a corpulent red-haired woman with a flushed face had only one concern: obedience. Punish the bad, reward the good, yet I was determined to provide a rich learning experience. I decided to move my kids out of the sterile classroom to the pre-school playroom where they were free to work with blocks, draw with crayons or play with dolls, as they chose. Then I began to make home visits. I took Amy out for ice cream or car rides, for which her beleaguered mother was grateful. Despite my efforts to turn that barren, sequestered classroom into a better experience for these kids, it did not work. My charges, so used to being punished and disciplined, became more difficult to manage. The principal intervened—I watched her swat Bobby, the back of her hand sweeping across his face; then she twisted Amy's arm until she went limp. It did not occur to me that this was illegal, only cruel and morally wrong. Bravely, I confronted my boss who called me too naïve and idealistic. I told her I could no longer work for someone so "unprofessional," and after a crying session back home, I quit. My first job and I was a failure. Soon I recovered enough to try again. Maybe teaching young kids was not what I am best at—maybe I should aim higher, teach college. To my surprise, at the tender age of 23, with no more than a master's, I was hired.

On a cold February evening I entered my first college class carrying my black attaché case, a gift meant to make me appear more mature. The 30 or so students, mostly men in the military seemed amused by my presence at this community college course for adult learners. Improvisation became my pedagogy as I stumbled along, managing to stay a week ahead in the assigned textbook. The course, "Introduction to Social Science," began with psychology, the subject I knew better than the other two: sociology and anthropology. When I presented the section on Freud and uttered the phrase "penis envy," my girlish blush must have broadcast my inexperience. With actual college teaching experience now on my resume, I was able to get my first full-time college teaching position at a nearby state university as a section instructor for a large lecture course in child development.

LESSON 2: CURRICULUM COMES FROM EXPERIENCE

Three years later I landed at Goddard College in Plainfield Vermont. It was the fall after Nixon's invasion of Cambodia and the National Guard murders of students at Kent State and the entire culture seemed to be in upheaval. Goddard College was founded by Tim Pitkin in 1938 as "a college for living" and it is still going today (http://www.goddard.edu/about-goddard/goddard-difference/college-history/).

Pitkin, a Vermonter who had studied with William Kilpatrick, a student of John Dewey's, had a direct lineage to the philosopher who wrote extensively about democracy, citizen education, experiential learning and the importance of the arts in society (Dewey, 1916). My students and I sat at the retired president's feet and heard just how he had come up with the Goddard idea. He had been inspired by the Danish Folk schools where students attended classes along with farmers and Artisans which eliminated the social distinctions of class and age. For an entire semester each year, Goddard students went off on a field experience where they participated in jobs or internships for which they received college credit. Like Summerville, Goddard had no grades; instead, the faculty handwrote a personal narrative evaluation of each student which said far more than a letter grade could express. Faculty teams met each semester to discuss the progress of their student advisees and make decisions about promotion to the next level. Finally, students completed a senior project, coached and evaluated by a faculty team.

In a brand new freshmen program called Skete, based on principals of communal living, students not only shared a home-like dorm, they also ordered food, cooked their own meals, and took dorm based courses offered by us, the young new faculty. My self-invented course "The Politics of the Family," focused on studying alternative ways to raise children, from Margaret Mead's *Coming of Age in Samoa* (1928) to studies of the Israeli kibbutz, and 19th century utopian experiments like Oneida and the Shakers. Driven by dissatisfaction with my own family and their problems, I was convinced there were better ways. A typical session took place, not in a classroom with neon lights and desks in rows or circles, but in the living room of a small dorm. Students would be sprawled on the floor or sitting on couches. Faculty were called by their first names and students felt free to argue and to disagree with each other and with me.

"You could never raise children communally in this country," argued Cindy, an outspoken young woman from Berkeley California. "Parents want to possess their kids and control them, just like expensive cars or houses."

"I disagree," answered Randy," my parents were divorced when I was two and I was raised by a group of aunts and cousins—it was great—I always had a bigger person to go to if I needed someone."

"I guess that's why you're so mature," Bruce answered sarcastically.

"Let's see if we can identify both the advantages and the disadvantages of communal child rearing, "I suggested. A student volunteered to record our list on sheets of newsprint and a good discussion ensued.

LESSON 3: ADULTS ARE LEARNERS TOO

The Adult Degree Program at Goddard College goes back to the 1960s when Goddard President Tim Pitkin's assistant Evelyn Bates invented a degree completion program aimed at women who had attended college but dropped out to raise a family. I do not know if she was inspired by Betty Freidan's *The Feminine Mystique* (1963) but the students were mostly frustrated, intelligent woman suffering from "the disease that has no name." They came to campus for two weeks each semester, attended workshops and lectures and were assigned a tutor. Students left with a syllabus custom tailored to their interests and then studied from home, receiving detailed responses to each assignment from their tutors over the following six months. Fewer in number, male students increasingly attended after going through drug or alcohol rehabilitation. Resuming the interrupted narrative of their lives was essential to their recovery. These adults were able to fulfill distribution requirements in humanities, social sciences and even science through their own topic of interest. For example, someone focused on 20th century women artists might explore developmental psychology and gender, novels about women artists, and the science and chemistry of color, thus exploring her subject through a multidisciplinary lens. Since the program began before e-mail or the Internet, snail mail, and telephone were the means of communication, and students could live anywhere. Today there are many similar hybrid and low-residency bachelor's and graduate degree options that rely on electronic communication.

At the end of the semester, students returned to campus, completed their work with a formal presentation to the community and started a new semester with a new tutor. During their final term each person prepared a thesis, a lengthy piece of written work, sometimes accompanied by artistic products. Though they were working toward a bachelor's degree, many students were operating at an advanced level and went on to complete graduate degrees. When the curriculum is driven by the interests and passions of the students, this approach can produce powerful results. If one begins with an interest derived from her lived experiences, she can work backwards to research and master the basics needed to fully answer her question. Critics may argue that this narrow approach sacrifices breadth for depth. I would answer that these students learn how to learn. Consider these examples of adult students who graduated having done a major piece of work, often with a socially significant impact.

A quadriplegic man attended with a full-time aide. His speech was very difficult to understand and computers were in their infancy. He typed his papers using his head, which astonished all of us, but he wrote well in his chosen topic of history, graduated, and gave us all a different understanding of disability.

A Saudi woman with four deaf children discovered that deafness is inherited due to consanguinial marriage. She ended up reforming education for deaf children in her country.

A nurse used hands-on Reiki to treat cancer patients and went on for a master's degree.

A Cuban born gay man with thalidomide caused birth defects wrote a children's book about what it is like to be disabled.

A stockbroker, who lost his job, became a life coach and started a newsletter on coaching.

A divorced mother of two volunteered in a prison, fell in love with an incarcerated man and wrote a novel about his life.

The semiannual residencies were held in an old estate manor house, making students feel like guests. Friday evening began with a lively cocktail hour where new and returning students and faculty mixed freely. The final evening was given over to dancing, with faculty fully participating. Divorce became so common among these students that the program was jokingly referred to as "the adultery degree," yet ending a stultifying marriage or finding new love could be the happy result of being reborn through education. Those years of cultural upheaval added to a deepened sense of community that supported students through their studies and creative work. When I began teaching there, I was barely thirty and my students, often 10 to 20 years my senior, helped to equalize the mentor/student relationship. Rather than hide behind my credentials or my years, I learned how to seek information and ideas with, rather than reigning over my students; I became what educator Elizabeth Minnich calls, "a critical friend," and this approach has served me well (Minnich, 2004).

Today we live in a far more repressed environment with administrators worrying about lawsuits, sexual harassment, and potential violence. Under these dystopian conditions where students and faculty can legally carry guns into the classroom, we have moved far from the educational community I remember—yet that approach is as relevant as ever. If the right conditions are established: a community with dedicated faculty open to learning with students rather than talking at them, building the curriculum from the needs, personal histories and interests of the individuals and the availability of digital sources, people of any age can become skilled life-long learners who know how to find the information they need.

LESSON 4: HOW TO PASS (AT HARVARD)

In contrast to the ultra-progressive (often called "alternative") educational programs I had been immersed in, I made a drastic change. By then I had published enough articles, short stories, and a novel to be considered qualified to teach writing. I applied for a position at Harvard College in the required freshman composition course. One could not ask for better students—the cream of freshmen, drawn from elite schools as well as secondary schools across the country in an effort to create a diverse student body. In my sections, students were reading and writing essays on social science topics making it more than a routine English composition course. Students could choose from a list of course options on fiction, science, or history. My teaching colleagues were primarily journalists, novelist, and poets; thus the model of practitioners teaching their craft was valued over having academic composition specialists as faculty, though we were not employed on a tenure track. Classes were kept to 15–20 participants and personal student/teacher conferences took place three times per semester. I met with each student at a small table and together we went over their last paper line by line. This created a face to face connection between the 18-year-old and their 30 or 40 something teacher, even if the student might care little about their essay arguing that student athletes should be paid or marijuana legalized.

My favorite assignment was a step by step sequence of moving from a personal issue to defining a researchable topic that emerged from their story, to ultimately producing a research paper. Curtis Chang won a freshman award for his research paper challenging the stereotype of Asians as the model minority (Chang, 1987). His topic came from an essay he wrote about being forced to study Chinese when he really wanted to play basketball with his friends. From reflecting on his own rebellious urges he went on to wonder about the pressure he had felt as an ABC (American born Chinese.) After completing his research, he cited statistics on the number of Asian students left out of higher education or involved in the criminal justice system. This writing assignment represents how honoring a student's personal narrative can lead to research that means more than going through the motions.

At least two of my students from those years went on to establish national reputations as writers, appearing in *The New Yorker* and on the best seller list. This may have happened without their Harvard pedigree, but the networking such affiliation gave them certainly helped. Despite Harvard's effort to be inclusive, students recruited from mid-Western or Southern public high schools often struggled to make it through the course, necessitating the creation of a remedial section for the small number who lacked skills. Ultimately, for most Harvard students the required writing course was viewed as a necessary hoop to jump though and the satisfaction I gleaned from teaching there diminished as my allotted eight years came to an end.

LESSON 5: CREATE COMMUNITY

Though I went from Harvard to Lesley University in Cambridge, Massachusetts, less than a mile up the street, the facilities, the faculty and the student body were entirely different. Lesley began as a seminary for teaching young women to become early childhood educators, but when laws were established that prevented married women from working as teachers the school changed its focus to helping them become good housewives and mothers. When I started there in the mid-1980s, they were pioneering adult education programs offered during evenings and weekends as well as short residencies so that working adults could attend. With my experience in the Goddard adult program, this seemed like an ideal fit for me. Lesley also began the first expressive therapies master's program that combined dance, visual art, and drama as therapeutic modalities, as well as an integrated arts program that trained teachers to use the arts in all subjects, from science to math to reading. Another innovation was the creation of national and international satellite programs using intensive weekend classes with Lesley faculty flown out to teach on site in Washington, South Carolina, Nevada, Israel and other locations.

Entering students took a course called "Lives in Context" in which they read and studied memoirs and autobiographies and wrote a chapter of their own life stories. My students consulted a newspaper from the day they were born in order to put their own lives into a wider social context. While teaching a multicultural group, my eyes were opened by what I learned when a mixed race woman from Zimbabwe wrote about the discrimination she had experienced as a light skinned person in a dark skinned county. A woman from Morocco begged me not to let other students read her paper since women were not permitted to disclose any personal information. An African American man objected to Maya Angelou's memoir *I Know Why the Caged Bird Sings*, insisting that she was not telling the truth about her experiences, though he could not articulate how he knew this. These student's contributions led to lively discussions about race, gender and cultural differences, educating me, their white, American teacher as well as their peers. Since most Lesley adult students were from working class families and with limited resources, the concept of foreign travel was a reach for them. To address this gap, we offered a weeklong travel-study course based at Homerton College at Cambridge University in England. Using the contrast between Cambridge Massachusetts and Cambridge England, we explored history, literature, and education in a comparative mode. What a surprise to learn that elite Harvard University was started by a group of religious dissenters, rebelling against the Church of England. Each student selected a research project to be completed and submitted a month after the travel concluded. Even this short glimpse across the pond expanded many students' assumptions, leading to the kind of transformative learning we hoped to achieve. Similar place-based courses have been offered in Guyana, Quebec and other sites.

For additional credit toward an undergraduate degree, adults coming back to college after many years spent working or volunteering could write essays that were evaluated by a faculty team for college credits. This prior learning portfolio exemplified Dewey's experiential learning theories—we were practicing what we preached. Learning in community and exploring problems that stem from personal experience is addictive for many who wished to keep studying. This led us to develop a master's program based on the model of short intensive residencies followed by faculty guided independent studies, culminating in the next residential experience. As I had learned at Goddard decades earlier, this model allows adults to engage in a campus environment, have night long conversations with peers, and feel freedom from daily expectations, all experiences most had missed as young people. In fact, maturity allowed them to value their learning all the more.

Though Lesley already offered an interdisciplinary PhD program, it became clear that a doctoral program designed for midcareer educators that focused on adult learning and development would be desirable. My long career ended as a professor and faculty advisor to men and women who returned to get that ultimate credential. For the majority their doctoral level research project emerged from their experiences as practitioners. Here's a small sample of what they accomplished:

An occupational therapist who taught basic adult education to rural Maine high school drop-outs saw the need to integrate occupational skills into the required math and reading courses her students took.

An educator in a medical school sought to understand and improve the patient simulation exercises students engaged in.

A teacher educator in Oregon wondered why so few Latina teachers were in the workforce despite the growing Hispanic population, so she sought out successful teachers and recorded their stories.

A disability educator explored the trajectories of learning disabled students who succeeded in college.

An early childhood educator in her 70s, undaunted by aging, spent years collecting the stories told by Native Alaskan women who had dedicated their own lives to teaching inside their communities.

The understanding that came from professional experience, along with a commitment to further research allowed these older adults to contribute to their professions well into midlife and beyond.

FINAL LESSON 6: REMEMBER THE BODY

My sabbatical was approaching and given my age I knew it would be the last one before retirement. Like my adult students, I had finished my PhD in my late 40s and later began to explore the role of the body in learning. Since computers engage such limited aspects of our selves, I sought to embody education by asking my students to move, stretch, and breathe at breaks during classroom sessions. After promoting experiential learning and becoming a yoga practitioner myself, I decided to deliberately integrate mind and body by taking a yoga teacher training course, open to all ages. Quite naturally I expected to be treated as a mature adult; instead I found myself in class surrounded by slender young athletes, taught by a teacher who led us through arduous day long practices with scant attention to individual differences or the personal histories each student brought. In my 60s as an adult student myself, I experienced the way one should NOT teach. I came away from that training and sought a more appropriate course that honored students as individuals. Today I teach yoga to healthy adults in their 70s and 80s. Having begun my career as a naïve 23-year-old, who lived mostly in the world of words, I end as an active 70 plus woman who views embodied learning as more than a slogan. At a time when online learning offers accessible, cheaper ways to be educated, I worry that face to face, highly personalized, community-based education will become available only to those who can afford such programs. The hybrid model which combines on-site with online studies offers hope, but only if the digital environment is used as a tool rather than determining the curriculum. If we reduce learning to metrics and eliminate human bodies sitting together in a face to face environment, full human participation in a community of learners will become a nostalgic memory.

REFERENCES

Dewey, J. (1916). *Democracy and education*. New York, NY: Free Press.

Chang, C. (1987). *Streets of gold: The myth of the model minority*. Retrieved from http://depts.washington.edu/college/mce/Myth1.pdf

Freidan, B. (1963). *The feminine mystique*. New York, NY: W.W. Norton & Co.

Goddard College. (n.d.) Retrieved from http://www.goddard.edu/about-goddard/goddard-difference/college-history/

Mead, M. (1928). *Coming of age in Samoa*. New York, NY: William Morrow & Co.

Minnich, E. (2004). Reflections of the wellsprings of interdisciplinary studies and transformative education. *Issues in Integrative Studies, 22*, 141–154.

Neill, A. S. (1960). *Summerhill: A radical approach to child rearing*. New York, NY: Hart.

CHAPTER 9

"I AM WHAT I DO"...

Professional Voices From the Field of Further Education and Training

Anne Graham Cagney
Waterford Institute of Technology

INTRODUCTION

Being close to the frontline of a changing educational landscape offers further education and training (FET) teachers opportunities to construct avenues that fully utilize their whole worldview while capitalizing on lifelong professional learning and development opportunities. The FET education system in the Republic of Ireland is currently subject to large-scale structural changes. Yet, FET teacher education and continuing professional development (CPD) is not well researched. As FET teachers experience an evolving professional identity, additional research is needed to understand the experience and impact of these changes from the perspective of practitioners. This study highlighted the evolving nature of FET teacher identity and the transformative learning spaces required to support their professional development. By exploring the nature of the pedagogical entry points provided for such learning experiences a contribution is made to knowledge about creating opportunities for transformative learning in professional lifelong learning and development.

The Postcompulsory Education Sector in Ireland

The Irish FET sector includes community, vocational, professional, technical education and training in state provided centers, vocational colleges, refugee centers, prisons, community centers and care/disability centers, and so forth. In some respects, this structure is not that different from community education in the U.S. and certainly mirrors a more informal and responsive "reaction" to local social and individual needs for lifelong learning.

Since 2013, SOLAS, the Irish government agency responsible for adult and continuing education has been tasked with building a "world-class integrated system of further education and training" (SOLAS, 2014–2019, p. 3). The subsequent structural and organizational changes have caused shifts in identity, ethos and objectives for teachers as FET emerges and develops from a fractured history to a formal recognized education sector. FET teachers are now required to hold a formal Teacher Education Qualification (TEQ) in order to continue working in the sector (The Teaching Council Act, 2001; and Regulation Five of the Teaching Council (Registration) Regulations, 2009). Traditionally less structured than primary, postprimary, or third level systems, FET teachers take pride in the fact that they do things differently. They tend to have had previous careers outside of academia and consequentially, are inclined to have a more practical, applied approach. This resonates with those who have felt excluded by the mainstream education system.

Existing teacher education programs (TEQs) did not meet the distinctive nature and challenges of teaching in this unique sector. Consequently, the Higher Education Authority (HEA) and the Teaching Council (TC) implemented sector-specific criteria for higher education institutions (HEIs) seeking approval to deliver FET TEQ programs. Currently, eight HEIs provide a range of programs at undergraduate and postgraduate levels for existing FET teachers, and for those who wish to become FET teachers. Exploring this specific context provides insight into how TEQ programs can best meet the emergent needs of participating teachers who face some of the most pressing demands in Irish society today.

Waterford Institute of Technology (WIT)

The study was based in WIT's undergraduate and a postgraduate part-time TEQ programs for new and existing FET teachers, delivered in an intensive two-day teaching block on a biweekly basis and supported by a blended learning platform. Designed specifically for FET teaching and learning contexts, the program encouraged application, facilitated critical reflection, collaborative in-class discussion, group projects, and online threaded discussions. A separate teaching practice (TP) development course formed an integral part of the TEQ program, focused on pedagogical training, curriculum development and design. TP program assessment comprised (per semester) of a teaching portfolio, structured reflective assignments and a TP tutor observation of students during a teaching placement or at the actual organization where they were employed as teachers.

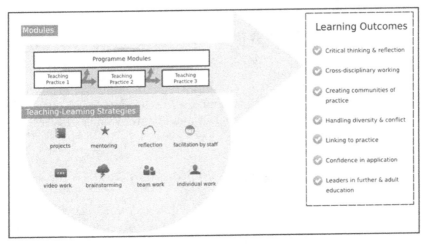

Figure 9.1. Conceptual map of the TEQ program.

Students on the program reflected the complexity and diversity of the sector. In general, they had prior knowledge and previous teaching experience, very often across several disciplines and subjects. The age profile was from early 30s to late 50s; many had worked in other professions and brought that experience to their teaching role. Their employment contracts and roles included voluntary, part-time, and full-time contracts of indefinite duration, and tenured/permanent employees. On graduation, students were entitled to register as teachers with the Teaching Council (TC), which in turn entitled them to join the Teachers' Union of Ireland (TUI) and be covered under union agreements and conditions of service.

The holistic nature of an adult learning experience is important to this study, particularly the intersections between the "inner self" and the "outer world" where our learning and experience occurs. This research study highlighted the evolving nature of FET teacher identity and the transformative learning spaces required to support their professional development learning environments. By exploring the nature of the pedagogical entry point provided by such experiences within the TEQ programs, this study contributes to what is known about creating opportunities for transformative learning to occur within FET teacher professional education.

In summary, while professional development provision for FET teachers in Ireland is changing, the changes are not necessarily detrimental to those teaching in the sector. In this context, the study investigated what FET teachers perceived as personal transformative learning experiences within a TEQ program and how these experiences supported their evolving teacher professional identity.

THEORETICAL FRAMEWORK

Constructivist research on the "inner" teaching-learning environment (Entwistle, 2003), perspective transformation (Cranton, 2006; Mezirow, 1991), and identity self-states (Higgins, 1987; Markus & Nurius, 1986), formed the overarching conceptual framework from which this research project is derived.

The "Inner" Teaching-Learning Environment (TLE)

The conceptual map of the "inner" TLE draws on constructivist research on enhancing TLEs and suggests that students' perceptions are strongly determined by the "a set of overlapping contexts that comprise of four elements: course contexts; teaching and assessing content; staff-student relationships; and aspects of the students and student culture within a particular programme" (Entwistle, 2003; Entwistle & McCune, 2009). The "inner" TLE map is an organising framework when considering how to achieve a higher quality of learning through the creation of transforma-tive learning spaces (Graham Cagney, 2011). Constructivist research into undergraduate education identified the need for further investigation into congruence between the various elements and components of the TLE. Additionally, by concentrating on using ways of thinking and practicing in a discipline area as a focal point, it is possible to identify fundamental subject goals and find the through lines as a set of overarching goals in a program. This is necessary in order for students to understand the "whole picture" and where the learning journey is taking them. They assist students in making sense of the various knowledge components of a program, and in approaching an integration of their understanding and learning.

High quality learning is associated with program environments that are congruent on a range of dimensions including those depicted within the "inner" TLE. This is essential in order to create the conditions in which students can achieve an integration of their learning with a deep understanding of their discipline. In every discipline, field or profession, mastery of a subject requires an integration of the network of relationships amongst the constituent parts. Much of the extant literature describes this integration in thinking as akin to a portal or doorway through which the individual must pass. It is similar to a conceptual gateway that opens up a new way of thinking about something that was previously inaccessible (Entwistle, 2003). This type of integrated understanding requires a shift in understanding of such significance that the individual "thinks" or "perceives," apprehends or experiences particular phenomena within a discipline or body of knowledge in a completely different way.

Perspective Transformation

Transformative learning (TL) theory adopts a cognitive/rational approach emphasizing the critical role that experience and reflection play

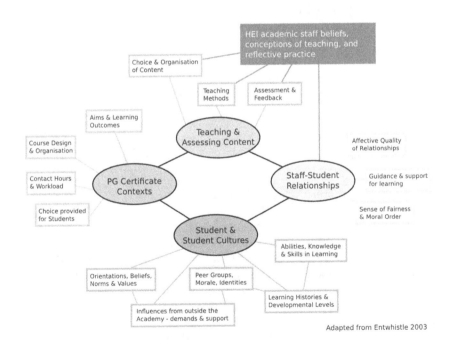

Figure 9.2. Conceptual map of the "inner" teaching-learning environment.

in existing assumptions about the world in order to arrive at a new worldview (Mezirow, 1991, 2012). TL theory and perspective transformation in particular depict the ways in which individuals identify and challenge their underlying assumptions, prompting changed perspectives leading to new roles and actions. Described as "a shift of consciousness that dramatically and permanently alters our way of being in the world" (O'Sullivan, Morrell, & O'Connor, 2002, p. xviii); it changes how we know (Kegan, 2009) and it leads to a more "inclusive, discriminating, permeable, and integrative perspective" (Mezirow, 1991, p. 14). During a TL experience, values, expectations and underlying assumptions are often challenged leading to perspective transformation and a corresponding shift in habits of mind. This different kind of thinking and being enables an individual to become open to revisiting their interpretations of the meaning of their experience and in turn guiding future action (Cranton, 2006, 2011).

Perspective transformation is a learning process with a sequential flow consisting of experience, alienation, reframing, and reintegration. Changes in habits of mind may appear to be sudden and dramatic or a slower, incremental change in points of view (meaning schemas), which eventually lead to a change in habits of mind. Mezirow and & Associates (2000) argues that it is only in adulthood that people develop the reflective judgment necessary to assess their own reasoning about their habitual expectations prompting changed perspectives leading to new roles and actions.

Figure 9.3.   Transformative learning process map.

There are four components essential to transformative learning namely, (1) experience, (2) critical reflection, (3) reflective discourse and, (4) action plans (Taylor, 2007). Other conditions are also necessary but Mezirow (2012) maintains that they are rarely fully realized in practice. However, to create a space for TL to occur within an educational context two further components are essential: (1) trusted relationships and (2) support from faculty and peer groups (Graham Cagney, 2011; Taylor, 2007).

In summary, TL theory is about change, dramatic fundamental change in the way individuals perceive themselves, and the world in which they live. They have to rethink some of their previous ways of understanding the world and interacting with it in order to engage with new knowledge and new experiences. This type of learning is more than just adding to what they already know; rather it is transformative because it shapes the individual in ways that result in changes that both now they and others around them can recognize. Changes in thinking that lead to new worldviews/perspectives on their personal and professional lives (Cranton, 2006) inform current debate on evolving professional identity and teacher agency in professional learning and development (Boylan, Coldwell, Maxwell, & Jordan, 2018).

Identity Self-States

Three seminal reviews of the literature on teacher identity in the last decade (Beauchamp & Thomas, 2009; Beijard, Meijer, & Verloop, 2004; Rodgers & Scott, 2008) highlight the importance of and interrelation of notions of identity, context, emotion and agency. Beijard et al. (2004) and Hamman, Gosselin, Romano, and Bunuan (2010) identify a strong preoccupation with investigating characteristics or content, namely what roles and values, constitute teacher identity and less attention on the situational and contextual factors within the broader framework of teacher professional development.

Identity self-states draw on a "motivational self-systems" framework that incorporates "possible" and "ideal" selves theory (Markus & Nurius, 1986, p. 954) and self-discrepancy theory (Higgins, 1987). Possible selves are "ideas which an individual has regarding what they could become (hoped for self), what they would like to become (ideal self) and what they are afraid of becoming (feared self)" (Markus & Nurius, 1986, p .954). They have a simultaneous impact on how one engages and expresses oneself in task behaviors that promote connections to work, others, personal presence, and job role performance. A person can move from the present toward the future by using their possible selves as "future self-guides" (Markus & Nurius, 1986, p. 957).

Self-discrepancy theory identifies three self domains (actual self, ideal self, and ought self) and two standpoints or perspectives on the self, one's own standpoint and the standpoint of a significant other. Higgins (1987) identifies a single ideal and a single ought self while Markus and Nurius (1986) examine multiple possible selves, including more than one ideal self. In an educational context, Dörnyei (2001) suggests which self-state an individual is motivated toward and their personally relevant self-guides will involve the desire to reduce the discrepancy between one's actual self and the projected behavioral standards of the ideal/ought self. Such a discrepancy would imply that future self-guides provide incentive, direction and the impetus for action. Finally, the discrepancy between actual and future selves initiates self-regulatory strategies to reduce the discrepancy. Learners who encounter and draw on different spaces of learning are more self-determined in their learning and are more willing to engage in new and multiple spaces of learning (Dörnyei, 2001).

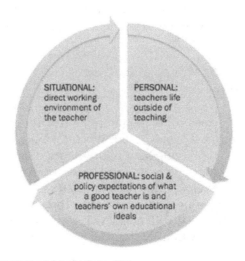

SITUATIONAL: direct working environment of the teacher

PERSONAL: teachers life outside of teaching

PROFESSIONAL: social & policy expectations of what a good teacher is and teachers' own educational ideals

Adapted from: Day et al 2006; Mannix & Graham Cagney, 2014

Figure 9.4.   Personal, professional & situational identity contexts.

Teachers balance three relevant dimensions in their work (Day, Kington, Stobart, & Sammons, 2006) namely: (1) personal dimensions, (2) professional dimensions, and (3) situational dimensions (Figure 9.4). Teacher identities are thus formed through the way such multiple dimensions interact. In recognizing the challenges and complexities of student teacher transformative identity formation and in keeping with international research, which has focused on the conceptualization of teacher motivation and the motivation to teach (Dörnyei, 2001), there is a strong need for a conceptual framework reflecting personal, professional, and situational teacher identity formation.

Possible selves theory may serve well as a framework, where there is a strong focus on the transformative nature of student teacher identity formation, reflecting past and present experiences, while adding to future orientated dimension of personal and professional agency (Conway & Clarke, 2003; Hamman et al., 2010). What is evident from the above research studies is that teachers' possible selves evolve from being task-based to quality based over time. The task-based dimension remains the most significant aspect of teachers' feared selves.

The above-cited research has yielded some understanding of the variables influencing how FET teachers perceive themselves, their work, their professional learning and development programs and the relation between all three. The understandings are general: they exist at some distance from the processes of people experiencing and behaving within particular work and study contexts. But none of them go to the core of what it means to be psychologically present in particular moments and situations that determine the driving force, for the type of learning underpinning an evolving professional identity. This is a critical factor in developing a different and fulfilling pathway toward professional development for FET teachers. Doing so requires deeply probing experiences and situations during discrete moments that make up a person's professional work life. Such probing relies on studying both people's emotional reactions to conscious and unconscious phenomena, and the objective properties of jobs, roles, work and professional development contexts, all within the setting of a TEQ program. The research questions were as follows:

1. What characterizes the student learning experiences of the TEQ program?
2. How can TEQ programs support FET teachers' readiness for change as they envisage future possible selves personally and professionally?

METHODS

The study emerged in an organic way, incepted during program evaluations when students reported significant learning experiences that had in some cases led to a change in their sense of self and identity as FET teachers. It was timely to explore the phenomenon and determine the nature of these learning experiences and how they may have supported changes in students' identity self-states. Exploring the existence of conceptual commonalities across both programs would, it was hoped, generate understandings about FET teacher identity and perspective transformation.

The research questions suggested:

1. Qualitative methodology: "learning experiences," "perspective transformation," and "identity" are not predetermined but are constructed by student teachers' personal, professional and situational roles and experienced by individual teachers;
2. Small-scale study: the focus on individual experience, therefore document analysis, a questionnaire and interviews were employed.

Following ethical approval 16 of the possible nineteen students in the research cohort participated in the study. Data were collected on fourteen women and two men, ranging in age from 30–57 years, from working and middle-class backgrounds. Most had previous work experience in the private and/or public sector, and had prior education, training and professional experience in a disciplinary or vocational area. Each individual was free to choose the extent of their participation in the study: questionnaire (5), interview (4), both questionnaire and interview (7), resulting in 12 completed questionnaires and 11 interviews.

Questionnaire and Interview Design

The questionnaire was designed to: (1) identify the stages of perspective transformation; (2) identify learning experiences that may have promoted a perspective transformation; (3) determine students' experience of the "inner" TLE; and (4) collect information on demographic characteristics that are suggested from the field of transformative learning theory (Brookfield, 1995; Cranton, 1996; King, 2009; Mezirow & Associates, 2000).

Follow-up interviews were considered a critical part of the inquiry and the researcher endeavored to get everyone to take part. Interview questions were sent to 11 participants in advance and sought to explore, (1) students' perceptions of their experiences of personal change and perspective transformation, (2) the "inner" teaching-learning environment, (3) professional identity and, (4) anything else they wanted to bring up in the discussion in respect of their TEQ experience. The interviews were recorded and lasted between 25 and 57 minutes (averaging 37 minutes). After transcription by the researcher, broad themes were identified. This proved to be somewhat challenging as each interviewee tended to have their own view of things. The Learning Activities Survey (King, 2009) combined with the conceptual map of the "inner" TLE (Entwistle, 2003) informed the primary research questions. These resulted in the most comprehensive framework to capture the full range of data gathered. This approach also offered an opportunity to compare across interviewee results to identify common themes and areas of significance.

Analysis

Data analysis occurred in three separate stages:

1. Immediately following ethical approval: program documentation, student personal statements and reflective journals, and researcher notes.

2. Following administration of the online questionnaire and completion of the follow-up interviews: responses from the structured questions, and the transcription of the open questions in both methods.
3. Final consolidation: resorting and reanalyzing of the artifacts (program and student document data) into more complex categories and concepts.

Experiences were identified and analyzed according to whether they clearly related to the TLE, a perspective transformation or a change in an identity self-state. Examples that did not clearly fit into any of the three categories were excluded. The collection finally included over 180 personal learning experiences. An independent coder similarly sorted a randomly selected sample of 30 experiences; there was a 95% inter-rater agreement on the sortings. These examples helped describe a model of personal transformative learning within a TLE that supported an evolving FET teacher professional identity.

FINDINGS

Across the different data resources (documents, questionnaire, and interviews) there was agreement about the positive effects of the program. However, the focus taken in the findings is on possible links between the TEQ program's "inner" TLE as a transformative space of learning and an evolving FET teacher professional identity. The following sections report on: (1) the learner experience of the 'inner' TLE; and themes that emerged from the consolidated data: (2) learner experiences of change, (3) perspective transformation in an educational context, and (4) possible and ideal selves (identity self-states).

(1) Learner Experiences of the "Inner" TLE

Staff-Student Relationships

The most important components for students in this category were the "affective quality of relationships" and "guidance and support." For those students who had not studied previously within WIT and were unaware of the critical reflexivity underpinning the school's philosophy, their experience of the quality of their relationships with WIT faculty was a significant surprise. For one learner, "Engaging with the lecturers over the year has been really, really huge for me." One description captures the majority of comments relating to support and the more informal aspects, acknowledging the importance of sharing experiences and sums up "A community of practice, you don't have to even explain what you're talking about. You just mention something and heads nod, people understand what you're talking about. There's an unconscious, a collective unconscious."

Students and Student Cultures

"Peer groups, morale and identities," combined with "orientations, beliefs, norms and values" and "influences from inside and outside WIT" were identified strongly by the majority of students. In considering the impact of other students and the student culture the universal view was that it was a combination of fellow students/classmates and in some instances, work colleagues; and their own students/adult learners. For example,

> Peer group, their experiences all added into it as well. And you know, it's like, I think in any adult education class I think the coffee breaks were as useful as the actual lessons at times; what we share in the breaks.

Another student describes the feeling of being part of a group of peers:

> When you're on your own ... you do feel isolated and you feel a bit lost. The fear creeps in and the certainty goes and you lose your flow of thought.... If I'd panicked about anything, I used to be ok by the time it came to Friday because I'd think, 'ok, I'm in Waterford....'" When I walked in the door and sat down, I didn't even have to talk to them. I used to think "Yeah, I know where I'm going again now". So that coming together is good.... I think meeting up is really important, I think just even when you come in and sit down and you're with everyone in the room. Maybe it's what you're subconsciously getting from everyone. I know what I'm doing— you know things occur to me ... it gives you inspiration.

Course Contexts

Learner expectations were directly influenced by how the program design was communicated ("aims and outcomes") to them. In some cases this led to false expectations about how much skills development and training would take place during the program ("course design and organization"). This was particularly important for those students who had little or no experience of teaching in the FET sector. For example,

> I expected to learn more "tricks of the trade," I suppose. And it's much more theoretical than I expected.... I thought I'd be learning things that I could really use to improve my performance ... as a teacher but it hasn't really given me very much of that. It's given me more just of a background to things. Personally, I'd like more practical stuff.

However, even for some of the very experienced teachers, their expectations were also directly related to the teaching task. One student says:

> I definitely thought it was going to be different.... I wanted the "right" answer.... I think I was very much in the mode that I was going to be told what to do here, rather than I actually need to trust myself to know what to do.

Some comments were made in relation to "contact hours and workload" and the scheduling of modules, particularly when the modular course assignments backed up into the TP program assessments and workload. The program design emerged as a significant aspect of the students' experience of learning and engagement with one another and the program:

> The immersive experience of the two-day workshop should be kept as an integral part of the programs in enabling students to network, work together, socialize and communicate and share knowledge and experiences.... There's something fantastic. We used to look forward to it. Who looks forward to going into class?

Eligibility to register with the Teaching Council represented formal recognition, "The TEQ qualification was the big thing ... no it was the teaching council thing because of the politics that's around that." Other students reported that their self-confidence and personal sense of self was enhanced. For example:

> I'm really enjoying it and delighted to get the opportunity to get a teaching qualification. Because, definitely for me well I am hoping it will validate what I do and hopefully make you a little more than—what did they used to call it—the "wooly jumper brigade" to actually have a qualification to back up what we do.

Teaching and Assessing Content

Students were most concerned with "teaching methods" and "assessment and feedback." These were seen as very important elements in creating a space to explore new ways of thinking and being, and of gaining support from those who understood the field.

The most influential learning activities within "teaching methods" were (1) class discussions and (2) critical reflection. Opportunities for discussion were created within class and outside the program within the peer group; while critical thinking was more individual and based within learning journals and assignments. Students spoke about relationships that developed through class discussion (profound discourse) as "amazing what you learn; and it helps you as well from the point of view of its great support for each other. It's amazing the support you can get from your fellow students." A second student valued the in-class work, "group work in class, more so than the rest of things." And, a third said "definitely, class discussions. I think they are probably one of the most powerful tools available, listening to other people's points of view, challenging your own, through their points of view."

Critical reflection occurred throughout the year, stated one student who said that while writing her learning journal, she began to realize how much she engaged in discussion and questioning in class; to the extent that she relates at one point, "I keep wondering, am I talking too much in class?" Another student stated, "Looking back I would say partially the learning journals—even though I don't like them—they force you to look at things. They are good." Some students identified a reluctance to engage with the process of critical reflection and writing their thoughts:

> The critical reflection, having to, this whole thing about journals, if you don't mark them they don't get done.... I'm not a journaller, you know? And I have found that going through those, it does embed all the stuff you do because you have to really, really think about what you're doing. You know? So, the practical observations and the critical reflections, the journals and stuff, I think now are very important.

In respect of "assessment and feedback" the area of most concern for many students was their TP assessment. There was an underlying theme of "being found out" or that their teaching practice would "not be good enough" in some respects. For example, one teacher shared her thoughts, "I was very nervous about what taking on the inspections would mean." Another very experienced teacher stated, "When we were first told about the observations and the visits and stuff, the whole thing terrified me." Although students were nervous and wary of the TP observation and assessment, they also appreciated the feedback as a way of improving their practice. One student said, "the teaching practice, the inspections: they were very good. Though, yet again I ... you're anxious coming up to them but at the same time you get so much from them."

(2) Learner Experiences of Change

Major life changes experienced by students included bereavements (including a miscarriage), separation and divorce, seeking mortgage approvals, coming out, trying to start a family and rearing a family while doing the program. For example, one student went through a divorce prior to the program and identified the development of confidence and testing new ways of going forward as part of her learning experiences, some of the girls in work said, that I've grown a backbone [laughs]. So, I think that was good, I don't know which comes first, the change but definitely, both have changed professionally and personally. I've learned a lot more about myself and have had to ... rely on myself and become more confident. And, um, I don't know, make sense of what I'm doing and why I'm doing it. My meaning in life, like why? What is important to me? What do I want to achieve?

Students reported their awareness of changes in their values, expectations and beliefs particularly about teaching and being an FET teacher. Some had begun FET teaching with no formal training and completed the TEQ program because it was interesting and offered an opportunity to learn more about teaching: "My expectations around the learning that I was engaging in and where I was going with it, I'd say definitely evolved over the last year." Others were working in the sector on a part-time basis but not really committed to it as a professional career, however this changed over time. For example,

So I suppose whereas before I'd kind of a fuzzy idea that I enjoyed teaching, and that I'd like to know more about how it was done so that I would be a better teacher than what I was doing. I have expanded my horizons and thought, well maybe I'm not just going to do part-time teaching in the evenings for a few hours a week. Maybe I can actually make a career out of this and move full-time into it.

Experienced FE tutors, expressed a sense of being "professional" in a way they had not been before; "I suppose a more professional approach to what I'm doing and also more confidence in what I'm doing." Others now realized that this was the career of choice for them.

(3) Perspective Transformation in an Educational Context

In order to verify that the perspective transformation was in fact related to educational experience, participants were asked, "What did your being in college have to do with this experience of change?" For one student the change in perspectives was incremental, a more gradual realization that their worldview had changed over time:

I cannot pinpoint a single event, a single disorientating dilemma.... There has been for me over the years a very comfortable gradual shift in perspective, which is still occurring. I am still in transition, on the threshold of meaning and I don't fully understand it all. I am not quite cooked yet!

Key factors drawn from extant literature on transformative learning in educational contexts (individual learning activities and experience of life changes) emerged from the data as significant elements in students' learning experience. In the first instance, some students were able to pinpoint a catalyst for their experience of a changing perspective during their program. For one student it was "being back in the classroom"; she described herself as trying to put herself in the place of the learners she was teaching (to put herself in their shoes) and says she "changed" as a learner. Her experience of the program changed her attitudes to learning and teaching. Another student clearly describes how she went through the testing phase of perspective transformation in adjusting to the changes brought on by the TEQ program:

> the stress and the volume of the workload and all of those things helped me cope with all the dysfunction. It did matter to your students and it matters to the services you work for, but outside of that it was more a personal development. I think it's where the new "me" was forming. The teaching-learning environment is a safe place where you can test out the new identity, the new you.

Finally, this student describes her realization of a perspective change during the program while she was travelling home.

> Awareness of change happened on second day [of] block three. Travelling home (by car) I had just heard about critical theory and was thinking about a new concept and relating it to a song on the radio. I thought, that's something I had never done before; brought learning out of the classroom and into a random part of my own world where I wouldn't usually be thinking about my learning. Previously, there was never any crossover into my personal life.

The majority of students described changes in predominantly three of the six habits of mind (Cranton, 2006). These were knowledge (epistemic), self-concept (psychological) and social norms and cultural expectations including roles in society (sociolinguistic). The following example indicates epistemic, sociolinguistic and psychological changes:

> Through learning and studying on WIT courses I have been able to apply new knowledge to my teaching and learning and have also been able to use my new found language, words, discourse to open up dialogues with my work colleagues on issues within a disadvantaged community that I think needs to change. I have found that once you can speak like your oppressors [laughs], educated colleagues, they take more notice of what you have to say. I also think that having done these courses your confidence in your abilities raises, your ability to reflect on your practice increases your insight and your ability to adapt and change. Perhaps not everyone has the same experience but this has been mine.

Another student focused almost entirely on the knowledge they had gained during the course (epistemic) and changes in their self-concept with a resultant impact on their identity self-state, moving from fear to confidence (psychological):

> The way we were taught has given me a new perspective on teaching. I am looking at the skills and techniques I am developing in a new way. It is also giving me confidence knowing that the things I know I do well are because I learned from experience, and many of them were based on sound theory even though I did not know it at the time. For these reasons the course was not like I thought it would be.

(4) Possible and Ideal Selves (Identity Self-States)

Using personal, professional, and situational dimensions for understanding a changing perspective helps to identify where and on what level changes are occurring in a self-state at any one point in time. One respondent links their learning to a growing awareness of their changing perspective and is clearly referring to their professional and situational dimensions:

> Engaging in learning, for me, meant I was ready for change. Being in college provided me with the skills and knowledge to reflect on issues, assumptions and power structures that I had previously taken for granted in a "this is how it is" attitude. College prepared me for the change that occurred in my way of viewing the world.

Critical reflection has an important role in perspective transformation in the context of an educational experience. Students reported that critical reflection impacted on the development of their identity self-states and particularly their future selves. Some said they engaged in "reflection for action" or future orientated reflection in relation to their teacher (ideal self) roles. They did this in order to visualize the kind of teacher they wanted to become:

> How I describe myself is changing. My confidence in my identity is growing. I am enjoying trying out the name "teacher" and also reclaiming "student". The tutors and group have been very supportive and have been useful sounding boards but rereading my journal entries and assignments, patterns in my attitude are obvious—as are the disruptions to those patterns. Particularly, my habit of recording negative experiences at the start of the journal, and the move to more balanced journaling including positive and negative experiences and my learnings from them.

Some students clearly represented ideas regarding what they could become, and what they would like to become confirming their professional identity was moving or evolving over time.

> I think it probably was towards the end of it and having discussions with some friends of mine who are teachers. And, realizing that while I would have agreed with them in the past that my worldview was so far removed from what their worldview was. I remember going home and saying to myself "Oh, why am I thinking so differently to what I would have thought in the past?" I think that's probably when I realized that I that my attitudes and my views had gone over to the other side (laughs).

Another student said her initial personal learning outcome was to increase her knowledge about how adults learn in order to rectify mistakes she made in the past and to learn what she was doing wrong. She identified that she "could have gone on teaching at the same level I was teaching forever," however, she clarifies her changed position by stating:

> The nub of the learning for me has been, insidious is probably the wrong word. Very quietly it has changed what I think about teaching, and what I think about me teaching, more specifically; and also what I think about how I learn and how my learners learn. So through being a learner it has changed a lot about how I would teach as well as what I have learnt.

It is clear that perspective transformation resulted in a corresponding shift in possible selves, specifically, from the actual to the ideal self. Many reported a conscious awareness of a difference in their thinking about themselves as professional teachers: "And I don't know if I've done it or how it's happened, but I've become defined by a qualification; a different person in my own right. I think differently; I think, I think differently." Another shared how they felt;

> How I view myself has also changed greatly. I am not apologetic when putting my opinions forward during staff discussions. The experience of studying has highlighted what I do know as much as what I don't, and the balance is convincing me that I do know what I am talking about.

DISCUSSION

Teacher Education Qualification (TEQ) programs must involve the whole person and cannot be separated out as a cognitive act or the application of skills or competences. Korthagen (2001) emphasizes pedagogy of realistic teacher education that combines formal academic knowledge with perceptual knowledge that is personally relevant and supportive in enabling an individual to understand their own behaviors in the light of beliefs, identity and the values that underpin them. Teaching is an enactment of the self in a holistic mix of academic and personal perceptual knowledge, skills, experiences, understandings, beliefs, and values. The development of a teacher's identity is therefore strongly connected to a "self-actualization" experience that ideally takes place within a transformative learning space that is personally safe, where one feels esteemed, has trusted relationships, combined with a sense of belonging socially.

On the basis of the empirical data, this discussion will focus on:

1. Specific components of the "inner" TLE (Figure 9.4) because they reveal the learning interactions that appear to be most power-ful, namely, trusted relationships, support from faculty and peer groups, critical reflection, and reflective discourse;
2. A "motivational self-systems" framework that incorporates "pos-sible" and "ideal" selves theory (Figure 9.5), because it offers some understanding of the shifts in habits of mind underpinning per-spective transformation and evolving teacher identity.

(1) The "Inner" Teaching-Learning Environment

The analysis of the data shows that the most influential aspects of the "inner" TLE on learning experiences were: (1) guidance and support for learning, and the affective quality of relationships (staff-student rela-tionships); (2) teaching methods—particularly the creation of discursive spaces and support for the development of critical thinking and reflection (teaching and assessing content); and (3) peer groups, norms and values and similar external work experiences (students and student cultures).

First, support for learning is an integral component in establishing a high quality TLE, but also a critical element in creating a transformative learning space. This is because the process of providing emotional, psy-chological, physical/educational assistance when needed is the foundation on which "trusted relationships" are built. Second, critical thinking assign-ments, when combined with class discussions focused on discourse and profound debate, provide the learning space to challenge changes in values and attitudes and develop the skill of reflective judgment. Third, a highly supportive peer group with embedded norms and values derived from similar external work experiences are needed in order for a transformative space of learning to be developed.

When these three learning interactions occurred within the overlapping contexts of the TEQ program "inner" TLE they created a transformative learning space. This explains the high level of reported experiences of

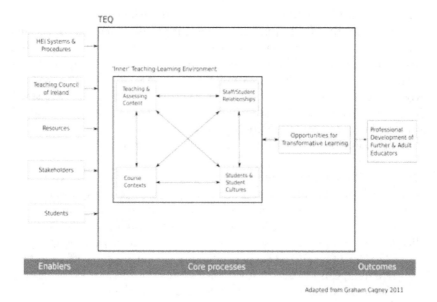

TEQ

Adapted from Graham Cagney 2011

Figure 9.5.   Conceptual map of the "inner" TLE of the TEQ program.

changed perspectives that led to an evolving identity for Future Education and Training (FET) teachers on the program.

(2) Possible and Ideal Selves (Identity Self-States)

Empirical evidence from the study suggests that some success was made in getting to the core of what it means to be psychologically present in particular moments and situations that determine the driving force, for the type of learning underpinning an evolving professional identity. As demonstrated in Figure 9.4, the learning interactions of peer group support and feedback promoted reflection by the students that included adjustments to their epistemic (knowledge), sociolinguistic (social norms and cultural expectations) and psychological (who we are and how we see ourselves) habits of mind. Possible selves appeared to act as a value-added lens providing information and critical awareness about identity in the past and present, but also about identity in the future (Hamman et al., 2010). It is clear that an evolving FET teacher identity was being supported by the overlapping contexts of the "inner" TLE and the components of a transformative learning space. Teacher possible selves were evolving from being task-based to quality based over time. The task-based dimension of teacher feared selves continued to be the most significant for where the individual is task focused and intent upon not failing in their role as a teacher. Both novice and expert teachers viewed observations as a source of considerable anxiety. This speaks to the extant literature on teacher identity self-states particularly the actual self-versus the feared self.

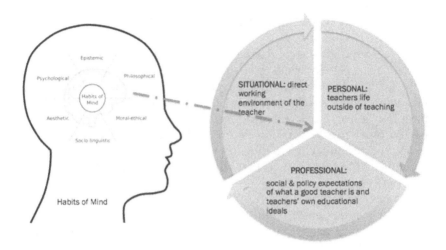

Adapted from: Day et al 2006; Cranton, 2006; Mannix & Graham Cagney, 2014

Figure 9.6. Evolving teacher identity formation.

The changes experienced by students in their professional identity appear to have happened as a result of their learning during the TEQ program. There is a general sense that changes were happening, one way or another; that these changes were organic and incremental within the sector but occurring in tandem with their college experience. However, for students, the changes experienced during their educational program were more visibly focused and directed into their personal lives and professional practice. Similar to Beijard et al. (2004) and Hamman et al. (2010) there was a strong preoccupation with roles and values and less attention to situational/contextual factors. Furthermore, Teaching Council recognition of FET teacher status had resultant implications for work, career and progression opportunities. This obviously relates very closely to professional and situational dimensions of FET teacher role and identity, as they would now be on a par with mainstream teachers in primary and second level education.

Concurrent with research into the use of reflective activities in teacher education programs to enhance teacher professional growth (Korthagen & Vasalos, 2005), results of this study posit the importance of critical reflection on the development of identity self-states, in particular future selves. Reflecting for action or future orientated reflection in relation to teacher roles enabled some students to focus on their professional and situational dimensions of growth.

CONCLUSIONS AND IMPLICATIONS

This research study was conducted with an open mind. It explored whether student teachers experiences of themselves and their learning contexts influenced moments when their perspectives changed regarding their professional identity as teachers. Overall, this chapter demonstrates that the program "inner" TLE created a transformative space of learning that supported a perspective transformation or shift in habits of mind resulting in a corresponding change in teacher identity self-states. Results identify a number of key dimensions that characterize the student TEQ learning experiences:

- Strong relationships emerged between personal, professional and situational mediating factors in the formation of possible future teacher selves;
- Reflection on action having experienced an eventful personal and professional life change is critical in the formation of teacher's evolving possible selves;
- Teacher possible selves evolved from being "task based" to "quality based" with teachers feared selves remaining predominately task based;
- The importance of transformative learning spaces to support students in creating links between perspective transformation and a conceptual framework of personal, professional, and situational teacher identity.

The implications of the study can be summed up in five principles. First, program aims, objectives, and assessments should always be made explicit for students. Second, early career students should be provided with extra supports to enhance their teaching skills. Third, transformative learning spaces should be created through program design that acts as a powerful motivator. Fourth, differences in motivation, learning experience, and personal change experiences occur within students that necessitate essential, for example, academic reading and writing workshops, mentoring, and learning teams. Fifth, the pace of delivery and student workload should be aligned across the full program to allow deep learning to occur.

Areas for future research include (1) an exploration of individual differences in experiencing identity self-states, (2) identify the connections between future possible selves, perspective transformation and habits of mind, and (3) discover pathways to personal and professional lifelong learning and development for FET teachers.

LIMITATIONS

The following limitations should be considered when drawing research and practitioner implications from this study. First, the qualitative nature of a study that incorporates self-reported data and the small sample-size of participants may limit generalizability of the results to other educational contexts, FET teachers and other TEQ program contexts. Second, in many countries FET teacher completion of TEQ programs is not mandatory in order to work in the sector. Therefore, scholars and practitioners are encouraged to be mindful of these limitations when drawing conclusions from this study.

REFERENCES

Beijaard, D., Meijer, P. C., & Verloop, N. (2004). Reconsidering research on teachers' professional identity. *Teaching and Teacher Education*, 20, 107–128.

Beauchamp, C., & Thomas, L. (2009). Understanding teacher identity: an overview of issues in the literature and implications for teacher education. *Cambridge Journal of Education*, *39*(2), 175–189.

Boylan, M., Coldwell, M., Maxwell, B. & Jordan, J. (2018) Rethinking models of professional learning as tools: a conceptual analysis to inform research and practice, *Professional Development in Education*, *44*(1), 120–138, doi: 10.1080/19415257.2017.1306789

Brookfield, S. D. (1995). *Becoming a critically reflective teacher.* San Francisco, CA: John Wiley & Sons, and Jossey Bass.

Conway, P. F., & Clark, C. M. (2003). The journey inward and outward: a re-examination of Fuller's concerns-based model of teacher development. *Teaching and Teacher Education, 19*, 465–482.

Cranton, P. (2006). *Understanding and promoting transformative learning: A guide for educators of adults* (2nd ed.). San Francisco, CA: Jossey-Bass.

Cranton, P. A (2011). Theory in progress. In S. B. Merriam & A. P. Grace (Eds.), *The Jossey-Bass reader on contemporary issues in adult education* (pp. 321–339). San Francisco, CA: John Wiley & Sons, and Jossey-Bass.

Day, C., Kington, A., Stobart, G., & Sammons, P. (2006). The personal and professional selves of teachers: stable and unstable identities. *British Educational Research Journal*, *32*(4), 601–616. doi:10.1080/01411920600775316

Dörnyei, Z. (2001). *Teaching and researching motivation*. Applied Linguistics in Action Series. Harlow, Essex, UK: Pearson Education.

Entwistle, N. (2003). Concepts and conceptual frameworks underpinning the ETL project. *OCC. Report 3, Higher and Community Education*, University of Edinburgh: School of Education.

Entwistle, N., & McCune, V. (2009). The disposition to understand for oneself at university and beyond: Learning processes, the will to learn and sensitivity to context. In Z. Li-Fang & R. J. Sternberg (Eds.), *Perspectives on the nature of intellectual styles* (pp. 29–62). New York, NY: Springer.

Graham Cagney, A. (2011) *'Finding the red thread': The role of the learning space in transformative learning in executive education* (PhD Thesis). Trinity College, Dublin, Ireland.

Hamman, D., Gosselin, K., Romano, J., & Banuan, R. (2010) Using possible-selves theory to understand the identity development of new teachers. *Teaching and Teacher Education, 26*, 1349–1361.

Higgins, E. T. (1987). Self-discrepancy: A theory relating self and affect. *Psychological Review, 94*, 319–340.

Kegan, R. (2009). What "form" transforms? A constructive-developmental approach to transformative learning. In K. Illeris (Ed.), *Contemporary theories of learning* (pp. 35–52). London, England & New York, NY: Routledge Taylor & Francis Group.

King, K. P. (2009). *The handbook of the evolving research of transformative learning based on the learning activities survey* (10th Anniversary Edition). Charlotte, NC: Information Age Publishing.

Korthagen, F. A. (2001). *Linking practice and theory: the pedagogy of realistic teacher education*. London, UK: Routledge.

Korthagen, F., & Vasalos, A. (2005). Levels of reflection: Core reflection as a means to enhance professional growth. *Teachers and Teaching, 11*(1), 37–71.

Mannix, V., & Graham Cagney, A. (2014, July 8–9). *Toward a conceptual framework of personal, professional and situational teacher identity: A study of multiple teacher selves in Further and Adult Education in Ireland*. The 4th Academic Identities Conference, Collingwood College, Durham University, UK. Retrieved from https://www.ee.ucl.ac.uk/~milanaga/abstracts/AICO45.pdf

Markus, H., & Nurius, P. (1986), Possible selves. *American Psychologist, .41*(9), 954–969.

Mezirow, J. (1991). *Transformative dimensions of adult learning*. San Francisco, CA: Jossey-Bass.

Mezirow, J., & Associates (2000). *Learning as transformation: Critical perspectives on a theory in progress*. San Francisco, CA: Jossey-Bass.

Mezirow, J. (2012). Learning to think like an adult: Core concepts of transformation theory. In E. W. Taylor, P. Cranton, & Associates (Eds). *The handbook of transformative learning: Theory, research, and practice*. San Francisco. CA: Jossey-Bass.

O'Sullivan, E., Morrell, A., & O'Connor, M.A. (2002). *Expanding the boundaries of transformative learning: Essays on theory and praxis*. New York, NY: Palgrave and Macmillan.

Rodgers, C. R., & Scott, K. H. (2008). The development of the personal self and professional identity in learning to teach. In M. Cochran-Smith, S. Feiman-Nemser, D. J. McIntyre, & K. E. Demers (Eds.), *Handbook of research on teacher education: Enduring questions in changing contexts* (3rd ed., pp. 732–755). New York, NY: Routledge, Taylor & Francis Group/Association of Teacher Educators.

SOLAS, Further Education and Training Strategy. (2014–2019). Further Education and Training Authority. Retrieved October, 20, 2019, from http://www.solas.ie/SolasPDFLibrary/FETStrategy2014-2019.pdf

Taylor, E. W. (2007). An update of transformative learning theory: A critical review of the empirical research (1999–2005). *International Journal of Lifelong Education, 26*(2), 173–191.

Teaching Council Act (2001 and Regulation Five (Further Education) of the Teaching Council (registration) Regulations. (2009). Retrieved October 20, 2019, from https://www.teachingcouncil.ie/en/Publications/Teacher-Education/Further-Education-General-and-Programme-Requirements-for-the-Accreditation-of-Teacher-Education-Qualifications.pdf

CHAPTER 10

MULTIFACETED IDENTITIES OF TEACHER EDUCATORS AS LIFELONG LEARNERS

Michal Shani, Pninat Tal, and Ilana Margolin
Levinsky College of Education

CONTEXT

This story is about us three women, Ilana, Michal, and Pninat, who were immersed in the process of becoming teacher educators in a large teachers' college in our home country, Israel. We form a rather small heterogeneous group of almost every criterion: age, seniority, expertise, background, working contexts, and subjects.

The starting point of our joint story was our meeting in the multitrack experimental program where together we planned and implemented an alternative program of teacher education. Ilana envisioned and founded the curriculum of this program and her first phase was attracting people who would be committed to the vision and the pathway.

The new program which Ilana asked us, Michal and Pninat, to join, brought about a profound change in the teacher education model, which had prevailed in our teachers' college until then. The new program was

Identity and Lifelong Learning in Higher Education, pp. 177–194

characterized by daring principals, thus being change agents towards a profound change in the existing teacher education system. The main innovations were: integration and connections among various domains, collaboration between the teachers' college and the field (schools), training and collaborative practice of students and teacher educators in various fields of study, research as an organic part of training and development of innovative technology saturated learning environments. This longitudinal process consisted of complexities and challenges of various forms, which each of us experienced, and eventually as a reification of our professional community we published a book with our studies (Margolin, 2010; Tal, 2010; Shani, 2010).

All three of us put in the center of our lives the community we joined, in which we were active over those four years. We entered an ongoing learning process, both as individuals and as a community. In this community relationships were established, our professional identities were reformed, entwined into our personal identity.

Our theoretical grounding is situated in the intersection of three main bodies of literature which are under the umbrella of the sociocultural approach: Learning communities of practice (Grossman, Wineberg, Woolworth, 2001; Watson, 2014; Wenger, 1998); Professional identity (Beijaard, Meijer, & Verloop, 2004; Taylor, 2017) and scholarship of teaching and learning (Felten & Chick, 2018; Miller-Young et al., 2015; Miller-Young, Felten, & Clayton, 2017). These literatures represent the longitudinal process of construction and reconstruction of our identities in the context of continual learning and acting since our participation in the professional community (Margolin, 2011) and afterwards up to the present moment.

Etienne Wenger, in his canonical book *Communities of Practice* (1998) maintains that a community is a joint venture, a shared enterprise and a mutual activity. He emphasized that the "Community of Practice" is not just a defined group of people, nor a synonym for a team or network. The goals and values of such Communities of Practice create relationships of mutual commitment between the partners, which become an integral part of the practice in the reality we live in.

Nowadays, we serve as leaders of different units and engage in an ongoing exploration of our practice within the communities of practice we established. These communities support and foster our collaboration in a collegial environment with the goals of transforming teacher education and improving schools significantly. We negotiate meaning, develop pedagogical knowledge, transform our conceptions as well as our actions and lead towards sustainable improvement in the multiple roles we fulfill.

As part of our professional development, we begin to focus not only on the change we generated in our environments, but on reshaping our multifaceted professional lives and professional identities that continue to develop and change throughout our lifespan. Moreover, we try to understand the interdependence between them and the various communities of practice we establish, each of us in her specific area. As a continuous phase of our mutual long life learning we decided to join the writing community of this present book *I Am What I Have Become, Building a Learner's Identity Throughout Life*.

Collaborative Narrative Self-Study

The question we are asking ourselves is: **Who we really are—Mentors, researchers, assessors, curriculum developers or boundary spanners?** In order to find answers to this question we decided to conduct a collaborative narrative self-study (Kitchen, 2009; Taylor, 2017) which is a multidimensional exploration of our experiences (Clandinin & Connelly, 2004). This study is a part of a longitudinal process in which we examine systematically and critically our practice in order to improve it and generate practical knowledge for and of teacher education. This process accompanied by research we conducted along the way is interactive, aimed at improvement of our practice and validated by critical friends (LaBoskey, 2004).

For the current study we collected data by audio recordings of our three narratives, we reverberated and scrutinized as critical friends each other's story. In addition, we read and reflected on the diaries each one of us wrote over the years.

We started by telling each other the winding path we made in order to become teacher educators, emphasizing the critical junctions throughout the way. We were excited about the opportunity to stop for a second, to look back, to listen to the different life story of each of us; the professional life as well as the life we have outside, away from the frequent, professional meetings in the college, where we still work, learn and develop. We were also excited about the opportunity to conduct a narrative research together, "Research Close to Home" (Leiblich, 2008).

A rich discourse took place between us in the days to come, resulting in the birth of three rich narratives of our becoming teacher educators. The stories revealed the inner world of each narrator. Our empathic, active listening to each of us, as a narrator, enabled her and us to bring her story in its fullest and most correct form.

We discovered that even with the unique story each of us told, we the listening two, would still hear and see it from a different point of view. In a narrative research, each case has as many versions as it does narrators; they also remembered the event in different forms and chose to tell it in different ways, even if the partners had witnessed the same event (Leiblich, 2015).

Two thoughts led us when we had to design our research. One thought illuminated immediately after listening to Michal, the first powerful story. We were convinced of the "narrative truth," in which the components of Michal's story are largely common in the professional development of each of us. The second thought relates to the fact that each of us was moved by the depth and wealth of our stories; in each story, there was a reference to the professional and human experiences we all had and which were experienced differently by each of us in her special world. These thoughts led us to the decision to focus on one story, Michal's story, as the central narrative in this study and show how we all reacted to it, enriched it, and brought different points of view to the analysis of the narrative. This one narrative is the story reflecting our becoming teacher educators.

Our data analysis revealed three main categories that represent the teacher educator's identity emergence. The first depicts a role with no preparation and training, where reality is described, exposing the absence of preparation and training for teacher educators. The second is dedicated to the ongoing learning, research and knowledge creation, and to critical events and decision-making processes, as they were expressed in the analysis and interpretation of the story of Michal. The third deals with leadership and agency, which characterizes teacher educators, as is depicted in Michal's narrative, as well as in Pninat's and Ilana's, which are interwoven in it.

Role With No Preparation and Training

> I came back from England after six years and had to rework my life. I was a special education teacher before and naturally I was looking for a job as a teacher. A friend suggested trying in a teacher education college. I sent my resume and was invited for an interview. I was asked what I wanted to do and said I did not care; I did not really have a clear agenda. I was told that there is a need for a general didactics course. I agreed although I did not know exactly what general didactics meant; for me being a teacher at school or a teacher in an Education College was at the same level. I started and soon got more courses and some hours as a clinical supervisor in the field of special education.

Michal accidentally found herself in a teacher education college, without any prior planning or intent, and like many other teacher educators, she did not even distinguish between teaching at school and teaching at a teacher education institution. For her both were teaching. Since there is no formal preparation for teacher educators, and as many of them were previously teachers, this was perceived as a continuing process; the teacher educators at the college teach similarly to the way they saw in their schools, and in a way experienced school like when they were students themselves.

Teacher education colleges do not have a formal admission process, in which someone explains to the new faculty the nature of the institution's role, vision and agenda, including the importance of teacher education. The only criterion for admission to the institution is a third degree, or coursework towards it, and a subject of expertise required at the College (Margolin, 2011).

> I was told that the course was taught by someone who was about to retire and that she had a whole booklet already written for it. Also, that I should take the booklet home and learn it, and that's what I needed. I came to her home, she gave me her two-penny' worth for an hour about general didactics and that was it.

Michal was accepted to the college, but she had no idea what to teach and how. And she is not alone. Teacher educators are not usually familiar with the entire program of the college, and therefore the connections between the subjects, between the courses, between college learning and field experience are loose. Moreover, there is no consensus about the basic knowledge required for a teacher or about the knowledge that a new teacher educator needs in order to build a course in the college, neither the disciplinary knowledge nor the pedagogical one.

Unlike Michal, Ilana arrived at the college after many years of work as a training coordinator for national projects, led by the chief scientist of the Ministry of Education. Thus, her motivation to become a teacher educator was different as she recounts:

> After a three-year intervention project, as part of the thirty settlements, in schools, in two developmental towns, we realized that ninety percent of our time was invested in re-educating the teachers in schools. I said to the chief scientist that maybe instead of re-educating teachers in the field, I should go work in a college and train them properly in advance. With this sense of mission, I became a teacher educator.

Ilana came then with a clear agenda and vision of teacher education, however, she had no idea about its congruence to that of the college and nobody had ever talked to her about these matters.

As soon as Michal began working in the college she felt helpless:

> The students mainly told me that I looked very young. Apparently, they were in the teacher re-training program, some were kindergarten teachers for years. I was their age or even younger. I often asked myself if I knew more than they did; … I didn't have a clue whether I am doing well.

Michal felt just what student teachers feel. Both she and they were taught how to teach by "apprenticeship of observation" (Lortie, 1975). They watched their teachers along twelve years of studying at schools. Michal taught a course with no strong theoretical, empirical basis or anything else that would help her teach.

> There was no one in the college to talk to about that. That's how I wandered around the college completely alone; I was not part of any team. Between me and myself, I felt I wasn't doing it my way, using a booklet of another teacher. In a way some of the things I was told to do with my students were quite the opposite of my values, which I brought along.

The loneliness Michal felt was even worse than schoolteachers', since in schools there are different affiliation groups of staffrooms, headmasters and inspectors, and continuing education programs, whereas in teacher education everyone does what she feels like. While there is academic freedom, the teacher educator is free in her decisions and choices. Michal's beliefs and values were clear and solid, therefore, unlike her personal identity, her professional identity as a teacher educator had not begun to formulate yet. In congruence with Beijaard's et al. (2004) notion about identity, Michal's professional identity refers in this phase of her life not only to the influence of other people, including accepted images in society about what a teacher should know and do, but can be attributed mainly to her experiences in practice and her personal background and values which she finds important in her professional work and life.

And if the college course was a mystery for Michal, then the requirement to mentor students in their field work, made it even more difficult for her:

> I was asked to substitute for a clinical supervisor who went on maternity leave; I went to observe her students in the field. I was told to give them feedback.

If the profession of teacher educator does not exist, the problem of mentoring students in the field experience is even harder. The difficulty is increased due to the persistent desire for connecting in a deep manner between the theories taught in college and teaching practice in the field. The term "clinical supervisor" is vague, thus each one builds a role for herself.

> The first time I learned something in the college with someone else was when I was invited to take part in the course named "the adult learner." The course was about andragogy. The meeting with others who did similar things to what I did in the college was for me an important experience.

The Head of The Teacher Retraining Program back then studied the subject of andragogy, (Knowles, 1998; Mezirow, 1996) and therefore decided to expose this important subject to the staff. She prepared a course for the faculty, similar to the ones given to schoolteachers and kindergarten teachers in the Ministry of Education. This program shows on the one hand that the learning patterns of teacher educators are derived from those of teachers in school; on the other hand, each position holder in the college acts upon his own discretion. Depending on the areas of interest and expertise regardless of the overall agenda of the college, each position holder can show an initiative by developing the faculty members of her department in the college. Michal enjoyed this opportunity to meet other staff members; however, this short experience was, unfortunately, a one timer:

> So, I wandered around the college feeling lonely until at some point, after some two and a half years I was fired. The new principal, who was there for a short time anyway, told me he couldn't give me tenure, so I left and went back to teaching for the Ministry of Education.

One of the critical issues in education in general and in teacher education particularly, which Fullan (2006) raises in his writings, is the lack of continuity and the lack of a succession of leadership and ongoing vision. Institutions and organizations sparingly provide tenure and after three years of teaching new employees are fired. Michal was fired by the college's new principal, who had been there in position for one year only; he did not know the people and acted by the book. He did not lead with a certain vision or a sustainable agenda. However, one year later, after a cooling-off period, she was invited again to come and teach at the college, though the same scenario repeated itself and she found herself teaching intuitively:

> I don't even remember talking to myself in terms of studying as that wasn't my genre, that I have to learn, or need to develop. Those are things I felt I did intuitively, not the kind of things I would nowadays, retrospectively, conceptualize. I did not say to myself: Michal, you must develop as a teacher educator; I didn't, it didn't exist, I didn't give it a name; I felt that it was my workplace, aside of The Ministry of Education. Here it was more prestigious and I could also tell that I was a teacher educator.

Just like other teacher educators, Michal did not get any formal preparation, as there is none; she also did not think she should train herself for the profession during her teaching duty. Moreover, even in the college there were no forums or functionaries who prepared the staff for their position or were engaged in developing them. Beyond the "respect and prestige," namely the respectful status teacher educators have, there was no difference between Michal's intuitive teaching at school and the expectedly different academic one in college. Until today a lot has been written about formal professional training for teacher educators, but there is no such training program (Loughran, 2014; Margolin, 2011; Murray & Male, 2005). Turning the teacher educator into a learner and a teacher at the same time is becoming a necessary condition, yet researchers and teacher educators are still searching for an efficient way to carry it out.

Continuous Learning and Research

> When I started my journey as a teacher educator, I agreed to teach every course offered to me. I planned the courses all by myself. I felt that I had no partners to think with, deliberate with, no one to ask and no one to consult with. There wasn't any forum in my college that offered a supporting learning community.

What Michal describes is the common perception about teaching in general and teacher education in particular. A teacher is the one who teaches, and the pupil is the one who learns. This is one facet of the story, but there is another facet that relates to the ethical-moral aspect—Who is a worthy teacher? What are the values and big ideas which teachers should be educated towards in a teacher education institution?

> After six months of teaching I faced an event that influenced my perception about being a teacher educator. It was the Holocaust memorial day and I took my students to the ceremony which took place in our college. One of the students, who sat next to me, was listening to messages on her mobile phone very loudly, while the president of the college told his moving personal story on the stage. I felt uneasy. I shared my feelings with the head of the faculty telling her that I have doubts about the adjustment of a student behaving like this to our program. She put her hand around my shoulders and said: Michal, you are still young, you will get used to it. I remember the uneasiness feeling I had. I told myself that I don't want to get used to it, never. I kept asking myself questions about who is a proper teacher but I did not do anything with these questions because I had no one to talk to. I came to teach my course and went home, that was it.

Michal felt frustrated when she realized that her values and what she personally experienced as good conflicted with the head of the faculty's norms. This conflict led to friction in Michal's professional identity because the "personal" and the "professional" were too far removed from each other (Beijaard et al., 2004). Though the great ideas of teacher education, the questions of suitability, the "proper teacher," the values and the vision of training are all of the utmost importance, they never came to the front of the stage. These big ideas and issues are much more important than any strategy, method, or even content, but there was no continuous deliberation or discussion about them at the college. It is almost certain that an individual cannot lead changes all by herself; this can only be done by a professional community.

> Then I faced a critical event. I was a clinical supervisor in the field of special education at that time. Ilana was in charge of the training department and as part of her job came to watch me in a school. Until then no one mentioned the word "feedback" in any forum in the college. I did what I knew, I was quite sure I was doing well. I gave my feedback to my student teacher and then Ilana gave me feedback on the feedback I delivered. I was dumbfounded. She told me difficult things, used a professional language I wasn't familiar with. It was the first time I began to ask myself what am I doing here, where did I come from and where do I want to go. When I arrived home I wrote a reflective paper about what I faced, felt and learnt from this meeting with Ilana and sent it to her. I consider this writing as my first "self- study research."

Michal describes a critical event that became retrospectively the first step of her long journey of studying her practice. It was the first time she had been offered the opportunity to work intensively with issues connected to herself and to her practice. This feedback led Michal to ask herself important questions about her goals, her self-identity and professionalism. She participated in a live example of getting feedback of a kind she had never met before, feedback that was based on a full documentation of the observation.

> After this event, a systematic study of practice, writing about it and learning from it has become a cornerstone of my professional development. I understood that practice should be the central thing to read about, learn about and inquire. It must be interpreted, understood, analyzed and mainly be in a constant state of continuous improvement. Right after the meeting with Ilana she invited me to join an innovative program she started to design. Everything about my professional life has changed since I joined the program Ilana offered me.

For Michal as well as for Pninat, who also was invited to join the professional community of the experimental program, this meeting with Ilana was a turning point. Both of them joined a group of teacher educators and became part of the community who built an alternative program for teacher education. In this community they, like all other participants, faced the challenge of becoming educational researchers in addition to their teaching and mentoring positions. This was a great challenge for most of them because the two roles—researcher and teacher educator—require potentially conflicting perspectives. In acting as a teacher researcher an individual is disrupting established boundaries between teacher and researcher. In this process of becoming a teacher researcher a teacher educator begins to merge the perspectives of teacher and researcher into a single dynamic one (Taylor, 2017).

Ilana describes similar feelings to Michal's:

> Like Michal, Pninat and most teacher educators I did not think at the beginning in terms of learning. Teacher educators have already completed their studies; have a diploma, a master's degree or PhD, and now come to "pass on their knowledge to others." The continuing interest in learning throughout life gained momentum later. To this day, much has been written about formal training for teacher educators, but there is no such training program. Turning the teacher into a learner and teacher at the same time has recently become a necessary condition. It was at the experimental program where the ongoing learning or even the training of teacher educators was established. Until then in our college and other teacher education institutions this ongoing mutual learning had not been arranged.

Both, Michal and Pninat found themselves for the first time part of a group that formed a professional learning community that focused, while building an alternative program of teacher education, on the development of professional identity of teacher educators. The practice of their development has become more scholarly, relying more on research and theory rather than only on anecdote and personal experience, the focus has changed from teaching only to learning (Felten & Chick, 2018). Teachers' professional identities are socially situated and legitimated; that is, teachers' professional development is not solely composed of their growing knowledge base and skills, but also includes their ability to define themselves and have others see them as teachers (Simon & Johnson, 2015).

> Everyone who was there taught me a whole world. I became a much more professional as a teacher educator. I came from the field of special education and held a position of an expert in this field among other experts in variety of subjects. To be part of this group was extraordinarily demanding, day and night seven days a week, but I remember the feeling of developing from minute to minute. In addition to the feeling of professional development I also began to understand that I wanted it. I want to be a teacher educator as a career. The participation in this group lasted four years. The end point was writing a book where I had an article of my own for the first time. The feedback I got was encouraging and I began to get confidence in writing as well. I started to write on a regular basis. I realized that in the development of my identity as a teacher educator I add another dimension—being a researcher. Something that had begun in this group and perhaps even in the encounter with Ilana. I understood that I am in a constant process of exploring what I am doing. My writing was and still is connected to what I do.

The thick book that was published at the end of the experiment (Margolin, 2010) was comprised of the self-studies and action research studies of the participants. It was one of the artifacts that represented the reification of the community (Wenger, 1998). The faculty members learned while studying their practice that the benefits of collaborating in self-study, as opposed to individual reflection, include the availability of a variety of perspectives on their concerns and interests related to teacher education. The community enabled the opportunity for collegial dialogue around teacher education practices in the safe space we created. Moreover, the faculty's studies served also as a way for the teacher educators to act as change agents, while becoming experts in their fields and building educational knowledge that extends beyond their individual classrooms. And most important, these studies and their collaboration empowered the teacher educators and their students so they could challenge educational contexts in order to change them according to their vision (Chang et al., 2016; Fecho & Allen, 2011; Margolin, 2013; Stosich, 2016).

Michal sums up her multifaceted identity:

> The three dimensions of my identity became clear to me—a teacher, a researcher, and a change generator leader.

Indeed, this story of Michal indicates that she "came out of the literature." She entered this profession by chance. Once she joined a learning environment meaningful and relevant to her practice she began to show interest in what she did and even like it.

She built her professional identity in the course of action. She faced a social learning per se, she learnt with and from colleagues. Her story illustrates the theory that self can arise only in a social setting where there is social communication; in communicating we learn to assume the roles of others and monitor our actions accordingly. Our concept of self can be defined as an organized representation of our theories, attitudes, and beliefs about ourselves (Mead, as cited in Beijaard et al., 2004).

Identity, Agency, and Leadership

> I remember the great place Ilana had given me in this group of experts in which each one was a knowledgeable and specialist in his/her field. She gave me the feeling that there was some sort of value to what I was saying, and slowly helped me to find myself within the community. With time I understood my professional value as a special education expert and that I held the issue of inclusive education within the group of experts. I began to grow into this role and began to crystallize myself to form some kind of say in this field that was coming into being. I developed a new professional identity.

Michal stresses the huge influence of the environment of the community. The professional and social support she got enabled her transformation in conceptions, beliefs and self-confidence. All of these factors were interrelated with the external contextual change which facilitated the development of her professional, social and organizational identity (Hokka, Vahasantanen, & Mahlakaarto, 2017).

In the new program where the three of us met, a professional learning community was built, in which we all learned, explored, and became leaders. However, in addition to the personal and professional identity that developed and re-shaped, we reinforced the shared identity and sense of mission and collaborative activism of all the teacher educators who participated in the experiment, as Michal put it:

> I held the position of an expert, I developed, I learned to build new and different courses; it was the first time I belonged to a community that helped me grow, taught me.

Michal like all her colleagues in the professional community, which enabled a reciprocal learning process, became a teacher and a learner simultaneously (Paredes-Scribner & Bradley-Levine, 2010).

About this learning environment within the professional community Ilana adds:

> The common denominator of most of the faculty members who joined the experimental program was their dissatisfaction from the traditional program and the desire to transform it. The participants were ready to take risks and commit to a new complicated challenge, that nobody knew its essence at the beginning. However, all members worked very hard and acted much beyond the regular standards in order to generate a sustainable change in teacher education. We did all we could in order to change the institutional and systemic cultures. However, while the project's principal aim was to construct an alternative and innovative school-based teacher education program and experiment with it, a major surprising finding was the significant professional development of the teacher-educators and the emergence of all the members as leaders.

> Thus, there is no doubt that the power of the community was crucial. Had each of the participants been alone, he/her would certainly not have dared to follow such a complicated path. Communities of practice have individual and organizational influences that impact institutions, curriculum reform as well as teachers, teacher educators and students' learning (Margolin, 2012). And indeed, Michal tells how, within this community, she grew to become a leader while accomplishing her roles.

I joined Ilana at a schools principals' meeting in one of the country counties in order to think together about a partnership with our college. This meeting has opened the door to a significant period of my professional life. I started to work with one of the principals in her school. I established there a learning community that included students, school teachers and clinical supervisors from my college. The work towards forming a learning community allowed me for the first time not only to focus on my professional development but also to start helping others developing theirs, within the setting of professional learning community. I started to think in terms of leadership; I felt that I influenced others. I shared my professional knowledge, I put the theory into practice, I shared my ideology about the ability of being simultaneously a teacher and a learner and the importance of being a reflective practitioner. All the ideas we were talking about in our experimental program became a living theory, part of me not as external ideas anymore.

As a result of her interactions with the environment and colleagues in the community Michal became conscious of the complex, multidimensional and dynamic system of representations and meanings of her professional identity. Moreover, in the new setting of a partnership between the college and one of the schools, leading meant for her engaging in interrelated new learning and leading through the process of constructive change (Fink, 2009; Lambert, 2009). This understanding of professional identity, as that which can be redefined based on her changing context makes an investigation of how teacher educators' professional identities shift to accommodate field-based experiences informative for the profession (Chang et al., 2016).

I was part of a team that was thinking about developing a new integration program focusing on inclusive education. I developed a model of inclusive education and considered myself an expert in this field. However, someone else was appointed to run the program; for me it was surprising and frustrating. I felt that it was not only professionalism that matters, not only what I knew, who I am and what I am from a personal and a professional point of view. On one hand I felt that I developed and got more and more professional in what I did while on the other hand I felt that I did not progress and did not break out, did not reach key positions in our college where I could spread my ideas and my knowledge. I missed the community I belonged to a few years earlier where the focus was on learning together and giving each other personal and professional support. I didn't find an alternative to this community and started to think whether I want to continue.

Michal has experienced other side of the professional development and being aware of it and understanding its rules are part of a leader's role. Issues like power struggles, ego control, people whose motives are not always in the interest of the matter take up a significant part of the leader's time. As a leader she must be aware of these micro politics, analyze them, understand them and navigate them in order to change them. She compared her current situation to the one she had experienced in the experimental program, when she was part of a professional community and missed the professional, supporting team. As she put it, she started to re-think her future in the college.

However, within this period Michal was offered an opportunity to lead a unique, program that was not part of the regular programs in the college: A national program of academic retraining and career change for university graduates who were selected from hundreds of candidates from all over the country for being teachers in the geographical and social periphery (Shani, Shadmi-Wortman, & Tabak, 2017). This was a dream role that allowed her to bring together her educational vision and all she dreamt about in accordance with the teacher education program. About that new context Michal spoke with excitement:

> It was the first time that I had taken on the role of a manager. It wasn't only the management role I was excited about it was also the opportunity to design a totally new teacher education program based on my dreams, my values, my vision and all the ideas about how teacher education program should look.

Michal transferred her identity into a new context as a resource that allowed her to envision new worlds, new activities and new ways of being (Beauchamp & Thomas, 2009). Michal's agency was her freedom to act in accordance with her individual desires and personal values.
Michal summarizes the multitask role she plays:

> This role allowed me to bring myself in the three channels, as a professional teacher educator, as a researcher and also as a change agent leader. The three of them are based on my set of educational-social values.

The sociocultural approach conceptualizes teacher agency as embedded across social circumstances, tools, and people. This means that what Michal believes, and how she thinks and acts, is always shaped by historical and sociocultural practices. The knowledge she built, the professionalism she experienced and most important her multifacet identity which she reorganized and reformulated—all these brought her ripe and ready to this significant leadership role. The mixture of identities and roles she mentioned contain the two main areas of leadership and management, which are not always consistent within the same person. Michal is a manager who knows how to take care of the organization's active and regular flow, but also her leadership deals with innovation, experimentation and sustainable change.

Ilana sums up this life narrative from her point of view.

Michal's living theory (Whitehead, 2008) is unique and important in her improving her and others' practice, generating knowledge and influencing others and the contexts in which she lives and works. Her story is a fascinating story that represents, on the one hand, a process of "becoming" a teacher educator, and on the other hand, the development of the professional, organizational and social identities of an intelligent, ethical, diligent, and talented person. Very modestly, I feel that I have had a part in Michal's fascinating development, and perhaps I implement Fullan's criterion for defining a good leader as one who leaves behind a generation of leaders who are going further than him/her (Fullan, 2006).

Michal's narrative is a "story to live by" that conceptually brought together her personal practical knowledge, her professional knowledge, landscape and identity (Clandinin, 2003; Connelly & Clandinin, 1999). It also illustrates how her agency and identity are closely intertwined and enable her power to act, to affect matters, to make decisions and choices, and to take stances in relation to her work and professional identity. Given her interaction across organizational and professional boundaries of the college and the field she is a border-crosser (Vähäsantanen, 2015).

Final Thoughts

Personally, looking back at our evolving identities, through the lens of Michal's narrative, we can answer our research question and say that we are teachers, mentors, researchers, assessors, curriculum developers and most of all change agents who are passionate to transform the culture of our college as well as of the whole educational system. As boundary spanners striving to make a difference, we utilize our pedagogical, research, relational and theoretical expertise by blurring the boundaries between them in order to contribute to the coconstruction of knowledge by teacher educators, teachers and student teachers.

Professionally, looking back at our stories retrospectively reveals a kind of layout of teacher educator's development. While processing and analyzing the data of our evolving identities, we understood that our challenging paths could be a basis for a teacher educator's induction and development framework. However, the challenge for future teacher education is not to devise a generic development program but to create an environment that affords time, safe space and abundance of opportunities for dialogue, collaborative research and reflection, continuous intellectual engagement and experimentation. In other words, leaders have to build professional learning communities in their institutions and support teacher educators' leading the cultural shift that is needed in the colleges and in schools.

REFERENCES

Beauchamp, C., &Thomas, L., (2009). Understanding teacher identity: An overview of issues in the literature and implications for teacher education. *Cambridge Journal of Education, 39*(2), 175–189.

Beijaard, D., Meijer, D. P., & Verloop, N. (2004). Reconsidering research on teachers' professional identity. *Teaching and Teacher Education, 20*(2), 107–128.

Chang, A., Neugebauer, S. R., Ellis, A., Ensminger, D., Ryan, A. M., & Kennedy, A. (2016). Teacher educator identity in a culture of iterative teacher education program design: A collaborative self-study. *Studying Teacher Education, 12*(2), 152–169.

Clandinin, D. J. (2003). Stories to live by on landscapes of diversity: Interweaving the personal and professional in teachers' lives. Keynote paper presented at the 11th conference of the *International Study Association on Teachers and Teaching* (ISATT). Leiden, The Netherlands.

Clandinin. D. J., & Connelly, F. M. (2004). Knowledge, narrative and self-study. In J. J. Loughran, M.L. Hamilton, V.K. LaBoskey, & T. Russell (Eds.), *International handbook of self-study of teaching and teacher education practices* (pp. 575–600). Dordrecht, The Netherlands: Kluwer Academic Publishers.

Connelly, F. M., & Clandinin, D. J. (1999). *Shaping a professional identity: Stories of education practice*. London, England: Althouse Press.

Fecho, B., & Allen, J. (2011). Teacher inquiry into literacy, social justice, and power. In: D. Lapp, & D. Fisher (Eds.), *Handbook of research on teaching the English language arts* (3rd ed., pp. 232–246). New York, NY: Routledge.

Felten, P., & Chick, N. (2018). Is SoTL a signature pedagogy of educational development? *To Improve the Academy, A Journal of Educational Development, 37*(1), 4–16.

Fink, D. (2009). Leadership for mortals: Developing and sustaining leaders of learning. In A. M. Blankstein, P. D. Houston, & R. W. Cole (Eds.), *Building sustainable leadership capacity* (pp. 41–64). Thousand Oaks, CA: Corwin Press.

Fullan, M. (2005). *Leadership & sustainability: System thinkers in action*. Thousand Oaks, CA: Corwin Press.

Fullan, M. (2006). *Turnaround leadership*. San Francisco, CA: Jossey-Bass.

Grossman, P., Wineburg, S., & Woolworth, S. (2001). Toward a theory of teacher community. *The Teachers College Record, 103*, 942–1021.

Hokka, P., Vähäsantanen, K., & & Mahlakaarto, S. (2017). Teacher educators' collective professional agency and identity: Transforming marginality to strength. *Teaching and Teacher Education, 63*, 36–46.

Kitchen, J. (2009). Passages: Improving teacher education through narrative self-study. In D. L. Tidwell, M. L. Heston, & L. M. Fitzgerald (Eds.), *Research methods for the self-study of practice* (pp. 35–51). New York, NY: Springer.

Knowles, M. S. (1998). *The adult learning* (5th ed.). Houston, TX: Gulf.

LaBoskey, V. K. (2004). The methodology of self-study and its theoretical underpinnings. In J. J. Loughran, M. L. Hamilton, V. K. LaBoskey, & T. Russell (Eds.), *International handbook of self-study of teaching and teacher education practices* (pp. 817–869). Dordrecht, The Netherlands: Kluwer.

Lambert, L. (2009). Reconceptualizing the road toward leadership capacity. In A. M. Blankstein, P. D. Houston, & R. W. Cole (Eds.), *Building sustainable leadership capacity* (pp. 7–28). Thousand Oaks, CA: Corwin Press.

Loughran, J. (2014). Professionally developing as a teacher educator, *Journal of Teacher Education, 65*(4), 271–283.

Leiblich, A. (2008). *Arak for breakfast*. Tel Aviv, Israel: Shoken. (Hebrew)

Leiblich, A. (2015). Self-narrative as a prologue. In R. Josselson (Ed.), *Interviewing for qualitative inquiry- A relational approach* (pp. 9–28). Tel Aviv, Israel: Mofet Institute.

Lortie, D. C. (1975). *Schoolteacher: A sociological study*. Chicago, IL: University of Chicago Press.

Margolin, I. (Editor). (2010). *Crossing the beyond: A multi-track teacher education program—An ongoing discourse*. Tel Aviv, Israel: Mofet Institute. (Hebrew).

Margolin, I. (2011). Professional development of teacher educators through a 'transitional space': A surprising outcome of a teacher education program. *Teacher Education Quarterly, 38*(3), 7–25.

Margolin, I. (2012). A coterminous collaborative learning model: Interconnectivity of leadership and learning. *Brock Education, 21*(2), 70–87.

Margolin, I. (2013). Nurturing opportunities for educational leadership: How affordance and leadership interconnect. *Higher Education Studies, 3*(3), 77–89.

Miller-Young, J., Dean, Y., Rathburn, M., Pettit, J., Underwood, M., Gleeson, J. ... Calvert V. (2015). Decoding ourselves: An inquiry into faculty learning about reciprocity in service-learning. *Michigan Journal of Community Service Learning, 22*(1), 32–47.

Miller-Young, J., Felten, P., & Clayton, P. (2017). Learning about learning—Together. *Michigan Journal of Community Service Learning, 23*(2), 154–158.

Murray, J., & Male, T. (2005). Becoming a teacher educator: Evidence from the field. *Teaching and Teacher Education, 21*(2), 125–142.

Mezirow, J. (1996). Contemporary paradigms of learning. *Adult Education Quarterly, 46*(3), 158–172.

Paredes-Scribner, S. M., & Bradley-Levine, J. (2010). The meaning(s) of teacher leadership in an urban high school reform. *Educational Administration Quarterly, 46*, 491–522.

Shani, M. (2010). Towards an ecological approach to inclusion. In I. Margolin (Ed.), *Crossing the beyond: A multi-track teacher education program- an ongoing discourse*. (pp. 148–170). Tel-Aviv, Israel: Mofet & Levinsky College of Education. (Hebrew).

Shani, M., Shadmi-Wortman, S., & Tabak, E. (2017). The case of Hotam Neomi: More than a teacher education program. In S. Fiman-Nemsar & M. Perez (Eds.), *Getting the Teachers we need: International perspectives on teacher education* (pp. 23–34). Lanham, MD: Rowman & Littlefield.

Simon, N. S., & Johnson, S. M. (2015). Teacher turnover in high-poverty schools: What we know and can do. *Teachers College Record, 117*, 1–36.

Stosich, E. L. (2016). Building teacher and school capacity to teach to ambitious standards in high-poverty schools. *Teaching and Teacher Education, 58*, 43–53.

Tal, P. (2010). *The graduate students point of view in a multi-track teacher education program.* In I. Margolin (Ed.), *Crossing the beyond: A multi-track teacher education program- an ongoing discourse* (pp. 489–516). Tel-Aviv, Israel: Mofet & Levinsky College of Education. (Hebrew).

Taylor, L. A. (2017). How teachers become teacher researchers: Narrative as a tool for teacher identity construction. *Teaching and Teacher Education, 61*, 16–25

Vähäsantanen, K. (2015). Professional agency in the stream of change: Understanding educational change and teachers' professional identities. *Teaching and Teacher Education, 47*, 1–12.

Watson, C. (2014). Effective professional learning communities? The possibilities for teachers as agents of change in schools. *British Educational Research Journal, 40*(1), 18–29.

Wenger, E. (1998). *Communities of practice: Learning, meaning and identity.* Cambridge, UK: Cambridge University Press.

Whitehead, J. (2008). Using a living theory methodology in improving practice and generating educational knowledge in living theories. *Educational Journal of Living Theories, 1*(1), 103–126.

CHAPTER 11

THE PROFESSOR
AND THE CLOSET

Teacher Educators and Coming Out

Lesley N. Siegel
West Chester University

I remember going downtown and meeting with the school district folks, and being much more closeted in those meetings and the times I was in schools looking at my classrooms, supervising my teachers. And that was interesting to me that even then I was slightly fearful that if people found out, they wouldn't let me run these programs. I wasn't doing the casual coming out. I wasn't just naturally talking before or after the meeting saying something about my wife, and I remember being surprised at myself that I reverted. (Participant I, 2017)

Teacher preparation holds an interesting place in higher education; faculty are charged with the responsibility of developing future educators to build safe and welcoming schools, while the lesbian, gay, and/or queer identified faculty who are doing this work may feel neither safe nor welcomed. This chapter details an ongoing qualitative study exploring the experiences of gay, lesbian, and/or queer identified faculty working in teacher preparation.

Identity and Lifelong Learning in Higher Education, pp. 195–212
Copyright © 2020 by Information Age Publishing
195

Three narratives from gay and lesbian faculty members are detailed in this chapter, their accounts of working in schools of education presented as a discussion with the author serving as moderator. Multiple facets are explored through voices of the study participants including the sociopolitical climate of the individual's institution, being queer in the academy, and the intersection of sexual identity and teacher preparation. Of particular interest is how university faculty make their sexual identity visible to students and how the unique work of preparing future teachers interplays with the faculty member's queer identity.

For queer faculty, sexual identity can be a silenced identity. Unlike more visible marginalized identities, queer teacher educators can bear the burden of silence having to calculate both the personal and professional consequences of "coming out" (Herman-Wilmarth & Bills, 2010; Turner, 2010). On the first day of class, queer faculty often walk into the classroom carrying not only a syllabus, but the question of if, when, and to what degree to make their sexual identity visible to students.

As teachers of those who will teach, there is a trained as well as unspoken commitment for faculty to model best practices for our future educators. The belief in teacher preparation is that ways in which professors of education build relationships and facilitate educative experiences in the university setting will set the example for our preservice teacher candidates to do the same in their future K–12 classrooms (Loughran, 2013). The stakes are higher and the obligation is greater; professors of education teach not only university students, but set in motion the ways in which K–12 students will be educated for years to come.

Many a K–12 school's motto reads some variation of, "creating a community of lifelong learners." As the national debate rages on school funding and structures, teachers continue to understand one of the central purposes of education is to facilitate the development of critical thinking and curious citizens. Professors of education are at the center of a concentric system of teaching and learning. Like the first drop on the water's surface, faculty in schools of education begin a teaching and learning progression that will extend far beyond their college classroom to students in K–12 classrooms over multiple years. Professors will never see the extent of the ripples, of just how far the learning radiates.

As an initiator of an extended learning cycle, teacher educators feel tremendous responsibility to their students. How does this professional responsibility interplay with the social, cultural and institutional forces that weigh upon queer teacher educators? This study explores the ways in which queer faculty assume this burden in a way that moves beyond the pedagogy of curriculum and instruction.

THE CLOSET AND THE IVORY TOWER

The Closet

Coming out has been a central pillar of the gay rights movement in the post-Stonewall era. Bringing one's marginalized sexual identity out of the closet has been made not only a personal, but also a political act (Rosiek, 2016; Whisman, 2003). Coming out is often intended as an affirming act for gay and lesbian persons; we are coming out of the closet, the assumed place of darkness and isolation into what is assumed to be a healthier and more affirming space. We are also often coming out into uncertainty.

Thirty years ago, at San Francisco's Gay Freedom Rally, Harvey Milk (1978) pushed coming out as the first step toward gay persons gaining political footing,

> Gay brothers and sisters, what are we going to do about it? You must come
> out. Come out to your relatives. Come out to your friends, if indeed they
> are your friends. Come out to your neighbors, to your fellow workers.

Milk posed coming out as an obligation; the visibility of one's marginalized sexual identity was needed for the public good. This might be seen as a foreshadowing of the implied obligation for educators to come out to their students for causes greater than themselves.

In many ways, the coming out experience has been embraced as a seminal milestone of the gay experience (e.g., National Coming Out Day; It Gets Better Project). Coming out is not a single incidence (Hill, 2009), a proclamation of, "I'm here and I'm queer." As queer persons move to new situations and meet new persons, they must decide if and when to come out to their current audience. For educators, this might mean every class, every semester.

The Tower

What it looks like to be queer in the ivory tower varies greatly across institution, compounded by a vast array of variables including: sociopolitical climate; geography; institutional affiliation, and diversity on campus. These structural variables are coupled with variables inherent to each individual's intersecting identities, personal relationships, and professional positioning. The ways in which lesbian and gay faculty are supported in institutions of higher education greatly varies (Blumenfeld, Weber, & Rankin, 2016). There is no census data on sexual orientation and being a sexual minority is not considered a measurable dimension of diversity (Renn, 2010). Gathering data on gay and lesbian faculty relies both on the desire of someone (e.g., institution, researcher) to collect the data and the willingness and ability for queer faculty to come out and be counted.

Across the variance of institutions, a cultural homophobia (also referred to as heterosexism) continues to pervade higher education. Cultural homophobia or heterosexism refers to the exclusion, negative or stereo-typical depiction of gay, lesbian, bisexual, and trans persons. Outside the walls of the gender studies department, heteronormativity is often the norm. Great strides have been made in gay rights over the past 15 years, but these strides are uneven; many institutions remain entrenched in cultural homophobia while others embrace queer faculty as a dimension of diversity and encourage the inclusion of queer content across depart-ments (Blumenfeld et al., 2016).

Current Scholarship on Queer Faculty

The vast majority of existing research on gay and lesbian faculty creates a single category of "LGBT(Q+)" persons, easily making all persons with a marginalized sexual or gender identity into an easy to categorize dichotomous variable. Much of the scholarship on queer faculty in higher education is centered on the degree of harm faculty experience as a result of their marginalized sexual identities with measures of campus climate most frequently used as a barometer (Blumenfeld, Weber, & Rankin, 2016; Renn, 2010). Research on institutional climate reports an exceptional range of experiences, from faculty who report feeling completely accepted at a department and institutional level to faculty who feel both emotionally and professionally compromised (Anderson & Kanner, 2011; Blumenfeld et al., 2016; Douglass, 2016). Larger studies both qualitative and mix-methods in orientation tend to look at faculty across the spectrum of the LGBTQ community and is neither discipline nor identity (i.e., sexual identity or gender identity) specific, but rather lumps faculty together as a single demographic employed in a single profession (Blumenfeld et al., 2016; Renn, 2010).

The research is fairly lean on the individual experiences of lesbian and gay faculty working in higher education (Blumenfeld et al., 2016; Renn, 2010; Sapp, 2001). The existing research relies almost exclusively on autobiography and auto-ethnography (Hermann-Wilmarth & Bills, 2010). Some scholars choose to "out" themselves in the pages of books and journals (e.g., Sapp, 2001; Dejean, 2007; Turner, 2010), demonstrat-ing the power of personal narrative in developing an understanding of how various individuals navigate their queer identity while teaching in higher education (Renn, 2010). Across time these studies have leaned heavily on the authorship of gay men and their personal journeys from personal to professional coming out (e.g., Sapp, 2001; Turner, 2010).

Even less studied is the unique experience of lesbian and gay faculty working in teacher preparation. Over the past 20 years the vast majority of writing on gay and lesbian faculty working in teacher preparation is autobiographical or auto-ethnographic in nature (e.g., Sapp, 2001; Turner, 2010). Some researchers are concerned with the experiences of preservice teachers (e.g., Hynes, 2012, Hermann-Wilmarth & Bills, 2010), but little concern is paid to the teacher educator.

To Teach ...

Faculty in schools and departments of education are uniquely positioned. Preparing future educators with the technical skills and abilities to teach academic content is only one dimension of teacher preparation. To teach is to engage in a highly personal act that calls for teachers to build relationships with their students and to share their vulnerabilities. As bell hooks (1994) writes,

> Any classroom that employs a holistic model of learning will also be a place where teachers grow, and are empowered by the process. Empowerment cannot happen if we refuse to be vulnerable while encouraging students to take risks. Professors who expect students to share confessional narratives but who are themselves unwilling to share are exercising power in a manner that could be coercive.

Many scholars echo hooks in the call for professors to be open with their students, to share vulnerabilities as a way to engage in relational and empowering pedagogy. Paulo Freire's (1970/2000) critical pedagogy is built on a foundation of dialogical experiences between student and teacher; teachers must become partners with their students. Teacher educators have an even greater responsibility to engage in an empowering pedagogy with their college students; faculty are modeling the practices they expect will be transmitted through school systems for years to come.

This can be an exceptional charge for gay and lesbian educators; how does one hold what is known to be 'best practice' when one's vulnerabilities can be so very great? What does it mean if your "confessional narrative" (hooks, 1994) is the core of your identity and can lead to judgment and discrimination? It is this tension that drives this research study.

CURRENT STUDY

Teaching while queer to those who teach is a phenomenon experienced by few, but that impacts many. The research tradition of hermeneutic phenomenology looks to understand human experiences shared by a group of persons who have similar characteristics and who experience a similar phenomenon (Cresswell, 2007; Padilla-Diaz, 2015) and is therefore particularly well suited for this study. As a lesbian researcher working in teacher preparation, I experience the same phenomenon as my participants. During the research process, I had to constantly balance the value of my insider status with the potential risk of bias. I took guidance from lesbian researchers Wilkinson and Kitzinger (2013) on the use of insider/outsider status in qualitative research. As with all researchers I hold both insider and outsider status, depending on my research participant. As a queer academic in a college of education, I am an insider, but depending on the participant I will hold various degrees of "insider/outsider" status with respect to race, ethno-religion, dis/ability and class. However, I believe that without holding group membership to this marginalized and at times vulnerable population, this work would not be possible.

Study Participants

Participants were recruited for this study using "purposive sampling" (Cresswell, 2007), a method often employed in phenomenological research in order to build a pool of persons who experience a similar phenomenon but may be dispersed or difficult to identify. Faculty members were eligible to participate in this study based on the following inclusion criteria: lesbian, gay or queer identified faculty, works in a school or college of education, holds a terminal degree in her/his/their field. Of particular importance to this study is a participant pool that represents faculty from sociopolitical and geographically diverse regions of the country, various types of institutions (e.g., private colleges, public universities), and faculty in various positions (e.g., pre-tenure faculty, tenured faculty, adjunct faculty). Information on this study was shared via my professional networks and organizations. Interested participants were asked to contact me directly. The study participants do not know me as the information often reaches them through a colleague of a colleague or a professional organization's message (e.g., organization newsletter). The topic of queer visibility in academia is highly personal and not without consequence. In order for a participant to place their trust in a researcher unknown to them, it is critical that I not just understand the way queer identity is marginalized in higher education, but live it.

Data Collection and Analysis

In the form of semistructured interviews, study participants were asked to describe the phenomenon of working in a school or department of education as a queer person. A particular focus was on the ways in which each participant makes her/his/their sexual identity visible to students. In semistructured interviews, each interview touched upon four central themes: institutional climate towards queer faculty; interplay of the personal and professional; visibility of sexual identity at institution and to students; and teacher preparation in particular. Each of the participants was interviewed individually and then each interview transcribed by the author. After transcription, participants corroborated the data in line with validation procedures for phenomenological studies (Cresswell, 2007; Padilla-Diaz, 2015).

Each participant was treated an individual case, supporting eventual cross-case analysis. Individual transcripts were inductively In vivo coded to maintain fidelity to the participant's words. The codes were then reviewed holistically to look for emerging themes within case. The focus of this data analysis was to explore the interplay of each participant's queer identity and their work in schools of education. This process was replicated for each case, followed by cross-case analysis to further my understanding of the ways in which these particular themes manifest across participants at varying points in their careers at unlike institutions of higher education.

A conversation was constructed using the words of three study participants by adapting Miles, Huberman, and Saldaña's (2014) poetic display of qualitative data. Miles et al. encourage the use of a range of literary devices to display data when neither summary nor matrix will bring the reader close enough to the data to fully grasp its meaning. I realized that in order to make meaning of the shared phenomenon of "teaching while queer" thematic presentation of the interview data would immediately bring the reader proximate to the participants. The participants' words are presented verbatim from the interview transcripts; I have excerpted from each interview and arranged the text to facilitate interaction between the participants. More than just presenting the participants' words organized in themes, I wanted to highlight the ways in which the participants' experiences are simultaneously similar and yet so very different. Each participant who joins the conversation has distinctly different experiences, yet as the conversation develops, there are multiple instances in which their voices dovetail. It is in these moments that the use of a conversation is at its most powerful.

THE CONVERSATION

As the author I act as moderator and host to this conversation, using my voice to frame questions and interactions. A single letter refers to each participant and only descriptive characteristics of participants and their institutions are provided in order to maintain confidentiality. In the conversation an initial that is not associated with her or his name refers to each participant. Participating in this study and conversation are: "B," a gay male at a small private liberal arts college in New England; "I," a lesbian at a private university in the Mid-Atlantic region; and "M" a gay male at a large public university in the Southeastern United States. My contributions are designated "A" for the author. We begin the conversation with introductions.

A: Welcome to the conversation. Please begin by sharing where you are in your academic career at your current institution.

B: I'm a second year Tenure Track Assistant professor. I've been at this institution since fall of 2015.

M: I will go up for tenure in the next academic year, not this upcoming year but the following academic year.

I: I've been at my institution since 1991 and I am full professor at this point and this is my 27th year here. I came here ABD, right out of grad school.

A: What types of messages, both explicit and implicit, does your institution put forth with respect to inclusion for the queer community?

M: The grand rhetoric that they are starting to put out more of is broad. There is a list of things we are being inclusive of and we as faculty have been successful in saying although inclusion and diversity can mean anything, right? But in terms of queer specific things.... There's not a lot. I'm just trying to think about.... We have institutional data on who is Black, who is White, who is Asian—the six federal race categories. But counting people who are LGBTQ is a harder thing. Which I think leads to some invisibility of the issue

I: There used to be that thing where if we all turned purple on a day people would be surprised.

M: That being said, some of the university wide stuff how to support …. I mean everything they do is really problematic, I mean they brought Michael Sam (the guy who was in the NFL briefly) on campus to speak. Which is fine. I'm not sure I find that to be a meaningful intervention. It's something. There was a memorial thing on the anniversary of the Pulse shooting. We have a pretty active GSA here.

I: I think the college has gotten clearer about its explicit messages. So including partners was not something that was in the paperwork in the beginning. It emerged four or five years after I got here, a couple of other colleagues that came at the same time who were gay we all started, 'What about the partner policy? What about insurance?' And I think that's when things started to explicitly change.

B: The university where I teach is a little bit more socially conservative I would say, compared to the rest of the region, but maybe not the rest of the country.

A: What about the implicit messages around inclusivity for the queer community?

B: And so in terms of implicit messages— here is something that was brought up that perhaps reveals some of the implicit messages about LGBT topics. There is another out gay male faculty member, who about two years ago was adopting a child and had a lot of issues about getting time off to welcome the child in and get MLA type of considerations and the topic is still a little unclear as to whether or not that should be included and his position was that it should be included and it can be used as a benefit to recruit more highly qualified faculty period and LGBT faculty as well.

I: I don't know that the implicit messages have changed. I think inclusively was fairly open and fairly positive, but I think that has something to do with those of us who were initially here and our personalities.

Each of you shared in your interview that you are out with your university colleagues. What does that look like?

A: Each of you shared in your interview that you are out with your university colleagues. What does that look like?

M: For example if we have a department off campus or social thing, I'm really insistent that my husband is coming. If you're going to bring your husband and you are a woman, okay he's coming. I'm pretty open about, if you're inviting me to something, you're inviting both of us.

B: I'm the only out faculty member of my department of three and we are always talking about what we are doing over the weekends and home life and its kind of like, because we are small, we are all working in parallel too. In terms of where I get my sense of community in terms of belonging to a gay community? I would say that it's not necessarily being fulfilled here, within the university, but I get it in other areas through my home life and also my husband.

M: I know we have faculty in this college who are queer but are not out. And there are various gradations of outness, but I am by far the most assertively out in our college. I mean far and away. Other people you sort of know, but its not, its an open secret in a sense. We are all aware, but no one is going to mention it. In terms of faculty and staff, I would say I am aggressively out.

A: It seems that partners or spouses play significant roles in each person's queer visibility.

I: As a little baby dyke, I never thought I would get married, I never thought that those kind of things were open to me. So I do think that the more it came into the public discussion, the more comfortable I got. And also the more responsible I felt. So now, if it is in the public discussion, I want to weigh in.

A: With rights come responsibilities? And M, you speak to a level of responsibility with respect to your queer identity as well.

M: Part of that is for me I recognize that as a productive scholar with good teaching evaluations, so that as somebody who can push for it, it's got to be me. I can't wait for a disabled queer scholar of color to come along to have to do all that labor. So in a way, I feel that being aggressively out is my way of saying—I don't think there is anything you can say about me professionally. If you do try to do some sort of nonsense, it would be pretty clear that it is personal.

A: How does each of your sexual identity intersect with being an academic?

M: There will be a student who will come along and I will need a defense. This is going to happen at some point. I am sure of it. And so this is a degree of effort for people who aren't visibly out or marginalized in some other way don't have to think about how to develop their defenses. Which leads to some pedagogical choices that are problematic too.

B: Through talking with you about this, I'm reflecting a bit on the ways I'd still like to grow in being a first and second year faculty member—there are still professional vulnerabilities that could limit some things I suppose ... but once you are tenured, you have more carte blanch to go in even more areas. I guess the course evaluations do bring it back to the front and center.

I: The truth is, I still have—the first time I say it, in a "casual coming out" a physical reaction—a very slight—my heartbeat goes up, or something. Which is funny, because, I'm a full professor, I'm tenured, there's really nothing....

M: I almost feel like my workload obligation is 48% teaching 35% research 9% outreach 8% service. I feel like you need to trim some points off that and put in a 5% self-defense allocation.

A: I am going to shift the conversation towards outness and teaching. In what ways do you make your sexual identity visible to your students?

B: There's not necessarily a moment I can pinpoint where it's like, I out myself to my students. It's not that kind of a thing, but I'm not, not out.

I: I think in the beginning I did not really come out. And then I started to come out to my classes and to also have conversations with them about the subtle ways in which straight people can come out all the time.

M: I'm sure I've never said in a classroom that I'm gay. I'm sure of that. But I'm also pretty sure that they all know.

B: When we are talking about what we do in relationship building, I talk about my husband, walking the dogs, normalizing what my life is outside of my work through normalizing what my life is outside of my work through modeling that and through being there. That's how we get to know one another and so for me, there's not really a sense of closing off that aspect of my story, being out in that regard, without naming it, you know, "I am gay." It's through my own narratives and stories I share with the students.

I: Sometime in the first or second class I just mention that I have a wife, and I'm usually talking about some interaction thing. Casual coming out is a good way to put it.

M: I've given thought to maybe I should be more intentional saying something about it. But I don't know. I think that my sense is that they are all well aware. Both through that when I'll tell a story, I don't shield pronouns. I also think that a lot of them figure it out through context clues too.

A: How has this played out with students? Do you get backlash?

B: It is a very political thing, so just making it not political. When I do that, I'm not looking for feedback or validation one way or another. It's just this is where I'm at this is what I do. Not looking to read too much into my students' reactions one-way or another when I do that.

M: Not to my face, anyway. I don't know what they are saying to their other faculty or to other students. But my classes keep filling and there are other people who are teaching the same classes, so it can't be that.

I: I felt maybe 15 years ago, 18 years ago, maybe 10 years ago, before legality started. I always felt there was a little silence in the room, a little collective inhalation of breath. Now I feel like nobody really cares. I rarely see a student reaction to that news as being particularly upsetting to them or surprising.

A: Do you experience different reactions based on student population, perhaps undergraduates and graduate students?

M: I only teach graduate students who tend to be a little bit older, hopefully more mature, although that doesn't always go together. Our graduate students are also hugely more diverse than our undergraduate students.

I: Early on I think I would have said that I was more comfortable and coming out and talking about it with graduate students. Partly because they are already adults, legally and fully and partly because they have more experience. Now, it's interesting I tend to hit more conservative students in the graduate program than the undergraduate program.

M: My colleagues who teach undergraduate classes, especially I have two colleagues who teach social foundations courses for undergraduates, and I think they get huge amounts of pushback on talking about queer issues.

I: I feel like our undergrads are sort-of—we were talking and they were talking about they are asexual and they are a-romantic and that they are hetero-romantic, but asexual and there all these things and I was like, as a lesbian I am so boring. My sexuality is like old-fashioned, I guess. I think in some ways they are sort-of past us, or certainly past a 61-year-old lesbian.

A: Does the visibility of your sexual identity specifically connect to working in a school of education? Is being out for a professor of education different then for a professor in a math department (for example)?

I: I take very seriously that our students are going to go out and interact with real people. Real little people. Children or adolescents and a bad teacher can do so much damage.

M: I think part of it is just having to be okay just talking to someone who is comfortable being queer identified, be okay taking direction from someone who is queer identified, or respecting their authority on something.

B: I don't know how to quantify it but, so much of teaching is relational, you can't be a well-rounded person, let alone educator, if you are not owning all aspects of your story. That's how we get to know one another and so for me, there's not really a sense of closing off that aspect of my story, being out in that regard, without naming it, you know, "I am gay" it's through my own narratives and stories I share with the students with the hopes that they do that later on down the road with their students to the extent that they are comfortable and can.

I: I think pushing them to make sure they can interact respectfully and supportively with persons who differ from them, I think really matters. I've also had some students struggle with the intersection between their religious beliefs and the people that they know or that they see.

B: I could see some of the more conservative students engaging in non-verbals that were showing they were uncomfortable or it was challenging, so the bottom line that I came to (this is an area where I still want to grow) is that at the end of the day we are serving communities and this will be coming into schools and these are important discussions to be had and so we need to model ethics and civility of inclusivity, no matter how we may feel personally, we need to separate.

I: I remember one time a student said to me, basically you are the first lesbian I've ever really known and basically you're not as bad as I thought you would be. Which I remember thinking, how bad was I? I was hoping for, "you are pretty good." I think her perspective was so demonized that she was expecting something from me that was totally beyond my personality.

M: I think that is important when preparing people to go back into schools to respect other, that's part of how this ideological foundation happens, they learn that there's only certain ways of knowing and being those are the ones that are valid, other ones are dismissible. And so interacting with faculty who have other ways of knowing and being and representing knowledge is really important, even just in trying to respect and deal with.

B: My bottom line is that as public school educators, my students are preparing to be public school educators, we have to be inclusive—we don't get to handpick who is in our classrooms.

M: I think that we should be trying to have classrooms that have current or future teacher educators in them that are modeling in some sense what we hope they will build when they practice, or when they go back to practice.

B: I feel like that our success is interwoven with their success, that when we look to see how we are doing within education as teacher educators, we don't really look to see what we did as much as how it was brought back to us, do you know what I am saying? I don't know how to pin point it, but I don't really look to see ... I can see how that is unique, because in other faculty it is more like what did I do today, did I deliver this, was the message. I can see there is a different way of thinking about it. Success is maybe in different measures.

I: I want to talk to my students about how we are just like everyone else. I want to prepare them.

A: I am wondering, do you ever share that experience with your students? The tensions that persons who are gay or lesbian feel walking that line between when we can or can't be out, and what we can or can't say because there could be consequences?

M: I don't think I'm alone is this, is that as a visible queer person that I need to be careful about how much I talk about queer issues. Particularly because I'm not teaching queer issues courses and to not appear ideologically or personally driven or biased is what they will say, right?

B: One thing that did get brought up with LGBT topics is in my class is that I want my students to be aware of the politics of their community as first year teachers that may be vulnerable.

I: I don't usually, but I think I will. I think it is an important thing for straight people or people who fit into a homogenous culture to talk about because I don't think people actually know the low level of fear or anxiety that can sit in being different. And being secretive about being different.

REFLECTING ON THE CONVERSATION

Each participant comes from very dissimilar institutions both in structure and in sociopolitical landscape. Within these different structures, each participant makes their sexual identity visible to colleagues and students in different ways. What unifies the participants is that each person believes it is crucial for faculty working with current and future teachers to bring queerness into the college classroom.

Modeling Queer, Just Not Too Queer

Being out is seen as an obligation to the greater good. The voices in chorus suggest that teacher educators have an obligation to make their queer identity visible, not directly for the sake of their college students, but for the sake of the public school students their students in turn will teach. It is this ripple effect into K–12 classrooms that is of greatest concern. In order for K–12 teachers to build classrooms that are inclusive to gay and lesbian and bisexual students, university faculty must put queer front and center. As M said, "I think part of it is just having to be okay just talking to someone who is comfortable being queer identified" (interview, 2017). This idea that outness will eventually lead to inclusion lines up with Allport's (1954) theory that extended contact with familiar persons can lead to the reduction of prejudice.

Reducing homophobia and shifting teachers from an overly heteronormative orientation in the college classroom is not enough. Participants I and B are more deeply embedded in the comprehensive work of teacher preparation and both put an emphasis on modeling normality. With their students, they both intentionally blur the lines between their personal and professional lives, wanting to show students just how normal queers can be. There is an unspoken pressure to be just queer enough that contact will have the desired effect, but not too queer to scare anyone off. Our identity as queer persons is directly connected with the learning of classroom teachers, who in turn facilitate the learning of hundreds of K–12 students. It is a ripple effect of learning. And contact with queers is essential.

MOVING FORWARD

This conversation is part of an ongoing study that looks to give voice to a larger group of lesbian, gay and queer identified faculty working in socio-politically diverse schools of education. Further work will consider the experiences of faculty working in the Southwest and Pacific Northwest. In future phases of this study additional aspects such as: faculty who work in the field with preservice teachers; faculty who are not out to their students; and the relationship between the personal and professional will be explored.

Twenty-nine years after Harvey Milk led the defeat of Proposition Six, queer educators stand at an interesting juncture. We can marry on Sunday and still be fired on Monday. Publicly promoted proposition witch-hunts are less public and less supported. Replacing the forced closeting for faculty can be the repression exerted by the overly heteronormative world of teacher preparation (Rosick, 2016).

The work of 'teaching while queer' can be simultaneously empowering and terrifying, fortifying and isolating. Each semester the cycle starts again, new syllabus, new students, coming out again, the start of a new teaching and learning progression. For queer faculty in schools of education, their marginalized sexual identity is part of the learning ripple effect, extending from the university classroom into K–12 schools. By giving voice to the complexities of this experience we can challenge assumptions that there is a certain way to "teach while queer" and to build a conversation on the specific experiences of gay, lesbian, and queer faculty working to prepare future teachers.

REFERENCES

Allport, G. W. (1954). *The nature of prejudice.* Cambridge, MA: Perseus.

Anderson, K. J., & Kanner, M. (2011). Inventing a gay agenda: Students' perceptions of lesbian and gay professors. *Journal of Applied Social Psychology, 6*(41), 1538–1564.

Blumenfeld, W. J., Weber, G. N., & Rankin, S. (2016). In our own voice: Campus climate as a mediating factor in the persistence of LGBT students, faculty and higher staff in higher education. In P. Chamness Miller & E. Mikulec (Eds.), *Queering classrooms: Personal narratives and educational practices to support LGBTQ youth in schools.* Charlotte, NC: Information Age Publishing. Retrieved from https://www.academia.edu/23713223/In_Our_Own_Voice_Campus_Climate_as_a_Mediating_Factor_in_the_Persistence_of_LGBT_People_in_Higher_Education

Cresswell, J. W. (2007). *Qualitative inquiry and research design: Choosing among five approaches.* Thousand Oaks, CA: SAGE.

DeJean, W. (2007). We are the development we are looking for: Queer people and schooling. *Journal of Curriculum and Pedagogy, 4*(2), 58–62.

Douglass, B. J. (2016). Faculty trainings. In N. M. Rodriguez, W. J. Martino, J. C. Ingrey, & E. Brockenbrough (Eds.), *Critical concepts in queer studies and education* (pp. 87–94). New York, NY: Palgrave Macmillan.

Freire, P. (2000). *Pedagogy of the oppressed* (30th Anniversary edition). New York, NY: Bloomsbury. (Originally published 1970)

Hermann-Wilmarth, J. M., & Bills, P. (2010). Identity shifts: Queering teacher education research. *The Teacher Educator, 45*(4), 257–272.

Hill, R. J. (2009). Incorporating queers: Blowback, backlash, and other forms of resistance to workplace diversity initiatives that support sexual minorities. *Advances in Developing Human Resources, 11*(1), 37–53.

hooks, B. (1994). *Teaching to transgress.* New York, NY: Routledge.

Hynes, W. (2012). Class outing. *Teaching Tolerance, 41,* 54–57.

Loughran, J. (2013). *Developing a pedagogy of teacher education: Understanding teaching & learning about teaching.* New York, NY: Routledge.

Miles, M., Huberman, A. M., & Saldaña, J. (2014). *Qualitative data analysis: A methods sourcebook.* Los Angeles, CA: SAGE.

Milk, H. (1978). That is what America is … speech at San Francisco Gay Freedom Day. Retrieved from https://friendsofharvey.wordpress.com/2015/11/27/remembering-harveymilk-1978-san-francisco-gay-freedom-rally-speech-in-full/

Padilla-Diaz, M. (2015). Phenomenology in educational qualitative research: Philosophy as science or philosophical science? *International Journal of Educational Excellence, 1*(2), 101–110.

Renn, K. A. (2010). LGBT and Queer research in higher education: The state and status of the Field. *Educational Researcher, 39*(2), 132–141.

Rosiek, J. (2016). Visibilty. In M. Rodriguez, W.J. Martino, J. C. Ingrey, & E. Brockenbrough (Eds.), *Critical concepts in queer studies and education: An international guide for the twenty-first century* (pp. 453–461). New York, NY: Palgrave Macmillan.

Saldaña, J. (2009). *The coding manual for qualitative researchers.* Los Angeles, CA: SAGE.

Sapp, J. (2001). Self-knowing as social justice: The impact of a gay professor on ending homophobia in education. *ENCOUNTER: Education for Meaning and Social Justice, 14*(4), 17–28.

Turner, S. L. (2010). Undressing as normal: The impact of coming out in class. *The Teacher Educator, 45*(4), 287–300.

Wilkinson, S., & Kitzinger, C. (2013). Representing our own experience: Issues in "insider" research. *Psychology of Women Quarterly, 37*(2), 251–255.

Whisman, V. (2002). Coming out. In G. Z. B. Haggerty (Ed.), *Encyclopedia of Lesbian and Gay Histories and Cultures* (pp. 186–190). New York, NY: Taylor and Francis.

CHAPTER 12

BECOMING LEARNER-CENTERED

A Constellation of Identity, Reflection, and Motivation

Emilie Clucas Leaderman
Santa Clara University

RESEARCHER'S CONNECTION AND CONTEXT OF STUDY

In concentrating on the stories of learner-centered faculty, I have realized that support for faculty should be provided in ways that meet their needs. As faculty participants at a private liberal arts college shared their intentions for student learning, empowerment, and success, I, as an instructor new to teaching, identified with their narratives. In the process of teaching, I begin with the best intentions but often forget that I am learning too.

From the participants of this study, I learned that teaching growth occurs in isolation as faculty experience similar challenges, changes, and triumphs. In my judgment, this is unnecessary. It is my hope that by reading personal accounts of learner-centered faculty growth, educators will recognize themselves, the similarities among their teaching paths, and the opportunities for future learning and connection. This chapter focuses

Identity and Lifelong Learning in Higher Education, pp. 213–230
Copyright © 2020 by Information Age Publishing
213

on two findings that describe identity, reflection, and the motivational journeys of six learner-centered faculty, both full-time and part-time, who teach undergraduate and graduate students at a private liberal arts college.

In conducting this study, I wanted to learn from experienced educators how they became successful in their learner-centered approach and what helped them continue to teach this way. Taking on this topic came from my desire to be a transformative teacher and feeling inadequate. As an educator, success for me has meant creating an environment where students are empowered in their learning. I am personally and professionally inspired by the learner-centered faculty in this study. As a higher education practitioner interested in faculty development, I am in awe of their commitment to student learning. These faculty embody 21st century leadership in higher education in describing the multidimensional ways that students motivate their teaching. Their narratives of teaching growth validate that learner-centered teaching is both meaningful and worthwhile.

Through this research, I came to appreciate the faculty learner-centered learning process as difficult, nonlinear, and complex. The faculty participants in this study have tremendous passion and dedication as lifelong learners who take their teaching identity seriously. By their report, it is evident that they continuously integrate their personal and professional identities into their role as college teachers. As these faculty describe their learning experiences, I believe there is still much to discover about faculty learning identity and faculty voice in higher education. The two primary research questions that drove this study were: (1) what motivates learner-centered faculty at a private liberal arts college to develop and sustain their teaching? (2) what institutional factors do faculty perceive as supporting them in sustaining learner-centered teaching? For the purposes of this chapter, I will focus on the findings specific to faculty identity and lifelong learning.

HIGHER EDUCATION LITERATURE

Higher education stakeholders suggest that radical changes are needed in college teaching to address deficiencies in student learning and ultimately promote students' higher achievement of essential student learning outcomes. Accrediting bodies and higher education organizations have urged colleges and universities to reshape the traditional paradigm of teaching and learning towards a learner-centered approach (American Association for Colleges and Universities, 2002; Eckel, Green, & Hill, 2001; Wingspread, 1993). Similarly, scholars maintain that traditional methods of college teaching must change to improve the quality of student learning (Barr & Tagg, 1995; Boyer, 1990; Kuh, 2008). Moreover, in preparing undergraduate students for the 21st century workplace, employers and economic organizations support the need for higher education teaching to adapt (Hart Research Associates, 2013; Hénard & Roseveare, 2012; Spellings, 2006). Learner-centered teaching has been identified as one approach in creating a dynamic learning environment.

Learner-centered teaching prioritizes the learning needs of students by its design. Compared to traditional modes of teaching such as lecture, learner-centered teaching explains five key changes to instructional practice: (1) power is balanced between student and professor, (2) decisions about course content are made mutually, (3) the role of the faculty member is a facilitator (versus expert), (4) students are responsible for their own learning, and (5) the processes of assessment are focused on responding to summative and formative data, with the purpose of informing teaching decisions (Weimer, 2002, 2013). In addition, learner-centered teaching facilitates complex cognitive learning: students are empowered as active participants, receiving frequent feedback from faculty and peers through discussion and collaboration. Learner-centered instruction has been identified as an effective multimodal approach in engaging students in learning (Freeman et al., 2014; Kuh, 2008; Wohlfarth et al., 2008).

Research suggests that faculty who already use a learner-centered teaching approach have a different mindset about knowledge and the learning process (Åkerlind, 2007; Feldman, 2000; Kember, 1997; Kember & Kwan, 2000; McKenzie, 2003). Literature in the faculty development field asserts that instructors ready to implement new types of teaching benefit from the support of faculty developers and these efforts are most effective when faculty are involved, and their preferences are considered (Sorcinelli, 2002). In this study, it was essential to consult with learner-centered faculty directly to uncover what has shaped their mindset about teaching. From paying attention to faculty experiences, I learned that leaders in higher education will benefit from understanding what will be supportive for faculty learning and growth.

This study can provide higher education practitioners and educators with an experiential lens to help us understand how individual faculty have developed their teaching as learner-centered. Research suggests that faculty development will continue to be essential in changing the institutional culture to promote learning (Sorcinelli & Austin, 2010). As connections have recently been demonstrated between well-designed faculty development initiatives and student learning (Condon, Iverson, Mandora, Rutz, & Willett, 2016), it is critical that assumptions are not made about what faculty need (Diaz et al., 2009). By investigating the needs of learner-centered faculty and hearing their voices through research, this study provides a practical lens for higher education administrators who want to improve the quality of learning, and for educators who aspire to be learner-centered.

STUDY

Methodologically speaking, this study is grounded in the social constructivist paradigm (Lincoln & Guba, 1985, 2000) using qualitative case study to highlight and interpret the significance of faculty experiences (Denzin & Lincoln, 2008; Merriam, 2009). To better understand the motivational and institutional factors that influenced their learner-centered teaching commitment, I have chosen to include rich descriptions of faculty learning and growth in their own words.

To identify participants who were already learner-centered, I asked students to help. Since students play an important role in decision making in a learner-centered environment, I saw them as an essential part of identifying faculty participants for this study. Students at one private liberal arts college voluntarily completed an anonymous screening tool with five domains of learner-centered teaching, listing faculty they knew who exhibited these teaching behaviors. I adapted the five domains from Weimer's (2002) definition and Blumberg's (2009) expanded definition, to help frame the teaching behaviors in terms that students could easily understand and identify. Thirty-one students identified 81 faculty names from fifteen disciplines. Following identification of the faculty pool, I e-mailed 30 of these faculty, two from each discipline, using purposeful selection based on faculty characteristics. Six of the faculty who were nominated by students responded to an e-mail invitation and were recruited to participate in this study. Four of the participants were full-time and two were part-time/adjunct faculty. Two of the faculty interviewees have previously taught online and all six currently teach face to face undergraduate courses. Three of the faculty have been teaching for over 10 years. Each of the six faculty participants was from a different academic discipline: English, education, communication, criminal justice, nursing, and foreign language. The number of learner-centered domains identified by students ranged from two to five and the number of students who identified each faculty as learner-centered ranged from one to five.

Once faculty members were recruited from the learner-centered pool identified by students, data collection consisted of semistructured interview questions, document review, and reflexive journaling. My goal for the faculty interviews was to: (a) understand what motivational experiences influenced the development of their teaching as learner-centered and (b) to gain insight into how the institution supported faculty in sustaining this teaching commitment. Three documents were selected for review based on their potential to demonstrate evidence supporting learner-centered teaching at the college (mission statement, strategic plan, and academic priorities and undertakings). During data collection and analysis, I frequently journaled about my identity as a part-time faculty member and how my perspective was influencing the development of qualitative codes. I analyzed the data using an iterative process of looking both within and across participant transcripts and institutional documents. I used in vivo codes to respect participants' own words. Approximately 50 codes and 100 subcodes emerged and eventually combined into four main themes. Themes and patterns were then reduced further to answer both research questions. I have included two of the four findings that resulted from the original study (Clucas, 2016).

FINDINGS

The findings from this study provide a window into the learning experiences of learner-centered faculty. Faculty participants were passionate about keeping students at the forefront of their work as they discussed their teaching and enthusiastically shared: what motivates them as a learner-centered teacher; what matters in student learning, what they value in their classes, and what drives them to continue to grow and change. These faculty highlighted the meaningful ways they learn from students. In addition, participants spoke about the influence of personal and professional identity experiences on their teaching.

Learning From Students

Faculty participants identified strategies that motivate them to continue learning about their teaching: learning from student engagement and having an openness to student feedback. Faculty revealed that this type of learning helps them to strengthen their overall learner-centered teaching commitment. One participant, Cameron, shared learning from his students about what excites them in the learning process. As an example, he described enthusiasm from his students when he incorporated online discussion into his course, using tweet chats on Twitter and the discussion board feature on Blackboard (an online learning management system). In online environments that were familiar to them, students were participating more frequently and interacting in a deeper way than they had previously. This participant emphasized his reason for using social media: the value of engaging students at a comfortable level.

Similarly, participants described that a major aspect of how they learn from students includes meeting them where they are, to increase their engagement. Following her experimentation with using current music and song lyrics, Denise describes the student reaction in her course,

> How I knew it was successful is because more hands were going up, people
> that normally hadn't talked. One day, a student was walking by. He comes
> flying in the class and he goes, "Why are you playing that song? I love that
> song." I thought, Oh, maybe this is a good technique.

As Denise demonstrates, one way that faculty gauge and evaluate the effectiveness of their teaching practice is through trying out strategies that build excitement for learning and encourage students to collaborate with each other. As faculty see their students' engagement levels increase during learning activities, this success motivates them to continue to take risks in their teaching by involving students in new ways. Participants noted that increased engagement levels are not only indicative of student learning, but also of their own learning as a learner-centered teacher.

Faculty identified the importance of understanding students' perspectives as they progress in their learning as an incentive for reorganizing and improving their courses. All six faculty who were interviewed spoke about a firm obligation to assess student learning as an ongoing conversation, demonstrated by their explanations of how they continuously seek both formal and informal feedback from students at several points during the course and beyond. Participants noticed that sharing this feedback and decision making with students is an essential part of their learning, in that it informs faculty to make changes to their syllabi throughout the semester. This openness to course redesign based on student feedback was described by one participant, Betty, in tailoring the content and structure of her course syllabus based on the group's learning needs, "Every semester … I just do things differently. You have to. It's purposeful and intentional.... The student is in the center of the planning, not the content." As seen in this quotation, prioritizing student feedback not only influences course design, it propels faculty learning.

Similarly, Denise described the importance of collecting midsemester feedback and giving her own end-of-semester course evaluation where students write in their ideas about how the course can be improved. She states,

> I look to what the students, what the strengths of the course were, what
> they thought and then I look at what they think can be changed.... The
> other thing I do ask … is what can *they* do to make the course better."

From this perspective, Denise demonstrates the significance of sharing power and responsibility for learning with her students. Participants revealed that engaging students' voices is not only vital for course improvement but also for faculty learning.

Several participants emphasized their learning to include involving students in course changes and decisions through sharing course feedback with their classes and encouraging this type of dialogue informally throughout the semester. Based on reports from faculty participants, feedback from students appears to reinforce flexibility in keeping syllabi as works-in-process, redesigning their courses, and by having an openness to making significant course changes in the future. Denise summarized this process best when she shared, "Isn't that a piece of being learning centered? The role that the students play, I mean yes we have our list of expertise and experience but *they* [students] play an important part in this." As faculty learn what works, where students are having difficulty, and where students need more support and instruction, they adapt their courses accordingly. Paying attention to engagement levels and including students in course decisions continues to motivate and challenge faculty in their learning.

To visualize how the learner-centered faculty in this study described their learning from students, Figure 12.1 is included below. The color in the graphic lightens gradually (left to right) to represent the deep commitment and progression of faculty learning from their students. As faculty participants paid attention to engagement levels and enthusiasm for student learning in their courses, they reported having a greater openness to student feedback and intentionally involved students in course decision making. This type of flexibility in course design both sparked and fueled their teaching. As they noticed increased excitement during learning activities and solicited frequent student feedback, it gave them confidence to take new risks in their teaching and influenced the design and redesign of their courses going forward. As reported by participants, each of these components appears to reinforce and complement one another in faculty learning.

Reflection and Identity

All six faculty participants identified a combination of mentors and life experiences as having a significant role in helping them make sense of their learner-centered teaching identity. These faculty spoke about forming a strong connection with individuals in their professional lives, such as supervisors or colleagues who embodied good teaching. Faculty indicated the power of mentoring as going beyond feedback, prompting self-reflection on their role in the teaching-learning process, and ultimately facilitating their growth as a learner-centered teacher. One learner-centered faculty member, Betty shares the influence of meeting with her mentor to discuss teaching, "That reflective piece is so important. Someone has got to help you make sense of it all, otherwise it's *nothing*. I realized that's what I'm doing here.... I'm trying to help people make sense of it all." This faculty member demonstrates the reciprocal nature of developing as a learner-

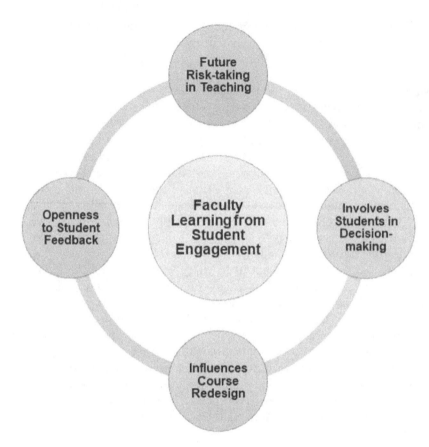

Figure 12.1.   Faculty learning from student engagement.

centered teacher; as she was guided by her mentor, she too is guiding her students to practice contemplation in their process of learning. Reflecting on the benefits of this approach for her students reinforced her teaching growth.

Several participants emphasized that reflecting with professional colleagues shapes their understanding of their teaching approach and validates what learning is. In referencing her connection with her mentors, Evelyn states, "To be able to look back and think, 'What did I do? What could I have done? What would I do different in the future?' That's the situated cognition that we try to teach students." Likewise, faculty in the current study explained that meaningful reflection on teaching involves examining their beliefs and core values about the purpose of teaching. By engaging with fellow faculty and individuals whom they respect to think deeply about teaching, it helps them understand how their current actions as an educator fit into their aspirational models. Eventually this type of reflection allows faculty to identify discrepancies in their teaching, make changes, and refine their learner-centered practice further.

Faculty participants in this study also highlighted the power of reflecting on their personal identity and professional experiences as essential in how they learn as educators. For instance, Annabelle spoke about the impact teaching incarcerated individuals has on teaching undergraduate students. She described how this professional role compelled her to ensure that college students have a voice in their classroom. To help them find their unique writing style, students in Annabelle's class individually identify areas in their writing that need improvement first, before she gives her suggestions. Students lead one-on-one conferences with her to share what they are working on, highlight their strengths, and navigate the direction of their writing. Annabelle explains her reasoning behind the activity further, "They [the students] have a lot to say ... even if they don't know that they do. It's my job to help them figure out what they need to say ... because it's their writing, it's not my writing." She describes her approach during the student conferences as careful listening and asking simple, probing questions to encourage students to own the perspectives and intentions embedded in their writing, which eventually prompts them to communicate more clearly than they have before. This faculty member emphasized the importance of empowering students to express their ideas by enabling them to first learn through their experiences. In turn, this piece of her professional identity validates and reaffirms her role as a learner-centered teacher.

Several faculty in the study described themselves as lifelong learners and later acknowledged that a major part of their teaching role is helping students establish their learning identity in their classroom. Betty shares, "yeah, I'm here to help them get a degree, but I think the most important aspect is ... It's personal. It's professional. It's personal growth. It's professional growth." This definition of the participant's own teaching identity influences her learning. Similarly, Annabelle expressed the importance of teaching undergraduate students about learning that happens outside the classroom and that gaining this self-awareness is essential for students' growth, "It's not just that you have a faculty member who is trying to get you to learn a particular subject, but that you're [students] there to be a learner ... about a lot of different things, and learning happens all the time." Annabelle later mentioned that she often has students identify current events articles to share with the class and stated that this activity joins her with students as learners. Having students share in this way informs her about their curiosity, what they find surprising, and helps them connect with each other on a deeper learning level as they think critically together about the larger implications of local and global events. In becoming learner-centered, faculty identities have a strong influence on their approach with their students, which compels them to continue to grow and change.

Faculty participants also attributed life experiences as having a major impression on how they make sense of their teaching values. These experiences influence their ability to reflect on how they work with students as partners in learning. Three participants elaborated on their experiences as parents and how this informs their teaching identity. Florence revealed her perspective in witnessing several of her children's negative educational experiences. In particular, she shared her disappointment with her sons' teachers and their educational philosophies,

> I've had a lot of experience vicariously, so that had had a big, big influence on how I teach because I listened to their complaining and I had to agree with a lot of the stuff that they didn't appreciate.

In seeing what was not effective as a parent, this faculty member was able to translate this experience into her teaching by choosing to know each of her students as individuals. Florence described intentionally using games to ask questions about her students' lives, developing a high level of respect among the students in her classes. Personal learning as a parent has influenced how she continues to learn from her students.

Similarly, another faculty member described that as she grieved the loss of a close friend, learner-centered teaching became an effective way to cope by channeling her energy into continuous improvement. Evelyn summarizes, "If you call having to recover from a friend's death inspiration, then that's what it is." In describing her interactions with students, it is evident that she views teaching as a serious endeavor; she is constantly looking for new strategies and ways to enhance her teaching. The personal experiences faculty bring into their teaching serve as an impetus for becoming better learner-centered teachers.

In essence, the identities of the learner-centered faculty in this study were defined by meaningful reflection (see Figure 12.2). All of these faculty enhanced their teaching identity through deep contemplation of the following: (1) discussions with colleagues or supervisors who embodied good teaching, (2) mentors who prompted self-reflection about their teaching role, and (3) personal experiences and professional identities. Models for good teaching inspired them to make sense of their teaching identity and carefully examine their core teaching values. Mentors encouraged them to develop a strong habit of self-reflection, comparing their decisions against their aspirational teaching models. Finally, their personal experiences and professional identities reinforced the roles they enact in their teaching and motivated them to continue to improve.

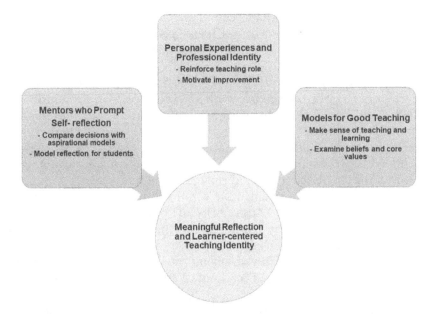

Figure 12.2.   Meaningful reflection and learner-centered teaching identity.

IMPLICATIONS AND RECOMMENDATIONS FOR PRACTICE

Student Involvement in Faculty Development

It is essential for higher education faculty and administrators to acknowledge the important contribution of students in faculty learning. In the current study, student-faculty relationships were powerful in inspiring faculty to make changes in their current practice and shape their working model of learner-centered teaching. A review of student-faculty partnership research in higher education reveals similar outcomes for both students and faculty: motivation and learning become enhanced; metacognitive awareness and an evolved identity develops; and the combination of both results in a heightened teaching and classroom experience (Cook-Sather, Bovill, & Felten, 2014). Student-faculty partnerships have also been cited as having a positive influence on faculty teaching relationships (Cook-Sather, 2008; Cox, 2001b), and faculty gain perspective from the advantage of giving focused feedback in their courses based on students' perception as learners (Sorenson, 2001).

Student-faculty partnerships seek to improve the teaching and learning process by highlighting the value of student voices, with student roles varying from teaching assistant, consultant, or fellow in a teaching and learning center. Key ingredients of these specific partnerships between teacher and student often include: (1) attitudes of bilateral respect, (2) reciprocal interactions, and (3) sharing responsibility for pedagogy (with students) and learning (with faculty) (Cook-Sather et al., 2014). Faculty developers suggest that giving students and faculty opportunities to connect with each other about teaching and learning provides mutual growth (Boye, Logan, & Tapp, 2011). Incorporating a student lens during and after a course ends provides faculty with new ways to design assignments and assessments, alternative forms of student interaction, and opportunities to make meaningful changes in their courses.

While partnership programs have continued to expand with promise in the United Kingdom and Australia for the past several decades, several models have emerged more recently in the United States. Both Brigham Young University and Miami University use the student-faculty partnership concept in their Student Consultants on Teaching program model to hire and train students in their teaching centers (Eliason & Nelson, 2019; Hodge, Nadler, Shore, & Taylor, 2011). Since 2005, faculty and academic development staff at Elon University have cooperated with students to implement several course design team (CDT) approaches that codevelop or revise an existing course syllabus, with several teams experiencing a moment when a student claims power in the process (Healey, Flint, & Harrigan, 2014). In their teaching and learning initiative, Bryn Mawr College developed a voluntary program that fosters continuous collaborative dialogue between faculty and student pedagogical consultants, Students as Learners and Teachers (SaLT). Action research conducted on the SaLT program concludes that faculty teaching evolved in substantial and enduring ways based on teaching practice insight gained from students through experimentation with student engagement tactics. Moreover, students are impacted by these experiences both directly and indirectly in their identity as learners: it deepens their course content understanding, builds their ownerships in the process of learning, and expands their future learning choices (Cook-Sather, 2010). These programs demonstrate the comprehensive value and impact of involving students in faculty learning.

Higher education administrators can initiate partnerships between students and faculty by first determining the level of interest among stakeholders at their institution. In their review of international research and current best practice, Higher Education Academy of the United Kingdom proposes a conceptual model for exploring ways to involve students as partners: in learning, teaching and assessment; subject-based research and inquiry, curriculum design and pedagogic consultancy; and scholarship of teaching and learning. These practitioners recommend that developing partnership learning communities can help guide practice and suggest further that critically engaging with some of the central themes identified in these communities: inclusivity, power relationships, and student and faculty identities- has the possibility for transformative learning (Healey et al., 2014). In taking first steps to implement partnerships between students and faculty, Cook-Sather and colleagues (2014) caution against taking on too much and making assumptions; and advocate for carefully considering diverse faculty and student roles, institutional culture, and context. Beyond the classroom, high-impact educational practices (Kuh, 2008) such as mentoring in undergraduate research or facilitating service learning, can also assist faculty with experiencing building mutuality with students using a partnership lens (Cook-Sather et al., 2014). With incentives, training, and encouragement, there are multiple ways that faculty can begin to voluntarily experiment with student partnerships, even on a small scale.

Fostering Social Learning Through Relationships and Meaningful Reflection

Faculty can benefit from collaborating with a peer or mentor who has experience with learner-centered teaching. In the current study, faculty reveal that through their relationships, stigma regarding talking about teaching improvement is reduced as educators share what matters most in student learning. Recognizing teaching as a true partnership involves social learning, a practice that has been considered effective at enhancing situated learning (Lave & Wenger, 1991), higher education teaching (Cox, 2001a), and community-level change (Chism, Lees, & Evenbeck, 2002). Higher education administrators can dedicate resources to increase collaboration and teaching partnerships among faculty, through offering grants for faculty learning communities or participation in mentoring. Mutual mentoring has been identified as a new model for creating networked partnerships between a variety of faculty, peers, staff, and students, even off-campus constituents, focusing on specific experiences or expertise, with partners having a reciprocal sense of agency and career development, and prioritizing individual preferences for contact (Yun, Baldi, & Sorcinelli, 2016; Yun & Sorcinelli, 2009). For faculty interested in taking an initial step towards mutual mentoring, they can: identify an area of interest, that is, a specific technology tool, or active learning strategy and ask a colleague for the name of someone they would recommend based on this area; find a colleague in a similar career stage; and identify potential internal and external partners beyond just faculty (National Education Association, 2009). Additionally, faculty developers can offer tools for critical reflection, such as Brookfield's (1995) reflective lenses in the design of their programs and services to provide structure in prompting faculty to think more deeply about their teaching and share these ideas with each other using a common language.

Integrating Personal and Professional Identities of Learner-Centered Teachers

As faculty continue to aspire towards a learner-centered approach, faculty can advocate for bringing their multiple lives into their teaching. O'Meara and Terosky (2010) assert that faculty learn based on how they see themselves and their identities, including: their definitions of their work (teaching, research, service, and outreach), the groups they interact with, and the context of their institution, suggesting that higher education institutions can enhance faculty growth through a focus on four factors: learning, agency, professional relationships, and commitments. Similarly, Neumann (2009) in her description of post-tenure faculty, refers to the importance of understanding the balance between scholarly learning (related to academic passions) with instrumental learning (necessary for service or administrative responsibilities) in how professors view themselves in their career and their work; a dichotomy that exists in prioritizing the amount of work that faculty produce. By intentionally focusing on the role of identity in faculty learning, faculty developers can enhance faculty growth in their teaching as learner-centered.

Faculty programs and services can incorporate personal and professional identities by first asking faculty to share experiences and commonalities with each other in informal ways. Some examples of integrating faculty identities could include creating forum opportunities online and in-person, hosting meal-time discussions in spaces designated for faculty, or providing multiple ways for faculty to connect in groups based on interests and commitments beyond their discipline. In implementing any of these initiatives, it is vital to have faculty identify and lead approaches that best fit their requisites for learning. Especially with the recent expansion of adjunct faculty, it is important that higher education administrators understand the multiple responsibilities and roles that faculty have outside of the institution and create flexible formats for community and support that reflect the diverse needs of faculty.

CONCLUSION

For institutions interested in moving towards a learner-centered paradigm of faculty development, administrators can benefit from reviewing their assumptions about traditional faculty roles. In addition to being researchers, teachers, and providing service to the institution, faculty have complex learning identities. Faculty interested in developing a learner-centered teaching commitment need opportunities to strengthen their learning. Faculty can develop an increased awareness of themselves and their identities as learners by monitoring levels of student engagement and enthusiasm during learning activities, incorporating student feedback through different forms of assessment and involvement in their course, and engaging in meaningful reflection with mentors or colleagues who embody good teaching. Faculty developers can help faculty foster mentoring relationships, facilitate partnerships with students in course design and collaboration, and encourage peer feedback on teaching with an emphasis on critical reflection. Administrators, such as deans and provosts can provide advocacy, funding, and incentives to formalize and promote an institutional culture of faculty learning. Teaching growth can be integrated with other parts of institutional change in higher education that prioritize learning. From this study, I have learned that at its core, success in learner-centered teaching emanates from faculty learning from students. Learner-centered teaching identities can be sustained when faculty have support from multiple communities that reflect their needs, both within and outside of the institution.

When I view myself as a learner instead of an expert, it inspires possibilities for exploration, deep reflection, and the ability to create teaching innovations. I can enhance my learner-centered approach by connecting with other faculty and asking them about their teaching values, personal and professional experiences, challenges, and success involving students in their courses. Together faculty can identify teaching strengths, better understand their commonalities, and figure out what they need to be effective learners.

REFERENCES

Åkerlind, G. S. (2007). Constraints on academics' potential as developing as a teacher. *Studies in Higher Education, 32*(1), 21–37. doi:10.1080/03075070601099416

American Association for Colleges and Universities (2002). *Greater expectations: A new vision for learning as a nation goes to college, National Panel Report*. Washington, DC: AAC&U. Retrieved from http://www.greaterexpectations.org/

Barr, R. B., & Tagg, J. (1995). From teaching to learning: A new paradigm for undergraduate education. *Change, 27*(6). Retrieved from http://www.maine.edu/pdf/BarrandTagg.pdf

Blumberg, P. (2009). *Developing learner-centered teaching: A practical guide for faculty*. San Francisco, CA: Jossey-Bass.

Boye, A., Logan, M. M., & Tapp, S. (2011). Learning from each other: Involving students in centers for teaching and learning. *Journal on Centers for Teaching and Learning, 3*, 65–82.

Boyer, E. L. (1990). *Scholarship reconsidered: Priorities of the professoriate.* Stanford, CA: The Carnegie Foundation for the Advancement of Teaching. Retrieved from https://depts.washington.edu/gs630/Spring/Boyer.pdf

Brookfield, S. (1995). *Becoming a critically reflective teacher.* San-Francisco, CA: Jossey-Bass.

Chism, N., Lees, N., & Evenbeck, S. (2002). Faculty development for teaching innovation. *Liberal Education, 88*(3), 34–41.

Clucas, E. J. (2016). *A constellation of faculty motivation, community, and culture: What it takes to build a learner-centered teaching commitment* (Doctoral dissertation). Retrieved from ProQuest Dissertations Publishing (10131630).

Condon, W., Iverson, E. R., Manduca, C. A., Rutz, C., & Willett, G. (2016). *Faculty development and student learning: Assessing the connections.* Bloomington, IN: Indiana University Press.

Cook-Sather, A. (2008). "What you get is looking in a mirror, only better": Inviting students to reflect (on) college teaching. *Reflective Practice, 9*(4), 473–483.

Cook-Sather, A. (2010, September). Students as learners and teachers: Taking responsibility, transforming education, and redefining accountability. *Curriculum Inquiry, 40*, 4.

Cook-Sather, A., Bovill, C., & Felten, P. (2014) *Engaging students as partners in teaching and learning: A guide for faculty.* San Francisco, CA: Jossey-Bass.

Cox, M. D. (2001a). Faculty learning communities: Change agents for transforming institutions into learning organizations. *To Improve the Academy, 19*, 69–83.

Cox, M. D. (2001b). Student-faculty partnerships to develop teaching and enhance learning. In J. E. Groccia, J. E. Miller, & M. S. Miller (Eds.), *Student-assisted teaching: A guide to faculty-student teamwork* (pp. 168–171). Bolton, MA: Anker.

Denzin, N. K., & Lincoln, Y. S. (2008). *Strategies of qualitative inquiry* (3rd ed.). Thousand Oaks, CA: SAGE.

Diaz, V., Garrett, P. B., Kinley, E. R., Moore, J. F., Schwartz, C. M., & Kohrman, P. (2009). Faculty development for the 21st century. *Educause Review, 44*(3), 46–55. Retrieved from https://net.educause.edu/ir/library/pdf/ERM0933.pdf

Eckel, P., Green, M., & Hill, B. (2001). *On Change V—Riding the waves of change: Insights from transforming institutions.* Washington, DC: American Council on Education, Center for Institutional and International Initiatives.

Eliason, S. C., & Nelson, K. M. (2019). Students Consulting on Teaching (SCOT): Moving toward a learning-centered paradigm. Retrieved from Brigham Young University: https://ctl.byu.edu/sites/default/files/moving_toward_a_learning-centered_paradigm.pdf

Feldman, A. (2000). Decision making in the practical domain: A model of practical conceptual change. *Science Education, 84*(5), 606–623.

Freeman, S., Eddy, S. L., McDonough, M., Smith, M. K., Okoroafor, N., Jordt, H., & Wenderoth, M. P. (2014). Active learning increases student performance in science, engineering, and mathematics. *PNAS, Proceedings of the National Academy of Sciences of the United States of America, 111*(23), 8410–8415. doi:10.1073/pnas.131903

Hart Research Associates (2013). *It takes more than a major: Employer priorities for college learning and student success. An online survey among employers conducted on behalf of the Association of American Colleges and Universities.* Washington, DC: Hart Research Associates. Retrieved from http://www.aacu.org/sites/default/files/files/LEAP/2013_EmployerSurvey.pdf

Healey, M., Flint, A., & Harrigan, K. (2014). *Engagement through partnership: Students as partners in learning and teaching in higher education.* York, UK: The Higher Education Academy. Retrieved from https://www.heacademy.ac.uk/system/files/resources/engagement_through_partnership.pdf

Hénard, F., & Roseveare, D. (2012). *Fostering quality teaching in higher education: Policies and practices, an IMHE guide for higher education institutions.* OECD: Institutional Management in Higher Education. Retrieved from http://www.oecd.org/edu/imhe/QT%20policies%20and%20practices.pdf

Hodge, D. C., Nadler, M. K., Shore, C., & Taylor, B. A. P. (2011) Institutionalizing large-scale curricular change: The top 25 project at Miami University. *Change, 43*(5), 28–35.

Kuh, G. D. (2008). *High-Impact Educational Practices: What they are, who has access to them, and why they matter.* Association for American Colleges and Universities. Retrieved from http://www.aacu.org/leap/hip.cfm

Kember, D. (1997) A reconceptualisation of the research into university academics' conceptions of teaching, *Learning and Instruction, 7,* 255–275.

Kember, D., & Kwan, K. (2000). Lecturers' approaches to teaching and their relationship to conceptions of good teaching. *Instructional Science, 28*(5/6), 469–490.

Lave, J., & Wenger, E. (1991). *Situated learning: Legitimate peripheral participation.* Cambridge, UK: University of Cambridge Press.

Lincoln, Y. S., & Guba, E. G. (1985). *Naturalistic inquiry.* Beverly Hills, CA: SAGE.

Lincoln, Y. S., & Guba, E. G. (2000). Paradigmatic controversies, contradictions, and emerging confluences. In N.K. Denzin & Y.S. Lincoln (Eds.), *Handbook of qualitative research* (2nd ed., pp. 163–188). Thousand Oaks, CA: SAGE.

McKenzie, J. (2003). *Variation and change in university teachers' ways of experiencing teaching.* (Unpublished doctoral dissertation). Sydney, Australia: University of Technology.

Merriam, S. B. (2009). *Qualitative research: A guide to design and implementation.* San Francisco, CA: John Wiley & Sons.

National Education Association Advocate Online. (2009, April). Mutual mentoring. Retrieved from http://www.nea.org/home/33677.htm

Neumann, A. (2009). *Professing to learn: Creating tenured lives and careers in the American research university.* Baltimore, MD: The Johns Hopkins University Press.

O'Meara, K., & Terosky, A. (2010). Engendering faculty professional growth. *Change, 42*(6), 44–51.

Sorenson, L. (2001). College teachers and student consultations: Collaborating about teaching and learning. In J. E. Groccia, J. E. Miller, & M. S. Miller (Eds.), *Student-assisted teaching: A guide to faculty-student teamwork* (pp. 179–186). Bolton, MA: Anker.

Sorcinelli, M. D. (2002). Ten principles of good practice in creating and sustaining teaching and learning centers. In K. H. Gillespie., L. R. Hilson, & E. C. Wadsworth, (Eds.), *A guide to faculty development: Practical advice, examples, and resources* (pp. 9–23). Bolton, MA: Anker.

Sorcinelli, M. D., & Austin, A. E. (2010). Educational developers: The multiple structures and influences that support our work. *New Directions for Teaching and Learning, 122,* 25–36. doi:10.1002/tl.395

Spellings, M. (2006). *A test of leadership: Charting the future of US higher education.* Washington, DC: Education Publications Center, US Department of Education.

Yun, J., Baldi, J. H., & Sorcinelli, M. D. (2016). Mutual mentoring for early-career and underrepresented faculty: Model, research, and practice. *Innovative Higher Education, 41*(5), 441–451. doi:10.1007/s10755-016-9359-6

Yun, J., & Sorcinelli, M. D. (2009). When mentoring is the medium: Lessons learned from a faculty development initiative. *To Improve the Academy, 27,* 365–384.

Weimer, M. (2002). *Learner-centered teaching: Five key changes to practice.* San Francisco, CA: Jossey-Bass.

Weimer, M. (2013). *Learner-centered teaching: Five key changes to practice* (2nd ed.). San Francisco, CA: Jossey-Bass.

Wingspread Group on Higher Education. (1993). *An American imperative: Higher expectations for higher education.* Racine, WI: The Johnson Foundation.

Wohlfarth D., Sheras, D., Bennett, J. L., Simon, B., Pimental, J. H., & Gabel, L. E. (2008). Student perceptions of learner-centered teaching. *InSight: A Journal of Scholarly Teaching, 3,* 67–74. Retrieved from http://files.eric.ed.gov/fulltext/EJ888411.pdf

CHAPTER 13

REFRAMING RESISTANCE

Understanding White Teachers in Multicultural Education Through the Course Identities Approach

Ellie Fitts Fulmer
Ithaca College

INTRODUCTION

Martin was particularly compelled by the Leonard Pitts (1999) article. Talkative and seemingly agitated, he shared with the rest of us—participants in a graduate education course on multicultural education, made up of five White students and myself, the White instructor—a depiction of his own upbringing: Italian parents who owned their own business in the medium-sized mid-Atlantic town where they had emigrated in the early portion of the last century. Martin's parents had recounted versions of the immigrant/bootstraps story to him over the years. Similar to the one the article discussed, Martin intoned, theirs was "the same old story" of White people looking to "justify their way of being ... their hard work" to explain their successes, when in reality, being White had a lot to do

Identity and Lifelong Learning in Higher Education, pp. 231–250
Copyright © 2020 by Information Age Publishing
All rights of reproduction in any form reserved.

with the opportunities offered them. Martin (all names and locations are pseudonyms) continued, as I noted in my field journal,

> He tells us it is difficult to grapple with "all the conditioning" he's had in his life as a White male and a member of the immigrant family to which he belongs, being "conditioned not to recognize" some of the issues about race in America that were revealed in the article we read for class that day. (fieldnotes, class session one)

In this moment, I reflected later that evening, Martin, a man in his early 40s who had been teaching for a decade, was working to recognize the existence of something that he, by his own estimation, had been conditioned over his lifetime not to see. I came to learn that this was not the first time that Martin had explicitly grappled with White privilege as it is tied up in the bootstraps story of his parents, but it was a keenly important moment to him in his racial development, as he explained to me in our subsequent conversations.

Yet, this positive moment of Martin's learning narrative was seemingly discordant with his participation at other points in the semester. Whereas this brief vignette seemed to demonstrate personal growth, there were other times Martin expressed something more complex and not so cleanly taxonomic. In fact, some of his utterances in class that semester were quite troubling, and I questioned, at times, his willingness to take up the course's more challenging material. As such, I found that it was not sufficient to depict Martin's overall participation in the course in a binary fashion: he didn't fit neatly onto either side of the "getting it" or "not getting it" calibration we instructors frequently use to understanding our students.

Through examining closely Martin's contributions and interactions over the semester, by adopting what I came to call a "course identities" approach, I learned to see Martin, and my other students, in an empathetic, more nuanced light that held potential for greater growth on the part of the learner as well as being equally transformative for myself. Indeed, "radical empathy" (Jordan & Schwartz, 2018) such as this has been shown to be an instrument of profound learning. The course identities framework urged me to reframe my assumptions of acceptance vs. resistance in students' engagement with course material and see the complexity involved in Martin's—and my other White students'—identities in the course. This chapter offers *course identities* as a new theory for unpacking binaries of resistance-or-engagement common to instructor interpretations of White students' engagement in courses on multicultural issues. The primary potential of the course identity framework is twofold: it can help us to complicate the picture of how White teachers learn about issues of race, privilege and systemic injustices, and more urgently, to articulate a new approach for teacher educators to help our White students unlearn the ways in which they have internalized and enacted racism in their personal and professional lives. This framework may be especially important in working with White teachers who we may deem close-minded, resistant, disinterested, passive, uninformed, or confused with relation to critical multiculturalism.

Drawn from a larger ethnographic study where, over the course of a 14-week semester, I examined the written and verbal responses of participants in a course on multicultural issues (Fulmer, 2012a), this chapter's significance resides in offering instructors alternatives to a resistance/compliance binary with consideration for lifelong learning processes. Elsewhere, I have examined more broadly the discourses of my students, as well as reflexive analysis of my own participation (Fulmer, 2010). Through that work, I came to see the urgency in stepping away from correctness paradigms (i.e., "getting it" or "not getting it") while students expressed and revised their own course identities. Similarly, I also came to see the potential for other teacher educators to analyze prominent features of students' course identities in the ways that I did. Through a process of teaching that included continuous reflection of my own assumptions, and recursively asking myself what my students were working *on* and *with* as they participated in my course as I sought narrative themes, I was able to see their contributions differently. I suggest that this process of systematically inquiring into students' course identities offers instructors a useful new tool. The course identities framework provides a method to reconceptualize student participation and reframe resistance by recognizing our students as lifelong learners.

Namely, course identities are constructed of the student's relationship with (1) the instructor, (2) others in the course, (3) course material, (4) the collection of discourse patterns and interactions over the semester, and (5) a student's own identity and personal history. Using a case study unit of analysis, grounded in practitioner inquiry (Cochran-Smith & Lytle, 2009; Lytle, 2006; Nichols & Cormack, 2017), this chapter extends the work of identity scholars whose contributions have drawn attention to transitional spaces (Dubouloy, 2004) where individuals (re)construct who they are, specifically in graduate school (Watson & Gammel, 2011). An instructor can cultivate a course identities approach by investigating a student's class contributions and demeanor across time, probing for themes, and comparing motifs to one another. Excogitating students' patterns in this way can help instructors understand students' responses to course topics, and respond accordingly, which is especially meaningful in the context of multicultural education classes.

Preparing educators for teaching in critical multicultural ways is an urgent need for multiple reasons. It is well known that the field of education is dominated by individuals who are overwhelmingly White, middleclass, monolingual, and female (Fox & Gay, 1995; Wiggins, Follo, & Eberly, 2007; Ingersoll, Merrill, & Stuckey, 2014), while student populations in the U.S. are increasingly diverse (Ingersoll et al., 2014). The racial, cultural, and social issues present in this cultural duality stem from the problems inherent within a White-dominant racialized society that sells a majority of its White citizenry on the notion of racial superiority (Kailin, 2002). Multicultural education, though, is not only urgent for White teachers of students of color and English language learners; it is additionally imperative for teachers of predominantly White student groups that likely represent home lives and communities possessing varying degrees of social capital and relationships to schooling (Grant & Sleeter, 2007), and who, it is likely, have not had consistent opportunities for their privilege to be questioned or brought to light (Derman-Sparks & Ramsey, 2011).

The construct of *course identities* emerges as a unique framework in reference to bounded aspects of identities expressed over a semester, which coalesce into students' complex and nuanced personal storylines that move beyond binaries of compliance or resistance. By asking ourselves urgent questions regarding our students—particularly those who present instructional challenges—instructors can gain perspective that will inform pedagogical decisions. Course identities can help us see the hidden frames within which our students are operating, and view these frames as artifacts consistent with processes for lifelong learning.

In this chapter, the case of Martin offers an example to assist in articulating the framework of this course identities approach. Implications are discussed in terms of what we can learn as instructors from applying this new theory to the way we teach adults. In the way that Himley and Carini (2000) advocate that seeing one student closely is to see all students differently, the story in this chapter about Martin helps us observe course identities in action.

THEORETICAL FRAMEWORK

The concept of course identities rests in the intersection of several literatures including: (1) sociocultural literacy (Gee, 1992; Giroux, 1988); (2) identity scholarship exploring individuals' (re)construction of who they are as teachers (Jalongo & Isenberg, 1995), and, specifically, as graduate students (Watson & Gammel, 2011); (3) critical and feminist perspectives regarding the import of autobiographical examination (Breault, 2017; Cochran-Smith, 2000, 2004; Phillion, 2002; Richardson, 1997; Kamler, 2001), and (4) inquiry-as-stance (i.e., Cochran-Smith & Lytle, 2009; Fulmer & Bodner, 2017; Simon, 2009).

Sociocultural Literacy, Autobiography, and the Course Identities Approach

The sociocultural tradition recognizes the existence of multiple and shifting selves which are shaped by socially constructed norms and practices. For instance, individuals carry with them their own "contexts and pretexts" (Richardson, 1997) to the "literacies of [their] teaching" (Lytle, 2006). In this tradition, literacy is understood to be an act of examining one's own ways of thinking, believing, understanding, and communicating in the world (Gee, 1992). Within multicultural education coursework, specifically, the sociocultural framework aids us in deepening our knowledge of the multiple identities participants may take on by enhancing our understanding that identities are not tacit, predetermined structures, but are, rather, dynamic and shifting as participants engage in and grapple with course material. By extension, it is a key facet of course identities that they reside squarely within the context of the course itself, and are limited to the bounded system of class time in which they are exhibited. In other words, course identities as I have come to define them may not be identities individuals express outside of the course, or beyond the semester; they are unique to the student's participation in the course itself.

Scholars of the critical, feminist, and practitioner inquiry traditions have upheld that the personal and autobiographical are too often excluded from academic content and professional discourse (Cochran-Smith & Lytle, 2009; hooks, 2000; Kamler, 2001; Richardson, 1997). And yet, autobiographical examination is an especially important practice in pre-and in-service teachers' development (Cochran-Smith, 2003; Cochran-Smith & Paris, 1995; Ladson-Billings, 2002). As Jerome Bruner (1986) tells us, narrative is a fundamental aspect of humans' process of making sense of the world. The perception (or creation) of narrative can work to bridge one's sense of self with one's understanding of larger society. By engaging in work with personal histories, the opportunity exists for teachers to expose and contend with perspectives and assumptions they bring with them to teaching, especially around culture and race (Breault, 2017). Excavating these types of "cultural fault lines" (Cazden, 1999, p. viii), it is suggested, will allow teachers to newly consider their positionality within a multicultural society and support moves toward making their practice more equitable.

The writing and examination of autobiographical narratives in the course offered space for the emergence of new and evolving narratives for each participant. Moreover, in keeping with philosophies of critical literacy, I have worked to maintain a level of uncertainty in extracting and scrutinizing these course identities: it is important to recognize the temporary and evolving nature of each student's utterances without binding them to these identities in tight and fast ways. It is the nature of course identities that they stand as flexible and evolutionary constructs.

Feminisms acknowledge that our autobiographies are always shifting, evolving, and never static. Negotiating our multiple selves, as researchers, readers, writers, and humans puts us at borders we are constantly moving between, as we find ourselves resting in and among our evolving plural identities (Anzaldúa, 1987/2007). Feminist perspectives on literacy implore us to consider substantive issues in the fabric of our research, such as researcher identity, participant representation, othering, and representation of voice in deliberate and ongoing ways. Feminist scholars maintain a curiosity towards mis/reading language, and we question who has the authority to do so in the first place. As such, the concept of course identities considers the weight of issues of representation alongside analysis of students' autobiographical work.

Inquiry-as-Stance in the Course Identities Approach

Drawn from critical and feminist realms, practitioner inquiry theory examines one's own researcher-, teacher-, and personal-self in a deeply analytical manner (Achinstein, 2002; Cochran-Smith, 2000, 2004; Cochran-Smith & Lytle, 1999, 2009; Fulmer & Bodner, 2017; Lytle, 2000, 2006; Nichols & Cormack, 2017; Simon, 2009). A central tenet of practitioner inquiry is the systematic examination of one's own positionality with regards to the research project, its participants, constituents served, and the larger political and social landscape to which the researcher belongs. Practitioner inquiry analysis includes the process of autobiographical meaning-making in relationship to the findings. Conducting an inventory of the self in such a way can be an avenue for teacher educators to begin to understand their students in new and unfamiliar ways (Fulmer, 2012a).

Jalongo and Isenberg (1995) examined pre- and in-service teachers' stories as a "context for unlayering" (p. 159) the experiences of their participants both inside and outside the classroom. They observed that personal narratives allowed the teacher/authors to "hear their own voices" (p. 85) by revealing perspectives that contributed directly to classroom behaviors and choices. This is particularly appropriate for understanding the presentation of students' course identity narratives because of the unique possibilities for development of student voice on personal autobiographical analysis.

CONTEXT OF THE STUDY

Course identities emerged out of a larger practitioner inquiry study examining the "bounded system" (Creswell, 2007, p. 73) of a 14-week, semester-long graduate level course for practicing teachers. The elective course, "Perspectives in Multicultural Education" included five graduate students who were all practicing K–12 teachers. I was the instructor as well as researcher studying my teaching and our classroom as we together formed a culture sharing group (Creswell & Poth, 2017). This dual participant-researcher role is the prominent feature of practitioner inquiry where the researcher is the instructor (and therefore coparticipant) within the research site (Anderson, Herr, & Nihlen, 2007; Cochran-Smith & Lytle, 1999, 2009; Nichols & Cormack, 2017). The students in the course were full-time, practicing teachers, and with this in mind I worked to understand how they took up course content, and operationalized it in their classrooms and lives.

Our setting was "Mulberry College," a small, mostly White, residential liberal arts college in a metropolitan area in northeast United States. All five students—Seth, Haley, Leah, Martin, and Olivia (all pseudonyms)—identified as White and middle class. This racial/cultural designation held some variation within it, as some students identified as White-and-Italian, White-and-Jewish, a child of immigrants, or other additional cultural, regional, or ethnic identities. For purposes of explicating the usefulness of the course identities framework, this chapter focuses on the story of Martin, as his course narrative provided a rich and especially multifaceted portraiture. Martin's course identity proved to be particularly complex and sometimes contradictory. Elsewhere I have explored in depth the course identities of other participants (Fulmer, 2010, 2012a, 2012b, and 2014).

METHODS

Data Collection

This research drew upon ethnographic sources of data collection, including fieldnotes, participant interviews, focus groups, documents, and member checks, within what can be understood as a "bounded system" (Creswell, 2007, p. 73) of participation in a semester-long graduate course. Participant-observer fieldnotes (Emerson, Fretz, & Shaw, 1995) provided the core of the data, and offered the opportunity to capture minute-to-minute interactions between participants and myself, which allowed for in-depth recollection and narrative interpretation of the culture of our interactions. I also wrote interpretive, subjective field journals (Carspecken, 1996) following each class session, and again each week in preparation for upcoming class sessions. These field journals allowed initial analytical calibration of macro and micro interactions in a constant comparative method of interpreting and comparing emerging codes in a beginning stage of data interpretation (Creswell & Poth, 2017). Focus groups and informal interviews provided opportunities for member checks on my understanding of their course identities. Informal member checks (Lincoln & Guba, 1985) were built into the fabric of the course, and also took place in the interviews and focus group. After formal data collection ended, I maintained contact with participants and asked them to weigh in on their recollections and opinions of events that transpired. I worked to write about participants in this study respectfully and in ways that honor their multiple and shifting identities as practitioners of multicultural education; yet, I also worked to remain honest in my representation of them, even when it meant writing something that may be uncomfortable for them to read (e.g., Michael, 2015).

Analysis

I initialized open coding analysis via analytic memos, beginning with salient units culled from data, drawing broader interpretations from these pieces of data (Lankshear & Knobel, 2004). Initial codes were applied tentatively: I began exploring provisional taxonomies early in the data collection process, using memos to identify and revise interpretations. Open coding provided the existence of multiple narratives to make their way into my synthesis, which came to be a core facet of recognizing students' course identities.

A second analytic tradition proved useful: narrative analysis. While open coding allowed me to see a micro-view of the data, narrative analysis commissioned a synthesis. I used this method to search for themes and plots that emerged in participants' spoken and written narratives, including their responses to autobiographical writing prompts. Lieblich, Tuval-Mashiach, and Zilbe (1998) write that narrative analysis requires the researcher to engage in close listening to three "voices" (p. 10): the voice of the narrator (the participant's narrative); the voice of the theories in which the study is grounded (the theoretical/conceptual narrative); and the voice of the researcher herself (researcher narrative), as she strives for reflexivity and self-awareness in her interpretation. For example, during member checks, participants gave voice to the ways in which their stances had changed over time. Parker-Webster (2001) proffers that searching for themes among multiple data sources grouped together is generative. Braiding together themes across sources leads to the understanding of students' shifting and varied narratives, leading to their course identity.

The work of a course identities approach is to assemble a flexible interpretation of possible ways in which students—in this case, White teachers in a course on multicultural education—take up the material, and it is my aim that this approach can be utilized towards understanding future students I or others may work with. "It is in the dialectic tension between individual experience and temporal, physical, and relational contexts that meaning is made in a narrative inquiry" (Phillion, 2002, p. 19). Thus, I sought out and listened closely for the dominant metaphors each student expressed, and attended to the roles each of them played within the classroom community. The result is a conscientious analysis that draws out each of the students' course identities in ways that conceivably position them as lifelong learners. This practice can be seen as one of many practices that set out to "intentionally disrupt social and cultural forces that distort and delimit adult learning" (Mezirow, 1997, p. 11) by urging mutually beneficial transformation (Jordan & Schwartz, 2018).

"GETTING IT RIGHT": MARTIN'S COURSE IDENTITY

Martin was a social studies teacher at "Concord Area High School," which lies within a suburb of Bradbury. Martin came to teaching after a career as a business owner and realtor, and possessed eight years of experience in his current position. Having grown up in the town of "Townsend" (a small hamlet adjacent to Bradbury, and home of Concord Area High School), Martin drew upon an intricate understanding of the vicinity where he lived and its demographic tensions. Townsend and Concord Area High School are mostly White, with diversity presenting itself most saliently in the form of economic and social divide between the "town kids" and suburban families who had more money, a distinction Martin observed his whole life, and talked about frequently in the course. He identified as both White and Italian-American, the son of immigrants. He was also one of only two men enrolled in the course. Martin's course narrative featured threads of humor, morality, and striving-to-get-it-right as he worked to become a "better White person," as he put it in one of our interviews. I explore each of these facets of Martin's course identity below.

Competing Narrative Threads

At times, in-class fieldnotes revealed an earnestness in Martin that was sincere and unexpected, as is shown in the vignette that opens this chapter, where he grappled with the realities of bootstraps mythology exposed in the Leonard Pitts (1999) article we read.

A year later, Martin recalled in a follow up interview that this experience had a great impact on his understanding of the way that privilege and racism operate in his own autobiography. He explained,

One of the biggest [moments from class] that I keep playing like a broken
record was right at the beginning of the course when you had given us a
hand-out that we had discussed, and it dealt with the story that is often
given that you have immigrants who have come to this country. And I
related to it so clearly because my father often pushes this mantra, which is,
and I love him, but that's just how it is, "When I came over here with nothing and this is what I made of myself and it took hard work and people
didn't like Italians very much," and on and on. And how we can agree with
that, and understand that it was tough and he's to be admired for his hard
work, but to try to equate that to the struggle of a Black person is not really
applicable because they are not in the group that is of influence or power.
Yes, there might have been people discriminating against Italians or Polish
people or Irish people, or whatever the race or whatever the ethnicity is
that you claim, [and that] was a difficult struggle for you, but it cannot
be compared to the Black experience. [...] It really, it did hit home with
me because I'd hear, I heard that a lot, you know, the bootstraps thing.
(Martin, one-year interview)

In this follow up interview, Martin recounted this experience from the
beginning of class as a moment that was highly meaningful for him because
it "hit home." In fact, it continued to impact him throughout the semester and, clearly, beyond, as it played "like a broken record" in his mind.
Students often experienced meaningful and perhaps jarring moments in
the class that contributed to their understanding and engagement in the
subject matter. Haley, another student, called these "epiphanies" on more
than one occasion, and the term seemed to stick, being taken up by others
to explain their experience (Fulmer, 2010). Early epiphanies that hit home,
like the one Martin experienced in reading and discussing the "bootstraps
article," as the Pitts (1999) piece came to be known in our class, were one
of the ways that students came to frame the course. Martin's own encounters with bootstraps stories in his life allowed him to read Pitts' article in a
powerful way that led him to question the ways he had been conditioned
not to recognize his own White privilege.

In another example, also early on in the course, Martin offered an
account of a moment from his childhood where his father disallowed a
friendship between Martin and another first grade child who was African
American. This was one of the earliest shared personal narratives of the
semester, and in many ways it set the tone for a classroom community
where such knotty, personal excavation could occur. In this moment, as in
the bootstraps discussions, Martin was willing to do the complex work we
undertook, laying out and examining his autobiography, asking vulnerable
questions about his teaching practice, and sincerely seeking feedback from
his classmates about his processes along the way.

However, at other times, fieldnotes captured Martin in a light of flippancy. He made jokes at times I deemed inappropriate, or remained noticeably silent for lengthy stretches while his classmates carried the bulk of the conversation. While these two aspects of Martin's course narrative may appear polarized, I examined them closely in juxtaposition with one another, returning to each element over time, as Ballenger (2007) and Carini (Himley & Carini, 2000) invite us to do. I asked what meaning was Martin making by these divergent expressions? In other words, what was he working *on*? And, I asked what was his personalized, evolving story-of-the-class? In other words, what was he working *with*? Investigating course identities offers a structure for finding linkages, and indeed, I came to an interpretation that suggests that these seemingly disparate expressions are very much connected: Martin introduced joking into otherwise serious spaces when the conversation turned towards more difficult discussions of racism—moments which may have become uncomfortable for him and possibly other students as well. While on the surface, Martin's tendency to joke came across to me as inappropriate and even offensive, I later understood that humor can open up otherwise unbearable conversations and make room for further delving into uncomfortable racialized territory (Fulmer & Makepeace, 2015; hooks, 2003). In this way, joking was potentially supportive of the goals of the course; however, the possibility also exists that these jokes were a sidetrack, detouring us from the uncomfortable moments at hand (Singleton & Hays, 2006). Martin's joking theme is further illustrated below.

By operating with a course identities approach, I saw that Martin revealed himself to be committed to the work of anti-racist pedagogy and autobiographical examination, in ways I had previously overlooked. But, I saw that work was deeply challenging for him, and jokes or silence were useful tools of relief, or even temporary avoidance.

An Internalized "Moral Code"

On more than one occasion Martin told me he worked hard to get things "right." He very closely adhered to requirements for written work, for instance, and he admittedly prioritized his grade in the course as a first rule of thumb, over pursuing his own subset of interests on course topics. In one poignant example, Martin wrote in his final paper about his relationship with authority during his upbringing, and reflected on the impact it had in his work over the semester in our work together. He wrote,

> I have always had a respect for authority, a trait which I believe has had an impact on my views of multicultural education and one that is reflective of

my upbringing (for better or for worse). I know for certain that this respect for authority continues to shape (or perhaps cloud) my judgment as I am proceeding on this pedagogical journey to answer my inquiry question. (Martin, final paper)

Martin went on to explain in this teacher inquiry paper how authority relates to his own personal history with race and racism, as well as lifelong learning, writing,

The rules of my household dictated that I was not to develop close friendships with those whose skin color was different from my own. Since the ultimate **authority** [bold text in the original] in my household was my father, I respected and obeyed that authority without question. As I have made my journey through adulthood, and with each year that passes for which I have not been subject to my father's rules [going on 20 years now], I have adopted my own set of moral belief systems, abandoning much of what I used to believe and obey in my childhood and adolescent years. [...] For me, it is a constant battle to adhere to what I know is right, even though the voices of my past keep telling me that it may not be quite right. (Martin, final paper)

In these excerpts from Martin's teacher research paper, he described a personal trait—adherence to authority—and connected this to the nature of his engagement in the course topics around multicultural education. Respect for the authority in his household growing up included avoiding close friendships with children who were not White. As it related to course material, Martin worked to unpack what he had internalized when he was a child to reconcile with what he had learned in his journey into adulthood, and would continue to learn. Martin had developed a new "moral belief system" that differed from that in which he was raised. However, an adherence to authority remains, though now the authority is an anonymous "moral code," to which Martin strives to obey, and apparently allows little room for error. In Martin's journey to grow as a practitioner of multicultural education, he has braided together antiracist pedagogy with a moral imperative. Though not incompatible, I contend that the two can be problematic when the latter is understood to indicate a singular, correct pathway, against which mistakes or wrong moves would be measured "immoral." In this way, Martin's course identity of working-to-get-things-right is understood to be intertwined with his adherence to authority and his ongoing quest for self-development.

Joking Around

A second element adds depth to our understanding of Martin's identity within the course. Martin's adherence to authority and efforts to get things right were sometimes alleviated by the insertion of jokes or light-hearted comments into strategic moments where he was becoming uncomfortable, or perceived one of his classmates to be. Joking was a common thread for Martin. On occasion, he invited humor into an otherwise serious space where the conversation about race, class, or culture had become challenging, and he used it to alleviate some of the internal discomfort he experienced (or the discomfort he perceived a classmate to experience). This can be seen in fieldnotes of a classroom conversation between Olivia, Seth, and Martin,

> As Seth was explaining to the class about his students [who are incarcerated youth in a juvenile correctional facility], Olivia interjected that she suddenly became aware that as Seth spoke, she had been "assuming that [Seth's] students were mostly Black and Hispanic." She told us that it wasn't until the moment when Seth briefly noted explicitly that his students were, indeed, mostly Black or Hispanic, that she caught herself in what she called "a sort of presupposition about the demographics of his school." This seemed to be a vulnerable moment for Olivia, and she was revealing something to us that she is not proud of, but nevertheless, wanted to think about some more. Martin interjected into this moment by quipping, "Well, I assumed it was all *Canadians*," with a grin, and this sparked a round of laughter among the group. (fieldnotes, class session two)

In this interaction, Olivia appeared to be working through her realization that she had possessed concrete and identifiable preconceived notions about Seth's incarcerated students. She was working to make her thinking transparent—a hallmark of Olivia's own course identity (see Fulmer, 2012b)—and in doing so, stepped into a micromoment that was quite possibly uncomfortable for herself or for others in the class. Her realization was thorny. Martin's response to Olivia's vulnerability had been to release some of the tension he perceived by injecting a short, quick, sarcastic statement. "I assumed it was all Canadians" is obviously not a literal truth: Martin in no way assumed Seth's students were Canadians, and thus this was met with laughter by all of us in the class. But, what did this joke do? I posit that Martin's move accomplished alleviation of his own discomfort, and perhaps the discomfort of his peers. Based on conversations with participants in one-year interviews, I came to see this particular moment, juxtaposed with his thematic thread of getting-it-right, as articulation of Martin's course identity. His comedy was an effort to relieve some of his own internalized pressure to make the right moves, and adhere to authority, while engaging with racial subject matter. Most participants shared this same viewpoint about what came to be remembered as the "Canadians joke," as I uncovered in subsequent interviews.

It is important to acknowledge that Martin's "Canadians joke" carries with it assumptions that would be neglectful to ignore. Implied in the sentence "I thought they were all *Canadians*" is the assumption that all Canadians are White. Alternatively, perhaps Martin's joke operated to remove race momentarily from the discussion altogether: if the majority of Canadians are White, perhaps Martin thinks of them, therefore, as *not* raced, in the same way that many Whites struggle to see themselves as raced individuals. As such, the underlying comedy intended may be to have indexed a nationality that is mostly White to make the joke not that Seth's students were of a *different* race than most of us assumed, but rather, that Seth's students were *un*raced entirely.

Also pertinent is what Martin's joke reveals about the assumptions of everyone else in the class: we were complacent in the unexamined presupposition that all of Seth's incarcerated pupils were Black or Hispanic. Martin's joke had surprised the class out of our assumptions about his students, and caused us to reflect on these presumptions in some way, furthering the goals of Olivia's original confession.

This small discourse moment that came and went so quickly within the scope of the class, became a significant exchange for critical analysis as I worked to understand the big picture of Martin's course identity. According to input I received from several of the other students, the joking moments that Martin contributed worked to create a space where deeper learning could be achieved. For instance, as another student, Leah, explained to me in a follow up interview,

> I think that [joking] alleviates discomfort, so it can open up a conversation.... [I]t helps to open up the conversation so that people then can maybe talk about something more personal or something that would make them uncomfortable or sad even, because, it did for me. (Leah, one-year interview)

Through Leah's description of the work that joking did for her—and what she indicated it did for others in the class—I came to understand Martin's joking in a different light. In my earlier assessment of Martin's comedy moments in class, the jokes disturbed me because I read them as inappropriate comments that perpetuated troubling and racist assumptions, and sidetracked the conversation. However, through continuous questioning about my own conclusions and through ongoing listening to Martin's classroom discourse, I was led to this additional interpretation about the existence of humor in our class. As Leah's statement explained, I came to understand, as Leah's statement explained, that humor could have the effect of opening up conversations for profound growth. In fact, this became the topic of a separate thread of classroom research I conducted with a colleague (Fulmer & Makepeace, 2015), inspired by Leah's assertions.

Bell hooks (2003) points to the forgiving nature of humor when the stakes are high. She explains, "Laughing together intervenes in our fear of making mistakes" (hooks, 2003, p. 63). Along this line, Martin's narrative thread of humor could be seen as a way for him to alleviate his own discomfort around making mistakes that would render him incorrect or even possibly immoral (per his own internalized high stakes), based on the feelings he expressed around his strong adherence to authority and his internalized moral code. While this moment continues to trouble me at times, I return to the idea that Martin used humor throughout the semester to create room for imperfection, or the working-out of his ideas within an otherwise unforgiving moral belief system he had constructed for himself. As Martin's other threads in his course identity suggest, he possessed an aversion to veering off what he perceived as the "right" course. When humor was introduced into a difficult or potentially stressful situation, as it was in the above exchange, the joke provided temporary relief, and perhaps even some room for forgiveness if a mistake was made, like Olivia's confession.

For Martin, who described himself as wanting to get it "right," and desired to be "a good white person" who wanted to avoid "wrong moves," his injections of humor provided room for him to take risks, and perhaps, give permission for him not to get it exactly right all the time. Michael (2015), Singleton and Hays (2006) and others (e.g., Gale, 2016) have noted the importance of safe spaces in which to make mistakes in multicultural learning. Most of the students commented on the benefit that humor generally provided in the course, and by looking at this issue through hooks's (2003) lens on humor in racial learning, I reexamined Martin's efforts at joking, and came to understand these instances for their possible affordances. The course identities approach urged me to reframe my assumptions of resistance to course material and see the complexity involved in Martin's narratives as an adult learner. Pasting him on a continuum of resistance and/or ignorance would likely have made few positive contributions to Martin's racial and critical autobiographical learning. But, coming to understand that Martin approached the course through his efforts to succeed at getting things "right," allowed me to build on this knowledge of him. From this new analytical interpretation—the *course identities* approach—I reconstructed a positive framework to guide my work with Martin.

CONCLUSIONS: WHAT WE CAN LEARN

In the way that Himley and Carini (2000) advocate that seeing one student closely is to see all students differently, the story of Martin helps to elucidate the construct of course identities. Martin's story offers a highly contextualized account of one of the ways in which White teachers may take up the subject of multicultural education. For Martin, this is centered on efforts to "get it right," including both moments where he dove deeply into personal accounts as well as cracked jokes that released tension. Analysis of classroom data, using open coding and a narrative analysis approach, revealed the themes Martin was enacting. As the instructor, by asking myself, recursively, what are my students working *on*, and *with*, I could see some of the hidden frames that Martin was operating with. If there are disparate themes, as in the case of Martin, teacher educators can seek out connectors between the threads in a process of investigating our own assumptions about our students. It is not wholly accurate to pin White students to labels implicating them in either ignorance or resistance to antiracist content. These are limiting and overused interpretations of students' engagement in such courses (Garrett & Segall, 2013). Rather, it is important to seek ways to understand our students beyond these pretenses if we are to guide them towards transformation as adults who are lifelong learners (Cranton, 1994).

This chapter relays the process of illustrating one student's *course identity* for the purpose of explicating the possibilities that this new approach offers. Through examining closely Martin's participation over the semester, by adopting what I came to recognize as a new approach towards under-standing students, I learned to see Martin in a subtle, more nuanced light that holds potential for increased learning on the part of the student, as well as being equally transformative for the instructor. The significance of this new construct resides in offering instructors alternatives to a resistance/compliance binary by coming to understand students' identities as con-stantly shifting, within and beyond the scope of a course. This framework allows us to see the urgency in recognizing how students express and revise their own identities within the bounded system of our course. A primary potential of the course identity framework for teacher education is twofold: it can help us to complicate the picture of how White teachers learn about issues of race, privilege and systemic injustices, and additionally, it can help teacher educators to support our White students in the ongoing process of unlearning internalized racism in their personal and profes-sional lives. This framework may be especially important in working with White teachers who we may deem close-minded, resistant, disinterested, passive, uninformed, or confused with relation to critical multiculturalism.

ACKNOWLEDGMENTS

The author would like to thank Sherry Deckman, Vivian Gadsden, Linda Hanrahan, Susan Lytle, Sharon Ravitch, and Kathleen Riley for their advice and guidance in various stages of this work.

REFERENCES

Achinstein, B. (2002). Conflict amid community: The micropolitics of teacher colloaboration. *Teachers College Record, 104*(3), 421–455.

Anderson, G. Herr, K., & Nihlen, A. (2007). *Studying your own school: An educator's guide to practitioner action research.* Thousand Oaks, CA: Corwin Press.

Anzaldúa, G. (2007). *Borderlands/La Frontera: The new Mestiza.* San Francisco, CA: Aunt Lute Books. (Original work published 1987)

Ballenger, C. (2009). *Puzzling moments, teachable moments: Practicing teacher research in urban classrooms.* New York, NY: Teachers College Press.

Breault, R. (2017). Dialogic life history in preservice teacher education. In J. Norris & R. D. Sawyer (Eds.), *Theorizing curriculum studies, teacher education, and research through duo ethnographic pedagogy* (pp. 63–84). New York, NY: Palgrave Macmillan.

Bruner, J. S. (1986). *Actual minds, possible worlds.* Cambridge, MA: Harvard University Press.

Carspecken, P. F. (1996). *Critical ethnography in educational research: A theoretical and practical guide.* New York, NY: Routeledge.

Cazden, C. (1999). Forward. In C. Ballenger (Ed.), *Teaching other people's children: Literacy and learning in a bilingual classroom* (pp. vii–viii). New York, NY: Teachers College Press.

Cochran-Smith, M. (2000). Blind vision: Unlearning racism in teacher education. *Harvard Educational Review, 70*(2), 157–190.

Cochran-Smith, M. (2003). The multiple meanings of multicultural teacher education. *Teacher Education Quarterly. 30*(2), 7–26.

Cochran-Smith, M. (2004). *Walking the road: Race, diversity, and social justice in teacher education.* New York, NY: Teachers College Press.

Cochran-Smith, M., & Lytle, S. (1999). Relationships of knowledge and practice: Teacher learning in communities. *Review of Research in Education, 24,* 249–305.

Cochran-Smith, M., & Lytle, S. (2009). *Inquiry as stance.* New York, NY: Teachers College Press.

Cochran-Smith, M., & Paris, P. (1995). Mentor and mentoring: Did Homer have it right? In J. Smith (Ed.), *Critical discourses on teacher development* (pp. 181–202). London, UK: Cassell.

Connelly, F. M., & Clandinin, D. J. (1990). Stories of experience and narrative inquiry. *Educational Researcher 19*(5), 2–14.

Cranton, P. (1994). *Understanding and promoting transformative learning: A guide for educators of adults.* San Francisco, CA: Jossey-Bass.

Creswell, J. W. (2007). *Qualitative inquiry and research design: Choosing among the five approaches* (3rd ed). Thousand Oaks, CA: SAGE.

Creswell, J. W., & Poth, C. N. (2017). *Qualitative inquiry and research design: Choosing among the five approaches* (4th ed). Thousand Oaks, CA: SAGE.

Derman-Sparks, L., & Ramsey, P. G. (2011) *What if all the kids are White? Anti-bias multicultural education with young children and families* (2nd ed). New York, NY: Teachers College Press.

Dubouloy, M. (2004). The transitional space and self-recovery: A psychoanalytical approach to high-potential managers' training. *Human Relations, 57*(4), 467–496.

Emerson, R., Fretz, R., & Shaw, L. (1995). *Writing ethnographic fieldnotes.* Chicago, IL: University of Chicago Press.

Fox, W., & Gay, G. (1995). Integrating multicultural and curriculum principles in teacher education. *Peabody Journal of Education, 70*(3), 64–82.

Fulmer, E. F. (2010, May). *"Wrong moves" and "epiphanies": Examining group and individual narratives expressed in multicultural teacher education.* Paper presented at American Educational Research Association Annual Conference, Denver, CO.

Fulmer, E. F. (2012a). *Autobiographical meaning making, practitioner inquiry, and white teachers in multicultural education* (Unpublished doctoral dissertation). University of Pennsylvania, Philadelphia, PA.

Fulmer, E. F. (2012b, February). *"False Confidence": Understanding white teachers' narratives in multicultural teacher education.* Paper presented at Ethnography in Education Research Forum, Philadelphia, PA.

Fulmer, E. F. (2014, May). *The course identities framework: A tool for investigating White teachers' engagement in multicultural education coursework.* Paper presented at Action Research Network of the Americas, Bethlehem, PA.

Fulmer, E. F., & Bodner, J. (2017). Detached and unsustainable: Central tensions in teacher research capstones and the possibilities for reimagined inquiry. *Inquiry in Education, 9*(2), article 5.

Fulmer, E. F., & Makepeace, N. N. (2015). "It's OK to laugh, right?": Toward a pedagogy of critical race humor in multicultural education. (With M. Abbe, S. Apgar, R. Strongin, S. Giarratano, & S. Shields.) *Perspectives on Urban Education, 12*(1), 38–53.

Gale, R. A. (2016). Learning in the company of others: Students and teachers collaborating to support wonder, unease, and understanding. *New Directions for Teaching and Learning, 148,* 15–23.

Garrett, H. J., & Segall, A. (2013). (Re)considerations of ignorance and resistance in teacher education. *Journal of Teacher Education, 64*(4), 294–304. doi:10.1177/0022487113487752

Gee, J. P. (1992). *The social mind: Language, ideology, and social practice.* New York, NY: Bergin and Garvey.

Giroux, H. A. (1988). *Teachers as intellectuals: Toward a critical pedagogy of learning.* Granby, MA: Bergin & Garvey.

Grant, C. A., & Sleeter, C. E. (2007). *Doing multicultural education for achievement and equity.* New York, NY: Routledge.

Heath, S. B. (1983). *Ways with words: Language, life, and work in communities and classrooms.* Cambridge, UK: Cambridge University Press.

Himley, M., & Carini, P. (2000). *From another angle: Children's strengths and school standards: The Prospect Center's descriptive review of the child.* New York, NY: Teachers College Press.

hooks, b. (2000). *Feminism is for everybody: Passionate politics.* Cambridge, MA: South End Press.

hooks, b. (2003). *Teaching community: A pedagogy of hope.* New York, NY: Routledge.

Jalongo, M. R., & Isenberg, J. P. (1995). *From personal narrative to professional insight.* San Francisco, CA: Jossey-Bass.

Ingersoll, R., Merrill, L., & Stuckey, D. (2014). Seven trends: The transformation of the teaching force, updated April 2014. CPRE Report (#RR-80). Philadelphia, PA: Consortium for Policy Research in Education, University of Pennsylvania.

Jordan, J. V., & Schwartz, H. L. (2018). Radical empathy in teaching. *New Directions for Teaching and Learning, 153,* 25–35.

Kailin, J. (2002). *Antiracist education: From theory to practice.* Oxford, UK: Rowman & Littlefield.

Kamler, B. (2001). *Relocating the personal: A critical writing pedagogy.* Albany, NY: The State University of New York.

Ladson-Billings, G. (2002). Fighting for our lives: Preparing teachers to teach African American students. *Journal of Teacher Education, 51*(3), 206–214.

Lankshear, C., & Knobel, M. (2004). *A handbook for teacher research: From design to implementation.* New York, NY: Open University Press.

Lieblich, A., Tuval-Mashiac, R., & Zilber, T. (1998). *Narrative research: Reading, analysis, and interpretation.* Thousand Oaks, CA: SAGE.

Lincoln, Y. S., & Guba, E. G. (1985). *Naturalistic inquiry: The paradigm revolution.* Newbury Park, CA: SAGE.

Lytle, S. L. (2000). "Teacher research in the contact zone." In M. L. Kamil, P. B. Mosenthal, D. P. Pearson, & R. Barr (Eds.), *Handbook of Reading Research* (Vol. III, pp. 691–718). Mahwah, NJ: Lawrence Erlbaum.

Lytle, S. L. (2006). Literacies of teaching urban adolescents *in these times.* In D. E. Alvermann, K. A. Hinchman, D. W. Moore, S. F. Phelps, & D. R. Waff (Eds.), *Reconceptualizing the literacies in adolescents' lives* (pp. 257–277). Mahwah, NJ: Lawrence Erlbaum.

McLaren, P. (2008). Critical pedagogy: A look at the major concepts. In A. Darder, R. Torres, & M. Baltodano (Eds.), *The critical pedagogy reader* (pp. 69–96). New York, NY: Routledge.

Mezirow, J. (1997). Transformative learning: Theory to practice. *New Directions for Adult and Continuing Education, 74,* 5–12.

Michael, A. (2015). *Raising race questions: Whiteness and inquiry in education.* New York, NY: Teachers College Press.

Nichols, S., & Cormack, P. (2017). *Impactful practitioner inquiry: The ripple effect on classrooms, schools, and teacher professionalism.* New York, NY: Teachers College Press.

Parker-Webster, J. (2001) Between the lines: Constructing parallel levels of meaning and identity in discussions about multicultural literature. In P. H. Carspecken & G. Walford (Eds.), *Critical ethnography and education* (pp. 27–60). Kidlington, Oxford, UK: Elsevier Science.

Pitts, L., Jr. (1999, March 27). The immigrant story: It says a lot about America, but still leaves a few things out. *The Philadelphia Inquirer,* n.p.

Phillion, J. (2002). *Narrative inquiry in a multicultural landscape: Multicultural teaching and learning.* Westport, CT: Ablex.

Richardson, L. (1997). *Fields of play: Constructing an academic life.* New Brunswick, NJ: Rutgers University Press.

Schultz, K. (2003). *Listening: A framework for teaching across differences.* New York, NY: Teachers College Press.

Simon, R. (2009). "We are all becoming teacher/theorists": Collaborative inquiry into the intellectual, relational, and political work of learning to teach. Retrieved from ProQuest Digital Dissertations. (AT 3381868)

Singleton G. E., & Hays, C. (2006) *Courageous conversations about race: A field guide for achieving equity in schools.* Thousand Oaks, CA: Corwin Press.

Watson, R. E., & Gammel, J. A. (2011). Exploring graduate students' identity work: The unspoken curriculum. *International Journal of Humanities and Social Science, 1*(5), 24–32.

Wiggins, R. A., Follo E. J., & Eberly, M. B. (2007). The impact of a field immersion program on pre-service teachers' attitudes toward teaching in culturally diverse classrooms. *Teaching and Teacher Education 23*(5), 653–663.

CHAPTER 14

I KNOW MORE THAN
I THOUGHT I DID

Enid E. Larsen
Endicott College

My office is a confessional of sorts. As a director of Prior Learning Assessment (PLA), I hear anxious, regretful, hopeful histories of undergraduate adult learners who are petitioning college credit for knowledge acquired in their workplaces and personal lives (Klein-Collins & Hudson, 2017). They have myriad reasons why they do not have their bachelor's degree or why they did not pursue or complete the traditional, high-school-to-college trajectory, reasons all well documented in adult learning literature (Tennant & Pogson, 1995). A common rationale is that they will get their degree later in life. But faced with life realities, the goal is put off, continuously. Fulfilling adult responsibilities is indeed a full-time occupation. Acquiring an education can seem adjunctive until the lack of one becomes a barrier to life's sustenance or soul. Vignettes of their life histories and manifestations of the imposter syndrome represent common, but private layers of adult-learner narratives. They state such things as:

"I partied too much in college. I don't know if I can do this now."

"No one at work knows I don't have a degree. What will they think when they find out?"

Identity and Lifelong Learning in Higher Education, pp. 251–266
Copyright © 2020 by Information Age Publishing
251

"I can manage multi-million dollar accounts but I don't know how to write a paper without bullet points."

"I am a first generation learner. I have a lot to prove."

"I'm being passed over for promotions."

"I'm proud of having been a parent all these years, but now what?"

"I have this nagging feeling of being less than."

"I want to be a role model to my children. But how can I without a degree?"

"I've lost a lot of time, including myself."

When I listen to my adult learners, I hear echoes of my own persistent narrative: "Sooner or later, someone, if not everyone, is going to figure out that I am not smart enough and that I am also not worthy, and then what?"

THE IMPOSTER SYNDROME

The imposter syndrome is common, yet rarely talked about in the academy. Who wants to admit they feel like an imposter? Authenticity, a relatively full disclosure of one's personal truth, holds a highly prized value in narrative theory and autoethnographic research, both embracing the study of one's self in culture (Ellis & Bochner, 1996; Tisdell, 2003). However, self-disclosure can be perceived as risky in the academy and the job site for obvious reasons. Academia is an enterprise where intellectual prowess is both process and product. Careers are typically built on leveraging brain power, not personal authenticity and transparency.

If someone had looked in a crystal ball when I was a teenager and predicted that I would achieve two master's degrees, a doctoral degree, and become an international educator and researcher, let alone graduate college, I would have thought they confused my crystal ball for another. My pedigree has humble roots that I thought I needed to hide well into adulthood. Yet, over time, these roots and my willingness to take risks have become calling cards for my work as an educator, researcher, psychotherapist, artist, and a lifelong learner. Paradigm shifts such as this, from concealment to transparency, unworthy to worthy, are accompanied by powerful stories. Rarely have I encountered adult learners who do not have a "big story" behind their return to education, myself included—an adult learner's "hero's journey" (Campbell, 2008). Adult learners, by virtue of life experience, come to the classroom with complex professional and personal narratives. Tennant and Pogson (1995) depict education and making use of these stories as a means of responding to some experience of meaning making, not just professional practicality.

A VIABLE PATHWAY

Adult learners returning to school for undergraduate degree completion now comprise the larger percentage of students in college compared to their traditional counterparts of 18 to 22 year olds (National Adult Learner Coalition White Paper [NALC], 2017). Petitioning proficiency credits through PLA is an appealing option for many adult learners, offering an opportunity to meaningfully and economically accelerate degree completion while validating college-level learning. In order to meet academic standards, PLA learners at my current institution become their own subject of learning in a three-credit course called *Assessment of Prior Learning*. Eligible learning is fit into a viable academic plan in which "experience is the adult learner's living textbook" (Lindeman, 1961, p. 7). Reflection is the model. Writing case studies of experiential learning for each course is the vehicle. A portfolio documenting college-level work and life learning is the product. To many adult learners, PLA is a radical, nontraditional, and welcome option for degree completion. Nationally, in a dramatic increase of interest, PLA is recognized as a viable pathway to strengthen America's economy by expanding educational opportunities for working adults (NALC, 2017).

WHAT DID I GET MYSELF INTO?

As my adult learners and I start exploring the concept and requirements of petitioning credit for workplace experiential learning, it does not take long for concerns about agency and self-efficacy to start surfacing. They wonder, am I capable of doing this?

Before embarking on writing case studies to validate their experiential knowledge, they write a Learning Autobiography as a first reflective dive. The Learning Autobiography introduces them as a learning person, creating an integral link to their case studies. Reflecting on their personal and workplace learning histories, they introduce who they are, including impediments to and support for their development, not only as learners, but also as generative, productive human beings. The critical thinking requirement is clear. They are to identify and articulate their learning and provide reflective and documentable evidence of their competencies. "The integration of former and new learning will not happen without learners engaging in critical reflection on their learning experiences" (Brewer & Marienau, 2016, p. 3). Secrets and worries about their capacity to fulfill the critical thinking and reflective first-person writing requirements are soon disclosed. Each semester I also hear some variation of the private lament that they are sure everyone else is smarter than they, especially the fresh younger employees with their newly minted degrees, despite their own years of grounded, experiential learning. Maybe it would be easier to just register for all those courses.

Dewey (1938), a foundational educational philosopher and reformer, noted it is cognitively demanding to think and feel one's way to new understandings of life experiences and to overcome deeply engrained perspectives and assumptions. No amount of rational assurance is persuasive enough, nor, as I have learned, is it respectful. The realization that one has undergone significant experiential learning, and then situating it in an educational context, is an impactful experience. As a director and advisor, I have learned that an empathetic and kind voice is a far more effective tool than either persuasion or reassurance of their capabilities and potential. They need to go on this journey and uncover their capacities themselves with compassionate and wise guidance.

A DISORIENTATION

As my advisees sit in my office, they read over my shoulder a predictive quote variously attributed to Oliver Wendell Holmes and a concept closely associated with portfolio assessment (Taylor & Marienau, 2016, p. 27), declaring a brain-based and culturally rooted concept of transformational learning: "A mind that is stretched to a new idea never returns to its original dimension." Before leaving my office the adult learners are on their way to a journey of discovery. However, what they will discover is unknown to both them and me. An anticipated disorientation has begun, starting as a tiny challenge to their perception of themselves. The Prior Learning experience is fertile ground for transformative learning; the kind of learning that has potential to change perspectives and create portals for new ideas and practices (Mezirow, 2000). PLA has potency also because adult learners have the opportunity to identify and reflect on their "big story" and their experience of integrating seemingly disparate personal and professional learning in the development of Self, considered here as an archetypal experience of the psyche as a whole (Jung, 1969).

Like me, adult learners are riddled with the imposter syndrome. The way they constructed or have been told their stories has left a lasting imprint on their learning history and feeling of agency and self-efficacy, or better understood as their "I can do this" feeling (Bandura, 1977). They feel, and often are, vulnerable, for indeed, the world is not always a kind, understanding place. But they are also brave. Becoming an adult learner is an encounter with ghosts that haunt educational memories. They take multiple risks as they navigate from experience to experience, course to course, and credential to credential. Completing a degree is hard work and takes guts on many fronts. Every time adult learners state "I learned" and "I know," and provide evidence of their learning in their case studies, they are claiming their place in the world of knowledge. While they may feel like "strangers in a strange land of higher education" (Taylor & Marienau, 2016, p. 27), they have already begun a journey as lifelong learners by virtue of their acquired learning and persistence. The journey may feel harrowing at times, but it can also be exhilarating and rewarding. I know this well. I understand my adult learners' potential, as well as their fears of inadequacy and exposure. It is my story, too.

MY STORY

In empathetic spirit and the style of writing a PLA Learning Autobiography, I now unpack my own narrative in the form of living inquiry research as an adult learner who became an interdisciplinary educator and evaluator of PLA. Living inquiry is a qualitative research practice in which knowledge is constructed in everyday encounters through experiencing and processing the world (Diaz & McKenna, 2004; Irwin & de Cosson, 2004; Springgay, Irwin, Leggo, & Gouzouasis, 2008). Living inquiry portrays certain kinds of knowledge to evoke empathy needed for instigating change and for providing insight into circumstances that are not best portrayed through statistical and scientific methods.

I am aware that even after decades of education and credentialing, I feel vulnerable, like I am shedding protective cloaks of persona. I ponder how my students feel creating their experiential portfolios for analysis and evaluation, peeling back and exposing layers of experience and hard won knowledge. My own adult learning story reveals encounters with risk taking, choice and consequence, unexpected turns, failures and celebrations, some explicit, others written obliquely between the lines and chapters of my life. A learning autobiography incorporates a form of narrative theory as a multifaceted means of exploration, telling a story, highlighting the voice from within (Tisdell, 2003). Stories touch our hearts and put a human face on the world of ideas but sometimes this can feel terribly exposing in higher education. That is why we construct personas that mask not only our vulnerability, but also our authenticity. What is true for my adult learners is also true for me.

Deeply Entangled Roots

I tell my students to start their story where it is most meaningful. For me, the impetus of my lifelong learning is rooted in struggles which began in childhood. Beneath my successful persona, I dragged deep feelings of inferiority into young adulthood; a complex of misperceptions, inexperience, and lack of support for finding a trajectory in life, all of which became challenges to my experience of agency and development of Self (Bandura, 1977; Erikson, 1994; Jung, 1969).

I am an American Norwegian whose education began in a one-room schoolhouse in Minnesota farm country settled by Scandinavian and German immigrants for whom a strong work ethic was an esteemed social value; a value deeply embedded into the construct of my psyche. Well-being, if not survival, depended on the fortitude of families who lived in harmony with nature and each other, and who were also at nature's and each other's mercy. This community formed a certain kind of knowledge that was innate, natural, and social. My childhood was lived out in woods and farmland where nature and animals were my first friends and teachers. The many neighborhood churches provided both spiritual and agreeable social sustenance to the community at large. I studied in the same one-room schoolhouse as my father 50 years earlier, and my older siblings and neighbors before me. I learned my lessons at the "little table" while students in grades above me had their turn at the "big table" and the coveted blackboard. I learned to learn by observation and osmosis with my learning cohort that included Dick and Jane, popular characters in reading texts in the United States in the 1930s through the 1970s. An abandoned chicken coop on the farm, salvaged as a playhouse, became a literal, and later, metaphoric vessel for my budding, indomitable creative spirit, and a prototype for an art studio and living inquiry research decades later (Larsen, 2010). My childhood was ideal by many standards. But I learned very early that my culture, personal, and social also had a shadow side with hidden, undesirable qualities at variance with the esteemed cultural, social, and spiritual values (Jung, 1973).

Shadow

I completed grade school at the tail end of the educational era of country schoolhouses. It was the sixties, and education reform was underway along with numerous social reforms. Little could I imagine how much I would be affected by these reforms and accompanying social disruptions. The Cold War was ominous and dominated American consciousness. Russia was an alien global Other—my first remembered experience of a social construction with which we dis-identify and fear (Bauman, 1993). Watching Sputnik silently arc across the star-studded Minnesota sky was intriguing and roused anxious questions that no one could answer. The Vietnam War, a national Other, was distant until a brother was deployed, and then it became excruciatingly personal. Racial discrimination and violence was abstract and puzzling and totally unfathomable to me. Why so much hate and disdain?

I had much to learn about the construct of social identities and the neat, comfortable means by which we organize and protect ourselves in culture (Bauman, 1993). The harsh outcomes of poverty and the consequences of alcoholism in my own family immigration history were hidden for decades. Why so much secrecy? As in the larger culture, the shadow of Otherness had slipped into a protective vessel of secrecy, leaving an anemic construct of social identity. I absorbed into a developing psyche my family's and my culture's wounds.

Otherness Emerges

Riding a school bus to "town school" was a developmental rite of passage in seventh grade. I was unprepared for learning my first big sociocultural lesson: Otherness and elitism is relative. Every culture creates its own lower class, its own Other (Bauman, 1993). In my town of 1,500 inhabitants located in the middle of farm country, the town students looked down on the country students as backward. I quickly absorbed feelings of shame and inferiority.

I also learned here, as in the country school, that friends could be really mean to each other. So adaptive was my survival behavior that I only learned to identify this bully behavior decades later when bullying became a nationwide social concern. I had to learn how to manage social survival, which I did with a strategic decision to kill everyone with a Midwest cocktail of kindness, fairness, integrity, popularity, and uniqueness, all the while acquiescing and conforming to the familial, social, and religious values. It was a developmentally treacherous navigation without overt guidance from anyone. I was on my own.

At this point in my learning autobiography, I take a deep breath, knowing that at some point, my students do the same. What do we make of our truthfulness? Do we continue? Some of these memories are painful. At this point, it is less about the assignment and more about Self truth.

I suffered and hated the unkindness bestowed on me. I often wished someone had taught me how to fight or at least stand up for myself. Familial, religious, and cultural norms trumped individual needs. Instead I compensated, if not overcompensated. I became a leader in every activity I took part in. I won music and speech contests. I almost failed my college prep courses, but I maintained my head cheerleader status. I became the Prom Queen.

But when my Lutheran church began to split over disagreements on church doctrine and who determines it, including management of threatening, changing social norms of the 60s, my teenage heart, too, split over what I experienced as hypocrisies and self-righteousness. I embraced new ideas rolling across the country because they spoke both to my needs and to the direction of the country, as I was beginning to perceive it. For that, I was outvoted as church organist because I introduced classical and modern music. I played too loud and too fast, and my skirts were too short. I got jammed up against the impulse of individuals, families, communities, institutions, and culture to maintain stasis in the face of change. Change is disruptive. Otherness is threatening. Comfort zones, social order, reigning values, and hegemony are all at risk (Freire, 2000). It took time, years, but I grew to appreciate how this experience laid down an early track for my interest in social sciences, mental health, and the arts, each with a unique angle of perception of human experience.

Approaching Edges of Knowing

Transitions and transformations can be harrowing. They push us to the edges of our knowing (Berger, 2004). My transition into young adulthood felt somewhat directionless. It seemed clear to everyone else but me that music was my field. I was indeed musically talented and I had intrinsic interest in the arts that fueled a passion for creative expression. However, rather than relishing hopes and dreams for a generative future, I harbored a private gnawing worry in my spirit. I did not feel smart. I had already internalized a "dumb" female identity cultivated by insensitive male-dominated family norms and the culture-at-large. All through grade school, I watched my siblings coming and going from college. They all followed the implicit expectation of our Norwegian immigrant mother. My parents achieved eighth grade education, but my mother longed for more. She highly valued education and was a lifelong learner within the bounds of her life, but could not fulfill her own longings or potential, let alone guide us. My father was mostly silent. We were each on our own to figure things out. I studied and studied a thick academic catalog in size 9 font from the University of Minnesota that lay around the house. It made no sense to me, which seemed even more confirmation that I was not smart. My private despair rooted early. This "not smart" identity already had long, tenacious roots intertwined with all the other promising generative roots—a complex slowly choking off necessary nutrients and growth at critical junctures of development (Erikson, 1994; Jung, 1969).

An Act of Individuation

At some point in writing their Learning Autobiography, my students identify a pivotal moment; a recognition of when their life path altered in an impactful, if not life-changing way. I found direction when I broke several social taboos on the "back of a motorcycle" when I met a young man from New York City who recognized my potential and flamed a passion for adventure in me. It triggered what Maslow (2014) and Jung (1969) might identify as a dramatic act to realize my potential and to become a whole person in my own right. Call it flight and/or a brave act of individuation—I got engaged in high school, married shortly after graduation, and moved to the East Coast, shocking everyone. They all waited to see if I was pregnant. "Good girls" don't do this. Well, this one did. This was the seventies, and social norms were breaking all around. I found numerous supports among other youthful migrants to embrace my new life, and I thought little of the profound impact my life change constellated in me.

New Possibilities

The whole of a narrative is greater than the sum of its parts, and some experiences stand out more than others as salient and transformational. All around me swelled a cultural renaissance fueled by rebellion, accompanied by new ideas in education, politics, values, and artistic expression. I relished it and experimented with my newfound freedom. I participated in political protest marches and international volunteer opportunities, taking me as far as the mountains in Guatemala during their civil war. I found a church on the East Coast that welcomed my arts-based talents. I directed teen groups and large-scale musicals. I augmented income as the female vocalist in a folk group, performing up and down the East Coast. Most impactful, I was fortunate to encounter the generative, life-expanding construct of Carl Jung's concepts in depth psychology. This became a fertile construct to understand human behavior through archetypal motifs (Jung, 1969). Archetypes, as universal models of people, behaviors, or personalities, dynamically activated in daily life, provided a way to understand and integrate seemingly disparate parts of the psyche and human behavior. It became a reliable and expansive frame not only for my individual and marital growth, but also core structure for what later became a career that included mental health, the arts, and higher education.

Individuation Is Not for Sissies

While at times it was excruciatingly painful to leave my culture, I learned to recognize that sometimes, for some individuals, one's culture of birth cannot support the individuation trajectory of its members. When any culture is constricting, inoculated by its own standards to the needs of its members, relating to or rejecting one or many of its members as an Other, or even simply instilling a lack of confidence, then one's life choices narrow. Countless midnight conversations, novels, and movies are made of this archetypal motif. Though risky, moving out of a culture and re-centering oneself into a place of agency can be a desirable, life-giving option.

> What was not modelled in the family of origin, what was not made available in the popular culture, becomes a personal task for each of us in the second half of life. Breaking the tyranny of history is a heroic enterprise and a task that confronts each of us, no matter how oppressive the past. (Hollis, 2006, p. 148)

As my world expanded, I continued to lay down psychological and arts-based foundations that stand firm decades later. However, my migration to the East Coast also planted me in the middle of yet another sociocultural division. I swiftly learned about East Coast/Midwest cultural biases and discriminations. Each looked at the other's social, political, ethical, spiritual, and cultural values with distrust, superior/inferior complexes, and more than a modicum of disdain, equally distributed—a condition of mutual Otherness. How was I to manage my bicultural status? My inferiority complex experienced little relief; it just shifted contexts. The appropriate young adulthood query of "Who are you?" was undergirded by "Who do you think you are?"

A Pathway Opens Up

My adult learners are asked to reflect on the pivotal moments in their learning history to discern the impact on their experiential learning trajectory. While some adult learners matriculate with a "get me out of here as fast as possible" attitude, others, like me, take a longer, slower pathway out of necessity and strategy. Tapping into valued Midwest sensibilities, I stopped comparing myself to traditional learners. I recognized my potential as a later bloomer and embraced it as a viable path in life, which gave me time to "grow up" before starting a family. It gave me time to work on a college career. However, driven by the frustration of losing time and credits through transience, and intrigued by the opportunity to construct my own learning path, I finally took a huge risk for my "not smart, unworthy" identity. I enrolled in the Goddard College Adult Degree Program ("About Goddard," 2018), where I participated in a century-old experiment in education—theirs and now my own. I repeatedly constructed, executed, and evaluated my own program of study, validated by an institution known for its innovative, rigorous, and student-driven curriculum. I formalized my curiosity and inclination in arts, mental health, and Jungian psychology into structured learning through reading, writing, experiential projects, and more rewriting than I had ever imagined. Despite riding nearly constant waves of fear and doubt, I worked harder than I ever had, and I successfully experienced my first encounter with academic agency and transformational learning. According to Nerstrom (2015), "Transformative learning challenges learners to interpret their own meanings rather than to adopt uncritically the beliefs and judgments of others. The process begins with an experience that prompts crucial reflection on one's learned assumptions" (p. 8). I saw myself as a different person, a learning person, a thinking person, a creative person, a writing person. Well, if I can do this, maybe I'm not stupid. Maybe I am smart enough. Why, maybe I am even smart. Wait, what is smart anyway? What is worthiness? And who is defining it? I learned that critical thinking begets more critical thinking. It was the first time I realized that not only was I capable of more than I previously thought, but I also knew more than I thought I did.

Lifelong Learning as a Process of Individuation

Developing an identity as a lifelong learner is a complex, multi-textured, and multi-layered experience that involves so much more than completion of academic requirements. My migration to the East Coast opened up a world of ideas and opportunities simply not afforded me in my family of origin and its culture. However, while I may have left my culture, my mother's aching, heartfelt intone in handwritten poetry, found in her china cupboard among her linens and life ephemera, remained a constant inspiration. I remember reading it countless times in my childhood ethnographic hunts—a found literary ruin: Pushing past the bounds of our lives is an act of individuation, an impulse to fulfill the longings and potential of one's life (Jung, 1969). I understand my adult learners because, like them, I have lived through complications resulting from exertions of my developing Self. Cell asserts that "messages learned early in life are adopted as truths, rarely with a backward glimpse to understand how or why they were formed" (as cited by Nerstrom, 2015, p. 8). With the benefit of perspective garnered through reflection as a life practice, I learned to recognize my personal trajectory as part of both my national youthful cohort and my individuation process. It was variously exhilarating and confusing, deeply disorienting, and yes, sometimes, even messy, just like my cohorts'. The

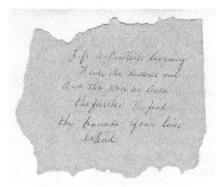

Life is constant learning
Never the lessons end
And the more we learn
the further we find
the bounds of our lives
extend.

Figure 14.1.   Handwritten poem.

transition from one culture to another, the deconstruction and reconstruction of belief systems, whether in developmental years, or later as adults, is typically a journey that includes disorienting dilemmas on numerous trajectories, crises of identity, and a massing of entangled life energies, better known as complexes; all of which can take a lifetime to untangle, if one chooses to undergo such a heroic undertaking (Campbell, 2008; Erikson, 1994; Maslow, 2014; Mezirow, 2000; Jung, 1969).

The Construction of Knowledge

Adult learners are typically patterned to having institutions affirm a curriculum of thought and knowledge rather than what we, as smart, living, breathing beings can affirm as our own hard-won experiential knowledge. Taylor and Marieneau (2016) note that adult learners do not recognize themselves as key players in constructing knowledge: "Much of their education to date has taught them how to 'do school'—largely to be passive recipients, to do what is expected of them, and to get the right answers" (p. 29).

At Goddard College, I experientially learned how learning occurs. Little did I know that this first significant academic journey and credential at Goddard would qualify me for establishing a PLA program at my current institution. Within an academic process, PLA, too, provides a structure and process to examine one's learning in a meaningful way. In PLA, adult learners experience an integration of what it means to construct knowledge, change perspectives, and transform what it means to experience something into what it means to learn something. Learning that has already been acquired through significant experiences now seeks affirmation and accreditation, an increasingly common practice in higher education since its inception in the 1940s (Klein-Collins & Hudson, 2017).

I seeded a love for learning because it was now driven by intrinsic motivation and a honed identity as a learner. I grew to love learning and the worlds, ideas, and opportunities that became available to me, in and out of the classroom. I identified with and internalized Goddard's pioneering spirit and its history of innovation and experimentation, growth, decline, and reemergence; a precursor to my later engagement with change processes and transformational learning. I know how learning occurs because I have engaged in it over and over again in my life. I began to take my seat in the academy long before the doctoral concept even entered my brain as another risky, thrilling, generative, paradigm-busting idea for professional and personal growth decades later. My mother's longing and prophetic words became my own and, in spirit, she continues to accompany me every step of the journey.

Freedom From Oppression Created Empathy

Upon completion of their PLA portfolio of experiential learning, my adult learners write a culminating Impact Statement to review and articulate what they learned in the reflective dive into their educational histories and experiential learning. In kindred spirit, in this living inquiry research, as I dig into layers of memory and experience, I realize that oppression experienced from the wounding in my early developmental years provides rich ground for understanding the imposter syndrome and also the resilience that powers not only my life but also my students' lives (Jung, 1969). I "get" my students and they feel it. In everyday vernacular, my "compost of crap," embedded in sociocultural, psychological, artistic, and spiritual development, is a superb source of empathy for my adult learners' learning journeys. Experience has taught me that the process of reflection in PLA is an opportunity to examine and rewrite life narratives, no matter how challenging. All along, I have admired my adult learners for their transparency and longing for freedom from the oppressive self-perceptions they harbor. In PLA, as in this living inquiry, while undergoing life-changing perspectives, wounds are often healed.

Each semester I bear witness to my PLA learners' marvel at the completion of their portfolios, whether face-to-face or online. It can be an occasion of delight and sometimes, quintessential separation as they reluctantly entrust their precious document into my care for the evaluation process. For some, it is a handover of relief and unburdening, including an exclamation and physical gesture of letting go. For others, the handover is a ritual of extreme risk and vulnerability accompanied by exclamations of fear, gestures of hanging on, including, amusingly, not letting go even as I attempt to receive it. I hear verbal or email expressions of "This is my baby! I don't want to let it go. Take good care of it!" In those moments, I know that I am a participant witness to a transformational declaration, a reclamation of Self into a new perspective as a generative, learning person. Their own private laments of "I am not worthy" have transformed into "I know more than I thought I did."

MAKING SENSE OF IT ALL

This living inquiry illuminates how my life is no different than my adult learners. Oppression comes in many forms. Through PLA, my adult learners affirm that lifelong learning begins, not in the classroom of formal educational processes and rituals, but in the act of everyday living in our work and personal cultures, as true to our nature as is possible, learning what needs to be learned, making meaning of its purpose, and becoming more conscious of the gestalt of it all.

The process of PLA, for me, is a metaphoric vessel constructed out of my own experiential learning, both personal and professional. It forms the belief that I hold for my adult learners: That PLA is a progressive, transformational, educational process of self-growth; affirming that we, as adult learners, indeed, know more than we realize. We have been life-long learners all along. It is wonderful and rewarding to have an institution validate one's learning and to obtain all the benefits that accompany a credential. But I, and my adult learners, know that it is also deeply satisfying to validate oneself through the reflection and meaning-making that results from recognizing our own learning, emancipating ourselves from our own oppression, and having the agency to continue learning that derives from within, not without.

REFERENCES

About Goddard. (2018). Retrieved from Goddard College Adult Degree Program, https://www.goddard.edu/about-goddard/

Bandura, A. (1977). Self-efficacy: Toward a unifying theory of behavioral change *Psychological Review, 84*, 191–215.

Bauman, Z. (1993). *Modernity and ambivalence*. New York, NY: Wiley.

Berger, J. (2004). Dancing on the threshold of meaning. Recognizing and understanding the growing edge. *Journal of Transformative Education, 2*(4), 336–351.

Brewer, P., & Marienau, C. (2016). Maintaining the integrity of portfolio assessment through theoretical understanding. In E. Bamford-Rees, B. Doyle, B. Klein-Collins, & D. Younger (Eds.), *Experiential learning and assessment for today's learner: The link between theory and practice* (pp. 1–7). Chicago, IL: CAEL.

Campbell, J. (2008). *The hero with a thousand faces* (3rd ed.). Novato, CA: New World Library.

Dewey, J. (1938). *Experience and education*. New York, NY: Touchstone.

Diaz, G., & McKenna. M. (Eds). (2004). *Teaching for aesthetic experience. The art of learning*. New York, NY: Peter Lang.

Ellis, C., & Bochner, A. (Eds.). (1996). *Composing ethnography. Alternative forms of qualitative writing*. Walnut Creek, CA: SAGE.

Erikson, E. (1994). *Identity and the life cycle*. New York, NY: W.W. Norton.

Freire, P. (2000). *Pedagogy of the oppressed*. London, England: Bloomsbury Academic.

Hollis, J. (2006). *Finding meaning in the second half of life*. New York, NY: Avery.

Irwin, R., & de Cosson, A. (2004). (Eds.). *a/r/tpgraphy. Rendering self through arts-based living inquiry*. Vancouver, BC, Canada: Pacific Educational Press.

Jung, C. G. (1969). *The archetypes and the collective unconscious* (2nd ed.). Princeton, NJ: Princeton University Press.

Jung, C. G. (1973). *Memories, dreams and reflections*. New York, NY: Pantheon Books.

Klein-Collins, K., & Hudson, S. (2017). Executive summary. *What happens when learning counts? Measuring the benefits of prior learning assessment for the adult learner*. CAEL self-study of the academic outcome of Learning Counts students. Chicago, IL: CAEL.

Larsen, E. (2010). *Text and texture: An exploration of transformation in adult learning* (doctoral dissertation). Lesley University, Cambridge, MA.

Lindeman, E. (1961). *The meaning of adult education*. Montreal, Canada: Harvest House.

Maslow, A. (2014). *Toward a psychology of being*. New York, NY: Sublime Books.

Mezirow, J. (2000). *Learning as transformation. Critical perspectives in theory on progress*. New York, NY: Jossey-Bass.

National Adult Learner Coalition White Paper (NALC). (2017). Strengthening America's economy by expanding educational opportunities for working adults. *Policy opportunities to connect the working adult to today's economy through education and credentials*. Chicago, IL: CAEL.

Nerstrem, N. (2015). Caution—University experience could change your life: Transformative learning in adult students. In E. Bamford-Rees, B. Doyle, B. Klein-Collins, & D. Younger (Eds.), *Advising the adult learner* (Vol. 1, pp. 8–13). Chicago, IL: CAEL.

Springgay, S., Irwin, R. L., Leggo, C., &, Gouzouasis, P. (Eds.) (2008). *Being with a/r/tography*. Rotterdam, Holland: Sense.

Taylor, K., & Marienau, C. (2016). Why the adult brain likes PLA: Part II. In E. Bamford-Rees, B. Doyle, B. Klein-Collins, & D. Younger (Eds.), *Why the adult brain likes PLA: Part II* (pp. 27–30). Chicago, IL: CAEL.

Tennant, M., & Pogson, P. (1995). *Learning and change in the adult years: A developmental perspective*. San Francisco, CA: Jossy-Bass.

Tisdell, E. (2003). *Exploring spirituality and culture in adult and higher education*. San Francisco, CA: Jossey-Bass.

CHAPTER 15

HOW DO YOU FORM AN IDENTITY FROM SWISS CHEESE?

Anjali J. Forber-Pratt
Vanderbilt University

INTRODUCTION

Cheese has always been a favorite food of mine; I was nicknamed the mouse in the house growing up. Those mice have left my core looking much like a piece of Swiss Cheese. There are gaping holes in my identity, pieces that will never be filled in. That is an absolute fact, one that I had to come to terms with. I do not know or know names of any blood relatives, including my birth mother or father. I come face-to-face with this every time I answer a questionnaire and it asks about family history. What happens when things you have reconciled about your own past and identities are thrown into the spotlight? The news of the Indian child-trafficking ring from the city of my birth implicates the nursing home where my brother was born and speculation of my orphanage is growing (Rowlatt, 2016; Walker, 2016). Though my identity as a person with a disability is often the most salient, my adoptive identity has resurfaced due to current events.

Identity and Lifelong Learning in Higher Education, pp. 267–276
Copyright © 2020 by Information Age Publishing
All rights of reproduction in any form reserved.

Incidents may happen somewhat far removed, like in the news, or may be more personal. When an incident escalates and you feel discriminated against, it is like being shoved down a black hole where you temporarily lose all faith in humanity. As a multiple minority, I am often left with these lingering unanswerable questions: Did this happen because I am disabled? Because I am a woman? Because I am a person of color? The purpose of this chapter is to illuminate this triple whammy through story telling. Stories are powerful tools that allow us to organize and share our experiences as they connect to the political, social, historical constructs in which we live. Stories have the potential to allow for debate and discussion through interrogation and deep questioning (Denzin, 2006), or simply to question the very world in which we live, where we have come from, and where we are today.

THE TRIPLE WHAMMY

My identity development has been sequential rather than simultaneous. One of the earlier chapter titles for this was The Triple Whammy. As a kid, teen, and adult, there are certain days when certain atrocities of humanity irk me so much. The incidents themselves are largely irrelevant—ranging from being denied access to board an airplane to being inconvenienced or teased. When the incident escalates and blatant discriminatory comments come out of somebody's mouth directed at you, it is like being pushed down that black hole. It is in the aftermath of such incidents when I feel the weight of the world bearing down on me, and yet I am often left with those lingering questions of, did this happen because I am disabled? Because I am a woman? Because I am a person of color? I would yell this at the top of my lungs, asking, "Why?!" to my mother, telling her that she did not get it, she had no right to try to console me because there was no way ever that she, a White woman without a disability could ever understand what I was going through. I would cry asking why was my life a triple whammy? Life is not fair, and I learned this very young. Thankfully, my mother was affirming and did not try to dispute my rant, rather, she told me I was right, and that some things are not fair and that she did not truly understand.

Disability Identity

For me, disability was always a piece of my identity. I acquired it at such a young age, it is a part of who I am. I rarely questioned it, it just was the deck of cards I was dealt. At age 7, I started public speaking (albeit at my older brother's class) but as a 7-year-old going up to the middle school to give a talk, it was a big deal. My talk was about how "I can do different things." It was about my acceptance of my disability and how I never let it stop me from achieving what I wanted to, it was a healthy part of who I am, but I also acknowledged the times when it was a pain in the neck, when it would frustrate me.

Part of my embodiment of my identity as a person with a disability was also the responsibility I felt and continue to feel to this day to educate others. I do not take this responsibility lightly, nor do I view it as a burden to me.

From an article in *Baystate Parent* (Roberge, 2011),

> "The educational piece is very important to me," she says. "That's how questions get answered." Whatever the question, Forber-Pratt prefers that parents find a constructive and positive way to help their children find the answers they seek. "It's a natural reaction for parents when their kids start asking about my wheelchair, they tend to shush them and pull them away," she says. "I would much rather the child be allowed to come and ask me. It could be a teachable moment, maybe for the parent too. (p. 1)

I will never forget one question that I was asked back in 1999 by a sixth grader from Long Island. He asked me, if there was a pill that I could take that would allow me to walk again would I take it? I paused at that moment on stage, because unlike every other question asked during most assemblies, I realized, I had to think about it. I used one of the oldest tricks in the book, re-stating the question, then stating, wow, what a really thoughtful question! (to give myself more time to formulate my answer). That question was one of the toughest questions I have ever answered, and I have continued to think about it years later.

I searched for this answer for years. In an odd sense, my disability has been a blessing to me. I have been able to find myself as an individual and also to make a difference practically everywhere I go. As I think about my life, the most important lessons that I have learned, such as how to deal with discrimination, would have been much harder for me to learn without being disabled. With this triple whammy sentence, these lessons presented themselves regularly. To me the student's question was almost like, if you could wave a magic wand and make all your problems disappear, would you? In my mind the obstacles that come about throughout life are what make you a stronger, well-rounded human being.

And so, my response today: no, absolutely not. My disability is a part of who I am. It is my identity and nothing that I have done in my life would have been possible without it; to me, my disability has opened doors.

As a woman, this piece of my identity was similar to disability, it just was always there and I was comfortable with that. There have been some roadblocks that may be because of my status as a woman, but which card is the ace? That is something I may never know the answer to.

As a person of color, for me this piece of my identity development has been intertwined with my status as an adoptee with two White parents. This story will be discussed in the next section.

To some degree, I always hoped the uphill battle would just one day get better. I dreamed that getting out of high school would mean the real world would be supportive of me for who I am; I dreamed that college would be better. I even as a young kid wholeheartedly believed that I would outgrow my disability! There is some level of realization though, a type of an ah-ha moment when you realize, you know what, this is my life. For me, this was the realization that I will *always* be different; a minority.

The downfall that many of us encounter with this realization, is taking on the negative projection of what this means. It is easy to say, life sucks and there's nothing I can do about it, woe is me, and to throw yourself a pity party. I have sent invitations out to my own pity parties before, I have been there. These are the days when you just want to slip away into a deep abyss and forget about it all; the days when I resent others who appear to have it so much easier than I do. It is also during this dark time when thoughts invade such as, what would happen if I did just slip away, would the world even notice I was gone?

I think the world would notice. They would be missing out on some great stories from me that's for sure! I will always be a minority, someone who is different, but I now realize that it is important to embrace these differences and to wear them boldly and with pride. So how do you do it? What is the secret ingredient, the recipe so to speak to identity formation? For me, it was about learning to let others in, to chip away at the fortress I had spent years building around my true core, to have conversations about social justice issues surrounding difference. By silencing your own true feelings, or only letting them come out as tears, it destroys you. There is a crucial role of supportive relationships and environments to navigate this. Even though outwardly, I have always been bold and daring, particularly with athletics, there are rules in wheelchair racing, and rules of ski racing that keep you somewhat on track; but there is no rule book for making this leap of faith to voice my true feelings.

I have come to realize that I have to strive to do the best I can with what I am given, holes and all. I recognize the gaps and the holes in my piece of cheese and *talk* about them. There are parts of all of our lives that we might not ever know the answers to, but I have learned that letting these unanswerable questions become all consuming, they will, quite literally, paralyze. Living with a spinal cord injury, I do not view myself as paralyzed by it, so I grew to realize that I couldn't allow this time of deep questioning to paralyze me either. I do admit that there were some dark months in there, some times of deep questioning and days where I literally could not get myself out of bed, and I wondered if life was even worth it. I got angry at professors, mentors and coaches who were telling me to live my life where my values were in alignment with my actions, because I felt it was an unfair expectation. It was unfair because I was a piece of Swiss cheese, not knowing all the pieces. Who were they to tell me to align something when I did not, and do not and will not ever have a full deck of cards?

For me, it was about putting my life under a microscope to identify the things in my life that grounded me, that were real. I also had to build with what I did know, and to stop fantasizing about what I didn't know in my past.

To form one's identity, I firmly believe it comes from your experiences, and your dialogue with others. As scary as it was, I knew in my heart of hearts I needed to get on a plane to India, to go back to where it all started to try to piece together what I could. The first trip back to India, that was a different trip; that first trip was the awe-struck-oh-my-god-this-is-what-India-is-like trip. You cannot process anything. It just is a whirlwind.

MY LEAP OF FAITH

My second trip, I went in with no plan, no expectations, no clue what I was doing. I just booked a plane ticket and went. That is pretty scary and slightly more difficult being disabled. But wrestling with the sleepless nights, and extreme depression, I knew I had to at least try. It was my attempt at filling in these gaps and holes in my identity. How do you do this without feeling so unbelievably vulnerable? You have to take that leap of faith and expose yourself despite fear of rejection, fear of loss and then, you will find that support in others. Every facet of my motto, *Dream. Drive. Do.*® can be seen in this small snippet of this Indian adventure.

The dream: To make a difference in the lives of orphans, those literally left on the sidelines of life. To show their teachers that they are worthy of attaining an education, of living life. My first time back to India I was heartbroken when I saw the orphans with disabilities essentially abandoned upstairs with no elevator in a room with no windows, very little stimulation, and minimal supervision. I needed that glimpse into what my life could have been like in India in order to grapple with my adoptive identity. Going there gave me that perspective in multiple ways. I witnessed and had my own everyday struggles and battles every moment that I was in India. I describe it to others as being a challenging trip to take, not just emotionally, but also challenging in the sense of having to go from being completely independent here in American culture to completely dependent. For example, I had to plan out my entire day for when I would have access to a somewhat useable, preferably Western style restroom and when somebody would be available to help me up the stairs to use it.

I saw, firsthand, the lack of educational opportunities and meaningful work experiences for people with disabilities. I would sit in a manually powered rickshaw taking in the scene of the dirty street, extreme heat, the invasion of the senses of the smells of spices, bright colors, honking of horns and lack of traffic rules and a man with polio would catch my eye. Amidst the chaos and sensory overload, I wondered, why was this man with the classic dropped foot gait due to polio working at least 20 times harder than a normal able-bodied person to walk infinitely slower up the street carrying that bucket, when to me, a wheelchair would be so much more enabling? And then I did a scan of my surroundings and realized, that man has a job and he does the best he can to hide his disability to be given the chance to be a contributing member to society. To him, on these streets, a wheelchair would be disabling.

It would be easy to feel guilty in these situations. I do acknowledge these experiences were powerful, meaningful and life changing. But I do not feel guilty about having them. The bottom line is: If I had not been adopted, I firmly believe I still would have gotten sick and acquired my disability, and I either would have died or been one of those kids trapped on the upper level of the orphanage shunned from society with hardly any language, no education and deprived of all opportunities. I firmly believe that these insights garnered happened for a reason. These experiences validate that I was put on this earth for a reason: To make a difference and to be a role model for others, especially those who face any type of adversity or who are left on the sidelines. I believe my mission is not just for people with disabilities, though that is one culture I am naturally well versed in and certainly passionate about.

My second trip to India was about filling in the holes in my own identity. It takes an immense amount of drive from within to go on such a trip, especially in my case. The laws and regulations pertaining to persons with disabilities are so very different in India. I am constantly faced with inaccessibility, lack of understanding and dumbfounded looks that I, as a person with a disability, would be traveling *alone* without help from a caretaker or a husband. There are little things, such as forgetting the fact that an aisle chair works better if the plane is not full of people. Or, asking to use the aisle chair to use the bathroom, but being told that there is a line. And then, having to explain that unless I get up and into the aisle chair and in the same line as everybody else, there will always be a line and I may never get to use the bathroom. Educating the world. That is what I am talking about. There are bigger things, like making a hotel reservation at a known 5-star hotel chain and being told enthusiastically that yes, they can accommodate a wheelchair and that they have a lift, only to discover that in order to get to the lift, you have to climb up five stairs.

This snippet of the next story (Forber-Pratt, 2017) also appeared in Hadler and Assaf's book, *Inclusion, Disability & Culture: Ethnographic Approach Traversing Abilities and Challenges*. One trip, I arrived in Mumbai, a totally foreign airport to me. As the plane approaches to land, it reminds me exactly of the scene from *Slumdog Millionaire* where you see the tent city up close, pan out, see more of it, pan out again, more. For as far as the eye can see, you see slums, yet the juxtaposition of life going on all around it with big commercial planes landing right overhead. Getting off of the plane, things seem to be going fairly smoothly, until I am in the aisle chair on the jet bridge and my wheelchair is nowhere to be found. I ask, patiently at first, but with an immense amount of anxiety in my voice. I am told, it is raining. That is the reason for not having my own wheelchair, is because it is raining a bit. It is times like this when you make the decision to rely on all those ounces of patience, and to just go with the flow. I inquire as to when I will see my wheelchair, will it be at baggage claim? Will I get it before customs? When will I have my independence back? I get an answer in Hindi that I do not fully understand, but I think it means that maybe it will be at luggage, to not worry and that this chair is fine … this chair that I cannot push or propel myself. I feel like I am a part of a factory assembly line as I get lined up with the other elders and pregnant women who are also using wheelchairs and am just left to wait for an "appropriate person" to come to push me through this foreign airport.

After some time goes by, I notice I am the only one left in the terminal building, sitting in a chair that I cannot propel myself. This is about the time when you start to wonder, have I been forgotten about? What now? All the other passengers are off the plane and on their way, it is now about midnight in Mumbai international airport and I am sitting in a wheelchair I cannot propel myself with my carry-on luggage decoratively placed like a Christmas tree. Great! Wow, what an opportunity! I just sit patiently, what else is there to do?

After some time goes by, a man comes over speaking in Hindi, I presume, and wants to know why nobody has come for me. I wish I knew the answer. He gets a bit irritated, then keeps rapid fire asking me questions I do not understand. I show him my boarding pass and tell him samaana? Meaning, luggage/baggage claim? Figuring if I got that far I could figure it out. We start on a long journey through the halls of the deserted airport, go through customs. I spot one of my favorite signs, "unaccompanied women, pregnant women, handicapped." It is in this moment I am keenly aware I am very low in the social stratosphere here.

These journeys to India started to fill in some of the missing holes in my identity; each journey has played a critical role in my own lifelong learning. Until visiting Calcutta, I did not truly identify with being Indian. I think this is one of the challenges adoptees who grow up with White parents may face; it is hard to gain a full appreciation of the culture you come from when you don't experience it until later in life. It was a bit of a paradox growing up in a predominantly White community and not fitting in there to then travel to India where everybody looked the same, but still not fitting in there either. On my trips to India, I learned that my story was different than how I had created it in my head. I was not just an orphan from a broken, poorest of the poor family; I was born in a nursing home (in American terms, like a hospital) which means my birth mother had some money and was likely from a middle-class caste. I have come to realize that for my birthmother to give me up was an act very similar to a mother turtle, where you want to protect and keep your babies safe but you know you cannot be the one to guide your child along every step of the way. It was more of an act of selflessness and wanting me to have a better life than her. I was also keenly aware that there were not enough records to ever know or search for blood relatives, and that is something that has never bothered me. I was not yearning for India to find my birthparents, I was yearning to process this aspect of my identity and hungry to learn more about India and Indian culture.

I had always previously only defined myself as a person with a disability, and I now realized I was also a woman, a person of color, and an adoptee. It was the first time I entertained the idea of allowing these multiple identities to truly develop. It may sound silly to some, but up to this point my identity development had been very sequential; I would spend a period of time in my life developing my identity as a person with a disability and set that aside, then there were rare times that I would dabble in developing my identity as a person of color, but I usually would just forget about it and resort to my White ways of living that came from my surroundings. These trips allowed me to finally develop these multiple identities simultaneously.

REVISITING MY INDIAN IDENTITY

Each trip I make back, I feel these strands of my identity getting stronger. However, it is not always a positive developmental trajectory and sometimes these strands are stretched when you least expect it, not on your terms. This is the hard work of lifelong learning! Let me explain. In November and December of 2016, a huge child trafficking racket was uncovered in Calcutta (Rowlatt, 2016; Walker, 2016). The allegations were astounding and made huge ripples on national and international news. Many news outlets, such as the *Times of India* (Ghosh, 2016) and *DNA India* (Mehta, 2016) reported that individuals were arrested for various crimes such as: kidnapping or abducting child under 10 years with intent to steal from its person, buying or disposing of any person as a slave, act done with intent to prevent child being born alive or to cause it to die after birth and criminal conspiracy. My brother, Ian Anand was also adopted from India (and lived in India for nearly eight years and his wife's family is based there). As the news of this child trafficking racket broke, it became evident that the nursing home where he was born was the main hub of the racket, Sree Krishna Nursing Home. We both shudder looking at photos of us together at and outside of the home on one of my journeys back. The corruption and the roots of this racket run deep. We were at the same orphanage, and it is quite likely that the orphanage was "supplied" by other nursing homes that were a part of this racket. This news rocked the Indian adoptee community. We cannot help but be a little emotional. Were we trafficked? Was *I* a victim of child trafficking? Is the narrative I have found peace with about an act of selflessness from my birthmother deciding to give me up for adoption false?

We will never know.

Secretly, or perhaps not so secretly, I am jealous of the fact that my brother was able to live a life in India, planted roots there and all that he has done and will continue to do there. Accessibility is scarce. This is always a constant struggle of mine going there and being a part of India. Many international adoptees talk about feeling a little bit as an outsider in America, and a little as an outsider in their birth country too. Though Ian Anand may feel some of that in India, he is very much an integral part of the community. That is something I am envious of; as a person with a disability and as a woman, it is not as practical for me to just go and live there. Though, I have begun to realize that instead of trying to figure out how to make me a part of India, there are ways that I can make India a part of me. For example, I have found ways to bring my research to India by conducting a case study to investigate perceptions and definitions of disability and inclusion. This is one way that my adoptee and person of color identities are able to stay alive and to connect with my identity as a disabled person as well as linking me to a broader community to process current events together. This also highlights the fact that this lifelong journey to reconcile and strengthen my identities is far from over. So, while my identity may have been formed from Swiss cheese, it's a good thing my favorite food is cheese.

REFERENCES

Denzin, N. K. (2006). Analytic autoethnography, or déjà vu all over again. *Journal of Contemporary Ethnography, 35*, 419–428. doi:10.1177/0891241606286985

Forber-Pratt, A. J. (2017). "Not everybody can take trips like this": A Paralympian's perspective on educating about disability around the world. In S. H Hadler & L. Assaf (Eds.), *Inclusion, disability & culture: Ethnographic approach traversing abilities and challenges* (pp. 59–75). New York, NY: Springer. doi:10.1007/978-3-319-55224-8_5

Hadlerm S. H., & Assaf, L. (2017) *Inclusion, disability & culture: Ethnographic approach traversing abilities and challenges* New York, NY: Springer. doi:10.1007/978-3-319-55224-8_5

Ghosh, D. (2016, November 25). Woman 14th to be held in baby trafficking case. *Times of India.* Retrieved from https://timesofindia.indiatimes.com/city/kolkata/Woman-14th-to-be-held-in-baby-trafficking-case/articleshow/55608447.cms

Mehta, P. (2016, November 24). West Bengal: 13th arrest made in connection with newborn trafficking racket. *DNA India.* Retrieved from https://www.dnaindia.com/india/report-newborn-trafficking-racket-uncovered-in-west-bengal-one-of-the-biggest-in-eastern-india-2276517

Roberge, A. (2011, January 1). Anjali's story: Sports are possible. *Baystate Parent Magazine,* p. 1.

Rowlatt, J. (2016, December 9). Trafficked babies, black money and India's values. *BBC News.* Retrieved from https://www.bbc.com/news/world-asia-india-38222672

Walker, P. (2016, December 24). 'Baby-smuggling ring' uncovered by police in India. *Independent.* Retrieved from https://www.independent.co.uk/news/world/asia/baby-smuggling-ring-gang-india-mumbai-children-kidnap-a7494101.html

CHAPTER 16

AT THE INTERSECTION OF IDENTITY, DISABILITY, AND POWER

Xóchitl L. Méndez
Lesley University

The self, when confronted with severe disability and pain, becomes vulnerable across social and, consequently, educational settings. In the struggle to make sense of disability and pain, some teacher-student interactions—though well-intentioned—rather than being empowering and self-affirming, can instead negatively affect students with disabilities. This may take place when teachers and mentors unintentionally impose dominant societal understandings that predetermine, and thus undermine, the student's own sense of agency. In the teaching setting, as in the personal setting, a common pitfall is assuming that the student's life-story should fit a redeeming narrative of struggle and success—often measured by external, socially defined scales. Furthermore, if the intrinsic unsayability of a lived experience of impairment and disability is brushed off, efforts to "help" or "save" the individual, could be seen, in themselves, as a form of oppression.

Identity and Lifelong Learning in Higher Education, pp. 277–288
Copyright © 2020 by Information Age Publishing

Focusing on the above, I relate a personal experience that can be characterized as a "mixed contact,"—a "social situation" (Goffman, 1986, p. 12), where identities and social categories are fraught with uneasiness and uncertainties. My physical condition currently makes it impossible for me to sit or stand for prolonged amounts of time, yet I engage with the world in a supine position with the help of a fully reclining wheelchair where I can lie down. My participation in the public sphere can be construed by the normal population as a challenge to the implicit rules of social interaction. Nevertheless, seeing these conventions as arbitrary obstacles, not as discrediting attributes (Goffman, 1986)—a courageous decision that is often the stance of an individual confronting disability—may result in "primal scenes of sociology" (Goffman, 1986, p. 13) that can lead to distress or vulnerability. I hope that the exchange I relate in this chapter sheds light on pitfalls and difficulties, as well as on perspectives and solutions that might be helpful to others, specifically to teachers and those interacting with individuals afflicted with a disability, and vulnerable populations in general, inside and outside the classroom.

Dovetailing with the narrative of my experience, sometimes interlacing theoretical concepts, I argue that effective support of students with disabilities, and of vulnerable populations, is very much a shared journey of accompaniment, a turning of the tables: the teacher learns from the student about what, within the limits of disability, can still be done and together engage in a conversation that allows the student to reconstruct an identity, to forge a new self—an opportunity for growth, affirmation, and self-determination.

NARRATIVE

The early New England winter afternoon was chilly, with skies a tad overcast, yet brightened by a colorful sunset. Sitting on my wheelchair, rolling into the room where I was to meet with an outgoing and kind-hearted teacher and author who I will refer to as J.B. (not his real initials), I was looking forward to talking about my studies, about scholars the like of Gadamer, Ricoeur, maybe Geertz. J.B. had kindly offered to engage in a conversation to help me solidify topics for my dissertation. I felt a discussion could be helpful, and though J.B. is not my advisor nor faculty at my university, and his work is outside of my field, he is also extremely knowledgeable and he kindly offered his time in a spirit of cooperation. I felt ready and confident.

It was not easy, however, to maneuver the wheelchair across the doorframe. Though I am only about 110 pounds, the wheelchair alone is 40 pounds—a big black heavy contraption. It has a reclining back and elevating footrests that I have covered with memory foam to make them more comfortable. My brother, who gave me a ride that day, assisted me with the wheelchair, as I cannot handle it on my own. J.B. was cordial, and he graciously waited as my brother and I set up the wheelchair. He seemed a bit taken aback when my brother proceeded to raise the wheelchair's footrests and recline the back. Wide-eyed, J.B. observed, his head tilted a bit. I assumed he had never met with a student lying down on a fully reclining wheelchair.

My brother left the room once the chair was set. I exclaimed, "Ready," setting up my backpack on the floor. J.B. and I exchanged some pleasantries, yet before I could say much, he asked bluntly, "Tell me about your condition. What happened?" He leaned forward on his chair, very attentively waiting to hear. "When did it start?" he asked, eagerly wanting to learn about a diagnosis he was not familiar with. "And how did it start?" He remained curious. 5 minutes, 10 minutes, 15 minutes, 20 minutes and counting, I still found myself answering questions about my illness. This is intellectually and emotionally a difficult task, forcing me to try to explain medical terms—allodynia, hyperalgesia, neuron responses to pain, the central nervous system, and so on—objectivizing my own body and setting aside the sadness of my diagnosis.

What about the conversation on narratives and interpretation we were going to have? Were we going to talk about Gadamer? Geertz? I glanced at the clock on the wall. It was getting late, thirty minutes into our meeting. Suddenly, I felt this conversation was beginning to box me in, and that whatever his interpretation of my disease was, it was now conditioning his impression of me.

J.B. was eagerly trying to understand, however. I had no recourse but to continue elaborating on my condition. "After I left the hospital, it took a while to be able to walk again. Now I can swim everyday, and I'm getting stronger. I need to build up my muscles, but because of the pain it's hard. So I have to go very slowly," I said. By the look in his eyes, he didn't seem too impressed with my partial recovery. "But I'm getting so much better!" I exclaimed.

He then continued, "I am being so intrusive, I'm sorry. But ... how do you support yourself?" I felt shame. "So your brother helps you?" He paused here. "I see," he added. My answers, I began to perceive, sketched an image of disability—a judgment, incomplete and distorted. No matter what questions he asked, in my replies I could not affirm what I *can* do, nor was there an opportunity to portray my life as seen from my own eyes. "Your brother is..." he turned his eyes towards the door through which my brother had left. "Is your brother married? Does he have a family?" His corollary, I felt, was that I was the cause of my brother being single. He seemed to feel bad for him. "To help you ..." he began. I suddenly felt bad for my brother too. From his statements, I knew I should infer I was the cause of the misfortunes of those around me.

"Can you earn a living?" "Could you maybe do some typing and make a living?" I felt more and more conflicted. I looked at the clock. I no longer felt compelled to explain many of the reasons and circumstances that bear on my life. Every minute I felt less and less trusting. I didn't want to share.

So I proceeded to attempt to ask questions about him too. "Next time," he replied. "We have so little time, I am so sorry. I have to leave early." (He had mentioned this at the beginning of our meeting.) "Next time…. We need to find a way to help you."

Most of what I could glean about J.B., given he volunteered nothing substantial, I gathered from his gestures, a look in his eyes, a comment here and there, and of course his questioning. Even though he tried to make me feel at ease by conveying an aura of warmth and concern, I felt powerless. My way of seeing the world, my own identity, the self-concept of capability I had created for myself, did not seem real to him. Only the "objective" reality of my disability—which he was creating with his very questions—seemed true to him. There was no dialectic. His attention and interest was on deficits as he saw them.

"So you can't sit up without reclining?" "I can't sit down for long periods of time because of the pain." "But for how long can you sit?" "And … you say you can walk. How far can you walk?" he inquired more deeply. "I can walk about four hundred steps per day," I replied. He paused here, he shook his head a bit, seeming to think, "So little?"

Trying to remark on the power imbalance of our conversation, I suddenly pointed out, "I feel like I'm in an interrogation room!" Yet to my surprise, he quickly retorted, "It's good for you," and then continued to ask more questions. I looked down.

As the conversation continued, I realized I began to perceive myself as he appeared to understand me. This reminded me of a passage by Hannah Arendt (1958) where she writes that reality is what can "be seen and heard by others" (p. 50). J.B.'s leading questions, and my inability to redress the imbalance in the power dynamics of our interaction, boxed me in a social category of disability. I tried to feel self-empowered but failed. "But there is so much I can do!" I thought to myself. Yet it seemed as if my recovery, in itself far more work than many an endeavor the healthy ever confront, had become virtually insignificant. "When, in this conversation, did I become my disease, and very little else, in the first place?" I thought to myself, "I'm much more than that! I'm more than my body!"

From where he sat, he seemed to consider the enormity, the vastness, the massive reality that separated us. I was taunted by his effortless ability to just sit normally. I suddenly felt I didn't measure up. My efforts and agency had no meaning given I lacked so much. "Identities [are] cognitive schemas—internally stored information and meanings serving as frameworks for interpreting experience," wrote Stryker and Burke (2000, p. 286). The identity I had built for myself, the accomplishments of transitioning from a young woman, bed-ridden and virtually immobile 24 hours a day to doing some walking (albeit very short distances still), my having completed two graduate degrees, all that significance, all that effort, suddenly felt insignificant. Indeed "distress may arise if feedback from others—in the form of reflected appraisals or perceptions of the self suggested by others' behavior—is perceived to be incongruent with one's identity" (Hogg, Terry, & White, 1995, p. 257).

He finally gave his judgment: "I think you must get out, go to the hospitals, make contacts. If you want a job in the future—you know jobs are not just handed out—you have to go and work on it." Though I do get out as much as possible, I found myself apologizing while trying to convey some of the very real challenges this represents, but based on his examining my answers, he seemed to think I was making excuses.

As the hour drew near, he apologized for needing to "rush off so quickly." He certainly seemed disappointed at having to cut our meeting short. He warmly took his leave, wished me the best and promised to email me to find a date to continue. I then found myself alone pondering about this experience.

INTERPRETING THROUGH THEORY

I preface my analysis by acknowledging that this meeting carried its own challenges for J.B., and that these likely contributed to his emphasizing my illness as the center of our discussion. Perhaps J.B., trying to help, felt he needed to address my disability first—a decision that might seem common sense yet is, as I will explain, unlikely to be conducive to an effective dialog. Furthermore, having to face a visible disability forces an interlocutor to confront his own vulnerabilities, bringing to the fore concerns regarding illness and aging, which can be difficult to confront.

In our meeting, J.B. kept returning to questions about symptoms, about manifestations, about causes. Goffman (1986) describes how individuals marked with severe visible disabilities or socially stigmatizing discrediting attributes are approached by others: "Strangers may feel free to strike up ... conversations in which they express ... morbid curiosity about ... condition[s], or in which they proffer [unsolicited] help" (p. 16). J.B. was doing this and trying—though without the certitude and training of a physician—to carry out a differential diagnosis. His intellectual curiosity began around knowing how my disease could be set apart from other diseases.

Just as Fritsch (2016) indicated, for J.B., impairments were "discrete categories of existence" (p. 346) that should be known to be controlled or at least understood. J.B. assumed that biology and impairment enact disability (Fritsch, 2016). He was, though unwittingly, carrying out an act of "biocertification" (Fritsch, 2016) that makes the disease, and the person, a subject within a category "functioning to create knowable social identities so as to govern them accordingly" (Fritsch, 2016, p. 345). My questions to him, though I was very polite and did not dare to articulate them, were "Why do you want to know?" "Why focus on my illness as an agent rather than me as a person?"

His interrogation, and the reductive process that this entailed, is unfortunately all too frequent. The disabled are commonly essentialized into a category that is passive and inferior, scientific, and naturalized (Hall, 1996)—a category based on an "objectifying taxonomy" where the body is a "static fact" (Snyder & Mitchell, 2001, p. 371). Indeed, for J.B., my body, as he perceived it, was an unmodifiable (i.e., static) fact with an undeniable meaning, one of limitation that he assumed he could categorize after a few cursory questions.

This entire process, of hastily imposing a category on the disabled, is in fact not based on biology. When examined critically, it can be seen that this categorization is mostly an exercise in power relations—of imposing societal perspectives that equate impairment with disability. These categories often presuppose uselessness in an ableist economy. Additionally, and perniciously, there is often the ableist suspicion of the disabled individual "faking" disability as a means to pursue gains such as Social Security payments, Workers Compensation, or simply seeking additional attention and love from family members. Imposing a category or identity of disability, rather than being based on facts of the body, is thus a normative judgment that revolves around the sort of biological essentialism (Lawler, 2014) that is often understood as "common-sense," that is, assuming that a "crippled body" is something so evident and so clear-cut that no further thought is needed before rendering judgment.

Identity is a social phenomena reenacted and reaffirmed, or denied and devalued, in the social domain (Blumer, 1969; Lawler, 2014). Fundamental to these meaning-making processes and enactments, social relations give rise to an intersubjective realm (Arendt, 1958) in which "reality" is defined as what can be seen or heard by society. Thus the individual's self-concept, akin to "subjectivities" (Gill & Scharff, 2011), depends on the social collective to achieve recognition (Jackson, 2013). Identity cannot be understood separately from the social world in which humans spin their "webs of significance" (Geertz, 1973, p. 5). Identity is a result of intersubjective exchanges that are part of a social discourse at the very intersection of disability, narratives, and power.

As I experienced that afternoon, and as is the case in most discourse, the sustainment of the many identities individuals believe define them is always negotiated, procured, and contested through speech and interactions often imbued with prejudice and power. In my exchange with J.B., our discourse served mostly as a vehicle for *his* conceptions of my identity, which I felt he disassembled into pieces in his analysis—with him evaluating every piece for value.

Metaphorically speaking, our conversation became a mirror that showed a reflection of myself as viewed from *his* point of view. In the case of individuals with disabilities, crucially, identity can also be interpreted as an exercise of exclusion. This reflects Hall's (1996) concept of identity as "points of identification … [functioning] only because of their capacity to exclude, to leave out, to render 'outside,' abjected" (p. 5). J.B. was, unintendedly, affirming difference that—once exoticized—became the most captivating topic for him to discuss.

Social identities are reinterpreted by each person and lived as "subjectivity," as concepts of self. This "makes it possible for any particular social identity to be lived either thoroughly or ambivalently" (Wetherell, 2008, pp. 75–76). My identity—or to emphasize fluidity and process, my identity-making—I elect to believe is a project accrued through a constellation of choices, adaptations, ability, talent, uniqueness, and potential. This personal exercise in meaning-making is the result of a long and protracted mediation that aims for a cohesive of two complementary sides always in tension: how I understand myself, and how can I project myself to others, especially when others easily fall in the trap of assuming that individuals with disabilities are mostly different, when in fact, it is the other way around, that is, the salience of difference is a result of an implicit bias pointing to an assumed superiority of the typical over the atypical, that is, of the so-called "abled-bodies" versus the disabled (Scott, 1992).

TOWARDS A VISION OF ACCOMPANIMENT

What perhaps made J.B.'s approach misguided, at least in my view, was his insistence on first locating me on a plane of the "objective" as *he* assumed it to be, that is, someone unable to sit or stand. Instead, he should have first created a space of trust, taken the time to nurture it, and then redress the inherent imbalances in our relation by sharing at least a modicum of information about himself. Perhaps he could have then striven to create a voice of connection (Cheever, 1995) relational in nature (Gammel & Rutstein-Riley, 2016; Miller, 1986)—not one of paternalism and interrogation.

As J.B. continued his interrogation and, though he was interested in me so much that he could not stop hearing and wanted to hear everything, he perplexedly never seemed centrally interested in my point of view nor in my narrative of selfhood. He seemed uninterested in how I defined my own agency, what I wanted to do, and how these wants were in fact based on what I could do. He saw me as an uncertain amount of untapped potential that—and here I hypothesize and speculate—needed to be emancipated.

A tendency to impose emancipation on others, well intentioned yet to an extent ironic, can in itself become an act of oppression. As difficult as it can be in practice, J.B. could have listened first, and later, in subsequent meetings, asked what I thought I wanted to do, and what I thought was possible, and then together, begin a common journey of accompaniment. A similar journey is referred to by Gustavo Gutiérrez when speaking of the poor. I believe this also applies to the person with disabilities. Gutiérrez speaks of this process as "walking with—not behind or in front—but beside a real person ... at his or her own particular pace ... in their struggles of survival.... There is no outside plan to be imposed" (Weiss Block & Griffin, 2013, loc. 276).

This accompaniment, this opening of hearts and minds, offers a true opportunity for growth that is patent to both student and teacher, but that places on the teacher, especially when teaching vulnerable groups, a higher onus on the act of decoding, balancing, and transforming oppressive social dynamics (Giroux, 1985), while truly demanding a role of "service-learning" (Grain & Lund, 2016) and of finding, at least in the interpersonal realm, "spaces of possible action" (Apple, 2011, p. 229).

This journey of accompaniment might evoke, at first, an appearance of indifference or passive resistance. Initially, the student might seem not to engage or respond. This is not a sign of rejection, but a result of the existential confinement that Arendt (1958) describes as being "imprisoned in the subjectivity of [one's] own singular experience" (p. 58). Persons with severe pain, disability, or serious illness, often have the conviction of living a reality that is unrelatable and thus often use silence or expeditious, superficial answers to questions and exchanges.

Indeed, the difficulty of expressing the challenges I have experienced across many years, that is, the indescribability of being disabled every day, the struggles, despair, obstacles, disappointments, the chronic pain—all that cannot be put into words. All of it can perhaps only be expressed as, quoting Moore (1988), "all that unsayable life!" (p. 237). Virginia Woolf (2017) echoes this unshareability when she writes "human beings do not go hand in hand the whole stretch of the way. There is a virgin forest in each; a snowfield where even the print of birds' feet is unknown. Here we go alone" (loc. 28632). Indeed, extreme pain and trauma can be "so fundamentally inaccessible and unshareable that any attempt at recounting one's experiences is haunted by the stark fact that one's suffering will always and necessarily be received by others with radical doubt" (Dauphinée, 2007, p. 142; Scarry, 1985, p. 4). Edkins (2003) expresses it so after traumatic experiences: "what we can say no longer makes sense; what we want to say, we can't. There are no words for it" (p. 8).

Confronted with this silence, it is often too tempting to force a narrative onto the student with disabilities—narratives that commonly revolve around the storylines of overcoming difficulties or regaining function. These stories of redemption and restitution are well-intentioned attempts that reflect a hope of uplifting finality and of finding solutions. However, we must be aware that, as Jackson (2013) says, "it is often the case that in times of extreme hardship people repudiate such legerdemain" (p. 39). Moreover, rather than the inherent power imbalance that a salvationist narrative entails, its greater offense is the imposition of a storyline with an extraneous finality on an identity that is vulnerable and in the making.

This is an unavoidable tension. The teacher and the outside world aspire to resolution, and compassion is naturally allied to the redeemer's impulse. Moreover, the teacher is justified in seeing his or her contributions and hard work as helpful, self-satisfying, and enriching to his or her own sense of self and professionalism. Nevertheless, in some cases where disability and illness are involved, and in particular when students face extraordinary social and physical barriers, the magnitude of adversity may make it impossible to comply with a teacher's expectations. In these cases, the individual with disabilities might be permanently unable to conform and fulfill social norms. Given this irresolvable conflict between the student's impairments and social expectations, the role of the teacher and mentor may not be of "liberating" the student, but of trying to reconcile (partially at best in many cases) some of these tensions by fostering a space of trust. To rephrase Jackson (2013), the existential question is then how can "immobilization, reduction and nullification of the person be resisted and transfigured, so that self-determination and power is regained" (p. 115).

A possible answer is for the student and teacher to join forces with sincerity in spaces of mutual respect and trust—even while rigor and performance are demanded from the student. Hopefully, when these voices of connection (Cheever, 1995) and mutual empowerment (Walker, 2013 p. 133) are established, in this mutual journey of accompaniment, the student may bolster his or her own agency as he or she defines it. Slowly, incrementally, and then suddenly, with skills and tools learned during this journey, with confidence regained, a new internal life-story of affirmation and a renewed self can begin to take hold.

CONCLUSION AND SUMMARY

When confronted with limitations and disease, over time, as adaptation, as self-narrative, as the rebuilding of their selves, persons with disabilities—as well as other members of vulnerable populations—strive to develop identities where impairments and discrediting attributes are no longer central, but a peripheral "accident" that is being overcome. Just like all individuals, students with disabilities create identities where they see themselves as valued, fully human individuals, living their own life-projects of action and affirmation. These personal stories of emancipation require recognition in the social domain if they are to be maintained. While teaching and mentoring, I argue that practitioners should pay heed to the pitfalls of power imbalances and to avoid dominant ideologies that belittle the particulars of a subjective life. Specifically in instances involving disabilities, examples include ideologies concerning passivity, dependence, and other stigmatizing moral judgments that are often applied as projections of a devaluing nature—rather than being clear and accurate representations of those who often steadfastly cope with impairment and discrimination.

Deep understanding of the precise effects of disability on the person can only happen as part of a true dialogue (Freire, 1985) that occurs within safe and trusting intersubjective spaces (Jackson, 2013) and as "voices of connection" rather than "voices of control" (Cheever, 1985). The creation of this trust and of this safe space is not very difficult to foster if certain straightforward considerations are kept in mind. A tendency to be curious about the level of ability, causation, and manifestations of impairments and illnesses in others is natural; it is best to temper these interests during initial meetings. Moreover, conscious efforts can be made to avoid defining a person by first-impression features we might initially perceive as salient or impactful.

This withholding of questioning and of conclusions, sometimes elusive in an environment focused on immediate results and efficiency, can be described as an exercise in humility. It is an openness of both mind and heart, an occasion to hear the uniqueness inherent in the voices of others, and a moment to accompany, shoulder to shoulder, as an expression of respect. Arthur Frank (1998) expressed this opportunity as the "gift of listening" (p. 198), conducive to worthwhile, content-rich dialogue that is buttressed by teachers who share a modicum of their own life-stories as an effective catalyzer to reciprocity—a foundation of a meaningful shared journey of discovery and self-assertion for both parties, of which learning and academic achievement are two of many components.

This is why reflexivity on the part of the educator is a must. Attempting to "save" the student runs the risk of obliterating the student's sense of agency and unintentionally dismissing and opposing the life-story and adaptations of the student. In like manner, efforts to force a progression of success narratives, conforming with redemptive arcs which are not propelled by the student's own volition, are equally counterproductive and damaging to the student's own agency. The objective is establishing relational interactions (Gammel & Rutstein-Riley, 2016) that foster a true encounter and an authentic exchange of the lived experiences of students and teachers in order to reinforce the educational process and a student's life-project. In this case the educator truly becomes a partner and facilitator while the student retains self-determination, overcomes difficulties, and continues to redefine his or her budding self in terms of self-motivated achievements and positive capabilities.

REFERENCES

Apple, M. W. (2011). Global crises, social justice, and teacher education. *Journal of Teacher Education*, *62*(2), 222–234. doi:10.1177/0022487110385428

Arendt, H. (1958). *The human condition*. Chicago, IL: The University of Chicago Press.

Blumer, H. (1969). *Symbolic interactionism, perspective and method*. Englewood Cliffs, NJ: Prentice Hall.

Cheever, O. L. (1995). *Education as transformation in American psychiatry: From voices of control to voices of connection* (Doctoral dissertation). Retrieved from UMI Dissertation Services. (UMI No. 9522271)

Dauphinée, E. (2007). The politics of the body in pain: Reading the ethics of imagery. *Security Dialogue*, *38*(2), 139–155. doi:10.1177/0967010607078529

Edkins, J. (1993). *Trauma and the memory of politics*. Cambridge, UK: Cambridge University Press

Frank, A. W. (1998). Just listening: Narratives and deep illness. *Families, Systems and Health*, *16*(3), 197–211.

Freire, P. (1985). *The politics of education: Culture, power, and liberation* (D. Macedo, Trans.). South Hadley, MA: Bergin & Garvey.

Fritsch, K. (2016). Blood functions: Disability, biosociality, and facts of the body. *Journal of Literary, and Cultural Disability Studies*, *10*(3), 341–356. doi:10.3828/jlcds.2016.28

Gammel, J. A., & Rutstein-Riley, A. (2016). A relational approach to mentoring women doctoral students. In J. B. Cohen, J. A. Gammel, & A. Rutstein-Riley (Eds.), *Transformative learning and adult higher education: New directions for teaching and learning* (loc. 653–840). [Kindle DX version]. Retrieved from http://www.amazon.com

Geertz, C. (1973). *The interpretation of cultures: Selected essays by Clifford Geertz*. New York, NY: Basic Books.

Gill, R., & Scharff, C. (Eds.). (2011). *New femininities: Postfeminism, neoliberalism and subjectivity*. Hampshire, UK: Palmgrave Macmillan.

Giroux, H. A. (1985). Introduction. In P. Freire, *The Politics of Education* (pp. 11–25). South Hadley, MA: Bergin & Garvey.

Goffman, E. (1986). *Stigma: Notes on the management of spoiled identity.* New York, NY: Simon & Schuster.

Grain, K. M., & Lund, D. E. (2016). The social justice turn: Cultivating 'critical hope' in an age of despair. *Michigan Journal of Community Service Learning, 23*(1), 45–59.

Hall, S. (1996). Introduction: Who needs 'identity'? In S. Hall & P. Du Gay (Eds.), *Questions of cultural identity* (pp. 1-17). Thousand Oaks, CA: SAGE.

Hogg, M. A., Terry, D. J., & White, K. M. (1995). A tale of two theories: A critical comparison of identity theory with social identity theory. *Social Psychology Quarterly, 58*(4), 255–269.

Jackson, M. (2013). *The politics of storytelling: Variations on a theme by Hannah Arendt* (2nd ed.). Copenhagen, Denmark: Museum Tusculanum Press.

Lawler, Steph. (2014). *Identity: Sociological perspectives* (2nd ed.) [Kindle DX version]. Retrieved from http://www.amazon.com

Miller, J. B. (1986). *Toward a psychology of women* (2nd ed.). Boston, MA: Beacon Press.

Moore, L. (1988). People like that are the only people here: Canonical babbling in peed oink. *Birds of America.* New York, NY: Picador.

Scarry, E. (1985) *The body in pain: the making and unmaking of the world* [Kindle DX version]. Retrieved from http://www.amazon.com

Scott, J. W. (1992). Multiculturalism and the politics of identity. *October, 61,* 12–19.

Snyder, S. L., & Mitchell, D.T. (2001). Re-engaging the body: Disability studies and the resistance to embodiment. *Public Culture, 13*(3), 367–389. doi:10.1215/08992363-12-3-367

Stryker, S., & Burke, P. J. (2000). The past, present, and future of an identity theory. *Social Psychology Quarterly, 63*(4), 284–297.

Walker, M. (2013). Power and effectiveness: Envisioning an alternate paradigm. In J. V. Jordan (Ed.)., *The power of connection: Recent developments in cultural-relational theory* (pp. 123–138). New York, NY: Routledge.

Weiss Block, J., & Griffin, M. (2013). Introduction. In J. Weiss Block & M. Griffin (Eds.), *In the company of the poor. Conversations with Dr. Paul Farmer and Fr. Gustavo Gutierrez* [Kindle DX version]. Retrieved from http://www.amazon.com

Wetherell, M. (2008). Subjectivity or psychodiscursive practices? Investigating complex intersectional identities. *Subjectivity, 22,* 73–81. doi:10.1057/sub.2008.7

Woolf, V. (2017). *Complete works of Virginia Woolf* [Kindle DX version]. Retrieved from http://www.amazon.com

CHAPTER 17

SELF-PORTRAIT

A Study of Value, Perspective, Space and Composition

Ann Mechem Ziergiebel
Salem State University

INTRODUCTION

The girl I am trying to save is me and I offer her portrait in this narrative. This rescue is not, as I once thought, for my two daughters or the hundreds of adolescent girls who have sat in my classroom. My personal work of saving myself requires constant scrutiny of power differences and gender bias. As I journey beyond my doctoral program at Lesley University and expand my responsibilities working with preservice educators at Salem State University, my rescue work offers a canvas for identity development and self-portraiture.

I was introduced to gender bias when I was 15, my first year of Newton High School. The year was 1965. I was excited about Mr. Bailey's Algebra II class. I knew my linear, quadratic, and exponential functions and I was looking forward to tackling statistics and probability. My sophomore math class, however, proved to be a unique challenge—not due to content or

Identity and Lifelong Learning in Higher Education, pp. 289–300
Copyright © 2020 by Information Age Publishing

computation but because of my persistent feelings of frustration and discouragement with how I was treated. Contrary to what I believed at the time, being the principal's daughter was not the source of this treatment. I was in a classroom that did not value girls' asking questions and seeking new pathways towards solutions. Furthermore, at the instigation of Mr. Bailey, bias towards me and other girls increased the more we offered correct answers to problem solving. Boys were encouraged to participate in this behavior—jeering, booing my correct answers and blocking entrances

I still remember that class, even the room number, 3314, for two reasons: there I would meet the boy I eventually married, and from then on I would carry forward a bruised intellect. John, who would become my husband of 36 years, was witness to this damage. My favorite subject, math, was the scene of my intellectual bruising and contributed to my daily discouragement. Merging with my intellectual discouragement was a sinking identity. I started wearing black and losing weight. I wanted to be invisible. Talking to friends about these feelings, I discovered frustration and discouragement occurring in many girls. Pathways of striving, questioning and creative thinking seemed to be closing for us.

Over 50 years later, I seek and research spaces for questioning and creativity as a preservice teacher educator at Salem State University, Salem MA, having recently completed a doctorate in Educational Studies at Lesley University, Cambridge, MA. Attending my first event as a doctoral candidate, the speaker I had the honor of hearing was education scholar, Diane Ravitch, talking about her new book, *The Death and Life of the Great American School System* (2010). She offered a public repudiation of positions she once staunchly advocated. I remember being moved to tears. I also remember having many questions. Is it okay to question your way of knowing in such a public space? How do we know what we stand for if we keep changing our stance? The theme of identity continues to lure me.

Classes at Lesley University were beginning in two weeks and I remember feeling a bit unsteady in my white, middle class, female teacher perspective —unsteady in my own beliefs and assumptions, both personal and professional. Here I am, 28 years in education, 23 teaching middle school, and counting. I am regrouping from immense personal loss (the death of my daughter, Jane, and husband, John) and leaping to new ways of knowing. Additionally, I feel confusion around my sociocultural identity —do I understand my own beliefs and assumptions enough to be free to comprehend the realities of others? Ravitch (2010) was modeling humility towards the nation and empathy towards school children while discussing her disaffection with the choice and accountability movements she previously endorsed. I find her journey inspirational.

CONTEXT

Over 50 years later, I continue to wrestle with intellectual bruising and identity. I choose the metaphor of portraiture to create context for my journey of self-examination. Portrait art symbolizes the deep artistic roots planted by my family running through three generations of talented artists working in watercolor, oil, mosaic, sculpture, stained glass, and block print. As I design my portrait, I employ the lenses of value, perspective, space and composition. These lenses reflect the prominent through-lines helping me understand myself as I navigated periods and relationships in my life. Discouragement, reflection and growth seem rooted in these lenses while providing the discipline to learn from mistakes, missteps and mishaps!

Integrating theoretical frameworks and the insight and experience by historically and artistically renowned artist, Emile Gruppe, the following sections paint portions of my life story through the depth and scope of the lenses mentioned above—value, perspective, space, and composition. Value involves changing majors from mathematics to American Studies and teaching middle school humanities—most recently, teaching pre-service secondary education, honoring growth and service. Continuing, perspective opens space for processing personal traumatic losses (death of daughter, Jane, and husband, John) providing context for discovering new ways of being and knowing at both Lesley and Salem State Universities.

Further, my third lens, space (pedagogical space), explores critical pedagogy (Freire, 2001) through the domains of caring, power, and relationships—my dissertation explores space, using the guiding question, "what happens when space is created for middle school students to engage in *photovoice* participatory action research and narrative self-construction?" Finally, composition arranges the intersectionality of systems of privilege and oppression into my narrative (along with Lesley undergraduate scholar mentors) of disorientation and transformation through the context of The Girlhood Project (TGP), Lesley University.

Value

"Never consider an object in isolation—always see it in relation to its surrounding" (Gruppe, 1979, p. 15). As a theoretical construct, discussing value in art (lightness or darkness in relation to context) and life is rooted in the work of educational reformer Dewey (1934) around imagination and meaning. Dewey asserts that imagination is the gateway through which meanings derived from past experiences work their way into the present. The melding of past experiences into current situations in a relational way framed many routines I established as a middle school humanities teacher, specifically an emphasis on discussion. Opening, expanding, listening, perspective taking and knowing is the synthesis I seek for myself, adolescents and undergraduates in communities of learning—spaces where perspectives are cultivated and voices are heard.

Literacy coach Gee (2008) calls for maintaining equitable discourse in a community of learning. Gee establishes value with the notion of "Big 'D' Discourse" ("Discourse" spelled with a capital "D") capturing the ways in which people enact and recognize socially and historically significant identities. His notion stresses how "discourse" (language in use among people) is always also a "conversation" among different historically formed Discourses (that is, a "conversation" among different socially and historically significant kinds of people or social groups). I strive to value thoughtful, sustained conversation in learning communities as teacher power becomes diffused, relationships are established, democratic norms are practiced, and all voices are valued as students grapple with difficult and engaging issues.

A through line in my academic journey is the value of interdisciplinary studies. While a teacher at The O'Maley Middle School, Gloucester, MA, our house team model values interdisciplinary studies through their eighth grade unit—Place Influences Perspective. Eighth grade social studies, my former teaching assignment, commences each year with a review unit on the relationship between Massachusetts geography and history. Five themes of "Geography as History's Stage" are reviewed: place, regions, movement, human-environment interaction, and location. In conjunction, English Language Arts (ELA) begins each fall with an introduction to a yearlong examination of perspective. ELA teachers model perspective as being embedded in all teaching and learning. How does place value individual perspective? This overarching question spirals through history, economics, geography, literature, and art. Backward design takes us to topical questions connecting to both social studies and ELA content:

- How does value deepen when ideas and subjects are examined from opposite views?
- How does practicing perspective taking through the lens of art help us understand and adopt different perspectives in all our disciplines?

Further, our topical questions are the building material of understanding. And, art is a wonderful way to deepen understanding around value and perspective. In Gloucester, Massachusetts, as in most communities, artists paint scenes that capture their unique perspective. Students discover that the paintings of Fitz Henry Lane, a renowned local artist from the mid-1800s, are a powerful entry into a big idea—how does place value individual perspective? Our students can view Lane's original paintings and then visit two sites along Gloucester Harbor where Lane's opposite harbor perspectives (looking in, looking out, below) are recorded in his work.

Figure 17.1. Looking in: "Gloucester Harbor from Rocky Neck." by Fitz Henry Lane.

Figure 17.2. Looking out: "Ten Pound Island from Pavilion Beach," by Fitz Henry Lane.

Lane's shifts of perspective become visual maps of interpretation and observation. Domain-specific vocabulary in geography of relative and absolute location, physical and human characteristics, environment, movement, and regions can connect with the art concepts of luminism, realism, perspective, and vanishing point. Student sketches recorded on site become artifacts that can be exhibited as student perspectives are valued, revised, and critiqued. Shifting perspectives seems to be at the heart of my identity development—when do my intersectional perspectives give me up power or down power?

Perspective

"This is part of what we call atmospheric perspective" (Gruppe, 1979, p. 14), visible equity—honoring all voices—in the classroom environment. Educational researcher Gehlbach (2013) adds that perspective taking is understanding the thoughts, feelings and motivations of others. However, inhibiting factors towards perspective taking can often be present in the most stimulating classrooms. My thinking on perspective taking draws from the theoretical framework for understanding the social development of self, articulated by psychologist Mead (1934). The ability of an individual to take the attitude of another toward herself/himself allows the individual to become self-aware—in Mead's (1934) words, *reflexive*.

Currently, as a teacher of preservice educators, I examine reflexiveness as it cultivates the development of self-awareness in myself and my undergraduates. Reflexiveness is fostered through the use of language to communicate and through the ability to switch social roles. By switching roles, an individual takes on the perspective of the other person in that role, including the perspective a person has of herself or himself. Cultural theorist Appiah states, "We can learn from each other's stories only if we share both human capacities and a single world" (Hansen, 2011). My personal struggle of integrating multiple perspectives and axis of power often leaves me disoriented and powerless—specifically in gender struggles in family and educational leadership.

Thus, I introduce narrative self-construction into my preservice classrooms—both for me and my students. However, telling stories can be scary, risky, and make us uncomfortable. As Yugal-Davis (as cited in Riessman, 2008) states, "identities are narratives, stories people tell themselves and others about who they are (and who they are not)." Myself and my students become uncomfortable because identity is revealed as our stories are being told. Yet, stories serve purposes, several being: remembering the past; persuading a skeptical audience; entering into another's perspective; and mobilizing others into action (Riessman, 2008). Preservice teachers need space to uncover their biases and acknowledge their sociocultural perspective to develop an emerging practice for the wonderful and complex challenges of diverse classrooms – our social justice stance demands this.

My past experiences as a middle school English/language arts and social studies teacher and mother of four adolescents (a classroom without walls!) connects me to the postmodern orientation of researcher/teacher as interpreter, describer, and discoverer. Whether in the classroom, living room, or lacrosse field, all my ideas regarding race, gender, class, ability, sexual orientation, and other axes of identity must be challenged and given space for reflexivity – self-reflection on my own biases (Chase, as cited in Luttrell, 2010).

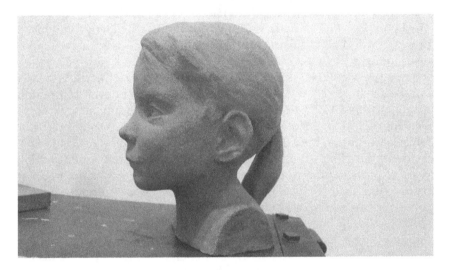

Figure 17.3. Ann Norton Mechem, Terra cotta sculpture, 1955, by Frederick H. Norton (Ann's grandfather).

Space

"Don't feel that you have to get everything in!" (Gruppe, 1979, p. 79). I love this creative and life stance—leave space open for discovery. Urban educator, Delpit (1992), reminds me to speak the truth about dominance structures and their consequences; Brown (2009), Gender and Women's Studies professor, shares a vivid vision of space, "a privileged outlaw space," creating a vibe within a community. The construct of space, as a meaning making environment, is at the heart of TGP, a multilayered community-based service learning and research program focused on the exploration of intersectional girlhoods in the context of intergenerational feminist girls' groups. My five year involvement in the TGP space continued my journey towards identity development as I was safe to tell the truth about my own identity struggles.

First, as a graduate student in the class, and most recently as a doctoral fellow, my exciting participation in TGP has involved multimodal layers of scholarship, relationship, and mentorship. Components of TGP include: an undergraduate course, *Girlhood, Identity & Girl Culture*; a companion advanced seminar course, *Teaching and Research in Girls and Girlhood Studies* for teaching and research assistants; and intergenerational girls' groups focused on the themes of identity development, critical media literacy, and body image. Girls' groups are a community collaboration between the Principal Investigator (Lesley University), and Somerville and Cambridge MA Public Schools, and are informed by feminist pedagogy and group process, critical race theory, intersectional feminism, and positive youth development.

Over the last 11 years TGP has delivered seven week girls' groups to middle school girls and college students, resulting in over 150 middle school girls and 170 college students participating. A unique and central element of TGP is the opportunity for both girls and college students to return each spring (until they graduate) to participate in TGP. What results is opportunity for both girls and college students to return for multiple years of participation to experience self-exploration, collaboration and partnership, dialogue about the lived experiences of girls and women in contemporary society, and opportunity for personal, academic, and professional transformation. This emerging girlhood scholar model provides opportunity for undergraduate and graduate students to participate first as students, then as teaching and research assistants (TA/RAs), and then as collaborators in the development of new teaching and learning strategies about identity development, intersectional feminisms, and girls and girlhood.

I work (if imperfectly) at extending Brown's (2009, p. 107) creation of "space" and suspension of judgment where women, young adults and girls come together to try and be positive, try new things and relate to each other in ways that challenge the status quo. The wide spaces created in the undergraduate course, *Girlhood, Identity & Girl Culture*, encourage mentors, undergraduates and middle school girls to experience disorienting dilemmas and explore new roles, relationships and actions. Further, this rich, relational space encourages our TA/RAs to examine what happens between college students and middle school students, and how the intersection of identity, body image, relationships, sexuality, and race surface from the girls' group sessions. This examination allows our TA/RAs to explore their own intersectional identities and coach both Lesley undergraduates and middle school students in coconstructing counternarratives that better represent their own lived experiences. This authentic work, bringing your own lived experiences into the TGP space, affected me profoundly, exposing counternarratives challenging the dominant cultural representations of girls and women in contemporary society. I began to build on the experiences of others, seeing me experiences in a different light—my composition of self.

Composition

"In a good composition, it's everything in one thing" (Gruppe, 1979, p. 79). Everything in one thing describes the social theory emerging from a social construction developed by law professor Crenshaw (Cho, Crenshaw, & McCall, 2013)—intersectionality. Cho, Crenshaw, and McCall offer intersectionality as a social theory that examines how various biological, social and cultural categories such as gender, race, class, ability, sexual orientation and other axes of identity interact on simultaneous levels. This interaction can create multiple systems of oppression and discrimination (Crenshaw et al., 2013) Crenshaw's theory grows out of her attempts to conceptualize the way law responds to issues involving both race and gender. She adds:

> What happened was like an accident, a collision. Intersectionality simply came from the idea that if you're standing in the path of multiple forms of exclusion, you are likely to get hit by both (or many). (p. 2)

During TGP, I examine what happens between myself, college students and middle school students, and how the intersection of identity, body image, relationships, sexuality, and race surface from the girls' group sessions. Exploring my own intersectional identities—White, middle class, senior, heterosexual, struggling Catholic—I acknowledge that both accidents and inspiration have shaped my context, fueled my recoveries and forged my current portrait.

PORTRAITURE AS PERSONALITY

Art is personality—"loose, spontaneous work is full of accident and inspiration" (Gruppe, 1979, p. 138). The two images, above, are a happy accident—I found myself looking across the room at this mirror reflection. I'm struck by the similar energy in my great-aunt Julie's watercolor and my

Figure 17.4.   Ann Norton Mechem, 1953, watercolor by Julie Turner (Ann's great-aunt): Ann Mechem Ziergiebel, 2017, photograph.

current stance. Might we be growing, shrinking, rising, falling and looking for inspiration all our lives? My current photographic portrait carries this life-long work and reflects a personality that could well have been shaped at age three (1953, for me). Noted artist and teacher Nicolaides (Maletskos, 1995) stated about portrait painting, "study (the person) it for 5 minutes—draw it for 5 minutes—and check it for 5 minutes" (Maletskos, 1995, p. 7). Observing, enacting, and reflecting seems to define my application of the lenses discussed above—value, perspective, space and composition—under the guise of identity construction. The spiraling of gender bias to intersectionality along with interdisciplinary middle school pedagogy and practice to preservice educator's creating meaning-making spaces speak to a life-long mission—to make space for ME.

My lifelong journey to understand my own beliefs began my sophomore year in high school, as previously shared. I thought I had a math identity but the overt gender bias in Mr. Bailey's math class bruised my intellect and silenced my voice. This bruising and silencing stuck for many reasons and I continue to struggle in these two areas—scholarship (the power of ideas) and advocacy—over 50 years later. Fortunately, during my first year in the Lesley Doctoral Program, I was introduced to feminist philosophers who speak to struggling women. In reading philosopher and educator Minnich (2005), I examine dominance systems, from Eurocentrism to Social Darwinism to privatization. Minnich (2005) teaches me that knowledge is derived from responsive, complex thinking with lenses that check for bias, prejudice, assumptions and half-truths. I am emerging stronger and more open—embracing my intersectionality (specifically gender and up and down power). Perhaps through the practice of observing, enacting and reflecting, my self-portrait emerges, deeply rooted in my three-year old glance.

REFERENCES

Brown, R. N. (2009). *Black girlhood celebration*. New York, NY: Peter Lang.

Chase, S. (2010). Narrative inquiry: Multiple lenses, approaches, voices. In W. Luttrell (Ed.), *Qualitative educational research* (pp. 208–209). New York, NY: Routledge.

Cho, S., Crenshaw, K. W., & McCall, L. (2013). Toward a field of intersectionality studies: Theory, applications, and praxis. *Signs, 38*(4).

Delpit, L. (1992). Acquisition of literate discourses: Bowing before the master. *Theory into Practice, 31*(4).

Dewey, J. (1934). *Art as experience*. New York, NY: Minton, Balch.

Freire, P. (2001). *Pedagogy of freedom*. New York, NY: Rowman & Littlefield.

Gee, J. P. (2008). *A sociocultural perspective on the opportunity to learn*. Retrieved from http://www.scribd.com/doc/5576300/

Gehlbach, H. (2013). Social perspective taking: A multidimensional approach. Retrieved from www.uknow.gse.harvard.edu/teaching/TC104-607.html

Gruppe, E. (1979). *Gruppe on color.* New York, NY: Watson-Guptill.

Hansen, D. (2011). *The teacher and the world.* New York, NY: Routledge.

Luttrell, W. (Ed.). (2010). *Qualitative educational research.* New York, NY: Routledge

Maletskos, C. (1995). *Mary Magna Maletskos—A rare spirit.* Gloucester, MA: Blueberry Hill.

Mead, G. H. (1934). *Mind, self, and society from the standpoint of a social behaviorist* (C. W. Morris, Ed.). Chicago, IL: University of Chicago Press.

Minnich, E. (2005). *Transforming knowledge* (2nd ed.). Philadelphia, PA: Temple University Press.

Ravitch, D. (2012). *The death and life of the great American school system.* New York, NY: Basic Books.

Riessman, C. K. (2008). *Narrative methods for the human sciences.* Thousand Oaks, CA: SAGE.

CHAPTER 18

INVISIBLE LIFE IN
THE ACADEMY

African American Women
Staff in Higher Education

Kimberly D. Johnson
University of Missouri

INTRODUCTION

The value of lifelong learning was modeled for me at an early age. My fondest memory of education was eagerly walking to elementary school as I anticipated each day of learning. I received rewards for good grades. When I received my report card, we would celebrate at the place of my choice. This instilled in me that hard work and consistency came with rewards. My dedication and desire for learning has continued throughout my adult years. However, through my research I discovered that lifelong learning encompasses many perspectives with several modalities different from my own.

This chapter examines formative learning and professional experiences as an African American woman staff member in higher education at a

Identity and Lifelong Learning in Higher Education, pp. 301–322
Copyright © 2020 by Information Age Publishing

predominantly White institution (PWI) in the Midwest. In addition to the sound of my personal experiences, the voices of African American women members articulate their life experiences through critical self-examination and self-reflection during semi-structured individual interviews. The theoretical frameworks of Black feminist thought and critical race theory are viewed through the lens of African American women staff in higher education. Qualitative research results illustrated the experiences of African American women staff in the workplace and the impact on their identity and lifelong learning. Finally, a framework is presented for practical strategies and implications for higher education leadership.

AFRICAN AMERICAN WOMEN AND LIFELONG LEARNING

Identity development and lifelong learning for African American women often comes with challenges. Many African American women at universities across the country face a multiplicity of personal and professional issues that may affect their desire for career advancement in higher education. Even with the issues these women encounter, their quest for knowledge and education remains a high priority in their lives. When faced with experiences that may threaten their self-concept, they affirm their identity in other areas. African American women staff turn to friends, family, and mentors among others, to cope with the everyday struggles of working in higher education and pursuing lifelong learning. Collins (2001) notes that while Black women in academic institutions have differing experiences, backgrounds, and beliefs, "they are connected in their struggle to be accepted, respected and have a voice in an institution with many views" (p. 20). Furthermore, Black women, especially at predominantly White institutions (PWIs), are often slighted by underprivileged consequences—meaning they often do not enjoy the same treatment in the workplace—in contrast to their White counterparts. The preferential treatment sometimes granted to White counterparts is a challenge to African American women in the struggle for racial and gender equity. In addition to their quest for justice, the women experience personal and professional barriers that attempt to inhibit their success.

Education is critical to the success of African American women and their desire for lifelong learning and visibility in higher education settings. Although many of these women have achieved educational success, they remain invisible to those in higher education leadership. There is the assumption that once higher education is obtained, African American women will have a seat at the table in the workplace. However, this is often not the case. According to Robinson (2012), African American women have a history of struggle and perseverance for education and opportunity; however, their opportunities for leadership and recognition within higher education have been slow to materialize and barriers to equity remain, including barriers to job promotion.

PURPOSE AND RESEARCH QUESTION

Researchers have investigated the burden and responsibility placed upon African American women in higher education to serve as the female and African American representative in various campus settings (Henry & Glenn, 2009). Black women have long understood that the intersection of race and gender places them in a unique position to be continuously misunderstood. Support staff are often invisible and not seen until it is necessary to be called upon to do work related to diversity or to meet the quota for people of color needed on a committee. Many colleagues in higher education do not necessarily understand the complexity for African American women of dealing with being both Black and female. As a result, Black women in the academy often stand out while being ignored in their quest to simply do their work. One of the main objectives of this study was to bring greater awareness to the underrepresentation of the experiences of African American women staff in the literature.

There are many studies that have examined and exposed the experiences of blatant racist and sexist discrimination and harassment (Gregory, 2001; Guillory, 2001) from White counterparts who benefit from White privilege (Harley, 2008). However, while there are various studies on African American women in higher education, there is a gross underrepresentation of studies specifically on staff (Crawford & Smith, 2005; Patitu & Hinton, 2003). Even though all women of color in the academy may face the barriers of inclusion and lack of support, the focus of this research was solely on African American women staff. This research was necessary to learn more about the workplace experiences of African American women staff employed at PWIs and to reveal how these experiences affect their advancement within the academy.

While previous research has focused on the challenges of Black students and Black faculty (Hughes & Howard-Hamilton, 2003), few research studies focus solely on the experiences of Black women staff in higher education. In addition to highlighting the workplace experiences of African American women staff, this study was significant because it contributed to the limited body of research with this group within higher education. The absence of such literature provides the foremost reason for the research. There is a necessity to comprehend the workplace experiences of African American women staff and challenges that may persist in PWIs. The voices of African American women staff in higher education should be heard. Listening to their stories and understanding their challenges can lead to effective strategies implemented to move these women forward at their institutions and in their desire to pursue higher education.

This study provided African American women in higher education, specifically staff at three PWIs, an opportunity to utilize their voices to share not only workplace experiences, but also personal experiences that revealed information that helped to shape their identity. This study focused on staff in support positions who described how their workplace experiences assisted them on a personal level. Although some of these experiences may have been obstacles, several participants described how they had a better sense of self, realized their worth and gained the courage to advocate for themselves and others as a result of meeting obstacles.

Typically, African American women support staff are not given the opportunity to have their voices heard, tend to be less influential, and hold the least political power within the academy. They are often invisible workers. While race and gender make Black women visible on the outside, when they are devalued, ignored and disrespected they are left feeling invisible inside as well. African American women often feel invisible at their institutions and this is even more prevalent at PWIs. Insight gained from study participants may be an avenue to provide effective strategies for other African American women to succeed. These strategies may affect change for women who seek assistance in their efforts to navigate institutional issues that may be barriers to their advancement in higher education and their quest for lifelong learning while maintaining their identity as African American women.

Given the purpose of the study, answering the research questions exposed the depth of these experiences. The study aimed to answer the following questions:

1. What are the workplace experiences of African American women staff in higher education?
2. What challenges exist for African American women staff in a PWI?
3. What coping strategies are utilized by African American women staff to navigate interactions and workplace experiences in a PWI?

The research questions led to the development of the theoretical framework, which provided the foundational knowledge to support the research design.

FRAMEWORK FOR UNDERSTANDING AFRICAN AMERICAN STAFF IN HIGHER EDUCATION

An emphasis of the literature review focused on the challenges of African American women within the academy. Although Black women have been essential to American higher education, they have also experienced some oppressive conditions in the workplace. Identifying a theoretical framework to explain the experiences of African American women was challenging (Hughes & Howard-Hamilton, 2003). The term theoretical framework focuses on the beliefs and assumptions of the researcher, concepts and theories, experiential knowledge, and existing literature (Maxwell, 2005). In essence, it attempts to integrate key aspects of information especially variables in a logical manner. Stephens and Phillips (2005) contend that theory grounds how researchers identify, name, interpret, and write about the unique experiences of African American women. Furthermore, Stephens and Phillips state that it is important to identify a theory that reflects African American females' social isolation (2005). Given the focus of this study, Black feminist thought and critical race theory were appropriate frameworks for the research.

Black Feminist Thought

At the core of Black feminist thought (BFT) is the concept of standpoint, which suggests that the struggle against racism and sexism is a shared bond among African American women (Collins, 2002). Collins (2002) contends that while all African Americans experience racism, they do not experience or respond to racism in the same way due to the diversity (i.e., class, age, religion, sexual orientation) that exists among these women. Additionally, race and gender are often internalized in ways that contribute to a significant portion of one's worldview (Smedley, 2007; Zamani, 2003). Maintaining the invisibility of Black women and their ideas have been critical in maintaining social inequalities (Collins, 2000). Clarifying Black women's experiences and struggles is at the core of BFT.

Critical Race Theory

Critical race theory (CRT) was used in this study as a lens to explore the workplace experiences of African American women staff in higher education. Many theories created by the dominant majority do not take into account the societal, environmental, and developmental factors of African American women. CRT was developed in response to racial oppression in society and seeks to "deconstruct the racialized content" (Howard-Hamilton, 2003, p. 7) of institutional practices, curriculum, and research. It is a theoretical construct identified as a mechanism that can address the specific experiences of African American women. CRT also helps to understand and reshape the organizational culture within the academy. In particular, the theory deeply values the knowledge of people of color as grounded in their daily life experiences. African American women higher education staff and the researcher were able to capture the voices recounting their perceptions of current workplace challenges and their strategies for success.

SILENT VOICES OF AFRICAN AMERICAN WOMEN STAFF

Racism, sexism, and classism are barriers often cited as three salient forms of oppression that bruise self-confidence and shatter dreams of African American women (Collins, 2000; Gregory, 2001). These forms of oppression lead the American public to feel that Black women's voices are the least compelling when serious issues are at the forefront (hooks, 1999). Although these women have varied experience and education, they still are invisible to some when critical issues need to be discussed. This critique has also caused Black women to protect and maintain face by remaining silent about their stories, stories also referred to as their struggles (Boylorn, 2013). Despite the achievements of African Americans, their voices are still not heard within the sometimes cold nature of the academy (Holmes, Land, & Hinton-Hudson, 2007; Robinson, 2012; Thomas & Hollenshead, 2001; Valverde, 2003).

African American women tell stories about their lives that are different from the stories that other people tell about them (Bobo, 1991). The voice of African American women reveals details of their identity. Voice allows the opportunity to share their stories of how their experiences have impacted their education and quest for lifelong learning. According to Boylorn (2013), her project *Sweetwater* offered her a unique opportunity and responsibility to review the language used about Black women's lives, and the language that Black women use to not only tell about their lives, but also to make sense of them. Black women focus on strength, resilience, and their daily struggles. For years, Black women have overlooked themselves as they have been overlooked, accepting, without critique, the versions of their lives and realities offered back to them by others (Boylorn, 2013). Listening to language and voice was important in the data analysis of the stories shared by African American women staff members. Collins (2000) noted that understanding the interconnectivity of both gender and race must resonate from the voices of the lived experiences of these women. Listening for evidence of interconnectivity of race and gender was also important in this study.

TABLE TALK: COFFEE, HOT CHOCOLATE & CONVERSATION

As a child, I was encouraged to have an inquisitive spirit and be intellectually curious. I recollect sitting at the table with my mom. She would give me hot chocolate or a cold beverage in the cup matching hers and we would discuss several topics, mostly of my choice. I learned, as my feet dangled from the chair, that someone wanted to hear what I had to say. This conversation, and many others, taught me the importance of my value as a person and discourse. At a young age, I learned that I not only had a seat at the table but also a voice. I realized that what I said mattered. I was confident that my contributions would be taken into consideration. My identity development included the goal of pursing education and lifelong learning. African American women often see lifelong learning as a critical part of their identity. The quest for learning starts early on and never stops for many women. While I was seen and heard at home, I learned that it is possible to become invisible at work in the academy.

THE STUDY: INVISIBLE LIFE IN THE ACADEMY

Methodology

The approach to the study was to understand lived experiences and it is an appropriate tradition because it supports seeking the meaning and understanding of the experiences of each participant (Creswell, 1998). The purpose of this study was to understand the lived experiences of African American women staff members employed at PWIs of higher education. Heuristics also allowed me to share my own experiences and participate in the reflective processes of this study (Moustakas, 1990; Patton, 2002). My personal experiences enabled me to relate to the stories of the participants. These personal insights on workplace experiences provided the rationale for utilizing the heuristic inquiry approach.

Participant Selection

As a qualitative research approach, purposeful sampling was used to identify women whose workplace experiences could provide critical information and rich responses related to the key research areas. African American women from three PWIs in the Midwest were solicited for their participation. Criterion-based selection also was used to identify attributes required by participants to be included in this study. Criterion sampling includes standards that each case must adhere to (Gall, Gall, & Borg,

2007; Miles & Huberman, 1994). For this study, participants had to meet the criteria developed for the study. Each staff member was invited to participate based on the following criteria: (a) their ethnicity—African American; (b) position at their institution—employed in higher education as a staff member; (c) years of employment at the institution—working long enough—a minimum of one year—to be generally familiar with the climate of the institution. The participants were also selected based on their responses to an initial survey, which indicated their ability to articulate meaningful information that would shed light on the questions under study. The selected participants were contacted via e-mail to further explain the intent of the study and to confirm if they were willing to participate in one-on-one interviews. Sixteen African American women, classified as support staff members below director level at their institution participated in the study.

Data Collection Methods

There were three data collection methods used for the study. The first method was a survey to participants to collect demographic information and brief information about their overall workplace experiences. The second method was facilitating in-depth interviews to gain additional knowledge about their workplace experiences and challenges they encountered. A third strategy for data collection included obtaining documents about job postings on the human resources website at the institutions. The purpose of searching the websites was to review the job descriptions to see if the wording appealed to diverse candidates. Participants in the study mentioned that job postings are not appealing or after reading the description they did not think they were qualified. Some women mentioned that they did not think internal candidates had a chance at some positions because the postings seemed geared towards external candidates.

In an effort to enhance the validity of the study, the data sources were triangulated to assist with identification of recurring themes. Merriam (2009) asserts that one of the characteristics of qualitative research is that the researcher is used as the principal instrument to help understand the phenomenon through the perception of the participant.

Data Collection: Interviews

The interview participants were very enthusiastic about their participation in this study and expressed their appreciation for being allowed to share their experiences. In addition, I had established collegial relationships with two of the participants, which made the interview process more relaxed and comfortable. Participants' workplace experiences and feelings were captured through semi-structured, open-ended questions in order to elicit answers related to their experience at a PWI. Semistructured interviews utilize a general set of questions with all participants, however, interviews vary with the context of each situation and the researcher is allowed to capture the worldviews and new ideas of each participant (Merriam, 1998). All participants were given pseudonyms for the study and were assured that confidentiality would be maintained throughout the process. Contact information regarding the study included the researcher's information, dissertation advisor, and contact information of the Compliance Office in the event a participant had questions at any point during the study.

Data Analysis

A heuristic approach was selected to analyze the information collected. The process involved a review of the surveys, interview transcripts, and job descriptions on human resources websites to identify emerging themes. Miles and Huberman (1994) defined codes as labels for assigning units of meaning to the descriptive or inferential information compiled during the study. The main goal was to search for patterns and trends in the responses so the researcher could develop conclusions regarding the content of the data.

Creating counter-stories was necessary to understand how these women navigate the higher education system. Counter-stories are an opportunity for Black women to share their experiences with one another in welcoming and hospitable counter spaces (Hughes & Howard-Hamilton, 2003, p. 101). During the study, it became apparent that those in the majority at the institution told the current narrative. This study allowed the participants to reflect on their personal narratives and to offer this as a counter narrative to how their stories are told. Implementation of the counter stories into the current workplace can be achieved by allowing participants to have safe spaces to share their stories.

The meaning and comprehension of the participants' perspectives were interpreted through my lens as an African American woman professional who serves in a staff role. My professional lived experiences caused me to ensure that my predisposed biases did not interfere with interpretation of the data or my interactions with the participants. It was important for me to avoid allowing my personal experience as an African American woman staff member to influence how I interpreted the data. In order to alleviate research bias I used member checking which allowed participants to review their interview transcripts to confirm that their stories were presented without the influence of the researcher. At the conclusion of each interview, the data collected was reviewed with a special emphasis on the workplace experiences.

The participants' stories were consistent with findings from other studies conducted pertaining to African American women in higher education, especially in administration.

FINDINGS AND DISCUSSION

The phenomenon being explored was the workplace experiences of African American women staff in higher education. Overall, the study participants enjoyed the work they do on a daily basis when asked directly about their experiences working at a PWI. The phrases and words used by the staff members to describe their daily experiences were analyzed. This section reveals the emerging themes and how they relate conceptually to Collins's (1991) BFT thought. Black feminism was used in analyzing and interpreting the data to explore the challenges that African American women experience as staff members in public institutions of higher education and the strategies they employ to cope with the resulting conflicts.

Overview of Themes and the Relationship to Black Feminist Thought

Participants expressed personal pleasure and comfort working in higher education institutions, even though the experience could be challenging at times. They stressed the importance of a commitment to the value of creating a positive environment for others in institutions of higher education, especially for African American women. Collins (1991) suggests, "Black Feminist Thought consists of specialized knowledge created by African American women which clarifies a standpoint of and for Black women. In other words, BFT encompasses theoretical interpretations of Black women's reality by those who live it." This contends that African American women have common experiences because of race and gender and that certain themes will be in black women's standpoint (Becks-Moody, 2004). Based on the words, phrases, and similar characteristics, I identified the following four themes:

1. Experiencing obstacles to advancement and promotion;
2. Impact of colleague interactions in the workplace;
3. Importance of support and coping mechanisms to deal with issues; and the

4. Importance of mentoring and networking in the lives of African American women.

Although the participants did not state these themes verbatim, the underlying message was present throughout the discussions. The participant responses were used to identify broad categories and then later to determine subcategories. Emerging themes provided evidence that African American women staff in PWIs have challenges in the workplace and that they employ different strategies to cope with them.

Experiencing Obstacles to Advancement and Promotion

Scholar Audre Lorde (2007) noted the lived experiences of African American women in society as an insider versus outsider phenomenon and discussed obstacles such as oppression as an intersectional construction in their lives (Collins, 2000). Bailey (2010) applied this analysis to the experiences of African American female professionals working in higher education and found that Black women experience a lack of support in career advancement, isolation, and discrimination as compared to their White colleagues. These experiences may often make African American women feel that their identity as Black women is an obstacle to lifelong learning and advancement. In reality, identity is a tool to learning about yourself as an individual and learning about others. This study allowed African American women staff at predominantly White institutions who might feel marginalized and isolated, to share their stories and recount their workplace experiences. The findings revealed that the participants did experience obstacles to advancement which were in line with other research on the experiences of African American women in higher education.

Study participants shared their observations, which illuminated the lack of promotion into leadership. Nadine stated,

> In my experience, I've seen Black women with degrees passed over and the job given to someone with very little to no experience. Getting promoted at the university sometimes appears to be a matter of who you know and not what you know.

Janine also shared her opinion on obstacles at the institution and commented:

> I feel that is it wrong of the university to not allow the women who have been at this institution, much longer than I have, to have trained faculty and clerical staff coming in and out of their department and these women are overlooked to move up in positions that have been vacated.

The participants discussed the lack of promotion opportunities and the challenges of other African American women colleagues with the same issues. Samantha provided a synopsis of her sentiment by expressing her feeling of why there is a barrier to advancement for so many African American women staff at PWIs:

> I think an obstacle to advancement is because of the people who are hired in the higher-level positions, the people with authority, and I do not want to sound like I am racist or discriminating but they are mainly white men. In addition, I feel that with that being said, the white men first of all do not have a whole lot of respect for the African American women to acknowledge them to the point where they want to promote them. Therefore, I think this is a barrier.

Another participant described how she would constantly apply for positions within her department but was never offered the position. She then was expected to train the new hire in that position. Another described how she was given basic clerical duties but not allowed to work on any project related assignments that would allow growth within the department or the university.

African American women staff are often trapped in what is termed as the "Sticky Floor (Iverson, 2011). This refers to the challenge that staff in clerical positions have with moving into professional positions. Findings in the study revealed that staff often will not ask to attend conferences because they are afraid to approach their supervisor. One study participant explained her experience with speaking up. She said,

> In the first five months of my employment, instead of being trained in a uniform manner, the trainer often shared materials with my coworker apart from me. I finally brought it to the attention of my supervisor when I recognized that my coworker was able to respond to certain questions/issues, although we share the same duties.

As a staff member, my quest for knowledge in higher education was evident early on when I entered the field of higher education and this was recognized by my supervisors. My goal in every position was to learn more and increase my knowledge of the field. Although higher education was not my initial path for a career, I quickly learned that this was an area where I could not only increase my lifelong learning but I could also impact the learning of others including students and staff. My conversations with students and staff always include encouraging them to know who they are and to strive for excellence in education.

The Impact of Colleague Interactions in the Workplace

Leadership in difficult times can serve as a means of moving forward towards your goal of lifelong learning. My middle school years proved to be the most challenging of my entire educational experience as I was the only black student in the school during my sixth grade year. I quickly learned how cruel other students could be to someone who was different and what it felt like to be the "only one." To combat the negativity, education was my best defense as I often scored the highest grades in class. Once in college, "the only one" syndrome continued as there were courses where I was the only African American student. Being the "only one" often is being seen as only the frontline staff, the note taker or the girl who gets the coffee in the workplace. African American women's self-value can be eroded through unfairness or invisibility in the workplace. Being the only one sometimes forces you into leadership because you may not necessarily be invited to the table on many occasions. Therefore, you must insert yourself into areas that will give you leadership opportunities to grow and advance your career.

Some African American women encounter psychologically damaging racism at institutions of higher education creating a climate where they struggle to succeed. The bulk of the incidents described in this study are what social scientists call microaggressions. Microaggressions impact not only faculty and students, but also staff. While these are more covert than blatant forms of racism, the actions cause stress and may often have African American women staff questioning their place at PWIs.

Franklin (2000) links the experiences of microaggressions directly to what is called "invisibility syndrome," a syndrome defined as an "inner struggle with the feeling that one's talents, abilities, personality, and worth are not valued or even recognized because of prejudice and racism" (p. 33). Franklin also contends that these covert slights are deceptively subtle but carry enough weight to "force the individual into a mold structured by stereotypes and the negative associations attached to them" (p. 36). The study gave examples of White coworkers making comments about what type of car they drove, their hairstyle, the type of expensive clothes they wore and also in one instance a White coworker said she understand Black people because the neighborhood she lived in had Black people there.

Participants discussed the impact that these daily interactions with coworkers within their areas had on them at their institution. One study participant, Sheila, noted the perception that some colleagues have of her as she is the only African American in her department. She stated,

> Being the only one [African American] in my area, I have noticed some
> people assume I have limited education. I have also noticed that sometimes

people assume they know how I will respond to a situation and limit what they really want to say.

Rachael, another participant, expressed her perception of interactions with some colleagues. She shared, "The way certain situations are handled by the different races is sometimes frustrating. Also, there are times when those who are degreed seem to feel superior. I don't know if it has to do with race or job title."

These critical conversations were significant for African American women staff members. The conversations allowed the staff to reflect on their interactions with coworkers and also who they are as a person and how their identity impacts their daily work. Sharing their experiences may enable the study participants to obtain support for advancement at their institutions.

Importance of Support and Coping Mechanisms

The significant challenges, often times inherent in small numbers, coupled with institutional racial and gender inequality, have prompted Black women in academia to employ a variety of coping strategies that have been key to their academic and professional advancement (Thomas & Hollenshead, 2001). Black women should have an established supportive network of colleagues both within their areas and outside of their departments (Gregory, 2001). It is important for African American women staff to have a network of resources and support on predominantly White campuses. This allows them the opportunity to feel safe with someone in order to share their experiences and to help guide them through any challenges they face on campus. Several of the participants mentioned family, spirituality, and friends as their support systems who were instrumental in coping with challenges in the workplace.

Spirituality was mentioned by the participants as one of the main coping strategies. Jones and Shorter-Gooden (2004) poignantly portray the day-to-day challenges and triumph of 'sisters' at work, in relationships, and in their spiritual lives." Rachael stated "there's a way to do everything so you know I am a spiritual person so I pray and that helps me cope." Candace also described the impact of spirituality in her life,

I just pray a lot. I don't really have any support, I'm relying more on my faith. I did have a prayer partner and I'd go and talk to her and we would pray and she would also give me good advice.

Connecting with other women that participants could identify with was also critical as a support mechanism. According to Hughes and Howard-Hamilton (2003), Black feminist perspectives suggest that creating and sustaining strong connective relationships with other Black women are essential to their social and psychological well-being. Several of the participants mentioned how connecting with other African American women on campus helped them as they navigated higher education. These women who helped them cope served as someone who assisted them along their journey. Some were coworkers, friends, or supervisors. Brittany explains how close coworkers help her to cope with issues. She stated:

> I kind of just link myself with like-minded people and they happen to be women of color because we experience the same things and we can relate. I think I distance myself from the other [White] staff to a certain point as far as like personally and sharing personal information ... So to cope, I just don't talk to them at that level. We do work together, we have meetings together, and I'm polite. You know, I speak in the hallways but I'm not going to go any further than that.

Connecting with other African American women who can support you on your journey is critical to success in higher education, especially at PWIs. As I reflect on my own educational path, there were several seasoned professionals who took time to assist me with learning not only my job, but also learning about the culture of the institution and strategies to advance. My first supervisor at my institution was an African American woman and she always encouraged me in all of my endeavors. I will never forget the impact she had on me because it was her initial support and encouragement that allowed me to succeed at the institution. She told me that she would never hold any employee back who wanted to advance. Identifying someone to talk to about my challenges, issues, and even successes was a coping mechanism that has helped me along the way and is still an important factor today.

Importance of Career Mentoring and Networking

Mentors can often provide an avenue for staff to seek advice and counsel on a wide variety of issues which will allow the staff members to feel that they have been heard. The women in the study indicated that having a mentor in their life was critical to their success at their institution. Throughout the discussion the women indicated that they felt it was important for them to give back and to serve as a mentor for other African American women as well.

Mentoring can serve as a beneficial resource for staff who are seeking to build their career (Garvey, Stokes, & Megginson, 2014). African American women could benefit from having a mentor to assist with guiding them in their professional career and providing insight into strategies to navigate the different situations in the workplace. Montgomery, Dodson, and Johnson (2014) suggested that mentoring is necessary for career advancement. Mentors can assist with providing mentees an opportunity to meet new people, be exposed to new opportunities, and network with other professionals.

According to Hughes and Howard-Hamilton (2003), "a major source of frustration for African American students is the lack of African American role models in visible leadership positions" (p. 97). Guiffrida and Douthit (2010) contend that connections made between Black students and Black role models who have been successful in higher education can increase self-efficacy of Black students and lead to academic success. Just as the students need support, the participants in this study shared examples of their need for professional support in the roles they were asked to perform. They discussed support systems, mentors, and colleagues who assisted them with navigating through the system. Crawford and Smith (2005) suggested that the essence of mentoring is the development of individuals on both professional and personal levels. For many of the participants, mentors were friends who provided leadership and career advice. These friends were central to helping participants with networking and often served as role models.

Role modeling is a function that the mentor plays in relation to the staff member. Staff members may see behavioral or personality traits exhibited by a mentor that they wish to emulate. At PWIs, African American women often deal with a lack of role models as a major hindrance as they often do not see African American women in leadership roles. One participant, Rachael, mentioned that one of her sources of support was having people who look like her on the campus. She stated, "Women who look like me are very supportive and I'm able to discuss certain situations and they let me know if I'm off target. It's very important to have role models so you don't feel so alone." Another study participant, Taylor, further describes role modeling for African American women staff. She shared:

A role model can help you stay true to who you are and this is especially important and I feel that at a predominantly White institution it's not always necessary to say "hey, I'm the Black woman in the room" but knowing who you are and staying true to your values and understanding the importance in this game. The reason I said it's a game is because of the importance of knowing who the players are and their roles and an understanding of their objectives. Understanding their role is critical so you can figure out a way where your role can be in a participatory process so everyone knows that you are strong in who you are and you will not waiver from your standpoint.

I have often encountered African American women staff at institutions who do not engage with other staff members. Many have indicated that networking is not authentic, takes too much time or they feel they do not have an initial connection with anyone to get them started. One of my personal goals has always been to make at least one connection whether I'm at a meeting, event, or conference. My passion is helping other women succeed. If I can connect them with campus resources or assist them in their journey, then this is what I strive to do daily. Many of the study participants described challenges in the workplace and one participant spoke about the many positive experiences at her institution. Overall, even though I identified with much of the information shared by the participants, I can also say that I have been fortunate to have supportive supervisors who allowed me the opportunity to participate on committees, gain professional development and serve students when time allows.

IMPLICATIONS AND RECOMMENDATIONS

This study sought to explore the unique and varied experiences that African American women face as staff in higher education. This included their perceptions of campus climate and any workplace challenges. This study provided a platform to share their stories and to explore and to reflect on their overall experiences. After reflecting on their experiences, participants were encouraged to pursue higher education to enhance their opportunity for advancement. The conversations also gave them confidence to take leadership roles on campus.

The research findings illuminate important implications regarding the experiences of African American women staff while working in PWIs. The major implication of this research is that voices of staff matter in institutions of higher education and we should seek ways to gain knowledge about their experiences. Entering the workplace with the goal of advancement within the institution was noted, yet several staff mentioned that because of barriers they often stay in the same position or are unable to further their education and pursuit of lifelong learning.

As an African American woman staff member, it was imperative to hear the stories of women who look like me. I wanted to allow a space for them to share their challenges and successes and gain a perspective on what they need from their institutions in terms of support.

Overall, the views presented in this study are part of an array of perspectives that need to be heard. The perspectives offered are valuable because they come from revealing points and allow the workplace experiences of African American women staff at PWIs to be expressed in their own words. The major proposition for institutions is to acknowledge the voices of African American women staff, thus making their invisible contributions more visible. Acknowledgement can include recognition for their work, for service to the university, and for any campus service activities such as work with students, mentoring other staff, or additional projects they take on within their department. Hopefully, this acknowledgement will lead to change and more inclusion of this group of women.

The goal of researching African American women staff in higher education was to help to fill a gap in the research literature and to hopefully serve as a catalyst for more in-depth research on staff in academic institutions.

Based on the findings, this study suggests several practical strategies that universities can implement to benefit and support African American women staff members and that may also provide tools to assist women of color overall. The following recommendations will assist institutions move toward the goal of improving the climate and workplace experiences for African American women staff at PWIs:

1. Advancement Programs: Institutions should consider career and leadership development programming specifically designed for African American women staff. The programs are necessary to assist staff with their desire to advance. So often, African American women staff become stagnant in positions when they do not have opportunities for promotion. This recommendation could also help institutions increase the retention rate of African American women staff.

2. Job Posting Language: Enhancing the language in job postings could serve as a mechanism to increase the number of staff in support staff roles who transition to next level positions. Institutions should ensure the language in descriptions is inclusive and welcomes diverse applicants. Job descriptions should include language that acknowledges that professional work experience has value even if the applicant has no formal degree. This would encourage those without a degree but have years of work experience to apply for positions for which they may be qualified.

3. Formal Mentorship Programs: Institutions should consider formal mentoring programs for African American women staff. Mentoring opportunities are common for faculty and students, but not necessarily for staff on campus. African American women staff could learn about the unwritten campus rules, responsibilities of administrators, and the role of faculty at the institution.

4. Informal Mentoring Relationships: Institutions should encourage informal mentoring to help staff get acclimated to the campus culture. Staff could reach out to their peers to assist them in becoming familiar with the campus culture. This is a relationship that would be beneficial to African American women staff.

5. Affinity Groups: Programs designed specifically for African American women staff, such as affinity groups, will enhance the experience of African American women staff. These groups could be a step toward reducing the isolation that staff feel at their institutions. Some institutions have Black faculty and staff associations which are essential to creating safe spaces for women to network and connect.

6. Networking Opportunities: A critical component of networking is recognizing who has the influence and power to assist a person with moving their agenda forward. Networking is essential, and these relationships can often lead to job opportunities, sharing resources, and conference presentations.

7. Create Inclusive Climate: Institutional climate is a particular concern for staff of color at predominantly White institutions, particularly African American women. Institutions should consider ongoing assessments of their climate. This would be a step towards ensuring that staff feel included, welcomed and respected.

8. Supervisor Training: Institutions should have mandatory training related to cultural diversity and equity for all supervisors, so they are knowledgeable about the experiences of people of color. Supervisors should have the capacity to work with people who are not like themselves.

9. Curriculum Changes: Include courses regarding staff issues in higher education for graduate students. Many programs have courses which highlight the faculty and student experience in higher education, but it would be helpful for students to also learn about the experiences of staff. This would be especially beneficial for those students who aspire to become administrators in higher education.

10. Engaging in conversations with African American women staff to inform leaders of the staff member's workplace concerns and their potential for leadership. These conversations with staff can take place by having university leadership: (1) attend staff governance meetings (2) conduct focus groups, or (3) offer professional development opportunities.

Support is vital to African American women staff who work in environments at PWIs as the climate at an institution also can affect staff satisfaction; climate is of particular concern for staff of color at a PWI. The strategies and coping mechanisms generated by the study participants may also assist other African American women staff in navigating barriers in higher education through the use of meaningful accounts of workplace experiences.

CONCLUSION

Lifelong learning does not always come from textbooks; it can come from life experiences. Listening to the women share stories confirms that I am not alone in this struggle for visibility. African American women have much to offer institutions, but we must first be recognized and validated as a resource. Conversations with participants reinforced my belief that African American women must support each other and offer mentorship in our quest for advancement and education.

Although we may have different histories and identities, we share many of the same struggles and similar obstacles. African American women must utilize their voices to advocate for themselves and take advantage of learning opportunities. Self-advocacy is key to lifelong learning as women must be confident in their abilities and take every opportunity to learn in order to move to the next level.

My hope is that knowledge gained from these women may be an avenue to actions that support African American women staff in their efforts to navigate barriers to their professional and educational advancement. Understanding the unique challenges faced by African American women staff is necessary to assist them in combating challenges related to the underrepresentation, isolation, and marginalization they face in higher education (Moses, 1997).

REFERENCES

Bailey, K. M. (2010). *The hidden leaves of the baobab tree: Lived experiences of African American female chief academic officers* (Dissertation thesis). University of Texas, Austin, TX. Retrieved from http://utexas.summons.serialsolutions.com

Becks-Moody, G. (2004). *African American women administrators in higher education: Exploring the challenges and experiences at Louisiana public colleges and universities.* Dissertation. Louisiana State University, Baton Rouge, LA. Retrieved from http://www.etd.lsu.edu

Bobo, J. (1991). Black women in fiction and non-fiction: Images of power and powerlessness. *Wide Angle, 13,* 72–81.

Boylorn, R, (2013). *Sweetwater: Black women and narratives of resilience.* New York, NY: Peter Lang.

Collins, P. H. (1991). Learning from the outsider within: The sociological significances of Black feminist thought. *Social Problems, 33,* 14–32.

Collins, P. H. (2000). *Black feminist thought*. New York, NY: Routledge.

Crawford, K., & Smith, D. (2005). The we and the us: Mentoring African American women. *Journal of Black Studies, 36*(1), 52–67. Retrieved from http://www.jstor.org/stable/40027321

Franklin, A. J. (2000, January). Invisibility syndrome: A clinical model of the effects or racism on African American males. *American Journal of Orthopsychiatry. 70*(1), 33–41.

Gall, M. D., Gall, J. P., & Borg, W. R. (2007). *Educational research* (9th ed.) Upper Saddle River, NJ: Pearson Education.

Garvey, B., Stokes, P., & Megginson, D. (2014). *Coaching and mentoring: Theory and practice*. Thousand Oaks, CA: SAGE.

Gregory, S.T. (2001). Black faculty women in the academy: History, status, and future. In F. B. Bonner & V. G. Thomas (Eds.), Black women in the academy: Challenges and opportunities [Special issue]. *Journal of Negro Education, 70*(3), 124–138.

Creswell, J. W. (1998). *Qualitative inquiry and research design: Choosing among five traditions*. Thousand Oaks, CA: SAGE.

Guiffrida, D. A., & Douthit, K. Z. (2010). The Black student experience at predominantly White colleges: Implications for school and college counselors. *Journal of Counseling & Development, 88*(3), 311–318.

Guillory, E. A. (2001). The Black professoriate: Explaining the salary gap for African-American female professors. *Race, Ethnicity and Education, 4*(3), 225–244.

Harley, D. A. (2008). Maids of the academy: African American women faculty at predominantly white institutions. *Journal of African American Studies, 12*, 19–36.

Henry, W. J., & Glenn, N. M. (2009). Black women employed in the ivory tower: Connecting for success. *Advancing Women in Leadership Journal, 27*, 1–12.

Holmes, S. L., Land, L. D., & Hinton-Hudson, V. D. (2007). Race still matters: Considerations for mentoring Black women in academe. *The Negro Educational Review, 58*(1/2), 105–129.

hooks, b. (1999). *Remembered raptured*. New York, NY: Henry Holt.

Hughes, R. L., & Howard-Hamilton, M. (2003). Insights: Emphasizing issues that affect African American women. In M. F. Howard-Hamilton (Ed.), *New directions for student services. Meeting the needs of African American women, 104* (pp. 95–104). San Francisco, CA: Jossey-Bass.

Iverson, S. (2011). "Glass ceilings and sticky floors: Women and advancement in higher education" *Women as leaders in education: Succeeding despite inequity, discrimination, and other challenges, volume I: Women's leadership in higher education*. Retrieved from http://works.bepress.com/susan_ivefrson/21/

Jones, C., & Shorter-Gooden, K. (2003). *Shifting: The double lives of Black women in America*. New York, NY: HarperCollins.

Lorde, A. (2007). *Sister outsider: Essays and speeches*. Berkeley, CA: Crossing Press

Maxwell, J. A. (2005). *Qualitative research design: An interactive approach* (2nd ed.). Thousand Oaks, CA: SAGE.

Merrriam, S. B. (1998). *Qualitative research and case study applications in education*. San Francisco, CA: Jossey-Bass.

Merriam, S. B. (2009). *Qualitative research: A guide to design and implementation.* San Francisco, CA: Jossey-Bass.

Miles, M. B., & Huberman, A. M. (1994). *Qualitative data analysis: An expanded sourcebook* (2nd ed.) Thousand Oaks, CA: SAGE.

Montgomery, B., Dodson, J., & Johnson, S. (2014). Guiding the way: Mentoring graduate students and junior faculty for sustainable academic careers. *SAGE Open, 4*(4), 1–11.

Moses, Y.T. (1997). Black women in academe: Issues and strategies. In L. Benjamin (Ed.), *Black women in the academy: Promises and perils* (pp. 23–37). Gainesville, FL: University Press of Florida.

Moustakas, C. (1990). *Heuristic research: Design, methodology, and applications.* London, UK: SAGE.

Patitu, C. L., & Hinton, K. G. (2003). The experiences of African American women faculty and administrators in higher education: Has anything changed? *New Directions for Student Services, 2003*(104), 79–93. doi:10.1002/ss.109 24

Patton, M. Q. (2002). *Qualitative research and evaluations methods.* Thousand Oaks, CA: SAGE.

Robinson, K. (2012). *Institutional factors contributing to the under-representation of African American women in higher education: Perceptions of women in leadership positions.* Electronic Theses & Dissertations. Paper 811. Retrieved from http://digitalcommons.georgiasouthern.edu/etd/811

Shorter-Gooden, K. (2004). Multiple resistance strategies: How African American women cope with racism and sexism. *Journal of Blacks Psychology, 30*(3), 406–425.

Smedley, A. (2007). *Race in North America: Origin and evolution of a worldview.* Boulder, CO: Westview Press.

Stephens, D. P., & Phillips, L. (2005). Integrating Black feminist thought into conceptual frameworks of African American adolescent women's sexual scripting processes. *Sexualities, Evolution, and Gender, 7*(1), 37–55.

Thomas, G. D., & Hollenshead, C. (2001, Summer). Resisting from the margins: The coping strategies of Black women and other women of color faculty members at a research university. *Journal of Negro Education, 70*(3), 166–175.

Valverde, L.A. (2003). *Leaders of color in higher education: Unrecognized triumphs in harsh institutions.* Walnut Creek, CA: AltaMira Press.

Zamani, E. M. (2003, Winter). African American women in higher education. In M. F. Howard-Hamilton (Ed.), *New directions for student services. Meeting the needs of African American women.* San Francisco, CA: Jossey-Bass.

CHAPTER 19

THALIA'S STORY

A New Perspective of "Non-Traditional" Undergraduate Students

Kristen Linzmeier
University of Wisconsin–Whitewater

I am a person that likes to work *hard*. I like to challenge myself to try to not stay [in] the same place at all. I always try to walk ahead a little bit. Maybe take a longer time, but I like to do that. I like to try and find the ways to get better. In this case, I think my English, it wasn't so good. So I say, I try … ok, let me try [college]. We'll see how hard it is and if I can do it, I can continue, if not, then I [am] gonna stop. At least I can say I tried. (Thalia, 1/13/11)

In these words, Thalia, a 46-year-old Mexican immigrant and "non-tradi-tional" undergraduate student, summarized her educational experiences and expressed her determination to succeed in college and become a certified teacher. "Non-traditional" students such as Thalia are often viewed from a deficit perspective—focusing on what they are not: "*not* tra-ditional, *not* prepared for higher education, *not* in a position of privilege or advantage" (Smit, 2012, p. 370). This type of deficit thinking has created a focus on students' inadequacies and has perpetuated stereotypes among

Identity and Lifelong Learning in Higher Education, pp. 323–344
Copyright © 2020 by Information Age Publishing
All rights of reproduction in any form reserved.

educators and policymakers (Delpit, 1995; Garcia & Guerra, 2004; Smit, 2012; Valenzuela, 1999).

Historically, the term "non-traditional" in reference to students is formatted in a variety of ways (e.g., "non-traditional," "nontraditional," nontraditional, non-traditional). I use "non-traditional" because I view the term as a category, and I "trouble" the term later in this chapter. "Non-traditional" students are also frequently labeled "underprepared," "disadvantaged," and in some places, "minority students" (Garcia & Guerra, 2004; Smit, 2012; Warren, 2002). This type of terminology creates a deficit discourse of adult undergraduate students.

While identifying the factors that explain poor academic outcomes among certain groups is a laudable goal, focusing solely on this type of analysis is problematic because it leads researchers to overlook the strengths of students in these groups. "Non-traditional" learners are a prime example of lifelong learning and yet the deficit perspective may lead them to problematize their identities, focusing on their weaknesses and overlooking their strengths.

In this chapter, I use a case study of a "non-traditional" student to document a process of lifelong learning, identify the ways in which "non-traditional" status affects educational experiences, explore themes of identity construction among "non-traditional" students, and present an alternative to the deficit perspective on education. Specifically, I use narrative inquiry to analyze data—gathered in the form of stories—and retell or "restory" Thalia's journey to complete her bachelor's degree.

BACKGROUND

To contextualize the analysis of Thalia's educational experiences and identity, I review three topics: First, I present an overview of the population of "non-traditional" students and the most common ways of classifying students as "traditional" and "non-traditional." Second, I review critical race theory, a theoretical perspective often used to counter deficit views of education. Third, I summarize the literature on identity as a theoretical concept.

"Non-Traditional" Undergraduate Students

Historically, educational institutions have categorized undergraduate students as "traditional" and "non-traditional." A "traditional" student is 17–22 years of age and enrolls in college immediately after high school graduation while a "non-traditional" student is typically over age 25 and attends college later in life. "Non-traditional" students make up an increasing proportion of undergraduates. The National Center for Education Studies projected that between 2012 and 2023 enrollment would increase much more among students over age 25 (20%) than among those under 25 (12%) (National Center for Education Statistics [NCES], 2015). Despite this trend, adult students continue to occupy a marginal status in research, policy, and institutional practices (Chao & Good, 2004; Kasworm, Sandmann, & Sissel, 2000; Taniguchi & Kaufman, 2005). Further, the curriculum and institutional culture was designed with "traditional" students in mind and continues to cater to these students. Because "traditional" students are viewed as the norm, those who do not follow the normative educational path are placed into the "other" category, which by default categorizes difference as a deficiency.

As an alternative to the binary classification based primarily on age, Horn (1996) defined "non-traditional" students as individuals who meet any of the following criteria:

- Delays enrollment (does not enter postsecondary education in the same calendar year that he or she finished high school)
- Attends part-time for at least part of the academic year
- Works full-time (35 hours or more per week) while enrolled
- Is considered financially independent for purposes of determining eligibility for financial aid
- Has dependents other than a spouse (usually children but sometimes others)
- Is a single parent (either not married or married but separated, and has dependents)
- Does not have a high school diploma (completed high school with a GED or other high school completion certificate or did not finish high school)

Horn's "trait framework" defines "non-traditional" students on a continuum ranging from minimally "non-traditional" to moderately "non-traditional" based on the number of these characteristics present (Horn, 1996). In the 2011–12 school year, approximately 74% of undergraduates had at least one "non-traditional" characteristic (NCES, 2015). Thus, in this framework, the majority of undergraduate students are defined as "non-traditional."

The term "non-traditional" has also been used to refer to various student background characteristics including ethnicity (Kim, 2002). Of the 17 million undergraduate students enrolled in 2015, 9.3 million were White, 3 million were Hispanic, 2.3 million were Black, 1.1 million were Asian/Pacific Islander, and 132,000 were American Indian/Alaska Native (NCES,

2017). The number of minority students in higher education has increased in recent years, and is projected to continue to grow rapidly in the future.

In sum, the students in today's college classrooms are "more diverse in terms of age, social class, and ethnicity as doors have opened to groups previously underrepresented" (Merrill, 2012, p. 163). Despite the doors opening, however, underrepresented students are often "othered" and viewed from a deficit perspective by the institution at large, faculty, and students. Barnett (2007) argued that for many "non-traditional" students, this negative stereotyping has created "uncertainties as to what it is to be a student" (p. 9).

Critical Race Theory

Critical race theory (CRT) challenges the dominant discourse on race, gender, and class as it relates to education by examining how theory, policy, and practice work to subordinate people of color (Delgado & Stefancic, 2001; Sólorzano, 1998). CRT has gained prominence as a framework that education researchers use to examine racial subordination (Ladson-Billings, 1998; Sólorzano, 1998; Sólorzano & Yosso, 2001), with CRT theorists in education seeking to explain the continued inequities that people of color experience in educational settings (Ladson-Billings, 1998).

Based on the work of Oliver and Shapiro (1995), Yosso (2006, 2005) used the concept of "community cultural wealth" to counter traditional deficit views and to describe a CRT-based lens through which to "see" ways in which Communities of Color nurture cultural wealth. Yosso's (2005) framework includes six forms of capital that overlap to create "community cultural wealth": aspirational, linguistic, familial, social, navigational, and resistant capital. Yosso (2005) emphasized the "cultural knowledge, skills resources, and abilities" (p. 69) that, students of color and their communities possess and countered traditional interpretations of Bourdieu's (1986) theory of cultural capital and the deficit thinking its adherents have often attached to the concept. Ultimately, "community cultural wealth" is a theory of empowerment that recognizes Communities of Color as "places with multiple strengths," (Yosso, 2005, p. 82) and thus shifts the focus away from a deficit view and toward communities' cultural assets and wealth (Yosso, 2006). Following Kress (2011), I draw on the tenets of CRT "to trouble [the] existing hegemonic notions of education" (p. 268) that existed at Assisi University (AU), and I utilize CRT as a tool to better understand "the dialectical process which is represented by the individual, the collegiate environment, and the broader world of the learner" (Kasworm, 2007, p. 5).

Identity

Identity as a theoretical concept is one of the most studied constructs in the social sciences (Patton, Renn, Guido, & Quay, 2016). Historically, the term *identity* has taken on a variety of meanings and many researchers have come to view identity as an "important analytic tool" (Gee, 2000) for understanding students and schools. In recent years, researchers have frequently used the concept of identity to study adults and their experiences as students in higher education (Moore, 2006). Simply defined, "identity is what we make of ourselves within a society that is making something of us" (Josselson, as cited in Jones & Abes, 2013, p. xv).

Because it is important to use a theoretical lens that highlights both the social and dynamic aspects of identity, this chapter uses social constructivism as a key perspective on identity. From a social constructivist perspective, identity refers to the concept "that one's sense of self and beliefs about one's own social group as well as others are constructed through interactions with the broader social contexts in which dominant values dictate norms and expectations" (Torres, Jones, & Renn, as cited in Jones & Abes, 2013, p. 57). Drawing on the work of Holland, Lachicotte, Skinner, and Cain (1998), Kasworm (2010) extended the theory of identity and agency in cultural contexts, finding that students experienced "changing student identities influenced by both the complex set of actors and structures of the classroom and college as well as their own self-constructions of college student behaviors and beliefs and the ongoing dynamics of adult role experiences" (p. 16). These findings suggest that for students, identity is connected to their interaction with other people and their environment; this understanding of identity stands in stark contrast to previous notions of identity as solely developmental and not significantly affected by social interaction.

In addition to using a social constructivist perspective, this chapter also draws on role theory as a conceptual framework to consider the various roles, or identities, that adult students simultaneously enact throughout their undergraduate experiences and to examine how individuals manage and prioritize the demands of these multiple roles. Role theory, as defined by Barker (1999), is a "group of concepts, based on sociocultural and anthropological investigations, which pertain to the way people are influenced in their behaviors by the variety of social positions they hold and the expectations that accompany those positions" (p. 67). In the current case, undergraduate students simultaneously enact a variety of roles such as student, worker, spouse, and parent. These roles often compete, or even conflict, with one another, which can jeopardize a student's ability to complete college (Jacobs & King, 2002).

For some individuals, their identity or role as a student is situated in invisibility and "otherness"; these students often experience a sense of being outsiders and feel unsupported by those within or associated with the university. This chapter uses social constructivism and role theory to examine how one "non-traditional" student constructed her identity within the context of the current higher education system (Burke & Stets, 2009). I argue that identity construction is a dynamic process that involves individuals, their educational environment (e.g., the university or college), and the broader societal context (Kasworm, 2010). In addition, I explore the implications of identity construction among "non-traditional" students for higher education.

STUDY SETTING

The data on Thalia's educational experiences are drawn from a larger study that sought to answer two central research questions: (1) What are the lived experiences of "non-traditional" students in an early childhood baccalaureate program? (2) What sorts of knowledge and experiences do participants in the study bring to their university? The project examined the lived experiences of three "non-traditional" undergraduate students in the early childhood (EC) program at Assisi University (AU), a small Roman Catholic university in Oakview, a suburb of Lake City. Lake City is a Midwestern city with a population of 600,000. At the time of the study, 27 students (in three cohorts) were enrolled in the EC program, which was designed to target students from diverse linguistic and socioeconomic backgrounds. All students in the program had an associate degree in early childhood education. Students were considered "non-traditional" based on their age and their status as full-time workers, and because they were completing coursework during evening and summer sessions.

The EC program was situated within the context of the larger university, which had historically catered to the needs of a more "traditional" student demographic. According to AU's website, in the 2009–10 school year, the university had a total undergraduate enrollment of approximately 3,070 students. About 30% of undergraduate students were "minority" students (22% African American, 5% Hispanic, 2% Asian, and 1% Native American). In stark contrast, 85% of the undergraduate students enrolled in the EC program were "minority" students, including many who reported coming from a low socioeconomic background. Latina students made up 54% of the total enrollment in the EC program. Because the demographic composition of the students in the EC program differed significantly from the demographic composition of the larger university, students and professors in the larger university community had certain perceptions of the EC program students as well as questions about who "these" students were and whether they had the ability to succeed in the program. Many AU faculty and staff believed that "non-traditional" students did not belong or that they lacked the skills to be successful students. Many of these assumptions resulted from AU's history of serving traditional students, and many faculty were not willing to change their beliefs or teaching practices to meet the needs of *all* students.

METHODOLOGY

Narrative Inquiry

I utilized narrative inquiry as a qualitative research method to gather, analyze, and interpret the narratives of the three "non-traditional" undergraduate students (including Thalia) in this study (Chase, 2000; Clandinin, 2006; Clandinin & Connelly, 2000; Creswell, 2007; Marshall & Rossman, 2006; Webster & Mertova, 2007). More specifically, I utilized life history interviews to examine how "non-traditional" students story their lives (Atkinson, 1998; Cole & Knowles, 2001; Goodson & Sikes, 2001; Linde, 1993). I conducted a case study as described by Bogdan and Biklen (2007)—as a life history in which I completed "extensive interviews with one person for the purpose of collecting a first-person narrative" (p. 63). As is common in case study research, the analytic strategy was to provide "detailed descriptions of themes within each case (within-case analysis), followed by thematic analysis across cases (cross-case analysis)" (Bloomberg & Volpe, 2011, p. 31).

Data Collection and Analysis

Each participant completed three to five life history interviews, each lasting approximately two to three hours and covering the participant's entire life span. All interviews were audio-recorded and transcribed verbatim; I also recorded detailed field notes from each session and then coded these for salient themes. In addition, I used document analysis to gain further information about each participant. At the start of the study, each participant completed a consent form allowing me access to the following documents: class assignments, student portfolios, grade reports, application materials, program disposition forms, performance inventories, and test scores. These documents further provided information about the participants' educational journeys at AU, including important details that participants did not share in the interviews.

Data analysis and data collection occurred concurrently. As I analyzed the data, I sought patterns and common themes. I also created an ongoing list of themes and topics that I wished to explore in future interviews. I viewed data collection as a cyclical process, in which there was "continuous movement between data and ideas" (Bloomberg & Volpe, 2011, p. 26). After collecting and analyzing the data, I created a life history for each participant, focusing on the forms of capital (Yosso, 2006) that participants utilized throughout their respective journeys.

To ensure credibility, I utilized triangulation, the process of using multiple sources to identify patterns and themes of the study (Creswell, 2007). My triangulation process involved comparing data I had collected via interviews, field notes, and document analysis. I also performed member checks by sharing my data and interpretations with the participants, and soliciting feedback on my emerging findings (Marshall & Rossman, 2006).

THALIA'S STORY

Thalia was born in Oaxaca, Mexico in 1965 and was one of seven children. Her father was a farmer and her mother cared for the children and the home. Since childhood, Thalia had dreamed of becoming a teacher. She recalled, "When I was in elementary school, my dream was always to be a teacher.... I don't know how long it's gonna take, but my dream was always to be a teacher." However, Thalia experienced educational challenges from a young age. Growing up, she spoke Mixteco, a dialect of Spanish spoken in the surrounding community. When she began school at the age of six, it was necessary for her to learn Spanish because instruction was solely in Spanish.

Throughout her early years in school, Thalia spoke Mixteco at home and Spanish in school, which created conflicting identities that Thalia described as feeling like being "two persons in one." Thalia was proficient in Mixteco but was slow to acquire Spanish. As an *emergent bilingual*, a term used intentionally here to here to highlight students' potential rather than their limitations (García, Kleifgen, & Falchi, 2008), a lack of Spanish proficiency was evident to her peers and marked her as an "outsider." As a result, she was often the target of ridicule by her peers:

> When I was in fifth grade, one of the teacher[s] was *so* nice to me...some kids started making fun [of me] and he stopped them. And he asked, "Do you speak two language[s]? Do you like to learn two language[s]?" And, I remember that boy, he didn't answer anything and the teacher [said], "She speak[s] two language[s], and you speak only one." He told him, "So she have more [value] than you, so don't make fun [of] any of those person who speak more than one language...."

For the first time in her life, Thalia was positioned as someone who knew *two* languages, rather than someone who *did not know* Spanish. Rather than embracing a deficit view of her language skills, the teacher focused on the *assets* she brought, in this case, the knowledge of two languages, an asset that few of her peers could offer. Until that point, others (including Thalia) had always viewed language skills as something Thalia lacked.

Over the next several years, Thalia completed secundaria (grades seven through nine) and design school, and worked in a textile factory. Although Thalia was successful in her role as a designer at the factory, her early aspirations to become a teacher persisted: "I still kept thinking, I'm *gonna* be a teacher. In Mexico [it] is hard to find a school in the evenings to go, almost all the school is during the day, so work and studies, and it's not easy." Despite her continued desire, she put her dream of becoming a teacher on hold to marry a man she had known since childhood. Her husband had a visa and had lived and worked in the United States for six years prior to their wedding. In order to be with her new husband, she had to travel to the United States without citizenship or a green card, which meant crossing the border without documents.

Starting Life in Lake City, United States

After she arrived in the United States, Thalia and her husband lived in Lake City, a large city in the Midwest. Over the next several years, her husband worked a variety of blue-collar jobs and the couple had two daughters. Thalia stayed home and cared for the children until her youngest daughter turned four. At that point, Thalia began to help in her daughter's classroom—it was the start of a job that lasted for the next 16 years.

Thalia enjoyed working at the same school her daughters attended; she also liked the school because it was bilingual and allowed her to use Spanish, which she now considered her primary language after struggling to learn it so long ago. She continued to wonder if being a teacher was her true calling and a career worth pursuing. She explained, "I really want to be a teacher. I always want to be a teacher ... one day I start asking [for] confirmation, is that what I really want or not. God, how can I know that this is my real passion...?" At the same time, Thalia's husband was encouraging her to apply for U.S. citizenship. Thalia was surprised and thrilled when she discovered that she had passed the citizenship test: "At first, I didn't believe myself that I passed the test and then I said, 'I passed it!'... So, that day was happy. That all changed everything!"

Earning an Associate Degree

After obtaining her U.S. citizenship, Thalia began taking classes to pursue her dream of becoming a teacher. Thalia learned of a program at Lakeview Technical College (LTC) that resulted in an associate degree in early childhood education. Some of the first courses in the program were offered in Spanish, which sparked Thalia's interest and increased her confidence in her ability to succeed. She explained: "In Spanish, I can do it. I can do it better in Spanish than English. Even though it was in Spanish, it was a little hard for me, because my brain was so lazy."

For the next few years, Thalia worked toward completing her associate degree in early childhood education. She continued to work full-time as a teacher's aide at the bilingual elementary school, as well as simultaneously caring for her husband and young daughters. Thalia worked hard to improve her English and developed a network of friends in the program, most of whom who were also Latina and emergent bilinguals. She was a dedicated student who earned A's in most of her courses. After three years, Thalia graduated with an associate degree in early childhood education, the first step toward achieving her lifelong goal of becoming a teacher.

Earning a Bachelor's Degree

Thalia was "proud" to be enrolled in the AU's early childhood (EC) program, a program she viewed as "not for regular students," but rather an "adult special program." AU considered Thalia a "non-traditional" student based on her age, full-time work status, and emerging English skills. Thalia described herself as a "unique" student compared to "regular," more traditional students. Her cohort consisted of 10 students and was quite diverse: four students identified as Latina, three identified as African American, two identified as White, and one identified as Native American. Like her fellow students at Lakeview Technical College, the students in her AU cohort had diverse work experiences and cultural and linguistic backgrounds. The students in the cohort consisted of females who worked full-time in early childhood settings including childcare centers, Head Start programs, and schools.

Like many "non-traditional" students, Thalia struggled to balance the responsibilities of both working full-time and studying full-time. Further, like most of the other women in her cohort, Thalia inhabited the "competing roles" of wife, mother, educator, and student as she cared for her family, worked, attended classes, and studied. On a typical day, she woke at 5:20 A.M. to get her children ready for school, worked until 3:30 P.M., and spent the rest of the afternoon and evening caring for her family and doing homework; she usually worked until midnight or even 1:00 A.M. Her weekend days were almost as long: she woke at 6:00 A.M. and usually worked on coursework until 10:00 at night. She reported that some coursework took extra time because she needed a "longer time to think and write." Thalia viewed her rigorous schedule as something that was simply necessary for her to succeed in school.

Given her competing roles and her age, Thalia saw herself as different than "traditional" students. She recalled telling her daughter that her (Thalia's) experiences at AU were very different than the college experience her daughter had at the University of Lake City (ULC) as a traditional student:

> I tell my daughter my [program] is gonna be different than yours because [you're] like a *regular* student because you start with K4 through now and you didn't stop. You didn't take any breaks and your brain is active and the class you take is as a full-time student. And, my case is different because we're adults who work full-time and we try to go back to school. So, [it's] a little bit hard. [It's] not like special program, but [an] opportunity for *other* person. I like the program, [it] give[s] opportunities to *other* person.

The categorization of "other person" was often used by Thalia to describe emergent bilingual and/or minority students and is significant because the phrase highlights her feelings of being marginalized within the program and society. The feeling of "otherness" had followed her since she was very young. Not only did Thalia assign the "other person" status to herself, but some of her classmates, specifically those who were not Latina, "othered" her as well. Tears flooded her eyes as she described her experiences early in the program: "At the beginning, they look at us, like what are you doing here? You not speak, very well English and you don't know how to write or whatever. They make us feel like that ... it's a little bit hard."

Despite the marginalization she felt from some of her peers, when asked what it was like to be a bilingual student in the program, her response was surprisingly positive: "I think, for me, it's a gift to stay here. To learn new stuff. Even if it's a little bit hard. This is an amazing program to give the opportunity for Latino or different ethnicities to continue their education."

More than anything else, Thalia sought respect from her fellow students and instructors. She explained, "It doesn't matter if they have different opinion, different ethnicities. I need to respect them and I would like them to respect me. So, I think the most important thing is to respect each other." For Thalia, respect included accepting cultural and linguistic differences and understanding the barriers that non-native speakers face: "I think, like a Spanish person, or Latina person or student, I gonna ask little bit of patience with us because it's not our first language, it's the second language, and so we take a little more time to learn." Thalia's comments show that she was simultaneously enacting the roles of student and emergent bilingual. To be considered a successful student, she had to perform both roles proficiently. Consequently, Thalia felt that her presence at AU was constantly under scrutiny.

As a student fluent in a language other than English, Thalia was in the process of acquiring basic English skills. She described the process of code switching, using her second and third languages:

> I took hours to read and I tried to translate and understand what the chapters talk about. Sometimes I have to think in Spanish first, or translate the rubric to see, to make sure I understand what she's expecting me to do, and sometimes I still have to write it in Spanish.

Thalia used this process throughout her studies. Like many of the students in the EC program, Thalia utilized the writing support services provided by Lara, a trilingual instructor in the writing center at AU. Lara was more than a writing coach for the students, she was often a lifeline because Spanish-speaking students could converse with her in Spanish about concepts or topics that were difficult to articulate in English. The value placed on Lara's ability to speak both Spanish and English is significant, because from an institutional perspective, Thalia's bilingualism was *not* valued.

Many "non-traditional" students such as Thalia faced considerable challenges because the university was designed to meet the needs of "traditional" students. For example, the university bookstore and financial aid offices were only open from 9:00 a.m. to 4:00 p.m., which made them inaccessible to students such as Thalia who worked full-time and attended classes in the evenings. Further, when Thalia did try to access services such as financial aid, she often became frustrated and discouraged by her experiences. She lamented, "they make me to feel stupid." Most alarmingly, many faculty members opted not to teach in the EC program. Many stated that they felt unsafe at the Central City Campus (even though the area was very safe); however, my observations suggest that many of these faculty members did not want to teach students such as Thalia based on their belief that "non-traditional" students were deficient and incapable of succeeding in their classes. Faculty members often made comments expressing their disdain for "those students" or students "who weren't up to par" based on their lack of English proficiency, once again "othering" students or categorizing them as deficient before even meeting them.

In addition to feeling "othered" by faculty and "traditional" students, Thalia also faced criticism from a group of fellow teacher's aides she considered friends. She recounted that when she began taking courses, these former allies began to turn against her:

They see me like a future teacher and they feel behind, even though I [do] not speak very [good] English.... You gonna be on the other side, on the other team. I think they see me like a future teacher so that makes it a little bit hard.

Thus, Thalia's pending graduation and transition to the "other side" created another identity clash. While transitioning from teacher's aide to certified teacher was her dream, she feared it would come at the expense of acceptance among her Latina coworkers. When I asked whether her friends' behavior bothered her, she replied that the experience had fueled her motivation to complete the program and become a teacher. She asserted, "No ... it doesn't bother me. It's *them*, it's not me. When I see the attitude they have, they push me a little bit more." Thus, the negative reaction of her friends became further motivation to complete the program.

Despite this group of critics, Thalia was surrounded by people who supported her dreams of becoming a teacher. Her family expressed a great deal of pride in her accomplishments. For example, her daughter said, "Don't you feel proud of you? You have to feel proud." Thalia's father was proud as well; she remarked: "Oh, my father, he is proud of me. Because he says, she's a teacher, she teaches and I say, No, I'm not. I don't have my *license*."

Thalia's father, her family, and the young students with whom she worked all regarded Thalia as a teacher. However, despite working with children as a teacher's aide for over 16 years, she did not identify as a teacher, because she believed that she wouldn't be a *real* teacher until she received her teaching certification. Thus, it was important to her to become a certified teacher.

Praxis Exams

During the last year of the EC program, the only thing keeping Thalia from achieving her dream of becoming a *certified* teacher was passing the state Praxis exams. She explained, "You have to have [a] license in order to be the lead teacher, so that's why I really want to pass those tests." Despite her determination, at the time of her graduation, Thalia had taken the exams several times, and though her score had improved each time, she had not yet passed. She continued to take practice tests and retest every few months.

As an emerging bilingual student, Thalia faced a variety of obstacles inherent to standardized tests. I concluded that it was not Thalia's failure to understand the material that kept her from becoming a certified teacher, but rather the fact that the Praxis exams, like most standardized tests, are first and foremost tests of English proficiency, and are not necessarily accurate measures of content knowledge (Garcia & Menkin, 2006). As a result, these exams usually result in students fluent in a language other than English being labeled as "failing."

For Thalia and other emerging bilingual students, it is problematic that high-stakes tests such as the Praxis exam "ultimately reflect a 'language-as-problem' or 'deficit model' orientation in recent US language policy, where language has become a liability for ELLs" (Menkin, 2008, p. 152). Within this "language as liability" framework, Thalia is viewed through the lens of the deficit model yet again. Despite all her accomplishments, Thalia is still labeled as "failing" in an educational system that utilizes standardized testing as a gatekeeping function that perpetuates the power of dominant groups (Menkin, 2008).

EXAMINING THALIA'S STORY: TIME FOR A NEW PERSPECTIVE

Like nearly two thirds of all Latinas, Thalia began her postsecondary studies at the community college level (Sólorzano, Villalpando, & Oseguera, 2005). Her experience at community college was positive. She was surrounded by other Latina women who were also emerging bilingual students, and much of her preliminary coursework was offered in Spanish. No one questioned her presence at the technical college or her ability to obtain a degree. The technical college, writ large, both accepted and *valued* her presence as evidenced by the supports provided to emerging bilingual students (e.g., bilingual coursework, support services, and bilingual instructors and administrators). In the context of community college, Thalia easily constructed an identity as a student.

Like Thalia, over 50% of students enrolled in two-year early childhood associate degree programs within community colleges represent cultural and linguistic minorities (American Association of Community Colleges [AACC], 2009). One critical function of community colleges is to provide access to higher education and also respond to the call to identify and support a more diversified teaching work force in the field of early childhood (National Association for the Education of Young Children [NAEYC], 2010). Interestingly, Early Childhood candidates in two-year programs are proportionately more diverse than in four-year programs and similar to LTC, most community colleges offer courses in English as Second Language and developmental courses for adult students who need additional support (NAEYC, 2010).

Unlike the supportive community college context, Thalia's student identity was constantly questioned during her four-year program at AU by the university, her peers, and at times even herself. In this context, she found it confusing and difficult to construct an identity as a student, even though she succeeded in earning a bachelor's degree. In the words of Patton et al. (2016), Thalia's experiences "shaped [her] identities within a framework of power and privilege" (p. 67).

Based on her current situation, many would define Thalia from a deficit perspective, describing her as a student who lacked English proficiency and who did not become a certified teacher because she failed the Praxis exams. What if, however, we used another perspective to assess the situation? From childhood, Thalia was determined to become a teacher. In Yosso's (2006) terms, she possessed *aspirational capital*, "the ability to maintain hopes and dreams for the future even in the face of real and perceived barriers" (p. 77) which fueled her determination to obtain her teaching license despite the many barriers she faced. Further, her ability to speak more than one language can be considered a *skill*. In fact, because she is fluent in her students' home language, she may be recognized as a "relatively more effective" teacher of emerging bilingual students than her monolingual counterparts (Loeb, Soland, & Fox, 2014).

The ability to speak more than one language is particularly important given the changing demographics of the U.S. population—NCES has projected that English Language Learners (ELLs) will compose 25% of public school students by 2025 (NCES, 2011). In 2009, the same time Thalia was enrolled at AU, one in four children in the United States lived in a first- or second-generation immigrant family and over one third of those children had at least one parent born in Mexico (Child Trends Data Bank, 2009). In fact, in the Midwestern state where Thalia resides, there is a growing shortage of ELL teachers. Some districts in the state have even recruited teachers from Spain to teach Spanish because they have been unable to find qualified bilingual teachers locally. The bottom line is that U.S. schools are in dire need of bilingual teachers and Thalia has much to offer the field of education. Furthermore, the increased diversity of children and families in early childhood programs, specifically those from culturally and linguistically diverse communities, presents the need to grow a more diverse early childhood teaching workforce (NAEYC, 2010). Thalia exemplifies a teacher that could respond to this call for action, that is, if she was given the opportunity to share all that she brings to the field of early childhood.

This situation once again highlights the need to describe students according to what they *are*, rather than categorizing them as what they *are not* (Smit, 2012). In this case, Thalia is a native speaker of Spanish who earned an undergraduate degree and is proficient in the content of early childhood education. She is a student who is trilingual. She is a mother. She has over 16 years of experience teaching in a bilingual early childhood classroom. Most of all, she is determined. Thalia has proven that she has all the qualities necessary to be a *good* teacher: She passed all her classes (indicating that she has the necessary content knowledge) and her performance in the classroom has shown that she is an effective teacher. Yet her dream of becoming a teacher remains out of reach solely based on her inability to pass the Praxis exam.

The fact that Thalia was unable to obtain her teaching certificate despite her extensive qualifications suggests a need to for educational researchers and the educational system to move away from a deficit perspective and create a new perspective focused on the skills that "non-traditional" students bring to the table. Minikel-Lacocque (2015) asserted that in order "to combat this deficit orientation, the experiences of underrepresented college students must be brought to the foreground of academe" (p. 104). Considering Thalia's skills and experiences from multiple perspectives—bringing her experiences to the "foreground of academe"—reveals a student who is prepared and ready to become a successful teacher.

IDENTITY AS A LIFELONG LEARNER

Thus far, I have argued against the deficit perspective often assigned to Thalia and highlighted the need to consider Thalia from multiple perspectives. There is no doubt that Thalia simultaneously enacts a variety of roles which are all a part of her identity and who she is. An important consideration is that identity formation does not happen in isolation, thus we return to the notion of identity as "what we make of ourselves within a society that is making something of us" (Josselson, as cited in Jones & Abes, 2013, p. xv).

As we reflect on Thalia's story, it is important to recognize that the part(s) of her identity that she enacts are coconstructed and dependent on the context and individuals within those settings. Put differently, it is not as simple as Thalia being able to create or choose an identity for herself. Her identity is dependent upon how she is defined by certain individuals, the environment, and the broader context of society. In some contexts, such as the community college or in the bilingual early childhood classroom in which she teaches, she is viewed as a person of value and that she has much to contribute. Contrastingly, in the context of the four-year University, she is considered to be lacking and deficient. Given those interpretations, what is Thalia to make of herself? At times, trying to create an identity for herself, based on the interpretations of others, is daunting. Yet, other times, it is empowering, and Thalia is pushed to persevere and become stronger.

While there may be no one identity that defines Thalia, one thing that is at the core of her being is her dedication to lifelong learning. Lifelong learning refers to "those activities and engagements representing lifespan learning beyond compulsory schooling" (Kasworm, 2012, p. 173). Her learning process began with her early schooling experiences in Mexico and continued throughout her lifetime, including both formal and informal school and life experiences. Both her formal education and her experiences are an essential part of her identity. Notably, however, identity is more than a response to the question "Who am I?" Other important considerations include "What do I contribute?" and "Why does that matter?" Thus, Thalia has a multifaceted identity and ultimately, she cannot be defined in any single way—no one identity fully encompasses who she is. She is a mother, a wife, a teacher, an immigrant, and someone who strives to help children.

CONCLUSION

There is a call for an "ontological turn" (Barnett, 2007) in the scholarly thinking about adult students in higher education. As Donaldson and Rentfro (2006) noted, the discourse on adult education has a significant influence on the identities of adult undergraduate students. Problematically, the current discourse positions adult students as "different" and in need of "adjusting" to the institution and its traditional norms. Additionally, this discourse of deficiency focuses almost entirely on what "non-traditional" students lack and gives little consideration to their experiential knowledge. Further, it places no responsibility on institutions to adjust their current models to meet the needs of *all* students. Donaldson and Rentfro have questioned the current discourse, asking: "Are adult students 'other,' different, and more needful and deficient when compared to traditional age students? Or, are adult students individuals who also belong in the academy and enrich it by virtue of their presence" (p. 6)?

Stories like Thalia's suggest that the answer to the latter question is a resounding "yes." Examining these stories is essential for creating a more nuanced understanding of the U.S. educational system. Her experience can and should be considered a success story. Thalia graduated from college and while she has not achieved her dream of becoming a certified teacher yet, I truly believe she will. Schools need teachers like Thalia in the field of early childhood education. The U.S. educational system needs bilingual teachers who reflect the culturally and linguistically diverse students in today's classrooms. A teacher is much more than her undergraduate teacher-training program; she is the sum of her life experiences, and teachers such as Thalia bring a wide range of valuable experiences to their classrooms, their students, and ultimately, to their identity.

It is critical for researchers, teacher educators, and institutions of higher education to work collaboratively to create an asset-based definition and understanding of adult students. As I have shown in this chapter, the binary of "non-traditional" and "traditional" students is outdated; in reality, "non-traditional" students outnumber "traditional" students, making them the majority, not the exception (Compton, Cox, & Laanan, 2006). This reality raises the question of why the term "non-traditional" persists and what the continued use of the term means for how adult students are viewed within institutions of higher education. An asset-based discourse (and new terminology) would consider how the extensive variation among today's undergraduate students—variation in characteristics such as age, ethnicity, gender, and sexual orientation—*enriches* (rather than diminishes) the undergraduate experience. Further, this type of discourse would more accurately reflect today's diverse population of undergraduates. Importantly, such a change in the discourse would facilitate a reconstruction of adult student identity as well. Older students, those who are members of racial and ethnic minority groups, and those whose first language was not English would be able to see themselves not as students who have deficits and are "at risk," but rather as lifelong learners who have something unique to offer the field of education.

REFERENCES

AACC (American Association of Community Colleges) (2009). Fast facts. www.aacc. nche.edu/aboutCC/Pages/fastfacts.aspx

Atkinson, R. (1998). *The life story interview.* Thousand Oaks, CA: SAGE.

Barker, R. L. (1999). *The social work dictionary.* Washington, DC: NASW Press.

Barnett, R. (2007). *A will to learn: Being a student in an age of uncertainty.* Maidenhead, UK: Society for Research into Higher Education and Open University Press.

Bloomberg, L. D., & Volpe, M. (2012). *Completing your qualitative dissertation: A roadmap from beginning to end.* Thousand Oaks, CA: SAGE.

Bogdan, R., & Biklen, S. K. (2007). *Qualitative research for education: An introduction to theory and methods.* Boston, MA: Allyn and Bacon.

Bourdieu, P. (1986). The forms of capital. In J. G. Richardson (Ed.), *Handbook of theory and research for the sociology of education* (pp. 241–258). Westport, CT: Greenwood.

Burke, P. J., & Stets, J. E. (2009). *Identity theory.* New York, NY: Oxford University Press.

Chao, R., & Good, G. E. (2004). Nontraditional students' perspectives on college education: A qualitative study. *Journal of College Counseling, 7,* 5–12. doi:10.1002/j.2161-1882.2004.tb00253.x

Chase, S. E. (2000). Narrative inquiry: Multiple lenses, approaches, voices. In N. K. Denzin & Y. S. Lincoln (Eds.), *Collecting and interpreting qualitative materials* (pp. 57–94). Los Angeles, CA: SAGE.

Child Trends Data Bank. (2009). Racial and ethnic composition of the child population. Retrieved from www.childtrendsdatabank.org/?q=node/234

Clandidin, D. J. (2006). *Handbook of narrative inquiry: Mapping a methodology.* Thousand Oaks, CA: SAGE.

Clandinin, D. J., & Connelly, F. M. (2000). *Narrative inquiry: Experience and story in qualitative research.* San Francisco, CA: Jossey-Bass.

Cole, A., & Knowles, J. G. (2001). *Lives in context: The art of life history research.* Lanham, MD: AltaMira Press.

Compton, J., Cox, C., & Laanan, F. (2006). Adult learners in transition. *New Directions for Student Services, 114,* 73–80. doi:10.1002/ss.208

Creswell, J. W. (2007). *Qualitative inquiry and research design: Choosing among five approaches.* Thousand Oaks, CA: SAGE.

Delpit, L. (1995). *Other people's children: Cultural conflict in the classroom.* New York, NY: New Press.

Delgado, R. & Stefancic, J. (2001). *Critical race theory: An introduction.* New York, NY: NYU Press.

Donaldson, J., & Rentfro, A. (2004). Adult undergraduates in higher education journals: A marginal and insecure status. *The Journal of Continuing Higher Education, 52*(3), 13–23. doi:10.1080/07377366.2004.10400291

García, O., Kleifgen, J. A., & Falchi, L. (2008). From English language learners to emergent bilinguals. *Equity Matters: Research Review No. 1.* [Research Report]. Campaign for Educational Equity, New York, NY: Teachers College, Columbia University. Retrieved from http://www.equitycampaign.org/events-page/equity-in-education-forum-series/past-events/from-english-language-learners-to-emergent-bilinguals/6532_Ofelia_ELL__Final.pdf

García, O., & Menkin, K. (2006). The English of Latinos from a plurilingual trans-cultural angle: Implications for assessment and schools. In S. Nero (Ed.), *Dialects, Englishes, Creoles, and education* (pp. 167–184). Clevedon, UK: Multilingual Matters.

Garcia, S. B., & Guerra, P. L. (2004). Deconstructing deficit thinking: Working with educators to create more equitable learning environments. *Education and Urban Society, 36*(2), 150–168. doi:10.1177/0013124503261322

Gee, J. P. (2000–2001). Identity as an analytical lens for research in education. *Review of Research in Education, 25,* 88–125. Retrieved from http://www.jstor.org/stable/1167322

Goodson, I., & Sikes, P. (2001). *Life history research in educational settings: Learning from lives.* New York, NY: Open University Press.

Horn, L. (1996). Nontraditional undergraduates, trends in enrollment from 1986–1992 and persistence and attainment among 1989–90 beginning post-secondary students. *U.S. Department of Education, NCES.* Washington, DC: U.S. Government Printing Office.

Holland, D., Lachicotte, W., Skinner, D., & Cain, C. (1998). *Identity and agency in cultural worlds.* Cambridge, MA: Harvard University Press.

Jacobs, J. A., & King, R. B. (2002). Age and college completion: A life history analysis of women aged 15–44. *Sociology of Education, 75,* 211–230. doi:10.2307/3090266

Jones, S. R., & Abes, E. S. (2013). *Identity development of college students: Advancing frameworks for multiple dimensions of identity.* San Francisco, CA: Jossey-Bass.

Kasworm, C. (2007, April). *Adult undergraduate student identity: Proposed model.* Paper presented at the annual meeting of the American Educational Research Association, Chicago, IL.

Kasworm, C. (2010). Adult learners in a research university: Negotiating undergraduate student identity. *Adult Education Quarterly, 60*(2), 143–160. doi:10.1177/0741713609336110

Kasworm, C. (2012). United States of America: Adult higher education and lifelong learning in the USA: Perplexing contradictions. In M. Slowey & H. G. Schuetze (Eds.), *Global perspectives on higher education and lifelong learners* (pp. 173–192). Abingdon, Oxon, UK: Routledge.

Kasworm, C. E., Sandmann, L. R., & Sissel, P. A. (2000). Adult learners in higher education. In A. L. Wilson & E. R. Hayes (Eds.), *Handbook of adult and continuing education* (pp. 449–663). San Francisco, CA: Jossey-Bass.

Kim, K. (2002). ERIC review: Exploring the meaning of "nontraditional" at the community college. *Community College Review, 30,* 74–89. doi:10.1177/009155210203000104

Kress, T. (2011). Stepping out of the academic brew: Using critical research to break down hierarchies of knowledge production. *The International Journal of Qualitative Studies in Education, 24*(3), 267–283. doi:10.1080/09518398.20 10.534116

Ladson-Billings, G. (1998). Preparing teachers for diverse student populations: A critical race theory perspective. *Review of Research in Education, 24,* 211–247. doi:10.2307/1167271

Linde, C. (1993). *Life stories: The creation of coherence.* New York, NY: Oxford University Press.

Loeb, S., Soland, J., & Fox, L. (2014). Is a good teacher a good teacher for all? Comparing value-added of teachers with their English learners and non-English learners. *Education Evaluation and Policy analysis, 46,* 457–475. doi:10.3102/0162373714527788

Lutton, A. (2012). Using the new NAEYC professional preparation standards. In A. Lutton (Ed.), *Advancing the early childhood profession: NAEYC standards and guidelines for professional development* (pp. 103–109). Washington, DC: NAEYC.

Marshall, C. & Rossman, G. (2006). *Designing qualitative research.* London, UK: SAGE.

Menkin, K. (2008). *Early learners left behind: Standardized testing as language policy.* Tonawanda, NY: Multilingual Matters.

Merrill, B. (2012). Non-traditional adult students: Access, dropout, retention and developing a learner identity. In T. Hinton-Smith (Ed.), *Widening participation in higher education: Casting the net wide?* (pp. 163–177). Hampshire, UK: Palgrave Macmillan.

Minikel-Lacocque, J. (2015). Getting college ready: Latin@ student experiences of race, access, and belonging at predominately white universities. New York, NY: Peter Lang.

Moore, E. (2006). Educational identities of adult university graduates. *Scandinavian Journal of Educational Research*, *50*(2), 149–163. doi:10.1080/00313830600575940

National Association for the Education of Young Children. (2010). *2010 NAEYC standards for initial & advanced early childhood professional preparation programs for use by associate, baccalaureate and graduate degree programs*. Retrieved from https://www.naeyc.org/sites/default/files/globally-shared/downloads/PDFs/our-work/higher-ed/NAEYC-Professional-Preparation-Standards.pdf

National Center for Education Statistics (NCES). (2011). *The condition of education*. Washington, DC: U.S. Department of Education.

National Center for Education Statistics (NCES). (2015). *The condition of education*. Washington, DC: U.S. Department of Education.

National Center for Education Statistics (NCES). (2017). *The condition of education*. Washington, DC: U.S. Department of Education.

Oliver, M., & Shapiro, T. (1995). *Black wealth, White wealth: A new perspective on racial inequality*. New York, NY: Routledge.

Patton, L., Renn, K., Guido, F., & Quaye, S. (2016). *Student development in college: Theory, research and practice*. San Francisco, CA: Jossey-Bass.

Smit, R. (2012). Towards a clearer understanding of student disadvantage in higher education: Problematising deficit thinking. *Higher Education Research and Development*, *31*(3), 369–380. doi:10.1080/07294360.2011.634383

Sólorzano, D. G. (1998). Critical race theory, racial and gender-microaggressions, and the experiences of Chicana and Chicano scholars. *International Journal of Qualitative Studies in Education, 11*, 121–136. doi:10.1080/095183998236926

Sólorzano, D. G., Villalpando, O., & Oseguera, L. (2005). Educational inequities and Latino undergraduate students in the United States: A critical race analysis of their educational progress. *Journal of Hispanic Higher Education*, *4*(3), 272–294. doi:10.1177/1538192705276550

Sólorzano, D. G. & Yosso, T. J. (2001). Critical race and LatCrit theory and method: Counter-storytelling—Chicana and Chicano graduate school experiences. *Qualitative Studies in Education, 14*(3), 471–495. doi:10.1080/09518390110063365

Taniguchi, H., & Kaufman, G. (2005). Degree completion among nontraditional college students. *Social Science Quarterly, 86*(4), 912–927. doi:10.1111/j.0038-4941.2005.00363.x

Valenzuela, A. (1999). *Subtractive schooling: U.S.-Mexican youth and the politics of caring*. Albany, NY: State University of New York Press.

Warren, D. (2002). Curriculum design in a context of widening participation in higher education. *Arts and Humanities in Higher Education, 1*(1) 85–99. doi:10.1177/1474022202001001007

Webster, L., & Mertova, P. (2007). *Using narrative inquiry as a research method: An introduction using critical event narrative analysis in research on learning and teaching*. New York, NY: Routledge.

Yosso, T. J. (2005). Whose culture has capital? A critical race theory discussion of community cultural wealth. *Race Ethnicity and Education, 8*(1), 69–91. doi:10.1080/1361332052000341006

Yosso, T. J. (2006). *Critical race counterstories along the Chicana/Chicano educational pipeline*. New York, NY: Routledge.

ABOUT THE CONTRIBUTORS

ABOUT THE EDITORS

Dr. Jo Ann Gammel

Jo Ann Gammel, EdD, is an Adjunct Faculty member in the PhD program in Educational Studies at Lesley University in Cambridge, MA. She earned her doctoral degree in Adult Learning and Leadership through the AEGIS program at Columbia University Teachers College. She has a master's in international administration from the School for International Training in Brattleboro, VT. She teaches courses in adult learning, leadership, and qualitative research methods. Jo Ann was founding director for Endicott College's first doctoral program in educational leadership and collaborator on three subsequent doctoral degree programs. She was an early collaborator designing a hybrid online and low-residency doctoral degree option in Adult Learning at Lesley University. She recently transitioned from Massachusetts to Florida, where she continues to teach online and sponsor dissertation writers. Her research and teaching interests include doctoral education and relational mentoring, coaching, advising and mentorship, program design and evaluation, and adult learning and leadership theory and research. Jo Ann has mentored doctoral students across a variety of educational and adult development topics, coached writers in various stages of development, and is committed to supporting adult learners in their doctoral study.

Dr. Sue Motulsky

Sue Motulsky, EdD, is an Associate Professor in the Division of Counseling and Psychology at Lesley University in Cambridge, MA. She teaches graduate courses in vocational development and career counseling, developmental psychology, and research methods, including doctoral courses in qualitative research as well as advising doctoral students. Her teaching, research, and writing interests include feminist, relational psychology; gender; multicultural and LGBTQ identity development; career development and transitions; and qualitative, constructivist, and narrative research as well as social justice issues in counseling education. Sue publishes and presents on relational career counseling and career transition, transgender career issues, qualitative methods in psychology, and social justice in counseling psychology. Sue earned her doctorate in human development and psychology from Harvard University, where her studies focused on adult development and transition, feminist and cultural perspectives on identity and development, and relational psychology. She also has master's degrees in culture, gender, and relational development and in English literature. She maintains a private practice in career counseling and has an extensive background in career development and transition in university, community, and human services settings. Sue's approach to teaching and counseling is based on a relational definition of a healthy psychological self as being in connection with the self, with others, and with the world.

Dr. Amy Rutstein-Riley

Amy Rutstein-Riley, PhD, MPH, is the Interim Dean of the Graduate School of Education at Lesley University in Cambridge, Massachusetts. She is an Associate Professor of sociology and Principal Investigator of The Girlhood Project (TGP). Amy teaches courses in girls' and women's studies, sociology, qualitative research methods, and adult learning and development. She is the co-chair of the Women's Studies Steering Committee and Women's Center, where she has initiated programming focused on women's health, sexual assault prevention, and most recently, a leadership enrichment and development study group for core women faculty. Amy is the Vice Chair of the American Council on Education National Network of Women Leaders in Higher Education of Massachusetts. The work closest to Amy's heart is The Girlhood Project, a multilayered community-based service learning and research program focused on the exploration of intersectional girlhoods in the context of intergenerational feminist girls' groups. As TGP enters its 13th year, Amy has mentored over 200 undergraduate and graduate students and is currently writing about the emerging girlhood scholar model, a central component of TGP. Amy can be found presenting locally, nationally, and internationally about this unique program. Amy's current research areas include girls' and emerging adult women's health and identity development, relationship-centered teaching and mentoring, feminist pedagogy, and leadership development of women faculty. It is the relationship between feminist theory, pedagogy, and praxis that is the essence of Amy's work with her students and faculty peers. Amy holds a PhD in educational studies with a focus on sociology and women's health from Lesley University, a Master of Public Health Degree in Epidemiology and Sociobehavioral Sciences from Boston University School of Public Health, School of Medicine, and a Bachelor of Arts in Psychology from Simmons University.

ABOUT THE AUTHORS

Anne Graham Cagney, PhD

Anne is a Fulbright Scholar and Senior Lecturer in Education at Waterford Institute of Technology (WIT), Waterford, Ireland. Following an early career in organization change management she became a university lecturer at Copenhagen Business School and then a full-time doctoral student at the Business School of Trinity College Dublin. From Copenhagen Anne moved to join WIT's School of Lifelong Learning and Education and has developed her research and teaching in professional learning and development. At WIT, in addition to her research and teaching, she is Research Officer for the Teacher's Union of Ireland. Outside of WIT she is a visiting professor at Henley Business School, University of Reading and the Vice-President of the Irish Fulbright Alumni Association. Her research in exploring the links between scholarly partnerships and research collaborations has contributed to what is known about useable knowledge and professional learning and development that support educational, business and organizational success.

Emilie Clucas Leaderman, EdD

Dr. Emilie Clucas Leaderman is an independent educational consultant for higher education programs, secondary schools, and nonprofit organizations to advance learning in Silicon Valley, California. She currently works as Assistant Director of Assessment at Santa Clara University and teaches as adjunct faculty in the School of Education and Counseling Psychology. Dr. Clucas Leaderman has also taught education and psychology courses at institutions in the greater Los Angeles and Boston areas. Prior to working in higher education assessment and teaching, she worked in student affairs as a prevention educator and as a substance abuse clinician in community-based organizations. Her current research focuses on exploring the role of disciplinary identity in higher education assessment practice.

Hyesun Cho, PhD

Hyesun Cho is Associate Professor of TESOL in the Department of Curriculum and Teaching at the University of Kansas, Lawrence, KS. She received her MA and PhD degrees from the University of Hawaii at Manoa. Prior to her graduate studies in Hawaii, she taught English in secondary schools in Korea. Dr. Cho is the recipient of the 2008 Outstanding Dissertation of the Year Award from the Second Language Research SIG at the American Educational Research Association. Her work has appeared in such journals as *Race, Ethnicity and Education, TESOL Journal, Language and Education, Computers and Education, Curriculum Inquiry*, and *Teaching and Teacher Education*. Her book on critical literacy pedagogy was published by Springer in 2018. She received the School of Education Faculty Achievement Award for Research in 2018. Her research interests include social identity, critical literacy, heritage language education, service learning, and teaching for social justice. She can be reached at hcho@ku.edu.

Judith Beth Cohen, PhD

Judith Beth Cohen, Professor, BA, English, University of Michigan, MA. Educational Psychology, University of Michigan, PhD in Literature and Creative Writing, Union Institute. She has been involved with innovative programs for adult learners for over 30 years. A core faculty member of the Lesley University Ph.D. program in Educational Studies, she has also taught at Harvard College, the Harvard Business School, Goddard College, Skidmore College and the Bard College Institute on Writing and Thinking. Her publications include: "Transformation in a Residential Adult Learning Community,"(with Deborah Piper), in *Learning as Transformation: Critical Perspectives on a Theory in Progress,* Jack Mezirow & Associates, Jossey-Bass: San Francisco, CA, 2000. Her novel *Seasons* was published by The Permanent Press of Sag Harbor, New York Her short fiction and articles have appeared in numerous magazines.

Allyson Eamer, PhD

ate Professor in the Faculty of Education at University of Ontario Institute of Technology, Oshawa, Ontario, Canada. She researches in the area of language pedagogy, and the reflexive relationship between language and cultural identity.

Anjali J. Forber-Pratt, PhD

Anjali J. Forber-Pratt, PhD, Assistant Professor in the Department of Human and Organizational Development at Vanderbilt University in Nashville, Tennessee. Her research adopts a social-ecological framework looking at issues related to identity development, inclusion, social-emotional learning, and school climate particularly for individuals who are different in some way, with a large focus on disability. She presents regularly at state, national, and international conferences and is author on over 25 peer-reviewed journal articles and numerous chapters. As a wheelchair-user herself for over 30 years, and a two-time Paralympian and medalist, Dr. Forber-Pratt is also nationally and internationally recognized as a disability leader and mentor. She was honored by *Diverse: Issues in Higher Education* as a 2018 Emerging Scholar. The White House honored her as a Champion of Change in 2013 and she had an opportunity to participate in a roundtable discussion with President Obama about disability policy issues.

Ellie Fitts Fulmer, EdD

Ellie Fitts Fulmer, EdD, MEd, is an assistant professor of education at Ithaca College, Ithaca, NY, where she teaches undergraduate and graduate courses in Literacy and Social Studies, and supports student teachers in the field. Her scholarship threads include identifying a subgenre of postmodern children's picturebooks, the topic of her recent article in *Dragon Lode*; and exploring life texts in college teaching, a focus of her recent co-authored chapter titled " 'Dangerous Black Professor': Challenging the Ghettoization of Race in Higher Education" in the edited volume *RIP Jim Crow: Fighting Racism Through Higher Education Policy, Curriculum, and Cultural Interventions*, published by Peter Lang. The author would like to thank Sherry Deckman, Vivian Gadsden, Linda Hanrahan, Susan Lytle, Sharon Ravitch, and Kathleen Riley for their advice and guidance in various stages of this work.

Morgan Halstead, PhD, MA

Dr. Morgan Halstead, Assistant Professor of English and Literature at Malcolm X College, Chicago, IL, has a PhD in Curriculum and Instruction from the University of Illinois at Chicago and an MA in Literature with a focus in Irish Studies from Boston College. Her research interests include the lived experiences of students to help inform their intellectual growth and development as life-long learners. She lives in Chicago with her husband and two daughters.

Kimberly D. Johnson, EdD

Dr. Kimberly D. Johnson currently serves as the Director of Special Projects to the Chancellor at the University of Missouri-Kansas City (UMKC). Her research interests focus on efforts to enhance the experiences of women staff in higher education with an emphasis on leadership, mentoring, professional development, and understanding the lived experiences of African American women. Johnson is an advocate for staff and seeks to ensure they not only have a place at the table, but that their voices are heard. Her passion is supporting the advancement of staff and women of color in the academy. Johnson has a Bachelor of Arts in Sociology, Master of Arts in Education, and an Educational Specialist Degree, all from UMKC, where she also received her doctorate in Education with an emphasis on Higher Education Administration.

Alyson E. King, PhD

Dr. Alyson E. King is an Associate Professor in the Political Science program in Faculty of Social Science & Humanities at Ontario Tech University, Oshawa, Ontario, Canada. She conducts research in the area of the social impact of education, student access to and success in higher education, and education programs for adults living with mental illness.

Enid E. Larsen, PhD, MSW, MEd

Dr. Enid Larsen is an international and interdisciplinary educator, researcher, and visual artist whose career spans education, depth psychology, organizational management, and art. This multidisciplinary mix provides numerous opportunities for exploring the transformative potential of education for adult learners. For over two decades, Enid has directed Prior Learning Assessment (PLA) at the Van Loan School at Endicott College, Beverly, Massachusetts, United States. As an experiential learner herself, she facilitates growth and change in adults who are seeking to further their professional and personal development through the challenge of petitioning college credit for work and life learning. Enid Larsen completed her Bachelor of Arts at Goddard College, Plainfield, Vermont; Master of Social Work at Simmons College, Boston, MA; Master of Education in Organizational Management at Endicott College, Beverly, MA; and a Doctorate of Philosophy in Educational Studies at Lesley University, Cambridge, MA.

Ji-Yeon Lee, PhD

Ji-Yeon Lee is the Korean Language Coordinator in the Department of East Asian Languages and Cultures at the University of Kansas, Lawrence, KS. She received her PhD degree in Curriculum & Instruction from the same university. Her research interests include Korean as a foreign/ heritage language education and Korean female students in U.S. higher education. She can be reached at jylee9@ku.edu.

Kristen Linzmeier, PhD

Kristen Linzmeier earned her PhD in Curriculum and Instruction from the University of Wisconsin-Madison, Whitewater, WI, and is currently an Assistant Professor in the College of Education and Professional Studies at the University of Wisconsin-Whitewater. She teaches courses in the Early Childhood Dual Licensure Program and her research interests include the lived experiences of nontraditional undergraduate students and early language and literacy development. She can be reached at: linzmeik@uww. edu.

Ilana Margolin, PhD

Prof. Ilana Margolin is a senior lecturer at the MEd programs at Levinsky College of Education. She is the head of a net inquiring teachers professional development programs for the Israeli Ministry of Education. Her main research interests include teachers' professional development, learning communities, leadership and organizational change.

Xóchitl L. Méndez, CAGS, MM, PhD Candidate in Educational Studies

Through her work, Xóchitl Méndez interrogates assumptions that permeate the definitions of ability and possibility as she explores the intersections of leadership and identity. As an educator, advocate, and researcher, Xóchitl strives to shed light on lived experiences ranging from disability and illness to the conflicts between social expectations and the individual's perceived reality. Xóchitl is a PhD Candidate at Lesley University's doctoral program in Education. She completed both her undergraduate and Master's of Music at Longy School of Music of Bard College. Xóchitl implements a multidisciplinary approach to research and pursues an alliance of the arts alongside rigorous scholastic inquiry in order to break intellectual boundaries. Her life trajectory resonates in her doctoral work, which draws inspiration from Hannah Arendt's call to a *Vita Activa*. Xóchitl interprets this exhortation for advocacy and leadership as a pathway to insightful academic inquiry that, in turn, imbues effective educational evaluation and successful program development.

Crystal S. Rudds, PhD, MFA

Dr. Crystal S. Rudds is assistant professor of African American literature at the University of Utah, Salt Lake City, UT. She received her PhD in English from the University of Illinois at Urbana-Champaign and an MFA in Creative Writing from Indiana University-Bloomington. Formerly tenured with Malcolm X College, she continues to write and collaborate with her community college colleagues.

Jeffrey S. (Jeff) Savage, EdD, SHRM-SCP

Dr. Savage is Dean of Business for Cornerstone University's Professional & Graduate Studies division, Grand Rapids, MI. A veteran of the U.S. Air Force, Jeff holds a BA in English from Culver-Stockton College, a master's degree in human resources (MSA) from Central Michigan University, and a doctorate (EdD) in higher education administration from Baylor.

Caren L. Sax, EdD, CRC

Dr. Caren Sax is Professor and Chair in the Department of Administration, Rehabilitation, and Postsecondary Education and Director of the Interwork Institute at San Diego State University, San Diego, CA. She conducts research to address systems change efforts that improve school-to-work transition services for students with disabilities, and access to assistive technology for individuals with disabilities to expand opportunities for employment, education, and community inclusion.

Jennifer Serowick, EdD

Jennifer Serowick is Assistant Vice President for Adult Learning at Lesley University, Cambridge, MA. She has worked in higher education for over 20 years in diverse institutions and positions including academic support, residence life, admissions, and for the last 10 years, adult degree completion. Passionate about creating pathways for adults to continue in higher education, Jen has led the development and delivery of programming for adult students both on and off campus in undergraduate and graduate programs. Jen grew up in Skillman, NJ; received her BA in English and theater from Hamilton College; a M.Ed. in higher education administration from the College of William and Mary; and an EdD in administration and leadership studies from Indiana University of Pennsylvania. Jen has worked at Lesley University in Cambridge, MA, as the Assistant Vice President for Adult Learning Programs since May 2016 where she is grateful for the opportunity to pursue her passion for the pursuit of social justice through education.

Michal Shani, PhD

Dr. Michal Shani is Academic Leader of Teach First Israel Teacher Education Program (Hotam Naomi) and lecturer at Levinsky College of Education in Israel. She serves as an academic leader of "Hotam Neomi," TFI's teacher education program. Her main research interests are teacher education, inclusive education and instruction and learning processes for students with special needs.

Lesley N. Siegel, PhD

Lesley N. Siegel is an Assistant Professor in the College of Education and Social Work at West Chester University, West Chester, PA. She teaches undergraduate and graduate courses in special education, culturally responsive practices, and qualitative research. Her areas of scholarship include: the experiences of LGBT faculty; the use of qualitative data analysis in the development of teacher dispositions; and the intersection of dis/ability studies and public pedagogy.

Marian Spaid-Ross, EdD

Dr. Marian Spaid-Ross, Department of Behavioral Sciences, Palomar College, San Marcos, CA: I am a lifelong learner who aspires to learn, lead, and apply ideas that will advocate new educational ideas and programs that focus on the older adult learner and educational access. My decision to return to college stemmed from a desire to understand and learn more about the specific needs of the older adult college student and their process in pursuing educational and social equity. My current research interests focus on the nontraditional student equity and access to services and resources that support a lifelong learning model by promoting the idea of a "social connectedness" within the college community. Teaching within the community college environment has provided me an opportunity to support the older adult student's college experience and the resources and services that contribute to their educational success. I discovered that institutions can play a significant role in developing and shaping older adult students' identities within our educational institutions.

Pninat Tal, PhD

Dr. Pninat Tal is the Head of BED early childhood Education Department in Levinsky College of Education, and lecturer at Levinsky College. Her main research interests are: teacher education, curriculum development, evaluation and epistemological views of teachers, expert in pre-school education.

Deborah (Debbie) Thurman, EdD

Dr. Thurman is a retired university distance education director from West Virginia and Tennessee. She attended Tennessee Technological University, earning three degrees: undergraduate degree in psychology, master's in educational psychology, and an EdS in educational leadership. Debbie also has a doctorate (Ed.D.) in educational leadership from Liberty University.

Ann Mechem Ziergiebel, PhD

Ann Mechem Ziergiebel, PhD, is an Instructor in the Department of Secondary and Higher Education at Salem State University, Salem, MA. Formerly, she taught middle school ELA and social studies for 23 years. Ann's participants in her dissertation research at Lesley University, Cambridge, MA - entitled *Adolescent Visual Voices: Discovering Emerging Identities Through Photovoice, Perspective and Narrative*—include suburban and urban middle school studentsvolunteering in after school programs. Her expertise in interdisciplinary curriculum development with middle school students is showcased in a recent publication with the citation: Ziergiebel, A. M. (2013). Digital literacy in practice: Achieving a cosmopolitan orientation. In J. Ippolito, J. Fahey, & C. Zaller (Eds.), *Adolescent literacy in the era of the common core*. Cambridge, MA: Harvard Education Press.

CPSIA information can be obtained
at www.ICGtesting.com
Printed in the USA
JSHW022313261219
3213JS00001B/4